The
Jazz
Collection

Made Possible By
and the Assistance
of Many Kind Friends

LISTEN

GERRY MULLIGAN

AN AURAL NARRATIVE IN JAZZ

LISTEN

GERRY MULLIGAN

AN AURAL NARRATIVE IN JAZZ

JEROME KLINKOWITZ

SCHIRMER BOOKS

A Division of Macmillan, Inc.
NEW YORK
Collier Macmillan Canada
TORONTO
Maxwell Macmillan International
NEW YORK OXFORD SINGAPORE SYDNEY

Schirmer Books
A Division of Macmillan, Inc.
866 Third Avenue, New York, N.Y. 10022

Collier Macmillan Canada, Inc.
1200 Eglinton Avenue East, Suite 200
Don Mills, Ontario M3C 3N1
LIBRARY OF CONGRESS CATALOG CARD NUMBER: 90-8668

Printed in the United States of America

printing number
1   2   3   4   5   6   7   8   9   10

Library of Congress Cataloging-in-Publication Data

Klinkowitz, Jerome.
    Listen—Gerry Mulligan : an aural narrative in jazz / by Jerome
Klinkowitz.
        p.   cm.
    Includes bibliographical references and index.
    ISBN 0-02-871265-X
    1. Mulligan, Gerry.   2. Jazz musicians—United States—Biography.
I. Title.
ML419.M79K6   1991
788.7'165'092—dc20   90-8668   CIP   MN
    [B]

For my son Jonathan,
who grew up with this music around him
and became a musician himself

CONTENTS

ILLUSTRATIONS

Photographs follow page 114:

1. Los Angeles, 1952
2. First pianoless quartet with Chet Baker, Los Angeles, 1952
3. Los Angeles, 1952
4. The Haig, Los Angeles, 1952
5. Lee Konitz joins Mulligan and Baker at The Haig, 1953
6. Lee Konitz records with Mulligan and Baker at engineer Phil Turetsky's home, 1953
7. Second pianoless quartet at Gold Star Studios, Hollywood, 1953
8. William Claxton's montage for a proposed LP cover, 1953
9. Gerry Mulligan Quartet and Sextet in San Diego, 1954
10. Quartet in San Diego, 1954
11. Sextet in San Diego, 1954
12. Backstage at San Diego, 1954
13. Quartet in Boston, 1956
14. With Father Norman O'Connor and Richard Bock, Boston, 1956
15, 16, 17. At the tailor shop in Cambridge, Massachusetts, 1956
18, 19. With Ben Webster, Hollywood, 1959
20. Hollywood, 1959
21, 22, 23. With Judy Holliday, Hollywood and Beverly Hills, 1960
24. The Concert Jazz Band, Newport Jazz Festival, 1960
25. *Concerto Grosso:* Mulligan, Bob Brookmeyer, and Zoot Sims supported by Concert Jazz Band, Newport Jazz Festival, 1960
26. In the early 1960s.
27. Circa early 1970s.
28. Recording soundtrack for "La Menace," 1982
29. With Zubin Mehta at New York Philharmonic, December 1989
30. New York, 1989

ACKNOWLEDGMENTS

Tracing and discussing Gerry Mulligan's music through his long career has been almost as enjoyable as listening to it all these years, and for making my work easier and, I hope, more reliable I am grateful to some very resourceful people. Wayne Jarvis, Senior Producer for the University of Northern Iowa's listener-supported public radio stations KUNI and KHKE, tracked down several fugitive LPs for me and clarified contexts for my research; at the university's library, Professor and Fine Arts Librarian Verna F. Ritchie was a guide to printed sources; the university itself supported my research with a summer fellowship; and our college's dean, Dr. Thomas H. Thompson (a jazz baritone saxophonist himself), offered additional support. *Down Beat* magazine, publicists at Fantasy and DRG Records, and the eminent photographer William Claxton contributed to the visual record. Producer Michael Cuscuna, whose hand has guided so many important reissues and expanded compilations, helped at several stages with my discography, as did critic Raymond Horricks and collector Gordon Jack.

Gordon Jack's archive of Mulligan materials is the world's foremost, comprising a treasury of nearly everything Gerry Mulligan has recorded, broadcast, and allowed to exist as private tapings; Mulligan himself is a frequent user of the collection. From his home in London, Gordon Jack bore patiently with the considerable nuisance of trans-Atlantic research to review my text and supplement the initial draft of my discography with descriptions from his own collection; moreover, he was able to solve problems that have vexed critics for decades, such as using historical and aural evidence to correct interpretation errors that have long stood as facts. Although Gordon Jack bears no responsibilities for any errors that might exist in my narrative, he does deserve credit for an immense number of corrections, clarifications, and pieces of new information. Short of having Gerry Mulligan himself on hand at all times, one cannot imagine a more complete resource.

As I have learned from doing books on such writers as Kurt Vonnegut, Grace Paley, and Donald Barthelme, a living subject is often faced with the prospect of, in Vonnegut's words, "therapeutic vivisection" at the hands of even well-meaning scholars and critics. Therefore I am especially pleased that Gerry Mulligan agreed to review my discography and clarify certain historical details. Completing my corps of researchers has been Julie Huffman-klinkowitz, who in addition to chasing down innumerable references had to bear with the stereo booming through the ceiling of my own study into hers just above.

My most personal affectionate gratitude is shared by everyone who buys jazz records—gratitude for the clerks and owners who keep shops stocked, who are often archivists themselves, who think of digging out an odd album that includes one's favorite, and—in the case of selling records to a kid just barely into his teens with collecting ambitions far deeper than his pockets—who give a break on the price. To Craig at Real Records in Iowa City, Ron and Bruno at Chicago's Jazz Record Mart, and Ron and Gordy at the old Radio Doctors Shop downstairs on Wells Street in the lost Milwaukee of my childhood, I'm thankful for making such listening possible.

Jerome Klinkowitz
University of Northern Iowa
Cedar Falls, Iowa

LISTEN

GERRY MULLIGAN

AN AURAL NARRATIVE IN JAZZ

INTRODUCTION

Milwaukee, 13 January 1959, during the inevitable week of winter's sub-basement, when the temperature is in the teens below zero and the wind whistles off the lake. A concert in jazz by the Gerry Mulligan Quartet at Downer College, not too lately the Milwaukee Downer Seminary. And the concert is in a snug, quaintly medieval hall—beamed ceiling, half-timbered walls, leaded windows, the works—providing a spot of warmth and light in this alien, forbidding world.

Alien indeed, here on the northeast side of Milwaukee, far from the southwest suburbs I'd rarely left before my freshman year of high school at Marquette downtown. Tom Repensek and I had seen Mulligan's picture in the *Milwaukee Journal* "Green Sheet" a few nights before—a jazz concert!—and phoned for tickets. The north side was new, jazz was new, and the whole atmosphere was something different. College girls in sweaters, full woolen skirts, perfume, and pearl earrings; every man bearded and smoking a pipe; a Mulligan LP, his first quartet album for World Pacific Records displayed like jewelry in a glass case, its abstract expressionist (I know now) cover speaking of a world as distant as those soft sweaters and whiffs of Chanel no. 5.

Never underestimate the effect of a jazz concert on a fifteen-year-old in the 1950s. A whole new world was being offered, based on aesthetic choices not yet available elsewhere in the culture. Rock music, for example, presented no great stylistic challenge beyond Bill Haley's "Rock around the Clock" of 1953, and it would be another five years before the Beatles and Rolling Stones would give rock what was

1

already present in jazz: an emphasis on technique, improvisation, and the wordless poetry of musical expression. Jazz brought a world of values along with it, as the ambience of that first Mulligan concert so amply testified. Newspaper stories told that the baritone saxophonist and some of his sidemen were playing and acting in two new movies, *I Want to Live!* starring Susan Hayward and an adaptation of Jack Kerouac's *The Subterraneans*. Replete with beatniks, interpretive dance (Janice Rule in leotards), poetry, and drugs, these films' night-life spoke of another universe, an underside to 1950s conformity. As we all grew up, this underside would emerge and become recognizable in our own lives as the 1960s. A deeply personal, idiosyncratic, expressive temperament seemed to be at the heart of all this, and taking the bus in from Hales Corners one cold night in January was as good a first step into it as anything a teenaged suburb kid could imagine.

Gerry Mulligan himself was at an apogee. Looking back over his hundred-odd albums and forty-some years in the profession, one sees that 13 January 1959 stands out. His quartet that night had Art Farmer (trumpet), Bill Crow (bass), Dave Bailey (drums), and himself (baritone sax), a master's version of the musicianship and structure he had experimented with since the early 1950s—a pianoless quartet, with the seldom-used upper register notes of the baritone sax interweaving with the breathy brass style passed down from Chet Baker and Bob Brookmeyer. By this date Mulligan's group was halfway through the sessions that would produce *What Is There to Say?*, the flawlessly executed album that caught the high point of his improvisatory lyricism. In addition, it was on Columbia Records, which meant it would reach a much larger public than his earlier discs for World Pacific (the first recorded in a friend's living room) and Fantasy (marketed out of critic Ralph J. Gleason's garage). Finally, there were the tunes: "Festive Minor," "News from Blueport," and those standards by Vernon Duke, Rodgers and Hart, and Comden-Green-Styne that were personalized by Mulligan's unique transpositions of commercial culture's surface, restructuring our lives according to artistic values not yet apparent to ourselves. Those songs, stripped down to just two melodic instruments and with nothing but Bill Crow's bass line to imply the chords, gave exquisite proof of Mulligan's gift as a writer and arranger, getting it all down to just this, yet with no sacrifice of sentiment or meaning. The night was pure Mulligan, as clear an insight into the man and his music as four decades of listening might provide. This was the night for both of us.

Next morning I found my high school bandmaster and asked if I could learn to play baritone sax. He gave me a clarinet—basics first, he said—and it took me three years to get from that instrument to alto and then tenor sax, finally picking up a "bari" senior year. It took even longer to move from the school orchestra through polka bands and rock groups to a real jazz combo. But by then it was 1965, and everything else was finally happening, too.

It's flattering to think that Gerry Mulligan got his start in music with similar misdirection: asking for a trumpet and getting the same infernal clarinet, the legacy of music teachers brought up on Benny Goodman and Artie Shaw. Born in 1927, Mulligan paid more dues in the swing bands of his adolescence. At age seventeen he was arranging for Johnny Warrington's radio band at WCAU in his hometown of Philadelphia, and a year later he was on the road with the even more unlikely outfit of Tommy Tucker. In 1946, when just nineteen years old, he signed on with a more hip aggregation, Gene Krupa's big band, which also employed such solid jazz instrumentalists as Warren Covington, Charlie Kennedy, Charlie Ventura, and Teddy Napoleon. But even with Krupa, Mulligan's writing showed a sense of humor learned from the Hal Kemp-style bands of his apprenticeship, and through the heady innovations of bop, cool, and progressive jazz Mulligan never lost it. In the late forties and into 1951 he played and wrote for Elliot Lawrence and then Claude Thornhill, but Mulligan's smaller combo approach was taking shape between tours. In 1948 he found himself hanging out with Miles Davis at Gil Evans's apartment on East 55th Street in New York. Their nine-piece group played at the Royal Roost for two weeks that year and at another club briefly in 1949, but the nonet maintained itself primarily as a rehearsal band, experimenting with ideas in writing and arranging for a new style of music, *The Birth of the Cool*, as the title of its 10-inch Capitol LP phrased it.

Rhythm section plus half a dozen or so horns up front: this was Mulligan's initial vision for the postwar jazz combo, its style grown out of the exotic French horns and mixed voicings of the Thornhill band, which in turn had followed from the section transcriptions of bop-style lines Mulligan scored for Krupa. It was the form he pursued through the Miles Davis sessions, then with the slightly smaller group featuring Jerry Lloyd (trumpet), Kai Winding (trombone), Brew Moore (tenor sax), and himself on bari ("Lestorian Mode," 1949), and finally with ten-piece groups in New York (*Gerry Mulligan All Stars*, 1951) and in Los Angeles (*Gerry Mulligan Tentette* [Capitol Jazz Classics, Vol. 4, M-11029], 1953). By filling out the trombone lines with French horns, pairing Miles Davis's spare trumpet with Lee Konitz's ethereal alto, and for occasional treats stacking the whole ensemble with the smaller horns on top and the tuba on the bottom, Mulligan was able to present the distinctive innovations that set the style for jazz in the fifties, especially as it came to be played on the West Coast.

Mulligan himself hitchhiked west in 1952. Here, working conditions led to the practicality of a different-sized group. Los Angeles was not the center for big bands New York was, and hence there was no supply of sidemen for off-time rehearsal groups such as the one Mulligan once set up in Central Park to save studio rental. Moreover, it was as hard to find work for a ten-piece avant-garde jazz group in Los Angeles as it was back East, with the added pressure that there were no larger organizations like Krupa's, Thornhill's, or Lawrence's forward-looking bands to fall back on for employment. Los Angeles did offer gigs, but they were in small beer-and-wine clubs like the Haig, which seated less than ninety people. Four-man minimums at union scale were the most overhead such clubs could afford, and musicians were challenged to think up orchestrations more promising than the typical single horn plus piano and rhythm. At the Haig Red Norvo made do with just vibes, guitar, and bass, letting the owner clear some space by storing the baby grand. When Mulligan agreed to fill in Mondays with no keyboard at all, the revolutionary form of the first Gerry Mulligan Quartet was born.

Mulligan, of course, had aesthetic justification for going without the piano. First of all, he needed a minimum of two equally strong melodic lines up front to set the contrapuntal effect he had achieved with the nonet and tentette. Given the economics of pay and space, baritone sax and trumpet would have to do, supported by bass and drums; for Mulligan, the pianist was expendable before anyone else in a five-person group, a principle kept intact when he later expanded his group to a sextet. On the positive side, he argued that combo-style piano had hit a stylistic dead end of merely feeding chords to the soloists. Those chords tended to be too limiting for truly expressive horn men, as Mulligan and trumpeter Chet Baker proved to be.

Dropping the piano was the first step toward a new aesthetic, something picked up in the larger musical style of the times and echoed by the other arts, especially painting and fiction. In 1960 Thomas Pynchon published a story called "Entropy," in which some musicians debate the meaning of Mulligan's orchestral amputation. Not "no chords," one of the characters speculates, but "no root chords. Nothing to listen to while you blow a horizontal line. What one does in such a case is, one *thinks* the roots." In Pynchon's story the combo takes the next logical step, "to think everything," and performs in utter silence. In the art world this approach yielded the dominant style known as minimalism, while fiction writers after Pynchon began to see how many conventions they could drop and still have novels and short stories. When art forms are challenged by outside competition—painting by the camera, fiction by newspapers, music by Muzak—the way they survive is by testing themselves down to bare essentials. The core that Gerry Mulligan discovered was a minimal chordal statement, sounded out by the bass, which in turn linked the chord's importance with the tune's ongoing rhythm, not with just the stratified, static sound structure. Along that basic line was played the *performance:* solo instrumentalists wailing with complete chromatic freedom of expression, owing allegiance only to an implied structure in the players' and listeners' heads. The art was participatory and interactive, with the emphasis on *doing.* We need to act out our art, not hang it in museums, the new age was saying. And the silence of Mulligan's absent piano said it first.

The quartet was structurally lean and spare, placing the emphasis on richness of individual expression, and this simple innovation let Mulligan work marvels within the limits of the commercial, three-minute song. "Lullaby of the Leaves," "My Funny Valentine," "Frenesi," and "The Nearness of You" were standards and let Mulligan assume that the listener would know the tune well—so well that the traditional first-chorus statement of melody could range from prettiness to stark abstraction in the trumpet-sax voicing. Sometimes he and Chet Baker would pass the melody back and forth several times in just eight measures; other times they'd play in low register mock-unison, making a good-time joke of "I'm Beginning to See the Light." They would split another chorus into two solos, one horn softly backing the other, then restate the melody in voicing reversed from what it had been the first time through—all in 180 seconds or less.

For all its historical and musicological importance, the original quartet with Chet Baker lasted only a year, from June 1952 through the following summer. What killed it was a narcotics bust, putting Mulligan on the sheriff's farm for three months and souring him on California life for many years thereafter. After his release he headed back East and, working out of New York, fronted a reorganized quartet with valve-trombonist Bob Brookmeyer, a group often augmented with a fifth or sixth piece (Jon Eardley's trumpet, Zoot Sims's tenor sax). By the mid-1950s the evolved unit known as the Gerry Mulligan Sextet was ready to cut three albums for Mercury Records. By now Mulligan could be considered *Mainstream,* as the title of the best of these three LPs suggested. West Coast jazz had developed into a cooler, slicker mode without him (although he would join Johnny Mandel and a group of Los Angeles regulars for the sound track of *I Want to Live!* in 1958, followed by some playing for music director André Previn and acting for director Ranald MacDougall in *The Subterraneans*). Meanwhile the most definitive East Coast jazz had acquired a harder, progressive edge, as characterized by Miles Davis recruiting Cannonball Adderley and John Coltrane for his legendary sextet of *Milestones* days. Mulligan's style was not reactionary, but there was an attempt in these Mercury sessions to get back to roots— including Mulligan's own in "Elevation," a tune he had written back in Philadelphia and recorded in 1949 with Elliot Lawrence, and to the roots of blues improvisation itself ("Blue at the Roots"). The sextet produced some of the finest sax, trumpet, and trombone solos recorded in this era, lyrical songs in themselves that push along the rhythm and emerge out of the ensemble playing like biomorphic figures from an abstract expressionist background. Again there was Mulligan's ability to make six musicians sound like the full Woody Herman Herd—like the essence of the Herman band, with nothing extraneous to clutter up the improvisation at the heart of each cut.

Meanwhile the Gerry Mulligan Quartet was getting better and better each time it played—with Brookmeyer in 1956 and 1957, then with Art Farmer on trumpet in the decade's closing years. For his own interest and to fulfill recording contracts with something more original than the quartet's third or fourth set, Mulligan announced a policy of meeting all comers, players in such diverse styles as Paul Desmond, Stan Getz, Thelonious Monk, Ben Webster, and Johnny Hodges. Each soloist brought out a different side of Mulligan in his own playing and allowed Mulligan the arranger to devise some particularly inventive pairings. The Desmond sessions joined high and low horns together, intertwining alto and baritone lines like a Jackson Pollock painting. With Getz it was more a case of straight blowing; on the flip side the two men traded horns as well as solos, revealing a previously undiscovered hard edge to Mulligan as tenor saxophonist while Getz coaxed unheard-of lyricism from the gutty bari. Monk forced Mulligan into more abstract regions, occasionally losing him in some of the more candid confusions ever released as finished takes, but Johnny Hodges brought him back into swing-style swinging. The Ben Webster set was bluesier and led to a club date and recording with Jimmy Witherspoon.

The next true innovation was Mulligan's Concert Jazz Band, financed out of his studio earnings and premiering in 1960. New York had plenty of clubs for jazz listening, but for listening to small combos. No one had thought of packing a thirteen-piece band into the Village Vanguard to play for a sitdown audience, but Mulligan did it with a group as startlingly new as the *Birth of the Cool* group was in 1948 and 1949. Two tactics figured prominently. For one, solos were not tossed around as in a riff-and-stomp band from the 1940s. Instead, the horn players from the quartet and sextet took spotlights roles, while Mulligan packaged their familiar solo styles with appropriate orchestrations. America's experience of listening to ten years of evolving Mulligan groups, by this point cataloged on nearly three dozen LPs, would now be dramatized, even ritualized, in an evening's performance of the Concert Jazz Band (CJB). Second, Mulligan didn't take the writer's spotlight, even though he was paying for the rehearsal time and even some of the performance fees himself.

The Concert Jazz Band's instrumentation was as important as the voicings in the 1948–49 nonet. Throughout the late 1950s Mulligan had experimented with a more traditionally organized band—seven brass, five reeds, four rhythm—but found the sound too heavy for the material he wanted to play and too inhibiting for his key soloists. In April of 1957 four numbers were cut for Columbia, but only one was released on a sampler (it and the others are now among the archival deposits mined on *Gerry Mulligan: The Arranger*). The CJB cut the roster down to thirteen, actually a concerto grosso structure that put the lead horns of the old quartet in a small orchestral setting. Clarity of sound and complex yet understandable interplay of lines were Mulligan's stated goals. The band would be there to color it all with Ellingtonian shadings and serve as a reminder that having fun with the song, as well as improvising, was what jazz could be about. To emphasize this clearness Mulligan put a clarinet on top of the band's instrumentation, and for richness he structured his trombone section with one valve, slide, and bass instrument each, while the trumpets were led as often as not by Clark Terry's mellow fluegelhorn. The tradition role of the big band in jazz was thus reversed, or more properly turned from hard swing to Duke Ellington's world of tonal shadings.

Mulligan and Brookmeyer did arrangements, but important pieces were also invited from George Russell, Johnny Carisi, Bill Holman and the young Gary McFarland. The idea was to build a book of true concert material, including long works that allowed the composer to use the band itself as an instrument, another Ellington touch. George Russell's "All about Rosie" ran through distinct changes in tempo and rhythm, almost like a miniature symphony, while Gary McFarland's "Weep" showed how the lyric could work its way up to epic in just six minutes. Mulligan himself had fun with standards: his scoring of "You

Took Advantage of Me" uses the quartet's practice of tossing the melody back and forth through different voicings and into improvised exchanges, as if the well-known tune exists not as a surface on which to represent but rather as an arena in which to act. Such instrumental action painting by baritone sax and valve trombone, here supported by an orchestra that occasionally gets in its own gesture, became Mulligan's major contribution to big-band music of the 1960s. His charts from the CJB years came off like animated conversations, brimming with the life jazz is supposed to have but loses too easily in a strictly academic big-band framework. There were moments of tender brilliance as well. "Come Rain or Come Shine" was initially a showcase for Zoot Sims's tenor, until Mulligan came to love the arrangement so much that he shaped his own solo performance out of the original orchestration.

The last Concert Jazz Band recordings feature Jim Hall on guitar, creating another new sound for big-band that Mulligan found easy to carry over into his small group. For the 1963 sessions that produced *Night Lights* and *Butterfly with Hiccups* he formed a basically new sextet consisting of guitar, baritone sax, fluegelhorn, and valve trombone supported by bass and drums. Hall's subtle style of guitar plus the breathiness of these two special brass instruments were softness personified, giving Mulligan at once a group capable of interpreting such quiet and introspective songs as Luiz Bonfa's "Morning of the Carnival" (from the film *Black Orpheus*), Chopin's "Prelude in E Minor," the earlier quartet's "Festive Minor," and such subdued standards as "In the Wee Small Hours of the Morning" and his own "Tell Me When." Even more so than before, the solos would creep out of the orchestrations; now the effect was like a wood nymph slipping from the foliage into a misty pond at daybreak. The effect was like Duke Ellington's "Dusk" or Claude Thornhill's "Snowfall," a reminder that pure voicing could make a song. If Mulligan's earlier effects were like Jackson Pollack's intersecting lines or Franz Kline's canvas-crossing clashes, the new performance glowed in silence like a Mark Rothko color field. Music, like art, could be made in more than one way, even with the same general school.

The balance of Mulligan's work in the 1960s was for many critics as difficult to deal with as the decade itself. For while the popular culture was radicalized, Mulligan's recordings become problematic, prompting some to say he's sold out to a lazy man's doodling. The ten-piece string section on *Feelin' Good* and selections such as the Frank Sinatra–like "The Second Time Around" and movie themes like "The Shadow of Your Smile" were hardly reassuring, and when his new small group album proclaimed itself as *If You Can't Beat 'Em, Join 'Em!* (1965) Mulligan's exodus to the reactionary realms of pop culture seemed obvious. But steaming along with "King of the Road" and "I Know a Place" while ignoring the blues-based popularizations by the Animals and the Rolling Stones was not the sellout it seemed to be, for Mulligan was taking an approach to this decade as original as his transitions from the forties to the fifties and into the first years of the sixties. Relationships were part of it—with singer and comedienne Judy Holliday and, after Holliday's death, with actress Sandy Dennis—because they brought the jazzman into more bourgeois film work and Broadway-based scoring, hardly the environs of cultural activism. Yet these interests anchored Mulligan to a segment of America his more radical cohorts were abandoning. While Ornette Coleman with Archie Shepp pursued one style, carrying forward the more extreme experiments of John Coltrane, Mulligan embraced a form of pop music so traditional that his very act became a radical gesture. By doing so he remained in touch with certain givens: that a Lennon-McCartney original could be as beautiful as a Gershwin or a Sammy Cahn-Jimmy Van Heusen classic and that such tunes might well turn out to be key items in the emerging generation's nostalgia bank, even though all the smoke and fire were at Stones Concerts. And while driving the avant-garde enthusiasts away, such work allowed Mulligan the freedom to do as he damn well pleased, such as helping Dave Brubeck reorganize the supposedly unchangeable Dave Brubeck Quartet.

While America rocked and jazz fused, Mulligan rolled through a mid-to-late-1960s of comfortable sessions and enjoyable tours. Pianos were now admissible; ever since Stan Getz had brought along Lou Levy for their horn-trading blowing session, Mulligan had repressed his skepticism toward the piano and eventually began making it a part of each nonquartet session. On *Something Borrowed, Something Blue* for Limelight in 1966, pianist Warren Bernhardt provided a subtle foundation for some pleasant interweavings between Mulligan and Zoot Sims, veterans of countless meetings in sextet and Concert Jazz Band formats but never before together for a face-to-face studio session. Though there was no horn trading, Mulligan did switch from baritone to alto sax on four of the album's six cuts, and by exploring the lower register of this instrument he managed to blend his borrowed voice with Sims's patented way of exploiting the tenor's breathier heights. By 1968 Mulligan was ready for the ultimate encounter with a keyboard master: not a confusing amusement like the Thelonious Monk session of a decade before, but a sustained, integrated engagement with Dave Brubeck. Beginning with the cautiously named group, the Dave Brubeck Trio Featuring Gerry Mulligan, Mulligan and Brubeck skirted several touchy issues, including Mulligan's historical reluctance to work with piano, Brubeck's dedication to symphonic-style work, and the absence of alto saxophonist Paul Desmond, key figure in the most famous jazz quartet ever organized and only recently disbanded so that Brubeck could do bigger yet more personal things. But the association lasted and grew. Two albums later the group was called the Dave Brubeck Quartet Featuring Gerry Mulligan, and the original Mexico tour that prompted Mulligan's work with Brubeck had grown to a floating, well-sponsored excursion to European capitals where the two were received as the heroic jazz legends they were—to the point that in 1972 Paul Desmond could be welcomed back for a tour album whose title tweaked the nose of short-sighted historical and linguistic purists: *We're All Together Again for the First Time.*

Mulligan's five LPs with Brubeck, dating from 1968 to 1972, frame the most recent breakthrough in Mulligan's development as a soloist, arranger, and organizer of musical groups. *The Age of Steam* on A & M Records (recorded through 1971, released in 1972) begins, for the Mulligan who apparently had been collecting laurels for his 1950s' work, with an amazing statement: electric bass and electric piano bringing up the lights on another fusion instrument, the reed-miked tenor and soprano saxes of youngster Tom Scott, whose recordings with the LA Express would bring jazz preciously close to rhythm-and-blues-based rock-and-roll. True, Mulligan had his friends along too—Bud Shank from the West Coast, Bob Brookmeyer from New York—and there was also Harry "Sweets" Edison for some showcasing on the aptly titled "Over the Hill and Out of the Woods," on which Mulligan played his percussively rhythmic style of piano as a way of structuring a score that spanned nearly half a century's style in jazz. The album's eight numbers were presented as a concept, demonstrating how instrumentation of the 1970s could be used to integrate solo and ensemble work. The keys were envisioning the expanded rhythm section—electric piano, bass, and guitar—as an ensemble in itself and artful miking of both the drum set and auxiliary percussion. Mulligan, who once played the beatnik priest in *The Subterraneans*, had graduated to reading Doris Lessing, and in "Golden Notebooks" he wrote a number letting him double-track his own electric-piano playing with his baritone sax line, recalling the percussive interaction he had achieved with Brubeck on the concert tours—a theft, perhaps, but as imaginatively compelling and instructive as the act of larceny described in Lessing's novel.

That *The Age of Steam* was a breakthrough became clear when, three years later, Mulligan rejoined Chet Baker for their 1974 Carnegie Hall concert. Baker's personal struggles were a story in themselves, and his ability to rephrase even a whisper of the original quartet's sound nearly a quarter-century later was at once cheering and heartbreaking. Part of the mid-1970s' promotional mystique with jazz giants of an earlier era, the Mulligan-Baker encounter would have allowed the players to fake their way through some decades-old head charts and leave early to start spending their big guarantees. Perhaps this was what Baker had expected, for he'd been playing some local clubs with an acoustic trio for backing. Mulligan, however, showed up with Bob James on electric piano and Ron Carter, a fusion superstar, on electric bass; part of his program included "K-4 Pacific" from *The Age of Steam* and the forward-looking compositions "Song for an Unfinished Woman" and "Song for Strayhorn," both of which would appear six years later as the most characteristically 1980–ish pieces on Mulligan's *Walk on the Water* LP for DRG Records. For the Carnegie Hall set Baker relied on early fifties' material: the old quartet's up-tempo "Bernie's Tune" and the soft-voiced, breathy trumpet standard he virtually owned, "My Funny Valentine." Announced to the audience with the lyrics from its most wistful stanza, this Rodgers and Hart classic reminded everyone of what Chet Baker had been and was striving to be again (appreciative applause), but it also emphasized the great amount of new work Mulligan had accomplished in the intervening years, and when "Song for Strayhorn" followed the applause was thunderous.

Since the Carnegie Hall reunion, Mulligan has pursued several interests. The Brubeck and the Baker experiences were part of a larger trend in 1970s jazz, highlighted by various all-star traveling festivals sponsored by tobacco companies, breweries, and distillers. The "Who's Who in Jazz" series of session dates was a parallel, and in 1977 this mini-label brought together Mulligan and Lionel Hampton for a respectably arranged set of six numbers that after first and second phrases turned into legitimate vehicles for free expression, emphasizing the soloists' most characteristic talents. Yet Mulligan could explore the more abstract realms of composition and solo work at the same time, going to Italy for albums with Enrico Intra and Astor Piazzolla and to the world of film for the soundtrack for *La Menace*. All of these albums were vastly different from the style of playing (and help with scoring) offered to Barry Manilow for the 1984 LP *2:00 AM, Paradise Café* (Arista), an undertaking in which Mulligan and other veterans of the 1970s' jazz tours were brought in to legitimize Manilow's belief that he was developing in their mode and following in their footsteps toward enshrinement himself. Mulligan's own mainstream, however, was more inventive: the freshly orchestrated world of music displayed in *Idol Gossip* (Chiaroscuro, 1976), *Walk on the Water* (DRG, 1980), and *Little Big Horn* (GRP, 1983), albums taking the *Age of Steam* concept and perfecting it for solo, ensemble, and compositional purposes. Here would be Mulligan's contribution to 1980s' jazz.

As always, it would feature the deep voice of baritone sax, surprising as ever in its lead role. This time around listeners found Mulligan's horn work integrated with the texture of electric instruments— guitar, bass, and the eighty-eight-key Fender Rhodes piano— supported by an acoustic piano playing more percussively than the other rhythm yet in time with tightly scored brass and sometimes interweaving lines with its electronic counterpart. Mulligan's soloing would be as strong as ever, trading passages with the larger group rather than being showcased by it and providing a lyric voice for his strongly melodic compositions. Here were tradition, continuity, and innovative developments in the same work, a combination serving as the artist's trademark through nearly half a century of jazz. What started as a tune for Gene Krupa—"Disc Jockey Jump"—would continue as songs for no less than four and perhaps five succeeding decades, during which Mulligan would continually reflect on both himself and his times—sometimes in harmony, sometimes at odds, but always productive of solid work for the present and an indication of things to come.

Little Big Horn ends with Mulligan's most playful, lively, and comically self-reflective song, "I Never Was a Young Man," which features his words, music, singing, and playing. Its story is a simple one. He never had a youth, forsaking sentimental sunrises and sunsets for the pursuit of a goal known as "downtown." No pushing or crowding; just a hard, steady climb. But now he wonders: Is there such a place as Heaven? Does he even care? No, because there's probably just another mountain there for him to climb. He'll have none of that, for what he wants is to be an old man, "I mean a really, really old man" who won't cry at a sunrise, might cry at a sunset, but will never be found climbing that mountain called downtown any more—because he's found nothing there. What remains is the act of climbing itself, to be celebrated in the relaxed, loping, yet vocally strong baritone sax style that has made him famous. It's there on over one hundred records, a sound that no audience can ever mistake. Listen: Gerry Mulligan.

CHAPTER ONE

ARRANGING A LIFE OF MUSIC

From the start, it was clear to Gerry Mulligan that some type of arrangement had to be made. Born in Queens, New York City, on 6 April 1927 and given a strict Irish-American Catholic upbringing, he had a traditional middle-class musical education financed by his father, a management engineer whose job transfers took the family from town to town until winding up in Philadelphia for part of Gerry's teens.

There were lessons on piano, the parlor symbol of bourgeois conformity and success. Then clarinet, that infernally difficult instrument despised by even the era's master jazzmen—one of Woody Herman's more sardonic comments in later years would be recalling how difficult it was for a young man to express himself on that demanding instrument, yet how the age demanded it as the sign of successful bandleading. Finally some schooling in the art of arranging, but learned in the studio of Sammy Correnti, master of the sweetly polite dance-band style—yet a talent nevertheless, one that would qualify the seventeen-year-old Mulligan for a staff arranger's job with WCAU's radio orchestra led by Johnny Warrington and then a traveling gig with Tommy Tucker.

Some called Tucker's style "society music," while others denigrated it as "Mickey Mouse," but the man was seeking to raise his band's musical quality, and so he took a chance with the brainy, rebellious young protégé. The experiment failed, sending Mulligan back to WCAU for more staff work. By now the station was featuring the big band of Elliot Lawrence. A forward-looking leader, Lawrence turned

Mulligan's pen loose and put him in the sax section as well, for his clarinet training meant he could pick up any other single-reed instrument at will: alto sax, tenor, even the cumbersome bari that only one other jazz musician, Duke Ellington's Harry Carney, had been able to develop as a lead and solo horn. At age eighteen Mulligan found himself an important voice in a jazz orchestra featuring such innovative opportunities as a brass section including French horn and a pianist-leader who enjoyed dropping in delicate fills and occasional light-touch solos, creating jazz concertos out of otherwise routine dance numbers. For Gerry Mulligan the artist, his paints and palette were ready.

Soon the band's book was filled with Mulligan's fresh, airy arrangements; but Lawrence knew enough to give the bright young kid some time off for trips up to New York, where he could hear the bop revolution taking place. Soon there would be a job in the big city—not with the beboppers just yet, but with a veteran big band needing some fresh blood to propel it through the first difficult postwar year of 1946. And so at age nineteen Gerry Mulligan signed on as arranger and fill-in alto man for Gene Krupa. This lasted just less than a year, from April 1946 through the following January, for in 1947 bandleader Claude Thornhill hired Mulligan to augment a book of truly innovative arrangements begun by Gil Evans. Evans, meanwhile, was getting to know Miles Davis quite well and invited Mulligan along for some discussion sessions on modern music. There was still time to do arrangements for Thornhill, but the movement toward Davis's style of small-ensemble jazz was a critical step: by 1948 Gerry was giggling with these people, and within a year he'd be both writing for and playing in the *Birth of the Cool* sessions with Davis's nine-piece group, leaving the swing-band era behind forever. American music was changing, and Gerry Mulligan had finally arranged things with life.

• *Elliot Lawrence and His Orchestra:* "Between the Devil and the Deep Blue Sea," from *"Sugar Beat,"* Big Band Archives LP-1219, 1945. Gerry Mulligan: arrangement and baritone saxophone solo; Red Rodney, John Dee, Paul Cope: trumpets; Frank Rodowicz, Joe Verrechico, Herb Collins: trombones; Ernie Cantonucci, Buddy Gentiles, Gerry Mulligan, Pete Sansone, Mike Donio: saxophones; Ernie Angelucci: French horn; Elliot Lawrence, piano and leader; Andy Riccardi: bass; Max Spector: drums.

For supposedly apprentice work, a great deal of Mulligan's arranging and even a spot of his playing from these big-band years can still
be heard. Indeed, when an attractive-sounding big band cranks up
today, chances are some of its more appealing voicings can be traced
to the innovations this rambunctious teenager first suggested back in
1945–1948. Elliot Lawrence's archival LP provides the first look at
Mulligan's arranging and baritone work: the Harold Arlen standard
"Between the Devil and the Deep Blue Sea" as recorded in 1945
(*Gerry Mulligan: The Arranger*, Columbia JC-34803, dates this as a
1949 performance, but the notes contain many errors; Mulligan himself recalls it as a 1946 air-check). This strongly melodic and thematically plotted song about being caught between the proverbial rock
and a hard place let Mulligan do things that would, a decade later, be
characterized as Shorty Rogers's West Coast style. Arlen's compositional habits, celebrated by Rogers's own treatment of *The Wizard
of Oz*, are invitations for a certain amount of hip whimsy, and Mulligan shows plenty of wit (later hastily categorized as California cool)
in redistributing the component parts of the song writer's popular
melody.

Mulligan's arrangement gives the devil's role to one part of the
band and the deep blue sea to the other, only to have this initial
distribution reversed the next time around. Meanwhile, the familiar
pattern of two statements of melody followed by a bridge and then a
single restatement is gradually replaced by an entirely new understanding of the tune's complexity. Lawrence's piano starts things off
with a thematic introduction of the melody, which the alto-led saxes
pick up and repeat from the top and on through the song's bridge,
with the brass section making counter-rhythmic comments in the
background. But for the last statement the saxes come back with an
entirely new statement of the melody as Charlie Parker might play it,
at which point the trumpets come in and take the boppish line to its
modernistic conclusion—which is no conclusion at all, but rather a
riffing introduction to a trombone solo played close enough to the
melody so that Arlen's song comes through intact. Then Lawrence's
understated piano takes the bridge, opening some space for a stronger, Harry James-like trumpet solo. Now the brass can take the number for its own, the traditional call-and-response pattern of big-band
arranging having transformed itself into the new style of challenge-
and-win. But only for a moment, for just when we think the trumpets
have taken it all, the most unlikely of reed instruments slips in for a
thoroughly surprising solo: Mulligan's baritone sax, played in the

upper register so that its weaving line can be as delicate as anything the alto saxes might have ventured earlier in the song.

After this the number really heats up, with brass initiating the bridge before turning the balance of it plus the restatement to a tenor sax solo. This time the song's structure finds the brass section showing off all its traditions, the trumpet players doing the classic ooh-aah while the trombones reach to the bottom for a bass-clef rendition of Arlen's melody, here given one last statement in its primal simplicity. But there's to be no bridge this last time through; Mulligan's bridges have been initiations to surprise, and now the arrangement's final innovation is that "The Devil and the Deep Blue Sea" can end with its melody alone, innocent even of Arlen's own tampering (which is what the middle part of any traditional song must do, playing a variation on the tune's first rendering). In three minutes and five seconds Mulligan has done almost everything: redistributing melodic statements from one section of the band to another, dropping the piano and then the baritone sax into the unlikeliest of contexts, and dividing bridges—themselves the logical division points within traditional composition—into even smaller elements, giving part to ensemble playing and part to a soloist. If this is how Mulligan wrote for Tommy Tucker, no wonder that band's radio listeners and dance-floor fans were confused. But the strength of Elliot Lawrence's orchestra carries it off.

When Mulligan moves on to his year's career with the Gene Krupa band, the sense of life changing with and around him is even more apparent. Music on the radio no longer had to fit an entertaining format like that of Kay Kyser or the other bands with a lease on network air time. Postwar exuberance had spread to the music itself, and with no need to thematize a coy yet traditional structure, performers such as Krupa could turn their organizations loose to swing and drive on their own terms. Audiences had graduated from the Kollege of Musical Knowledge to the real world of orchestral innovation, where arrangers such as Mulligan and Gil Evans were responding to the key lessons being taught on 52nd Street by the founders of bebop.

The boppers themselves understood the value of transition, and so their most frequently played songs would be old standards, transformed step-by-step into entities eventually so radically new that they'd be retitled. Mulligan captures this moment in the history of jazz by taking one of bop's favorite vehicles, "How High the Moon," and drafting an arrangement that celebrates its function as a bridge between two eras, in the process showing how well the Krupa band could handle such new material as Mulligan's generation was eager to introduce. The number's dance-band-style chord structure would provide the basis for Charlie Parker's "Ornithology," one of the first bebop reorderings of tradition. Mulligan's arrangement of the elementary "How High the Moon" for Elliot Lawrence in 1945 remains comparatively free of these urges, but when it comes time to adapt the chart for Krupa in 1946 the influence of Parker and Dizzy Gillespie shows through in the most dramatic way possible, as after an initial statement of the standard's theme by a muted trumpet section the saxes open up with a full-blowing rendition of Parker's new melody. In Mulligan's canon there are three archival versions to compare.

- ***Elliot Lawrence and His Orchestra:*** "How High the Moon," from "*Sugar Beat,*" Big Band Archives LP-1219, 1945. Gerry Mulligan: arrangement and baritone saxophone solo; Red Rodney, John Dee, Paul Cope: trumpets; Frank Rodowicz, Joe Verrechico, Herb Collins: trombones; Ernie Cantonucci, Buddy Gentiles, Gerry Mulligan, Pete Sansone, Mike Donio: saxophones; Ernie Angelucci: French horn; Elliot Lawrence, piano and leader; Andy Riccardi: bass; Max Spector: drums.

Mulligan supplied the chart for "How High the Moon" for the Lawrence orchestra dates from the same year as "Between the Devil and the Deep Blue Sea," but it sounds more traditional, as Gerry keeps the song's original form intact. The structure and tonality of 1945 are evident in the arrangement's first bars, introduced by a brass fanfare followed by a few notes of the sax section repeated by the leader's tinkling piano. After this, "How High the Moon" itself gets underway with muted trumpets stating the melody, supported by a traditional easy rhythm. There's a sweetly played second statement from the sax section with the altos on top, followed by the briefest of bridges, compliments of a single alto sax, before the trumpets open up for a loud final melody. Next time through the chorus Mulligan cues another fanfare and then gives the lead solo to Lawrence, who in turn passes the tune to the trombones (with the trumpets doodling quietly in the background), until a louder solo trombone concludes this part. Third time around a gritty tenor sax gets center stage, supported by some chromatically rising riffs from a subdued lower sax section and brass, before the spotlight shifts to the hard-hitting Harry James-style trumpet for a classic jump solo punched out against the high playing, chromatically descending saxes. Now, for the fourth and last time through, Mulligan calls for the era's standard jitterbugging conclusion, with a solidly voiced sax section blowing out the melody against a piercing trumpet barrage, all of which ends with a rousing fanfare.

Although the arrangement has showcased several good solos and provided an appreciable crescendo of excitement for eager dancers, this 1945 version of "How High the Moon" looks solidly to the present rather than to a bebop or cool jazz future, the hippest thing about it being Elliot Lawrence's verbal encouragement to the trumpet section as they play the song's melody at the start—"Hey!" and then "Sing it! Sing it!" They do, but that's about all the arrangement is meant to accomplish.

● **Gene Krupa and His Orchestra:** "How High the Moon," from *Gerry Mulligan: The Arranger*, Columbia JC-34803, 21 May 1946. Gerry Mulligan: arrangement; Red Rodney, Joe Triscari, Ray Triscari, Tony Anelli: trumpets; Bob Ascher, Dick Taylor, Warren Covington, Ben Seaman: trombones; Harry Terrill, Charlie Kennedy (alto), Charlie Ventura, Buddy Wise (tenor), Jack Schwartz (baritone): saxes; Teddy Napoleon: piano; Mike Triscari: guitar; Bob Munoz: bass; Gene Krupa: drums and leader.

When Mulligan gets his hands on Krupa's band less than a year later, the results are something else again. The opening fanfare is gone, part of ancient history consigned to the good old days of sweet dance orchestras; nor does Mulligan need it to announce the four clearly marked restatements of the tune's basic structure, as employed in the chart for Elliot Lawrence, to pace the dancer's energy. Big-band music can now be for listening as well, and the provision for Krupa's little high-hat swish followed by his sharp snare work becomes an entirely different kind of fanfare: an announcement with his signature that the leader plays drums up front, with no need for a subtle buildup to one rousing jump chorus at the end–this number will hop from the start! A lighter, tighter rhythm section gives the impression of everything taking place more quickly, and the second-time-through statement of Charlie Parker's "Ornithology" theme prepares listeners for the emphasis of the alto sax, trombone, trumpet, and tenor sax solos that follow. No more fanfare announcements here—just solid blowing all over the scale, with a quick nod at the end of each solo to the next instrument, helped along by the briefest of orchestral introductions. It is all very straight ahead, and by the time the piece ends with Krupa's drum display on the heels not of the standard's original melody but of Parker's reformulation of it, dancers can be grateful for the number's steady beat while listeners know they've been treated to a concert by a solidly swinging band.

● **Gene Krupa and His Orchestra:** "How High the Moon," et al., from *Gene Krupa Plays Gerry Mulligan Arrangements*, Verve MGV-8292, 20 October and 20 November 1958. Gerry Mulligan: arrangements. Al DeRisi, Ernie Royal, Doc Severinsen, Al Stewart: trumpets; Eddie Bert, Billy Byers, Jimmy Cleveland, Kai Winding: trombones; Phil Woods, Sam Marowitz (alto), Frank Socolow, Eddie Wasserman (tenor), Danny Banks (baritone): saxes; Hank Jones: piano; Barry Galbraith: guitar; Jimmy Gannon: bass; Gene Krupa: drums.

Although tenor-sax man Charlie Ventura had been the 1946 band's only superstar besides its leader, Krupa's players were always technically superb and intelligently spirited—the hallmark of working studio musicians Mulligan would attract and be attracted to throughout his career. It was the style of band Gene Krupa put together for the 1958 session that recreated the 1946–1947 Mulligan book, where "How High the Moon" and "Disc Jockey Jump" are done in a manner compatible with their original form on *Gerry Mulligan: The Arranger*, showing that a soloist could express himself well enough within the limits of arrangements over a decade old.

The twelve charts included on *Gene Krupa Plays Gerry Mulligan Arrangements*, totaling half the young writer's contribution to the drummer's catalog, compose an interesting literature of big-band music. "How High the Moon" proves as swingable for the late 1950s as it did for 1946, as does Mulligan's "Disc Jockey Jump," a hit after being recorded in January 1947, just as Mulligan was about to leave the band. Both songs are light and snappy, their pert melodies responding to Krupa's rhythmic punctuations in a way that makes the band's section work percussive as well as tonal. The style of "Disc Jockey Jump" is much like that of the Woody Herman hit "Four Brothers," though it predates that classic by several months and features not the tightly structured tenor saxes of Herman's band but rather similarly playing trumpets (muted in the 1947 recording, but open and joined by an alto sax in unison for the 1958 session). Primarily an up-tempo vehicle for tight section work and sharply executed solos, Mulligan's arrangement flatters Krupa's lyricism as well as his rhythmic talents by slotting the drum solo in the same format used to introduce the tenor-sax solo. Of the five Mulligan originals on this album it is by no means the most personally innovative chart; the trumpet voicings are those used on the more routine rendition of "Sugar," in which the muting of upper-register trumpets creates a distinct but unobtrusive sound, against which the individual soloists can characterize themselves—in fact allowing the featured alto sax (played in 1958 by Phil Woods) to be more piercing than the trumpets preceding it. This same contrast of softly muted trumpets versus individually cutting alto sax (for the bridge) appears again in "Yardbird Suite," one of the first Charlie Parker bebop originals scored for dance orchestra. A small Mulliganesque touch, however, provides the subtle anchor for these sweetly muted trumpets: the baritone sax accompanying their tightly packed high notes in its very lowest register.

The other Mulligan originals besides "Disc Jockey Jump" are two Parker-derived numbers, "Bird House" and "Birds of a Feather," plus a nicely textured "The Way of All Flesh" and the less melodically inventive but humorously played "Mulligan Stew." "Bird House" serves as a tip of the hat to the revolutionary alto saxophonist, creating a smartly thematic line, phrasing it with a boplike attitude, and carrying it through by means of a dialogue between the first half of a melodic passage and its symmetrical reversal. For this the sax section takes the lead, playing low behind the tenors and baritone, but with the brass standing ready to answer with rhythmic punctuations, the attack of which is sharpened by Krupa's rim shots off the snare. Not that old himself when he joined Benny Goodman in 1935, and proud to sport something of a punk-kid image in his early years as a stage-show feature, Krupa surely took delight in the way his sassy young arranger brought a new life to his band and to his own playing, as material like "Bird House" and "Disc Jockey Jump" kept the drums integral to each arrangement yet never sounding dated. A dozen years later, these remain the numbers leading off the A and B sides of the Krupa-Mulligan retrospective, setting the tone for the broader range of genius that follows.

"Birds of a Feather," like its sister tune "Bird House," starts out with a Parkerish solo alto, quoting the master's style of phrasing and intonation, before the trumpets take the lead in sounding out another bop-styled melody, this time played against an alto-led sax section filling in and backing up the more aggressive horns, until by the end of the first chorus the trumpets and saxes have assumed the roles taken by Gillespie and Parker in the bebop-quintet format emerging as these charts were written. Of the two other originals, "Mulligan

Stew" is barely more than a head arrangement based on the humorous interplay between the band's characteristically high and low sections, an approach Mulligan would find more rewarding when applied to familiar standards (as he'd done with "The Devil and the Deep Blue Sea" for Elliot Lawrence). More promising is "The Way of All Flesh," his first of several compositions throughout his career that cite the title of a famous novel. Here Mulligan presents an extremely smooth melody, played in sweet and easy harmony by a trombone section (underscored by a soft baritone sax whose lushness is first challenged by the harder-hitting introductory trumpets, who are soon persuaded to use their mutes for the bridge). The voicings are particularly rich, signaling the writer's intention to construct melodies and structural formats that would open the range for sound rather than provide opportunities for flashy instrumental pyrotechnics and raging riffs. Yet the number swings as resolutely as the snappier "Disc Jockey Jump" and "How High the Moon," proof that subtlety could survive both the bebop revolution and the closing days of the big-band era.

Attention to the texture of instrumental voice and dedication to giving big-band arrangement a few moments of blessed quiet amidst the traditionally incessant solos and ensemble work are Mulligan's chief contributions to the Krupa book, qualities he would take to Claude Thornhill's orchestra the following year and to his own Concert Jazz Band more than a decade later. From his apprentice work with the likes of Tommy Tucker he brought with him a sense of humor and an inventiveness that would often choose spunky wit and wry, even ironic comedy over the thundering-herd concept being developed by Woody Herman and the stampeding-elephants effect of overblowing massed brass of Stan Kenton's orchestra. These techniques are most easily measured when applied to familiar standards, of which the Krupa-Mulligan album boasts four noteworthy examples.

The most remarkable display of Mulligan's oddball humor comes with "Sometimes I'm Happy." The arrangement begins with a lavish double introduction, the first portion of which is played with a loud brassiness, the second more subtly with softer brass and saxes backing a solo trumpet. At the very end of this second portion comes the only warning that Mulligan has a trick in mind: a laughlike riff from the other trumpets, cup-muted for vaudevillian mocking effect and descending chromatically to introduce what listeners might otherwise expect to be the old predictable melody of this Youmans-Caesar-Grey standard.

The melody Mulligan delivers, however, is only as recognizable as a face might be in one of Picasso's more extreme cubist portraits, or perhaps as a human countenance can be discerned within the artfully arranged plate of fruits and vegetables painted by Arcimboldo. An even better image might be that of junk sculpture, and Mulligan's rendering of the tune's familiar line invites comparison with the era's junk sculptor in big-band music, Spike Jones. The melody is, in cubist fashion, broken down into minimally reductive parts and then redistributed among diverse sections of the band, which nevertheless plays it through as a coherent entity. The first two notes, corresponding to the word "sometimes," are given to the sax section; but the next one, matching the single syllable "I'm," is blatted out by a solitary trombone, while the next two notes (for "happy") are property of the trumpets, all of which is followed by an ornamental slide through a few extraneous notes by the saxes with an anchoring blat from the baritone sax in between. Like Picasso's and Arcimboldo's faces, the referential materials are there, only presented in a disarmingly different manner, causing the listener to reexperience what had become perhaps a too-familiar song and to hear parts that may never before have been recognized. *Sounds*, not just ideas, can communicate the feelings of such tunes, Mulligan shows, and to do it he resorts to a method bordering on that of Spike Jones's sound effects.

What does such humor accomplish for the arrangement as a whole? Sandwiched between the artful craziness of the melody's twin statements, the bridge—usually the intentionally odd-sounding part of a song—comes across here as a refreshingly smooth piece of music. Once into the body of the number, Krupa's band is able to combine section work with especially clear and biting solos by alto sax and trumpet, thanks to the rhythmic complexity established when the band presents the melody first time through. As backing for the trumpet solo, Mulligan has the sax section fill in with quiet riffs reminiscent of the herky-jerky handling of the song's main theme, while the alternating eight-bar sections given over to ensemble playing sound especially powerful, even as the drummer accentuates their percussive variations. Once again, Krupa himself is put back in the spotlight of his prewar glory days, but without setting the band aside (as it had to be in "Sing Sing Sing" with Benny Goodman). The leader must have felt ten years younger playing Mulligan's chart.

The same spirit of youthful invention pervades another standard, "Margie." Its introduction is much more concise, picking up what will become the melody's last few bars as a tag line played in full voice by the trumpets. The tune itself is presented in the fragmented manner of "Sometimes I'm Happy," with the theme's first bar sounded out in turn by all three sections: two notes for the name "Margie" played by the trumpets, followed by an echolike answer from the saxes, which is at once picked up by the trombone, before the sax section adds a little fill as a way of turning over the melody's remainder to the harmonizing trombones. After an ensemble bridge, a solo 'bone takes the melody one more time through, building up to the trumpets' tag-line ending that introduced the song. The central nature of this tag line becomes clear as the number proceeds with section work being showcased rather than solos. What the first solo (by alto sax) accomplishes is mirrored by some interchanges between the trumpet and sax sections; after this, when one might expect a second solo, the brass takes the first eight bars, sounding out a boppish line answered in turn by solo tenor. So far, solo instrumentals and full sections have shared the material. When, for the last time through, the full orchestra builds up to a high-register piece of solo trumpet virtuosity, the remaining trumpets stand ready to join in, at the piece's height, with the tag line that opened the number, followed by the full section quickly summarizing the theme at the horn's optimum range. The result is an integral partnership among the band, its component sections, and its individual solo instruments, all blended in a way that makes Mulligan's "Margie" a nonstop progression through what the Krupa organization has to offer.

If Mulligan takes advantage of "Sometimes I'm Happy" and "Margie" to show how witty he can be with old standards, "Begin the Beguine" and "If You Were the Only Girl in the World (And I Were the Only Guy)" let the young arranger construct virtual showcases for both the songs' qualities and the band's talent (not to mention his own aural artistry and intelligence). The first arrangement, in fact, is playfully overdone in parts, a sign in these bebop times that Cole Porter was becoming a bit campish for a high-powered group of swingers like the Krupa band to do. And so the introductory bars are laid on with a comic heaviness, the trombones, saxes, then trumpets intoning with a solemn, choirlike effect as the rhythm hangs in suspended time beneath them, as if the whole world is pausing while "Begin the Beguine" masses its forces to get underway. Once rolling, Mulligan resorts to another comic contrast—having the saxes play the melody in an extremely soft and light manner, clipping off Cole Porter's notes as if only the politest form of sophisticated understatement can be tolerated. But they no sooner get the theme stated than the trumpets intrude, stopping the beat until a solo trombone, again playing soft and sweet, reestablishes the tempo with a run-through of the song closer to the melody the saxes had been in danger of losing.

Full-blowing brass then pounds out the bridge until the baritone sax edges in to finish this middle part with an arhythmic bolero as the trumpets play a lavish rallentando in the background. Then comes an understated trumpet solo, which slowly builds to the trombones playing a soft melody while a solo alto reaches for new melodic variations as Charlie Parker might hear them. Here Mulligan plays his trump card, letting alto and orchestra trade notes until the atmosphere is sufficiently energized to let the number end with a grab bag of semiclassical techniques, including Krupa's snare drum signaling a march tempo for the trumpet section's concluding bugle call. The arrangement is at once hilarious and refreshing, showing that the colorful nature of Cole Porter's tune can still be exploited to several further degrees—and in the process letting Mulligan, just nineteen years old when this chart went into Krupa's book, make it clear that he not only has a great musical vocabulary but is not about to be intimidated by the sacrosanct features of a contemporary pop classic. The best of Cole Porter's compositions have a light but sharply edged wit to them, and in the young arranger's hands this sense of brightness is renewed for the coming, bop-tinged generation.

If Mulligan's first big-band charts are revolutionary, they are creatively so. Little of value from the previous age is destroyed in his works. Instead, he draws on the full range of techniques and approaches developed in the previous decade of the big bands' heyday, taking a little from Fletcher Henderson, a little from Jimmie Lunceford, and great deal from the stellar band-leader soloists of the time. Mulligan loves to feature a sweet trombone, showcased more like Tommy Dorsey's than Glenn Miller's, though there are plenty of chances for hard blowing that a player like Jack Teagarden would appreciate. Fascination with the emerging age of bop keeps him away from tailoring songs for clarinet, one instrument the 52nd Street crowd had little use for, but the Krupa charts give plenty of space to the pleasures of alto sax. Here Mulligan performs the remarkable act of thinking about mainstream leaders like Jimmy Dorsey and Woody Herman (on alto rather than the clarinet) and bebopper Charlie Parker at the same time. On the 1958 retrospective session Phil Woods exploits these facets, which only in a Mulligan arrangement come across as complementary rather than contradictory, the alto's potential for throaty richness rising at times to the wispy upperregister flourishes characteristic of Parker's playing. The elemental swing in these alto-led numbers is certainly a style pioneered by

Dorsey and perfected by Herman, but for that extra spurt of inventiveness—usually near the end of a solo phrase—Mulligan keeps the supporting ensemble work sufficiently open so that Charlie Kennedy (in 1946–1947) and Phil Woods (in 1958) can draw upon their instrument's full tradition, even as it was being extended by Parker when these arrangements were first unveiled.

He could also stand back from the fancy techniques and flourishes at his disposal and let the Krupa band and its soloists play pretty. "If You Were the Only Girl in the World," the familiar words of which are wrought with sweet emotion, prompts Mulligan to score a show-piece of instrumental voicing and texture. Like "Begin the Beguine," this standard gets underway with a clarion call from the brass, out of which the melody emerges with the tenderness of a spare, muted trumpet. After the first chorus, the brass retards the rhythm with another stunning call, debated for a moment by the alto sax; given the spotlight, the alto takes the full structure of the song for itself, rising out of the other sections' various choir effects to exploit the full register of sound available from this rich instrument. Amazingly, the tempo has been so lovingly slow that the number is over with the alto's final notes—the standard three minutes of a single's duration having allowed Mulligan to run through the chorus structure only twice. But thanks to the showcasing of the band's two most subtle horns—muted trumpet and sweetly played alto sax–the listener's full range of emotions has been explored. The band as a whole has intruded only twice—to get things rolling and to introduce the splendid alto solo. At the very end Mulligan plays a remarkable trick, taking the otherwise dead air following the alto's conclusion and filling it with a few isolated atonal bleats from the trumpets—another sound effect, like off-key auto horns sounding a distant cacophony across the late night of a city's exhausted streetscape. Analytically, the sound is bebop, the gesture Thelonious Monk would make by hitting two adjacent piano keys for an otherwise unobtrusive fill. Emotionally, the effect is languidly postcoital, a closing sigh after the heights and depths that Mulligan's arrangement has explored. Rarely has the total impact of a popular song been so thoroughly examined.

● *Claude Thornhill and His Orchestra:* "Jeru," "Rose of the Rio Grande," "Poor Little Rich Girl," and "Five Brothers," from *Two Sides of Claude Thornhill,* Kapp KL-1058, 28–29 April 1953. Gerry Mulligan: arrangements; Dale Pierce, Sonny Rich, Dick Sherman: trumpets; Owen Massingill, Billy Ver Planck: trombones; Al Antonucci, Sandy Siegelstein: French horns; Bill

Barber: tuba; Ralph Aldridge (tenor, clarinet), Med Flory, Gene Quill (alto), Dave Figg, Ray Norman (tenor), Dick Zubach (baritone, clarinet): reeds; Claude Thornhill: piano and leader; Barry Galbraith: guitar; Bob Peterson: bass; Winston Welch: drums.

The variations of tempos and the shadings of orchestral colors and dynamics anticipate Mulligan's next career development—writing for and playing in the decidedly forward-looking band of Claude Thornhill. In essence, the move to Thornhill signals Mulligan's transition from the characteristically prewar world of big-band jazz (of which Krupa had been a superstar) to the emergence of bebop and smaller group ensembles—a revolution lyricized three decades later in Martin Scorsese's film, *New York, New York*, and marked by jazz critics as the interface of two eras equaling the change from Dixieland to swing a generation before. It was a move at once historical, geographic, and musicological, both in substance and in implication. Bop was a New York City phenomenon, shaped by dictates of both sound and money as smaller groups were made necessary by the iconoclasm of new musical ideas and the difficult economics faced by postwar club owners, not to mention the initially small audiences for this bold new jazz. Mulligan heard it when Elliot Lawrence's band was called from Philadelphia to New York for a hotel engagement and again when Krupa's organization—often on the road—would pass through town. As the young arranger-saxophonist established himself as a professional, he fell in with the era's innovators, most of them just a few years older than he. This crowd lived, talked, and breathed music. They were dedicated to their own proficiency but were also concerned with new concepts for jazz. And they responded brightly to the breakthroughs happening almost every night in the 52nd Street clubs where small groups led by Charlie Parker, Dizzy Gillespie, and Miles Davis had begun the next identifiable epoch in the history of jazz.

These eager-to-learn musicians and arrangers—Mulligan, Lee Konitz, Brew Moore, Johnny Carisi, Gil Evans, and others—were drawn to bandleader Claude Thornhill, and he to them, in a momentary symbiosis that proved to be an important stage in the careers of the hardline beboppers themselves, including Davis (who would form a nine-piece group with them in 1948–50) and Parker (part of whose Carnegie Hall concert with strings in 1950 was scored by Mulligan). Thornhill, who was conservatory trained and had established himself as an arranger in the late 1930s with such top bands as Hal Kemp's, Benny Goodman's, and Ray Noble's, had devised his own subtly new approach to dance-orchestra music in 1940. Emphasizing a deftly understated touch and the rich dynamics of what at times seemed to be pure sound, Thornhill's own arrangements devised entirely new harmonies and textures for a big-band era whose tradition of antiphonal call and response between specifically defined and instrumentally distinct sections of brass and reeds had reached its full development with Fletcher Henderson's arrangements for Benny Goodman. Thornhill's choice for instrumentation exploded the customary form of four or five saxes and three trumpets and trombones by featuring as many as seven reed players—two on clarinet at all times, and four or five on saxes, making it possible through doubling to present a choir of seven clarinets on occasion (in Kemp's band, the entire reed section would at times play clarinets held inside Rudy Vallee-style megaphones, producing an eerie, ethereal tone radically different from Goodman's punching saxes or Glenn Miller's high-pitched saxophone section led by a single clarinet). There are also two French horns, and occasionally a single trombone or tuba would be scored to play above the trumpets rather than below them, the musician's sense of straining for these high notes making the ensemble work sound completely different from that when a trumpet would produce the same notes in its lower register. When the saxes worked alone, it was often in a subtone, the altos taking notes usually reserved for tenors, the tenor saxes doing the same for what otherwise belonged to the baritone, while the bari sax would come out on top in a reshuffling of conventional voicing (a practice that Mulligan would adopt in his small-ensemble work of the middle 1950s and again for the Concert Jazz Band in 1960).

If there was a tradition for such orchestral jazz, it was Duke Ellington's. But Thornhill's fate was impelled forward rather than backward by virtue of his association with another arranger, Gil Evans, who in turn became Mulligan's entrée to the bebop world of Miles Davis. The Canadian-born Evans had grown up in Stockton, California, where in the late 1930s he had formed a band soon taken over by Hal Kemp alumnus Skinnay Ennis. In 1939 he met Thornhill, who was working on the West Coast with Bob Crosby; by 1940 Thornhill was back East to start his own band, and in 1941 Evans joined him as an arranger. Here his role developed into adapting the patented Thornhill sound to the emerging bop rhythms and melodies of Parker and Gillespie; by 1947 the Thornhill band was making history by playing big-band arrangements of such Parker classics as "Anthropology," "Donna Lee," and "Yardbird Suite" (the latter of which prompted Mulligan to try his own hand with the number for Krupa).

Suddenly Claude Thornhill and his orchestra became the focal point for serious, forward-looking musicians. Thelonious Monk observed that Thornhill's was the only big band he found worth listening to, while Miles Davis began studying its orchestration with thoughts of expanding his own music from its initial quintet format. Thornhill in turn needed sharp young musicians who could play the technically demanding Evans arrangements yet also maintain a convincing sense of big-band swing. And so talents such as Mulligan, Lee Konitz, Brew Moore, Red Rodney, and later Nick Travis, Gene Quill, and Bob Brookmeyer assembled under the Thornhill banner, with the 52nd Street beboppers catching their sets even as Mulligan, Evans, and company were feasting on each new Parker-Gillespie-Davis single.

By 1948 Mulligan had joined the band to write arrangements and play baritone in a sax section including Lee Konitz on alto and Brew Moore and Phil Urso as heirs to the Lester Young tradition of wispy, breathy tenor. With Mulligan's affinity for the bari's top notes and Konitz's singularly brittle sound, Thornhill's 1948 sax section proved the perfect vehicle to be matched with his orchestra's soprano and bass clarinets and surrounded by the ethereal French horns, muted trumpets, and high-straining yet delicate trombones. Mulligan's experience writing for Tommy Tucker and his own whimsy in arranging "Margie" and "Sometimes I'm Happy" for Krupa gave him a ready-made affinity with the memories and ideas Thornhill and Evans brought from their years with Hal Kemp and Skinnay Ennis. In addition, his ear for the new phraseology of bop and feel for its intellectually impertinent rhythms and complex melodies made Mulligan the ideal new talent for what Thornhill had proposed in 1940 and Evans had begun perfecting a year later, before wartime service put the band on hold until 1946.

Though he left Thornhill's sax section in September 1948 to stay in New York City with the Miles Davis *Birth of the Cool* group, Mulligan continued to support himself by writing arrangements for the orchestra into the early 1950s, during which time he did the same for Elliot Lawrence. The four most important of these Thornhill charts are reprised on the 29 April 1953 session on *Two Sides of Claude Thornhill* (Kapp KL-1058). As with his writing for the Krupa band, Mulligan shows the range of his talent by doing two originals ("Jeru" and "Five Brothers") in the company of Noel Coward's "Poor Little Rich Girl" and the Leslie-Warren-Gorman pop hit "Rose of the Rio Grande," the unlikeliest of choices for a young man with his head full of Charlie Parker and Miles Davis. The album itself highlights Mulligan's talents for innovation within a smartly swinging context, for side A is devoted to six examples of Thornhill's soft and subtle Glen Island Casino mood music of the earlier forties, against which Mulligan's four cuts on side B seem all the more lively. The personnel remains authentic, with two veterans of the *Birth of the Cool* sessions drawn from the Thornhill band, Bill Barber on tuba and Sandy Siegelstein on French horn, still working for their old leader.

Of these Mulligan arrangements, "Jeru" is the most innovative, although the offhand abstraction displayed in "Rose of the Rio Grande" still turns heads four decades later. "Jeru" was the first composition, developed for Thornhill, that Mulligan took to Miles Davis for the *Birth of the Cool* sessions during this same period. Oddly enough, its version for the fuller Thornhill band features a more complex distribution of the same parts as used in the 21 January 1949 Miles Davis recording, thanks to the breakup of the traditional format by interpolating solos and section work. For Thornhill's book as with Davis's, Mulligan runs the song through four times. The first sixteen bars feature two statements of the melody, which in the larger band is carried by the saxes; the bridge begins with the sax and trumpet sections taking it together before a solo tenor extends the bridge with what amounts to a fill; then the last statement has the saxophones repeating the melody, which at the end becomes quite abstract. The second time through the tune's structure, trumpeter Dick Sherman takes a sixteen-bar solo but turns the bridge over to Ray Norman's tenor sax, which hangs on through the out chorus, its sixteen bars matching Sherman's in length but reflecting the different chord changes of the bridge. Mulligan's showcasing of tenor sax during the arrangement's first two bridges establishes a structural pattern that counterpoints the unconventional distribution of solos; it holds the number together and anticipates the pattern introduced in the third thirty-two-bar section, where a trumpet ensemble twice plays a rhythmic variation on the melody, answered each time by the tenor before taking its by now customary solo bridge, followed by Gene Quill's alto sax improvisation with the final eight bars. For the fourth and final time through, a much fuller voicing of the brass plays a variation of the melody; a surprising solo clarinet steps forth as a structural play on the second statement, and then, to close things, the eerie sound of high horns presents the out chorus in place of the missing bridge, leaving this final part of the arrangement one part short of its familiar structure, even as the listener is faced with the obvious sense of closure. The unusually high horns and the over-

looked bridge thus end things on a decidedly obscure note, sealing
the number's sense of unreality—just the impression Mulligan must
have wished to make in this self-proclaimed new age of jazz.

Obscure abstraction meets a bigger test in "Rose of the Rio
Grande," even in Thornhill's time a somewhat hackneyed cabaret and
ballroom standard, whose sing-song melody virtually demands a vocalist to sing the familiar words. To prevent the listener's memory
from taking control of the song, Mulligan boosts the tempo far beyond
the melody's ability to keep up so that ready-made assumptions must
be abandoned in order to keep up with what the band is doing. The
saxes open with a flourish, promising the number's anticipated broad
treatment, but the fast tempo soon forces them to play it through in
an exceedingly light and clipped manner, frustrating every shower-
stall crooner in the audience ready to sing along mentally with the
familiar tune. The trumpets add fills until one of them emerges to
take a solo. More section work among the brass leads to Gene Quill's
alto sax; then the solo piece by a muted trumpet over sax-section fills,
followed by tenor sax working among contributions from the brass.
All this time there has been no clear distinction between statement
and bridge; the changes are there, but the brisk tempo and light-
handed playing have done nothing to highlight them, and so they pass
by in a hasty blur, unnoticed in terms of structural effect. For what
turns out to be the last time through, the brass section presents a
more substantial variation on the melody, clear in rhythmic hitting
but quite distant from the tune's familiar features. With this ending
the band is playing clear and loud but establishing the song as Mulligan's own and thoroughly defamiliarizing listeners in the process. If
there were a big-spending drunk in Thornhill's audience laying down
a lavish tip to hear this old pop standard played, he could certainly
have felt cheated. But like Charlie Parker's similar response to a
request for "White Christmas," the result qualifies as bebop jazz
while keeping the song at least minimally intact—just radically altering the tempo could create a fresher-sounding piece.

Much the same happens with Noel Coward's "Poor Little Rich
Girl," another strange choice for an orchestra seeking to bring ensemble work into the bop revolution. Here again Mulligan speeds
things up and pulls out some old tricks, such as quoting the structurally critical tag line from his Krupa arrangement of "Margie" as one
of the ensemble riffs to introduce a series of hard-driving solos from
tenor sax and muted trumpet. The chart's greatest effect is one of
dynamics, building from the quiet solo piano among abstract section
fills that precede the full band's melody to increasingly bold and lively

section work that ends each phrase and takes over the final bridge as well.

"Five Brothers," Mulligan's response to the Woody Herman hit that had introduced the "four brothers" of the late 1940s' most famous and forward-looking sax section (Stan Getz, Zoot Sims, Herbie Steward, and Serge Chaloff), is, like many of his originals for the Krupa band, one of the more conventionally presented arrangements. Its melody is tailor-made for hip-sounding saxes, and although the tune can be regarded as a compositional variation on Guiffre's more famous melody, it is less mechanical in design than the refrain of "Jeru," a reductive complex of melodic possibilities (itself a customary device of bebop writing and an example of the era's hip intellectualism in music). As with many of his originals from this time, Mulligan would have more fun with it in later years, using its pert lyricism to get his smaller ensembles rolling and letting soloists ride free and easy along its clearly patterned changes, with two or three horns riffing in the background. When full sections do the work, the result is not terribly different from the way the Herman Herd stoked the fires for Stan Getz, Shorty Rogers, and Bill Harris. As such, "Five Brothers" gives the sometimes-placid Thornhill orchestra the chance to show how well it can cook. At a time when the leader's disposition toward tone poems and mood pieces threatened to have the band holding the same chord for what seemed like one hundred measures, Mulligan's brightness in providing a smart and snappy chart was surely welcome. This arrangement is patterned in a way that features the alto sax, which is handed the first bridge and all of the song for its second time through. The tenor solo that follows is reined in after the bridge, the penultimate chorus returning to the five brothers of Thornhill's larger sax section. Following their restatement of the theme Mulligan gives the trumpets half a chorus, but as in "Jeru" he suspends the bridge in favor of a grandly enlarged ending. Were Krupa the leader, here would be the chance for some fancy drum work; but with Thornhill's organization, the concluding emphasis remains on orchestral sound.

● **Elliot Lawrence and His Orchestra,** twelve arrangements by Gerry Mulligan, from *Elliot Lawrence Plays Gerry Mulligan Arrangements*, Fantasy 3-206 / OJC-117), 4 March, 1 July, and 5 July 1955. Gerry Mulligan: arrangements; Dick Sherman, Bernie Glow, Al DeRisi, Stan Fishelson: trumpets; Eddie Bert, Ollie Wilson, Paul Seldon: trombones; Fred Schmidt: French horn; Sam Marowitz, Hal McKusick (alto), Al Cohn, Ed Wasserman (tenor), Charlie O'Kane (baritone): saxophones; Elliot Lawrence: piano and leader; Russ Saunders: bass; Don Lamond: drums. Second and third sessions involve minor personnel changes, with trumpeter Nick Travis, French hornist Tony Miranda, bassist Buddy Jones, and trombonist Al Robertson replacing Sherman, Schmidt, Saunders, and Seldon.

His Claude Thornhill arrangements are Mulligan's last innovations in big-band work for a decade—until the Concert Jazz Band recorded and released its first album in 1960. The 1947–1952 period found Gerry increasingly involved in smaller groups, playing in and writing for the Miles Davis *Birth of the Cool* sessions, participating in recording gigs led by Brew Moore, Kai Winding, and Chubby Jackson, writing and arranging "Elevation" for Red Rodney's *Bebop* album with Keynote Records (later expanding the song for Elliot Lawrence), and placing an original titled "Young Blood" in the Stan Kenton library, following Lee Konitz's migration to that band in 1952. The catalog of Mulligan's 1950s big-band arrangements is less impressive than his 1940s work and implies why he was seeking new directions in smaller ensemble work in New York City and, after 1952, heading to California and the first Gerry Mulligan Quartet. The sessions issued as *The Elliot Lawrence Band Plays Gerry Mulligan Arrangements* feature the twelve charts Mulligan sold to his old leader after leaving Thornhill for Davis in the fall of 1948, while the archival Columbia release, *Gerry Mulligan: The Arranger*, presents four cuts (three of them never released and the fourth from a Columbia jazz-stable sampler) done by a conventionally orchestrated big band Mulligan organized in 1957 but abandoned when he became dissatisfied with its potential for new sounds and ideas. Each album is listenable, but together they show an arranger getting old in concepts and approach; in their company the first Concert Jazz Band albums sound like the work of someone a decade or two younger than the person writing these Thornhill and 1957 charts. But on each are several elements of technique and thinking that carry over into the small-group work of the 1950s into which Mulligan was pouring his heart, mind, and soul.

Seven of the twelve Lawrence pieces are Mulligan's own compositions, and their names anticipate a virtual anthology of his quartet and sextet material of coming years, from "The Rocker" (which he had also scored for Charlie Parker's concert with strings), "Mullenium," and "The Swinging Door" (done later as "Red Door") to such personal favorites as "Bweebida Bwobbida" and "Apple Core"; only the less-distinguished "Happy Hooligan" and overly mild "Elegy for Two Clarinets" escape the reharvesting of later years. The best known standards, "My Silent Love" and "But Not for Me," are run through a rather mechanical application of Mulligan's imaginative talents, his light wit playing with the different aural textures that his genius for scoring can now produce so facilely. Together, they serve as somewhat predictable bookends for his late 1940s' approach to familiar standards: taking George Gershwin's usually slow and sentimental "But Not for Me" and giving it a light but briskly swinging treatment, while cranking up the traditionally softer "My Silent Love" for a broadly voiced, Broadway pit-orchestra rendition. Hearing a tightly stacked sax section Parkerize Gershwin's pretty melody is a pleasant surprise, while the elements of sound (rather than just melodic improvisation) are featured in an Al Cohn sax solo that blends Cohn's mastery of the tenor's lower register with the similarly deep timbre of the supporting trombones. "My Silent Love," however, is all gesture, from the overly rich voices of the lavishly harmonic saxes to the self-conscious prettiness called for by showcasing one solo instrument from each section carefully improvising close to the melody. As a result, Mulligan's writing here approaches the "sophisticated swing" style Jimmy Dorsey carried into his last years of prominence in the mid-1950s—a rewarding fulfillment of 1930s and 1940s big-band swing, but with no interest at all in the future.

As usual, Mulligan shows his own talent for growth when it comes to scoring less intimidating standards. Here his choices verge on the comic: the 1930-ish "Bye Bye Blackbird" and the Gershwins' own witty comment on the music of John Philip Sousa, "Strike Up the Band." The former piece stands out by virtue of its solidly swinging presentation, but Mulligan is thinking in 1950s' terms as well as those of the later 1940s when he has a section of muted trumpets play a bop-phrased melodic variation in the company of a counterpointing sax ensemble with occasional fills from the trombones. For solos, the tenor sax trades fours with the piano—possibly the first time this pattern was used in a format larger than quartet or quintet. After a trombone solo yields the bridge and out chorus to alto sax and the tune is given one last run-through by the full band (which takes great license with the melody), Elliot Lawrence's piano reintegrates itself with Mulligan's arrangement at the very end, indicating that the interaction with solo tenor was no accident. "Strike Up the Band," prepared as a novelty introduction to the band's opening at New York's Paramount Theatre, is a standard swing treatment along the lines of Glenn Miller's "American Patrol," although Mulligan keeps the decks clear for more open blowing by the soloists, alternating Sousa-like trumpet riffs with boppish ensemble lines from the saxes (producing the humor of Al Cohn sounding like he's woodshedding behind the barracks of a marching band). In Mulligan's own canon this chart anticipates his composition "Bike Up the Strand" (recorded in 1956 with the quartet when it included Bob Brookmeyer), an example of the bebop practice of taking the chord structure from an old standard and reinventing its melody through inversions and mathematical permutations. This later version shares the same fast tempo as the arrangement for Lawrence and also its smooth voicing of the melody. For the big band, Mulligan plays with both the song's title and his previous association with Krupa by starting things off with a hip-sounding bit of cymbal and snare work, and even this little touch is recalled in 1956 by drummer Dave Bailey's opening brushes.

Of Mulligan's seven originals collected on the Lawrence album, five would become familiar staples of the smaller groups Gerry would organize in coming years, including his tentette recorded in New York during 1951, his subsequent California tentette (1953), the quartet he took to Paris with Bob Brookmeyer in 1954, and the sextet, which evolved when Zoot Sims's tenor sax and Jon Eardley's trumpet were added for a year-end engagement (leading to three sextet albums in 1955 and 1956). The others, "Happy Hooligan" and "Elegy for Two Clarinets," are distinctly backward-looking pieces, reprising the two extremes of Mulligan's big-band writing: the light touch and up-tempo swing of his Krupa charts for the first number, and the tone-poem subtlety demanded from time to time by Thornhill in the former. Lawrence's band could play either style, but neither shows the originality of Mulligan's best work for the earlier contrasting organizations, and as a result neither number reappears in Mulligan's later work. The "elegy" is a reference to the arranger's displeasure at having to write for the two clarinets in Thornhill's orchestra, and hence there are none in this piece—just the slow sustained ensemble sounds while an understated piano carries a quietly tinkling melody, with the tempo retarded even further when the trumpet section makes its entrance. Like the best of Mulligan's work for Thornhill, this later piece exploits the several qualities of voice and timbre available within the trumpet section and allows variations in sound to dictate the song's rhythm; solo work consists of the interwoven lines of two trumpets, one open and the other lightly muted, playing simultaneously while the exceedingly slow and subtle beat tolls softly in the back ground. Played too late in an evening's repertoire, it might well put an audience to sleep—a reminder of how special Thornhill's orchestra was and how hard it is for a conventional band to reproduce its effects, sympathetic as Lawrence's players might be.

Mulligan's direction is clear in a work like "Rocker," part of his second tour-of-duty's work for Lawrence but also serving as a contribution to the final Miles Davis *Birth of the Cool* session in 1950 (where the ensemble voicing of Davis's trumpet, Lee Konitz's alto, and the other horns playing underneath sounds more creatively original than the straight trumpet-section work here). "Rocker" also appears as a Mulligan arrangement for the Charlie Parker Carnegie Hall concert with strings later that same year (where oboe takes the lead over strings and Parker plays the bridge) and as one of the several originals characterizing the California tentette sessions in 1953. Its constant high-hat cymbal beat and interaction between drums and brass are reminiscent of Mulligan's writing for Krupa, showing that he could take this part of a big band's drive with him into smaller groups and even into Parker's string section. It is the score's openness, however, that shows how the young arranger was becoming more and more interested in opportunities to free things up for solo playing and more complex ensemble effects, both of which demanded an organization more flexible than the segregated sections of a seventeen-piece dance band.

"Apple Core" is the best chance Mulligan has to make the Lawrence band sound as free and open (yet also consistently driving) as his later sextet. By having the sections play in unison, he anticipates the single horns of coming years. But as the chart proceeds, its easy, loping rhythm builds into a predictably standard big-band effect, to which in this case the song's mechanically derived melody—so off-handedly appropriate as a head arrangement for small-group blowing—cannot remain equal. The same thing happens with "The Swinging Door" (here credited as a Mulligan-Sims collaboration but on later dates retitled "The Red Door" and ascribed to Sims alone). What in Elliot Lawrence's book sounds like a big-band chart of the Woody Herman era becomes for Mulligan's smaller group an especially sharp attack mounted by Gerry's and Zoot's complementary but still individually distinctive baritone and tenor saxes (years later the Concert Jazz Band would hang out while Mulligan and Sims reprised their classic interplay on this tune, written to celebrate their jamming in a rehearsal hall during the late 1940s and early 1950s). The greatest contrasts come with such soon-to-be Mulligan classics as "Mullenium" and "Bweebida Bwobbida." Within a year of scoring the former for Lawrence, Mulligan's 1951 New York City tentette would use a slightly revoiced version of this number to introduce its innovative, two-bari lead sound; but for Lawrence's band the number's natural smoothness is roughed up by an unsympathetic attack and somewhat rushed tempo. "Bweebida Bwobbida," which sounds as funny as its name when played in self-consciously herky-jerky abandon by the first tentette and later by the quartet with Brookmeyer, comes across in this earlier and larger format with the smooth slickness of a 1940s' zoot-suit number; comparing the Concert Jazz Band's version of it in 1960 will show how far Mulligan could travel in just ten years, as the song's heavily syncopated rhythms draw out extreme contrasts in instrumental sound rather than simply propelling a dance band's jump chorus.

These dozen charts for Lawrence—the way Mulligan earned a living while paying his first dues in progressive small-group jazz—are best appreciated as lingering traces of earlier interest and as a library of material that will demand radically different treatment by smaller, more innovative groups in coming years: treatment that shows these song's hidden strengths, buried as they are in big-band conventions of the late 1940s. Most of his originals for the Lawrence band come across more naturally when performed by Mulligan's sextet, even the well-regarded 1949 recording of "Elevation" preserved on *Gerry Mulligan: The Arranger*. Here solos are traded on an equal basis with sharply alert ensembles, the style Mulligan would exploit in the coming decade with his close group of favorite musicians: Bob Brookmeyer, Zoot Sims, Jon Eardley, Bill Crow, and Dave Bailey, most of whom would join their leader in the Concert Jazz Band. But even Mulligan's big-band writing at its best cries for a smaller group to open its sound and draw attention to more distinctive harmonic arrangements—not three sections overpowering each other and themselves, but the individually distinguishable voices of baritone sax, tenor sax, trumpet, and valve trombone jostling each other in friendly competition and mutual support, working their way through an arrangement to the point that their ensemble playing could be as rousing as a finale in the Krupa band at its cookingest best, yet with each player maintaining his own distinctive sound and instrumental style.

The Gerry Mulligan Sextet exists in embryo within such Elliot Lawrence tunes as "Elevation," "Apple Core," and "The Swinging Door," and also in the Mulligan arrangement of Lester Young's "Mr. President" that closes the Lawrence-Mulligan retrospective album. Here can be heard the relaxed melodic interweavings that would later characterize the sextet's four lead horns, together with the complex voicing used for Lawrence's sax section that—scored for baritone, tenor, trumpet, and trombone—would yield Mulligan's most personally identifiable sound in the 1950s. It is the sound he used a conventionally orchestrated big band to write large in 1957, its four cuts rounding out the *Gerry Mulligan: The Arranger* collection. But before devising the sextet's sound, Mulligan had much to learn about small ensemble writing and developing as a soloist himself. The first chance would come at the end of summer 1948, when Miles Davis called on Claude Thornhill's brighter and more experimentally inclined personnel to help him devise a new approach for jazz. Thornhill's chief arrangers—Mulligan and Gil Evans—would answer, Gerry bringing along his baritone sax for his first extended solo work. The results of these sessions made it clear that Mulligan's days as dance-band arranger were numbered. From now on the postwar world's job would be not just to dance to jazz, but to listen.

CHAPTER TWO

THE BIRTH OF THE COOL

Mulligan's shift from big-band work to progressively smaller ensembles provided him the chance to develop as a soloist, but it also allowed him to propose significantly new ideas as an arranger—ideas that would in turn vitalize his own playing. It was his talent as an arranger that brought him into the small-ensemble sessions. Unlike Lee Konitz, Kai Winding, and J. J. Johnson, who were recruited for their strengths on alto sax and trombone, Mulligan was not sought specifically for his skills on the cumbersome, awkward baritone—many of his solos from the 1949–1951 years suffer from tentative phrasing and uncertain tone and certainly show less of the smooth command characterizing the bari saxophonist most often hired for his horn work during this period, Serge Chaloff. But what caught the attention of Miles Davis and other small-group leaders of the late 1940s was Mulligan's writing. Alone among big-band arrangers, he was able to impart a lighter sound, opening up the big-band structure for the new approaches defining bebop. Mulligan's charts for these new, smaller groups proved how he could turn the tables, which is obviously what their leaders wanted: open, flowing lines for hard blowing, but with a coherent sense of swing that the more progressive Krupa and Lawrence scores had achieved when at their best. What gave Mulligan his chance on bari is that now he had only between five and nine colleagues to contend with. Obviously there would be more opportunities for everyone to solo; but also, with his writing adapted to this smaller, freer format, Mulligan the arranger could write charts not for sections but for individual horns, creating ensembles in which the characteristic timbre of each separate instrument could be heard, even as they played together. Thus idiosyncrasies of sound could now be featured as an integral part of each number. As a result, the distinctive aura of Gerry Mulligan's baritone sax was allowed to emerge and distinguish itself even before his first extended solo.

Between 1947 (when his work for Gene Krupa brought him to and through New York) and 1951 (his last year East before heading for California) Mulligan played and wrote for eight small groups and contributed arrangements to two others. His presence is noted on the seminal Red Rodney *Bebop* album not via baritone sax (here played by Serge Chaloff) but with an arrangement of his own composition, "Elevation." This 29 January 1947 session featured three horns up front (Rodney on trumpet, with Allen Eager's tenor sax and Chaloff's baritone) complemented by the piano, bass, and drums of Al Haig, Chubby Jackson, and Tiny Kahn. The tune itself is central to the Mulligan canon, purportedly the first he'd ever written (as a teenager back in Philadelphia), yet one that would be playable by both Elliot Lawrence's big band and the Red Rodney Be-Boppers and then show up again as the most representative number by Mulligan's mid-1950s sextet. In 1948 Gerry turns up on bari with Benny Green, Allen Eager, Al Haig, Jimmy Raney, Clyde Lombardi, Charlie Perry, and vocalists Blossom Dearie, Buddy Stewart, and Dave Lambert in a group named the Five Bops playing "Hot Halavah." On 4 September the Miles Davis *Birth of the Cool* group broadcast from the Royal Roost and by January 1949 had begun its recording sessions for Capitol. Throughout 1949 Mulligan was active with a group of musicians shaping music for the next two decades and established by the 1970s as the living legends of jazz: not just Miles Davis, but also Stan Getz, Kai Winding, and others who would become Gerry's favorite sidemen (Lee Konitz, Jerry [Hurwitz] Lloyd, Don Ferrara, and Zoot Sims). For Getz, Mulligan's contribution would again be arrangements of originals written to celebrate the session's peculiar assemblage: "Five Brothers" and "Four and One Moore" for the 8 April 1949 date on which Getz was joined by four other tenors (Al Cohn, Allen Eager, Zoot Sims, and Brew Moore) plus rhythm (Walter Bishop, Gene Ramey, Charlie Perry). The challenge here was to take the light but energetic swing of the Woody Herman "Four Brothers" sound and show how much more could be done with the saxes in a small-group format, something Mulligan accomplishes by giving the tenors a bit more range than in Jimmy Guiffre's orchestration and by distributing the melody's counterpoised lines to these two slightly different voicings. As with the "Elevation" chart for Red Rodney, Gerry anticipates the up-tempo yet unrushed swing of his future sextet, carefully integrating the horns in their ensemble work to highlight their individual sound when soloing—a strength drawn from the alternation of ensemble, solo, and free-form phases of a traditional Dixieland jazz number.

In April, May, and August 1949 Kai Winding included Mulligan's baritone in sessions with his sextet and septet, gatherings of friends whose leadership would rotate during its four recording dates among Winding, Brew Moore, and George Wallington. On their four studio sessions these groups featured a front line of trombone (Winding), tenor sax (Brew Moore), baritone sax (Mulligan), and, for the septet, trumpet (Jerry Lloyd), with a rhythm section of George Wallington, Curley Russell, and variously Max Roach, Roy Haynes, or Charlie Perry. Just as the arrangement of "Elevation" for Red Rodney forecast Mulligan's sextet sound of the 1950s, "Broadway" for Winding's septet signaled the style and approach Mulligan would be using with his own ensemble of trumpet, tenor, valve trombone, and baritone (indeed, half the repertoire of the sextet's first album, recorded 21 September 1955, can be traced to Mulligan's initial small-group writing in the late 1940s). The sound boasts a distinctive signature, using the tenor sax to sing the major melody but allowing the trumpet's bite to punch it through (again in the manner of Dixieland); harmony and bottom were shared by the trombone and baritone sax but with each occasionally reaching into its odd-sounding upper register to produce the weird harmonies and sense of strain employed by the Thornhill band. Most important, for Mulligan, was the sense that you could hear the baritone sax at all times—as clearly as the baritone or bass in a barbershop quartet, ensemble harmony now being a case not of ranked sections concealing individual identity for the sake of big-band-power but of four idiosyncratically distinctive voices accomplishing a collagelike effect in which a new entity was created without sacrificing the identity of any constituent parts. Winding and Moore were premiere soloists, each noted for his personal sound; even when all four horns played together, there was no doubt who was playing them (except perhaps for trumpet, an instrument whose challenge to individual expressivity was eventually met by the breathy tones of Chet Baker). In this context, the previously annoying nasal quality of Mulligan's baritone sound could be developed into an asset; compared to Harry Carney's work with Ellington, Mulligan's horn seemed almost wispy, but as a part of Winding's ensemble it became identifiable for its more lyrical timbre, a voice that would not so much anchor as lead the group.

The direction Gerry Mulligan chose for his small-group development is clear from the difference between two major precedent-setting ensembles with which he was involved at this time, the Miles Davis *Birth of the Cool* sessions for Capitol and the Brew Moore "Lestorian Mode" date for Savoy. The former work was self-consciously abstruse, abstract, and beboppish in its studied attempt to reform the dimensions of modern jazz, while the Brew Moore recordings are less organized yet still disciplined vehicles for solid, harder blowing. These two strains are apparent in Mulligan's work for Elliot Lawrence, from whose book Mulligan drew material for both styles of groups. "Rocker" and "Elevation" as played by Lawrence suffer from a certain amount of big-band leveling, as the peculiar nuances of each song take second rank to the band's impulsive fast-tempo swing. But the composition of "Rocker" shows through as a bop-tinged intellectual exercise, its melody formed by systematic permutations on a theme (much as a classical composer would approach the task, a fetish exploited by Parker and Gillespie in their more self-taken moments and feasted upon by precocious fans). This theme is stated by trumpets playing in bebop unison, holding back a bit but retarding the band's ongoing beat to emphasize their mathematical permutations as the melody methodically reaches up and down; for the bridge they're joined by unison alto saxes for an even more distinctive Parker-Gillespie touch. "Elevation," however, which was the first of his originals Mulligan reclaimed for small-group work, is even for the Lawrence band a completely different style of piece. The melody plays no tricks with composition theory but delivers its Woody Herman "Four Brothers" style of tune in direct, swinging fashion; rather than controlling the rhythm, the unison horns (trumpets fleshed out by trombone) seem anxious to work within it, as the major imperative is to lay down the solid eight beats to a bar as things rush on toward the solos, all of which are traded with sharply voiced ensemble work.

- *Miles Davis Nonet:* "Jeru," "Move," "Budo," and "Godchild," from *The Complete Birth of the Cool*, Capitol Jazz Classics M-11026, 21 January 1949. Gerry Mulligan and John Lewis: arrangements; Miles Davis: trumpet and leader; Kai Winding: trombone; Junior Collins: French horn; Bill Barber: tuba; Lee Konitz (alto), Gerry Mulligan (baritone), saxophones; Al Haig:

piano; Joe Shulman: bass; Max Roach: drums. "Venus de Milo," "Rouge," "Boplicity," and "Israel," 22 April 1949. Gerry Mulligan, John Lewis, Gil Evans, and Johnny Carisi: arrangements; trombonist J. J. Johnson replaces Winding; French hornist Sandy Siegelstein replaces Collins; pianist John Lewis replaces Haig; bassist Nelson Boyd replaces Shulman; drummer Kenny Clarke replaces Roach. "Deception," "Rocker," "Moon Dreams," and "Darn That Dream," 9 March 1950. Miles Davis, Gerry Mulligan, and Gil Evans: arrangements; French hornist Gunther Schuller replaces Siegelstein; bassist Al McKibbon replaces Boyd; drummer Max Roach replaces Clarke; vocalist Kenny Hagood performs on "Darn That Dream."

Gerry Mulligan's facility with two different approaches is evident in the Miles Davis Nonet's version of "Rocker" from its 9 March 1950 session and in the Brew Moore rendition of "Gold Rush" (a variation of "Broadway" later performed by various Mulligan groups as "Turnstile") recorded 20 March 1949. Close to beboppers' hearts, "Rocker" is the most characteristic Mulligan number in the Davis book and was the one piece by Mulligan that Charlie Parker chose to do with strings at Carnegie Hall (on 16 September 1950, while the Miles Davis recording was fresh). For the Davis nonet Mulligan provides a chart that emphasizes the lead players' distinctive voices, both in their solos and in the group's ensemble work. Like most of the *Birth of the Cool* sides, "Rocker" is structured so that the ensemble parts get as much attention as the solos—perhaps even more, since a great deal is made of the wispy, ethereal sound created for the six lead horns playing together, an atypical section sound characterized by those two Claude Thornhill additions of French horn and tuba.

As leader, Miles Davis naturally has the dimensions of Mulligan's tune tailored to himself, not just as a solo vehicle but as a number whose ensemble work reflects the distinctive sound of his trumpet— breathier than Gillespie's, softer than Kenny Dorham's, and not as driven as Red Rodney's. "Rocker" keeps these qualities in mind and joins Davis's horn with Lee Konitz's almost substanceless alto to create the impression not of raunchy beboppers blowing to beat the band but rather of angels gliding on tiptoes past a celestial throne. Their unison lead carries the boppishly logical melody over the fills provided by the other four horns, fills orchestrated in the manner of piano chords, the truth of which is demonstrated in succeeding bars when the horns drop out and John Lewis's piano supplies the same structure of notes. It is no small accomplishment making trombone, tuba, French horn, and especially baritone sax sound like a tightly stacked chord from the piano's treble range, and to pull it off Mulligan draws on the old Gil Evans-Claude Thornhill technique of pitching the lower-voiced instruments (here three of the four available) at the absolute peak of their range. If the group had been playing an ensemble melody, such scoring would make the baritone sax, trombone, and tuba sound overly strained, but by vamping little fills in the manner of a background piano their efforts come across as uncommonly clear, percussive rather than overly tonal.

Miles Davis gets the first solo in a context and tempo that emphasizes his soft touch. Lee Konitz follows with an alto sax whose understated beauty threatens to disappear into the mist at any moment, an effect Mulligan emphasizes by coming in with some extended ensemble playing by the full complement of six horns. The trumpet and alto could be delicate in each other's company and by themselves, and it is reassuring to learn what a full yet delicate sound they can produce when supported by French horn and the heavier brass instruments, particularly the noticeable harmony provided by Mulligan's baritone sax playing thirds beneath Davis and Konitz yet still near the top of his instrument's own range. This group effort continues as long as either of the previous solos and establishes the song's ensemble work as an element having at least equal time and weight as the featured horns' individual playing. But things are not to end yet, for Mulligan saves concluding emphasis for himself in a solo that emerges naturally from the ensemble melody to round out the tune's structure, bridging the transition to the ensemble's final statement of theme. More directly melodic than Davis's and especially Konitz's solo, Mulligan's improvisation displays his angular, loping approach to a song. He voices none of the hesitations and arythmic stutters of the trumpet and alto but instead swings through the bridge chords in a natural, good-humored way, taking obvious delight in the tune he's written and is now pleased to bring to a ringing close. Thanks to the directness of Gerry's solo, the last chorus of "Rocker" sounds a bit less ethereal than before, now that his big funny horn has shown how flexible the melody can be.

Mulligan's work on the *Birth of the Cool* numbers, which involved arranging five numbers, three of which he composed, and soloing on seven out of the twelve sides, is not atypical of his future evolution. But the more abstract and sound-oriented features of his contributions to the Davis group follow the logic of his development with larger groups, specifically the line from Claude Thornhill to the Concert Jazz Band of a decade later. He does open up the big-band sound for solos; the pieces for Davis have plenty of room for air, but so did his arrangements for Thornhill, Lawrence, and even Krupa. The emphasis on weird tonality and the loveliness of unencumbered sound is itself part of a larger alternative tradition in big-band writing dating back to Ellington and continuing with Gil Evans and the younger writers Mulligan would himself employ for the CJB. Mulligan was able to write so comfortably within this tradition that one of his arrangements, of "Darn That Dream" for the group's vocalist, Kenny Hagood, was for years ascribed to Evans, so completely did the younger arranger adopt the Thornhill veteran's style of almost atonal but unobtrusive sound (in this case an ideal choice for backing up the words and melody of this wistful Jimmy Van Heusen standard).

Of the five arrangers contributing to the *Birth of the Cool* repertoire, Mulligan is the most original. Evans looks back to the best of his Thornhill work, while John Lewis casts the group in terms of unison sections. Davis's own composition, "Deception," reflects his own playing rather than the group's, its clean lines recalling more of his approach to solo horn than to the ensemble work Mulligan's arrangement provides. Johnny Carisi's "Israel" is one of the album's most striking numbers, but it remains virtually sui generis in its highly idiosyncratic, almost cubist approach to melody (in this respect anticipating the work of Thelonious Monk). Mulligan's arrangements number the most, but in texture and tonality they also serve best to create a light, modern, ensemble sound from the unique instrumentations available. Lewis's, Davis's, and Carisi's charts could be played easily by a smaller group, just as Evans's work always seems to have the larger Thornhill orchestra in mind. Only Mulligan's pieces are uniquely suited to the six horns and three rhythm—when any of these numbers are done by larger or smaller ensembles, they loose a bit of their wit, sparkle, and originality and certainly sound less innovative. Mulligan's writing for the *Birth of the Cool* sessions is certainly a perfect match of inspiration and circumstance; there is nothing quite like it in the history of jazz.

Preserved on the Capitol Jazz Classics album *The Complete Birth of the Cool*, Mulligan's contributions are distinguished by their range. The high wispiness achieved in "Rocker" is only one of many ensemble sounds Mulligan proposes; it reappears near the end of the melody in "Jeru" and as part of the uniquely cascading harmony in the high-alto and trumpet work that slides in and out of the "Venus de Milo" theme, but in both cases Mulligan has much more to offer—a full ensemble in the former, with the baritone's sound in clear evidence, while "Venus de Milo" revels in the group's richest yet still delicately orchestrated ensemble sound, each of the six horns making its voice heard yet none of them dominating. "Godchild" goes to the opposite extreme, sounding the melody with tuba and trombone near their bottom ranges, a self-consciously humorous style of voicing (borrowed elsewhere by Evans, for just a moment), which is used only at the beginning, setting up not just the pure trumpet sound of Davis's solo bridge but making the trombone and bari seem even more lyrical until a full choral ensemble ends things on a decidedly rich note.

Compared to his other efforts of the 1949–1950 period, these *Birth of the Cool* numbers showcase some of Mulligan's finest emerging solo work. Although his writing for Kai Winding and Stan Getz opened things up for more spirited blowing (a style the baritone saxophonist would exploit himself in the later sextet), he plays most comfortably within these arrangements, which bear a characteristic personal stamp. There is nothing tentative about any of his seven solos. The finest are on his own compositions and arrangements, particularly "Jeru," where he trades fours with his own rhythm-breaking ensemble work. It comes across as a softly melodic solo in which his distinctive horn sound first expresses itself with none of the blatty harshness associated with the unwieldy baritone. His improvised melody blends perfectly with the number's tune, something not as apparent on the equally well-played solo from "Godchild" (where his individual lyricism contrasts with rather than complements the rougher melody). On "Moondreams" Mulligan emerges transparently from the quiet background, a context he had devised for soloists with the Thornhill band, just as in "Boplicity" he accommodates himself to Evans's easy understatement and unforced melodic range, sliding easily into the French horn-led ensemble following his solo. His least impressive appearance is on "Budo," where there is also the least orchestral writing; preceding Lee Konitz, Mulligan seems determined not to overblow him, which for Konitz's case means hardly blowing at all. Mulligan's very best work is on "Venus de Milo," an absolute masterpiece of composition in which his ensemble writing and solo playing literally emerge from the group's pure sound, all in all the Davis nonet's most flowing performance. Not the least notable is the fact that Mulligan's solo comes across as in the same league as Davis's, no small accomplishment for the young arranger who had been introduced to bebop only a few years before.

The *Birth of the Cool* sessions are remembered as well for the small touches, musical and historical, that surround them. There are the interpolated passages in $\frac{3}{4}$ time from "Jeru." These passages sent French critic André Hodeir into ecstasy, claiming that finally the tyranny of regular time would be broken (in fact, these measures only reaffirm the tune's basic $\frac{4}{4}$ nature). There is the program note that Davis insisted that Mulligan and Evans receive lead billing as arrangers and have their names listed on the signboards in front of the Royal Roost, where the nonet began its first engagement (for two weeks, in relief of Count Basie) on 16 September 1949. And it is significant that the Davis group presented possibilities sufficiently promising that Mulligan quit his steady job as a big-band arranger and horn man in favor of something as innovative (and risky) as the new world of bebop he'd been listening to only since coming to New York in 1946. Most important is the fact that Davis, an acknowledged leader in this bold new field, selected Mulligan to accompany him in his own next step, giving him the major voice in orchestrating his nonet and providing a good share of the solo as well. When Charlie Parker brought "Rocker" into his Carnegie Hall strings repertoire, the founders of bop were casting a solid vote for this still young (and even younger looking) white kid from Philadelphia to be counted as one of their own.

How interesting it is, then, that the direction Davis and Mulligan set in *Birth of the Cool* did not turn out to be the one Mulligan himself exploited in his own playing—until perhaps a quarter of a century later, when the new challenge of jazz-rock fusion in the 1970s would prompt him to devise a similar approach for his *Age of Steam* recordings, complementing the Evans-inspired work with the Concert Jazz Band during the intervening decade. Although the Davis nonet constitutes the center of Mulligan's work from 1949 to 1950, he spent an equal amount of time on record with the group that included Kai Winding (trombone), Brew Moore (tenor sax), and usually Jerry Lloyd (trumpet), plus a rhythm section centered on pianist George Wallington. Four sessions from April, May, and August 1949 (following the first two recording dates with Davis in January and April) produced fourteen tunes, four of which featured Moore while the rest showed Winding's leadership. Mulligan did virtually all of the arranging for these numbers, which included three of his own compositions. In all cases, his writing and the group's approach sound much more like the arrangement and execution of "Elevation" by the Red Rodney group two years before than anything in the *Birth of the Cool* material. The tempos are faster, the ensembles are more stacked (with each horn distinguishable by its patent sound within the ensemble, much like a Dixieland group), and the whole matter of business at hand is obviously to get to the hard blowing—the ensemble work consists of a brisk thematic statement at the start, setting the temperature for the cooking to follow. Unlike the *Birth of the Cool* numbers where the soloists literally creep out of the delicate orchestral effects, here the three or four horns punch out a melody in the same style as the hard blowing that follows. This tendency is especially noticeable in the numbers that carry over from the Davis group, Carisi's "Lestorian Mode [Israel]" and "Wallington's Godchild." Whereas the Davis nonet brought out each tune's exotic quality, Winding's players move through the cubist changes of Carisi's tune and smooth over the bass-clef roughness of Wallington's composition so that the soloists find themselves on a more stable plateau.

- *Brew Moore Septet:* "Mud Bug," "Gold Rush," "Lestorian Mode," and "Kai's Kid," two takes each, from *Brothers and Other Mothers, Vol. 2,* Savoy 2236, 20 May 1949. Jerry Lloyd: trumpet; Kai Winding: trombone; Brew Moore (tenor) and Gerry Mulligan (baritone): saxophones; George Wallington: piano; Curley Russell: bass; Roy Haynes: drums.

Reissued on the Savoy anthology that traces the postwar influence of Lester Young on tenor playing, the four sides by Winding and friends featuring Brew Moore sound very much like Gerry Mulligan's sextet of 1955–1956. "Mud Bug," trumpeter Jerry Lloyd's straight-ahead cooker that leads off the date, survives as the number Mulligan used to introduce his group six years later, in an identical head chart (save for some penultimate ensemble jamming) with the same lineup of horns (while dropping the piano). The first to benefit from this shift in emphasis from cool jazz to hot is Mulligan himself, whose full-bodied solo boasts the finest aspects of voice achieved with the Miles Davis Nonet while benefiting from the more straight-ahead tempo and dedication to swing. He takes his cue from the song's rhythm, winding in and out of its easy progression as the twelve-bar chord changes do their routine job of structuring the song. The Savoy reissue includes master and alternate takes for each of the four numbers, and while the other soloists (particularly Winding) are less original on the outtake, Mulligan benefits from having warmed up and plays with more confidence than ever, enjoying the familiarity of the tune rather than being bored with the memory of his first effort. If anything, his second-take solos are more creatively melodic, responding more to the tune than to the rhythm or changes, as with the first time through.

For both his own composition, "Gold Rush," and for the arranging of Lloyd's, Carisi's, and Winding's pieces, Mulligan foregrounds the baritone sax much more within the ensemble. It is most obvious in

"Lestorian Mode," where the baritone plays a second melody counterpointed to the tenor's lead, but in all cases it does more than just
fill out the bottom— a voicing accomplished by having that bottom
part played in harmony with the lead, rather than simply beneath it.
For "Gold Rush" and "Mud Bug" Mulligan delivers the four-equal-
parts ensemble sound that would characterize his sextet of the mid-
fifties; unlike the other two Winding sessions, where the trombone's
lead lowers the sound considerably and leaves less notable presence
for the bari, on this date Brew Moore takes not only the first and
longest solos but also (with Lloyd's trumpet) assumes the lead in
ensembles, giving the group a much lighter and also more cutting
sound. This brighter atmosphere perks things up for the soloists, and
even George Wallington forgoes his customary lapses into abstraction
and pounds out some aggressive solos, following in Brew Moore's
brisk, lyric, Lester Young manner, which in turn flows logically from
Mulligan's hard but happy ensemble scoring.

Where the tenor sax leads the ensemble of "Lestorian Mode" and
the trumpet stands out in "Kai's Kid," there is no baritone solo. But
when the bari makes its voice heard during the thematic statements—
"Mud Bug" and "Gold Rush"—Mulligan follows with a solo, almost as
if his horn's presence must be justified within the ensemble before it
can emerge as an individual voice. That Mulligan likes this sound is
evident in how he adds a thematic variation to the ensemble work
after the last solo of "Mud Bug" and before the out chorus, emphasizing even more the trumpet's lead voice, here harmonizing with the
relatively brassy sound of Moore's tenor. For "Gold Rush" he adopts
a technique magnified in the later sextet's works: having the other
three horns improvise a riff behind Brew Moore for the second half of
his solo, a deft reminder of the other horn's presence, which both
anticipates their own solos and recalls the tune's ensemble sound.
The practice signals Mulligan's cleverness and his temptations toward
anarchy—preciously little holds these riffs together, at any moment
threatening to dissolve into cacophony (a factor in Mulligan's writing
destined to drive a future employer, Stan Kenton, nuts).

"Gold Rush" remains the strongest number from the Winding
group's session spotlighting Brew Moore's tenor. Although Mulligan
did all four arrangements, this is the one in which his scoring is
matched to his own composition. Its rhythm and tempo, particularly
the song's melodic structuring around several rhythmic punctuations,
is a natural vehicle for sax soloing, although Jerry Lloyd delivers one
of his best efforts in a manner programmed by Mulligan's style of
up-tempo jamming (which with the sextet brought forth equally fine

solos from trumpeter Jon Eardley). It is a style developing within the Lester Young context, one that Brew Moore exploits here (as would Zoot Sims later) and that Mulligan proves can adapt to trumpet as well. That the cumbersome baritone sax manages to keep pace with these lighter instruments, especially in a context defined by Lester Young's bright style of rhythmic push and melodic inventiveness, shows how far Mulligan was coming on his horn—and, with the Davis sessions in mind, how he would have to be careful not to write himself into abstract corners but rather keep the floor clear for hard but good-humored blowing.

- *The Kai Winding Sextet:* "Bop City." "Sleepy Bop," "Crossing the Channel," and "Wallington's Godchild," from *Early Modern: The Kai Winding Sextet*, Jazztone J-1263, 10 April 1949. Kai Winding: trombone; Brew Moore (tenor), Gerry Mulligan (baritone): saxophones; George Wallington: piano; Curley Russell: bass; Max Roach: drums.

As the *Birth of the Cool* sessions incorporate the thinking of the bebop innovators—Miles Davis, Charlie Parker, Dizzy Gillespie, plus hints of the future Thelonious Monk and even Charles Mingus—the Winding sessions reach back into Lester Young's transformations of the Count Basie band (and of the role of solo tenor sax within it). The other ten numbers Mulligan recorded with this group lack the straight-ahead swing of the four cuts from 20 May 1949, but by drawing on more abstract elements of the musical times they keep Mulligan's direction pointed toward the future. The April session yields a study in dynamics, with the briskness of "Bop City" and "Crossing the Channel" contrasting nicely with the softer and slower approach of "Sleepy Bop" and "Wallington's Godchild" (the latter of which is given a much smoother treatment than with the Miles Davis group). Without Jerry Lloyd's trumpet leading the attack, Mulligan finds a somewhat broader palette of sounds available for the group's ensemble: in the four selections recorded, the unison of baritone sax and trombone dominates the first and second (with a bit more bari to "Bop City," while "Sleepy Bop" exploits the trombone's mouthpiece phrasing), until Brew Moore's tenor sax leads the other horns on "Crossing the Channel" and Winding and Mulligan coax a mellow unison sound from the lower registers of their horns for "Wallington's Godchild." If the May cuts favoring Brew Moore produced a more monolithic approach to hard swinging, this inaugural session gives Mulligan a wider range of expression.

The depth of that expression is clear in how the soloists emerge from Mulligan's ensembles. "Bop City" is the most Parkerish of anything the Winding group would do; named after the New York City club in which they played the majority of their engagements, it is a self-consciously intellectual romp through mathematically generated chord changes played against an alternately advancing and retarding rhythm. The front line of baritone, tenor, and trombone fits this mood well, its softer ensemble sound allowing Mulligan's depth, Winding's brassy burr, and especially Moore's lower-than-usual (and somewhat more metallic) tenor sax sound to come through. It is in this number that Winding shows off his expertise on trombone, structuring a solo around rhythmic pauses, melodic phrases, and dynamic builds—far different from poor Mulligan, whom the fast tempo leaves behind in a confusion of random doodles showing no strong melodic form. Pert bop rhythms are not the bari's cup of tea, but the slower tempo and much cooler approach of "Sleepy Bop" is just what Mulligan needs; here his solo comes across as made of the same materials as the easy yet intriguing trombone-baritone sax unison work in the song's ensemble (a voicing that occasionally splits into sweet harmony between the sax and trombone, and then again allows Mulligan and Moore to add a few bars' background for some solo notes by Winding— a reminder that the three horns could work together, in pairs, or by themselves). "Crossing the Channel" is streamlined modern, the horns playing fast but soft with the tenor dominating the tune's Lester Young-styled melody; everything seems made for Brew Moore's solo, and Winding follows with an understated yet appealing improvisation that allows him to show off his horn's more lyrical high reaches. But after a spiffy chorus by pianist George Wallington, Mulligan steps in with an unremarkable solo that soon proves utterly forgettable, his full sound holding up (as it does not in "Bop City") but inevitably losing control to the fast tempo that Brew Moore so enjoyed. One can certainly tell that the year is 1949 and that these young musicians are still in the first phase of a musical revolution, learning by trial and error just what combinations would work. The lesson here is that a fast-paced Lester Young jump number built around a soft-touch bop chorus would not be the best vehicle for Gerry Mulligan's cumbersome instrument.

Here is where "Wallington's Godchild" saves the day. A deliberately awkward tune that climbs out of the clef to present a barely singable melody, it seems tailor-made for Mulligan's rich sound (reaching from the horn's middle register to its very top, where no other baritone saxophone had played). The tempo isn't as slow as

"Sleepy Bop," but Mulligan is able to keep up because his playing assumes the loping manner of Wallington's theme and is able to mime its deliberate reaching over limits. Given the wide range of his instrument's sound, Mulligan loves to climb up and down its quite different registers, singing a lyric melody with its high notes, reaching into the middle range for more full-throated effects, and occasionally sounding a low note from its bottom (as a reminder that the horn's orchestral role is as a bass instrument). Placed between Winding's punched-out solo and Moore's soaring lyricism, Mulligan's spotlight performance helps knit the tune together as well as show off what he can do by himself. When he solos, one can tell his arranger's mind is still working, thinking of the number's overall effect as well as of his own expression.

- **The George Wallington Septet:** "Knockout" and "Igloo," from *George Wallington Septet*, Regal 1196 and Savoy XP-8112 and MG-12081, 9 May 1949. Jerry Lloyd: trumpet; Kai Winding: trombone; Brew Moore (tenor), Gerry Mulligan (baritone): saxophones; George Wallington: piano; Curley Russell: bass; Charlie Perry: drums; Buddy Stewart: vocal on "Knockout."

Two cuts recorded on 9 May 1949 under George Wallington's leadership show the arranger's cast of Gerry's mind, both in the way he writes and solos. For Wallington's boppishly breezy composition, "Knockout," he takes the scat-song line sung by Buddy Stewart and puts his own bari in unison with it, at once deepening the singer's voice and lightening up his own horn work; unfortunately, Mulligan's own solo fails to keep up with the pace set by the vocalist and the smaller, tighter horns, but all is saved by a fresh out chorus that takes the initial pitting of sharply tongued trumpet against tenor, trombone, and baritone to unify the sound around Buddy Stewart's voice. The piece thus winds up as a testament to the richness and variety of the human voice, which in the song's three minutes ranges from low bari to high trumpet in its instrumental sound, while prompting the more human elements from those horns as the arrangement proceeds.

Jerry Lloyd's "Igloo" reads much like "Mud Bug" and like it would become a staple of the Mulligan sextet. Though the tunes are similar and Mulligan's voicings of the ensemble parts take the same shape, "Igloo" is slightly more relaxed. As one might expect, the young baritonist benefits from the tempo, taking advantage of the relatively open space to slide in some triplets that keep his own playing on the

crest of the song's wave. This too would be a style of playing he'd exploit with the sextet, which in such numbers sounds closer and closer on the musical horizon.

● ***The Kai Winding Septet:*** "A Night on Bop Mountain," "Water-works," "Broadway," and "Sid's Bounce," from *Early Bones,* Prestige P-24067, 23 August 1949. Jerry Lloyd: trumpet; Kai Winding: trombone; Brew Moore (tenor), Gerry Mulligan (bar-itone): saxophones; George Wallington: piano; Curley Russell: bass; Roy Haynes: drums.

The Kai Winding sessions between April and August 1949 show Mulligan's own growth and the growth of the bebop idiom itself (which had begun with quick unison melodies, but which had now expanded into mini-orchestral effects). The 23 August set, which again included trumpeter Jerry Lloyd to form a front line of four horns supported by piano, bass, and drums, displays a strong variety of rhythms and ensemble effects, from the brisk drive of "A Night on Bop Mountain" and the slightly easier swing of Mulligan's "Water-works" to the more relaxed tempo of "Broadway" (later a staple of Mulligan's sextet) and the almost comic ensemble effect of "Sid's Bounce." No song sounds like one other, either in tempo or in voice, and all the players seem exceptionally confident in their roles. Of the three groups of recordings, this last session sounds the most like Mulligan's mid-fifties sextet. The horns play well together, their ar-ranger having found the perfect blend to make them execute the tune as one unit while still letting listeners hear the individuality of the tenor sax, trumpet, bari, and trombone sounding the notes (and not just that of the instruments themselves, but of Brew Moore's char-acteristic tenor, Winding's trombone, and especially Mulligan's throaty and occasionally adenoidal baritone sax). The only element yet to be developed would have to wait for the departure of piano (an after-effect of the pianoless California quartet) and the assumption of its filling-in duties by the four horns, probably the sextet's most dis-tinctive feature.

The four tunes present four different ensemble voices thanks to the instrument Mulligan chooses to lead (stacking it on top) but also because of how he ranks the other horns around it. For "A Night on Bop Mountain" he calls for the timbres most commonly associated with bari and trombone—harsh, metallic, and low (obviously a bow to the opening squib from Moussorgsky)—even though he and Kai

Winding rarely played that way. To emphasize this basal sound Brew Moore's tenor is called in for a few notes of sweeter harmony near the end of each chorus. Tenor sax leads the way on the more serpentine "Waterworks," inviting the loosest writing of the session and yielding an almost disorganized ensemble response to the lead sax. "Broadway" puts trumpet and tenor on top, in the voicing most characteristic of the sextet although the 1955 arrangement includes ensemble interplay for the bridge (which for 1949 is simply a baritone sax solo) and within the theme as baritone sax and trombone drop down for the little rhythmic fills here provided by bass drum and piano. For his last arrangement with the Winding group, "Sid's Bounce," Mulligan opens up for some self-consciously comic writing, taking the middle four bars of the first phrase and droning his baritone sax and Winding's trombone in bagpipe harmony. These measures are funny in themselves but also highlight by contrast the smooth ensemble sound of the opening and closing four-measure segments. For the out chorus Mulligan reaches the opposite way, to the trombone's and baritone sax's high registers for some outright honky-tonk harmony such as a Dixieland or small swing band would use to signal the finale. The horns also have fun responding to the tune's rhythmic irregularities. This is the only number without a Mulligan solo, but there is enough evidence of his personal bari sound in the out chorus to compensate.

There is a perceptible improvement among his solos on the first three numbers—perhaps because he warmed up and began to feel at ease in the studio, but more likely because Mulligan was learning which tempos and rhythms were to his personal liking. "A Night on Bop Mountain" is simply too fast for the ideas he wants to explore; the harsh, atypical sound of the ensemble carries over into his solo, which doesn't come across as Mulligan at all (Pepper Adams's work would be a better guess for a blindfold test). He is tentative with the song's pace and actually rushes a bit to keep up. It is sad to hear him struggling to find a melody and even squeaking when his reed won't play the notes his lip suggests. This same rough, harsh sound is heard again on "Waterworks," though Mulligan's playing is much more flexible and manages to swing in tempo with the song's somewhat easier rhythm. Thankfully, "Broadway" rescues Mulligan's solo work for this final session. Obviously a favorite, this number lopes along at the pace Mulligan has subsequently chosen for his most happy blowing—not too fast but not too slow, either, as his own horn and the others are able to sound out their full voices uncluttered by the need to play too many notes or change ideas with cascading chords and modal shifts. It is the tempo of brisk city walking, one of Mulligan's favorite pastimes and a habit memorialized in the title and feeling of his later composition, "Walking Shoes."

The material recorded with Kai Winding's sextet and septet is as different as small-ensemble jazz can be from the Miles Davis *Birth of the Cool* numbers. It is not simply because of the two groups' relative sizes; both feature a front line of trumpet, alto or tenor sax, trombone, and baritone, the extra instrumentation for Davis coming with French horn and tuba, two instruments Mulligan added to his California tentette in 1953. This tentette did not duplicate the *Birth of the Cool* approach but rather drew on Gerry's work with Winding and his New York City tentette from 1951. Mulligan's tentette from New York, which recorded six arrangements plus a side-long jam session on 27 August 1951, indicates the clear direction he was taking in the world of small group jazz; not the way Miles Davis pointed, but in the manner developed with Kai Winding, Brew Moore, and other white musicians who had studied at the knees of Parker, Davis, and Gillespie but who were now outgrowing the somewhat dated label of "bebop" in favor of what the fifties would call "cool" or "progressive" jazz—even though its swinging was of the hot variety and it revised a bit of the more extreme bop innovations.

The one feature of the New York tentette shared with the Davis group is Mulligan's distinction between his views of small-ensemble as opposed to big-band sound. The two charts he'd supplied to the Stan Getz "Five Brothers" session recorded 8 April 1949, in the midst of his involvement with both Davis and Winding, show how Mulligan could have proceeded with no distinctions at all, for both "Five Brothers" and "Four and One Moore" are scored in the big-band manner perfected with Krupa and Lawrence. Reissued as *The Brothers* (Prestige P-7022/OJC-008), this material looks to the Woody Herman style of late-forties big-band jazz rather than to the small-group work Mulligan was turning out this same year; it is definitely retrospective, for his work with Stan Kenton just a few years later would boast an entirely different sound. Both Getz numbers benefit from a light saxy style, lighter in fact than the "Four Brothers" style of arrangement Woody Herman was playing at the same time. However, the effect of "Five Brothers" depends on section work such as the horns would have provided for Elliot Lawrence, while the sole innovation of "Four and One Moore" is having the tenors divide up responsibility for what would otherwise be brass parts. Like the Miles Davis sessions, these cuts serve as an example of the wide range of talents Mulligan possessed—and chose not to pursue.

● **The Chubby Jackson All Star Band:** "Flying the Coop," "Why Not," "So What," "I May Be Wrong," "New York," "Leavin' Town," "Hot Dog," and "Sax Appeal," from *Chubby Jackson: Sextet and Big Band*, Prestige PR-7641, 15 March 1950. Tiny Kahn, Gerry Mulligan, Al Cohn: arrangements; Howard McGhee, Al Porcino, Don Ferrara: trumpets (section does not play on "So What"); J. J. Johnson, Kai Winding: trombones; Charlie Kennedy (alto), Zoot Sims, Georgie Auld (tenor), Gerry Mulligan (baritone): saxophones; Tony Aless: piano; Chubby Jackson: bass and leader; Don Lamond: drums.

Further evidence of the tentette's looming departure from what was essentially Gerry Mulligan's forties style is found in the eight tracks he recorded with the Chubby Jackson All Star Band for Prestige's New Jazz label. Although the session dates from the Ides of March 1950 and ranks as one of Mulligan's few recorded achievements during this year of difficulties with drugs and flirtations with other excesses of the bohemian lifestyle associated with these transitional years of "cool" jazz, it is essentially reflective of what he'd been doing during the fall and winter of 1949 after the last of the Kai Winding dates. The association was an important one, growing from hanging out with Zoot Sims and J. J. Johnson at a hotel-basement jazz club called Tin Pan Alley owned by tenor saxophonist Georgie Auld. This 49th Street venue was close enough to the action coursing back and forth between 52nd Street (of bebop fame) and Times Square (where the Miles Davis Nonet premiered) to catch a steady stream of musicians eager to listen and sit in; and from Tin Pan Alley bassist Chubby Jackson, a Woody Herman alumnus and veteran at organizing groups for recording dates, assembled a twelve-piece group of virtual (but young) "all stars" to cut the first big-band album for Prestige.

Although the musicians were forward looking and the recording conditions decidedly experimental (the Cinemart Studio was so small that the trumpet section had to be seated facing the wall so as not to overwhelm the saxes and trombones), the results are, much like Mulligan's scoring for Stan Getz's sax section, more retrospective than anticipatory of the styles Gerry would pursue with his tentettes. The band's structure was traditional, its three trumpets (Howard McGhee, Al Porcino, Don Ferrara), two trombones (J. J. Johnson and Kai Winding), four saxes (Charlie Kennedy on alto, Zoot Sims and Georgie Auld on tenors, and Mulligan on baritone), plus piano (Tony Aless), bass (Jackson), and drums (Don Lamond) approaching the material in the fashion made traditional by two decades of big-band arranging dating back to Fletcher Henderson and Jimmie Lunceford. Within this context Mulligan takes as big a role as any of the players, among whom responsibilities were divided as is proper to a true all-star group: four solos and two arrangements, including one of his own compositions. While his soloing is for the most part a bit tentative because of his obvious care in projecting a well-constructed line, its rather studied effect is mitigated by the lyricism and sharp tone he draws from the traditionally cumbersome and blatty bari. On Zoot Sims's tune "Hot Dog" (arranged by Tiny Kahn) can be found the same angularity that will distinguish Mulligan solos for the coming decade, and although he can't match Georgie Auld's smoothness on "So What," his playing shows a definite Lester Young influence when he joins up with Zoot Sims for a series of traded eights, fours, and even a concluding two-bar exchange.

Mulligan's own arrangements for the band reveal the stasis within which the creatively bleak year of 1950 found him arrested. His major contribution is "So What," soon to be recorded as "Apple Core" in an arrangement sold to Elliot Lawrence. For this chart the trumpets sit out, and their absence helps distinguish the piece from Elliot Lawrence's recorded version, which is slower and more precise in a conventional big-band manner. This Chubby Jackson rendition is less cleanly articulated and perceptibly faster, with its bari and trombone-section sound recalling the voicing Mulligan used for the Kai Winding recordings. Obviously arranged as a vehicle for himself and Zoot Sims, who had been spending most of the past six months jamming for audiences or, more often, in rehearsal halls, the number exudes the sense of relaxation these two professed to feel in each other's company and that would distinguish their work in the sextet five years later. But here the ensemble work shows none of the light spontaneity that would distinguish the coming six-piece group, and even without the trumpets there are simply too many instruments and not enough time (three minutes maximum allowed for a conventional single) for any experiments in the spontaneous polyphony that would be such an important element later. Mulligan's direction here is definitely back toward his work with Kai Winding, which had concluded just six months before but which nevertheless was failing to take advantage of the fresh direction his tentette would chart the next year.

His other chart is a dance-band style arrangement of "I May Be Wrong," a favorite tune he'd do with subsequent groups but which here draws on the muted trumpet-section work common to his Gene

Krupa charts and on Elliot Lawrence's conception of swing. It is surely an attractive number and gives Mulligan his longest solo so far, sixty-four bars taken a bit more carefully than the band's overall swing tempo but especially well phrased. On this chart there is room for some supporting riffs that, on Gerry's second time through, create the conditions for kicking along with the other horns' fills, a characteristic of the sextet. Though Sims doesn't have a solo here, his influence is obvious on Mulligan's playing, which is as smooth and lyrical as anywhere within his recordings from the 1946–1951 period. The overall judgment of this work with Chubby Jackson is that Mulligan was both writing and playing as well as he ever had, yet in no way as innovatively as he would just a year later. Although he could have continued in this mold—and did indeed round off the 1949–1950 period with some playing and arranging for Georgie Auld's big band, Stan Getz's and Al Cohn's smaller aggregations backing up Mary Ann McCall and Sarah Vaughan, and two all-star orchestras assembled by Gene Roland—Mulligan would have been falling victim to what he would always perceive as the greatest threats to his art: casual boredom and a consequent lapse into a drought of new ideas, ultimately losing the inspiration to play jazz at all.

• *The Gerry Mulligan All Stars:* "Funhouse," "Ide's Side," "Roundhouse," "Kaper," "Bweebida Bobbida," "Mullenium," and "Mulligan's Too," from *Mulligan Plays Mulligan*, Prestige 7006, 27 August 1951. Jerry Hurwitz [Lloyd], Nick Travis: trumpets; Ollie Wilson: trombone; Allen Eager (tenor), Max McElroy, Gerry Mulligan (baritone): saxophones; George Wallington: piano; Phil Leshin: bass; Walter Bolden; drums; Gail Madden: maracas. "Funhouse" and "Mullenium" omit trumpets and trombone; "Mulligan's Too" omits trumpets, trombone, and McElroy's baritone saxophone.

It is the New York tentette album that gives not only the clearest picture of the brighter side of Gerry Mulligan but presents the strongest and ultimately most characteristic work of his small-group efforts in New York during the postwar years.

The most impressive fact about this album is that all seven tunes are Mulligan originals and that his arranging takes special advantage of the group's unique instrumentation: two baritone saxes (which dominate the six-horn ensemble and provide an innovative lead orchestration for several tunes), two trumpets, (as if compensating for the baritones' bottom and assuring enough punch to keep the melody

on line), tenor sax, trombone, plus piano, bass, drums, and the unlikely (and not very successful) addition of maracas (played by Mulligan's girlfriend, Gail Madden). The two baris make things swing in
a straightforward but rolling manner, their broad sound sweeping any
rhythmic impediments out of the way (giving two sides from the
Lawrence band, "Mullenium" and "Bweebida Bobbida," a much
more forceful track than they had assumed with the larger orchestra).
Even when they don't have the lead, the force of their double-weight
presence makes the tentette a noticeably deep-voiced group, so that
when Mulligan takes a solo (coming first in every case but one and in
some cases preceding even this with a solo bridge during the theme's
statement) his horn does not seem so out of place. Instead, with the
song's lower timbre already established, his baritone sax emerges as
a distillation of the group's natural voice. The tempos are also easier
and somewhat more level than the range exploited by Winding's
group, and as a result Mulligan settles in comfortably for his most
confident and self-assured blowing yet captured on record.

Historically Speaking, as the Prestige reissue is titled, aptly captures the sense of this 1951 session—a great deal of material for just
one day in the studio and also a fine range of Mulligan's composing
talents (the original LP was titled *Mulligan Plays Mulligan*). Although
the tempos are somewhat level (to the benefit of Gerry's solos), the
melodies for each number remain distinct and even memorable, while
the voicings range from the two-bari sound of "Funhouse," "Bweebida Bobbida," and "Mullenium" to the tenor lead with brass background for "Ide's Side," the trumpet attack with sax bridge in
"Roundhouse," and the ensemble unison (with concluding harmony
for contrast) propelling "Kaper" into some of the session's most melodically inventive solos. Although performed by Elliot Lawrence
(with "Bobbida" spelled "Bwobbida," though the tentette's spelling
would carry forth through the canon), "Bweebida Bobbida" seems
written with the orchestration of the New York tentette in mind: the
full bari sound fills out the melody's odd contortions in a way that
higher-timbred horns cannot—plus the two big horns remain on call
for section fills that highlight the texture of the tenor, trumpet, and
piano solos and prepare the way for Mulligan to showcase his own
talents (in which he stretches out the song's lyric to new extremes,
before reaching up for high harmony to end the piece on a rousing,
horn-led out chorus bearing only slight relation to the curious tune
that started things off). The fugue-style play that Mulligan's and Max
McElroy's baritone saxes execute at the start of "Funhouse" is something previously unheard in jazz, a distinctive signature that boldly

announces Mulligan's choice of horns and orchestral sound. His solo in this number builds confidently on the song's chromatic progression; the bari solo comes across more naturally because the listeners have heard the melody played this way (with double force) and have also had their ears filled with the fugue that starts things off. Unlike his tentative efforts on some of the earlier Winding sides, here Mulligan sets the lyrical pace for Allen Eager's tenor sax and even for George Wallington's piano. As a result, the song swings in an unrelenting manner, keeping all soloists on the ball and not letting Wallington lapse into his customary abstraction. As opposed to Brew Moore's lower and more metallic sound, Allen Eager anticipates the sweeter lyricism of Zoot Sims, especially as Gerry would feature it in the sextet. And so another feature of Mulligan's later, most distinctive work falls into place.

There are no false moves in any of these cuts. On "Ide's Side" Mulligan's initial solo, as strongly melodic as it is, sets a pace that allows him and Eager to trade quick fours while still propelling things forward in a tuneful sense. The baritone's full flexibility is demonstrated as it keeps up with the more nimble tenor and also keeps the song's progression in mind, all of which leads naturally to a trumpet-led out chorus whose rousing variation makes the number even more snappy than its thematic introduction. "Roundhouse" is a typical Mulligan gesture in that it incorporates rhythmic pulses into the melody, pulses that the two baritones can emphasize within the trumpet-led ensemble. "Kaper" is the one composition relying on a unison ensemble, but even here Mulligan asks the horns to stretch into some subtle harmony at the end of the melody's phrase as a way of softening the attack; his own solo is especially responsive to their melodic phrasing, again setting the style for the tenor and piano to follow. Most representative of Mulligan's confident new presence is "Mullenium," in which the easy lope of the two-bari theme (with just a few touches of harmony to remind us there are two of them) sets the stage for Gerry's most characteristically angular solo, an indication of the humorous, witty playing he'd stamp as his trademark on the mid-fifties sextet sessions.

Looking back on the six arrangements of his own originals on side A of the Prestige LP, one notes a subtle break from the otherwise similar Winding-led numbers: although there's a trombone in the group (played by Ollie Wilson), it alone of all the horns is given no solos and is the one instrument not apparent in the ensemble work. Even the second baritonist, Max McElroy, is given solo space, and his contribution to the tentette's sound is absolutely central. But not the trombone, which makes these numbers sound distinctively different from the Winding cuts.

But there is a greater difference, one that easily would have suffered the inclusion of trombone solos and more prominence for that horn in the ensemble section. There are no self-consciously intellectual bebop numbers like "A Night on Bop Mountain" and "Wallington's Godchild"—deliberately awkward, inverted pieces meant to throw the swing off kilter and emphasize the new music's sometimes cubist effects. Instead, Mulligan shows his hand in the style of song he writes for this group: steady, deliberate swing, with melodies songlike in their simplicity but with chordal richness sufficient to inspire fully new songs from the soloists, all of whom could trip gracefully along the easy, not-too-fast but still moving tempo. The tipoff comes in the name Mulligan chose for his originals' publishing company: Pres Music, an obvious reference to Lester Young. Mulligan's compositions and solos both reflected the tenor man's easy lyricism and dedication to making his music sing. For Gerry Mulligan in 1951, leading his first group with full authority for choice of material and instrumentation, it is a decisive signal that his own tutelage within the Parker-Gillespie-Davis concepts of bebop had ended and that for the decade just beginning he would look back to Lester Young's own innovations, something no other leading young musician was doing. Others, however, would quickly join him, notably Zoot Sims, an obvious heir to Young's lyricism.

It would not be a question, however, of simply carrying on squarely in the path cut by Lester Young. The eighteen minutes of "Mulligan's Too" prove that. Trimmed down to baritone sax, tenor, plus rhythm, the New York group here faces the chance of anticipating Mulligan's other great advance of coming years: the California quartet (with Chet Baker). But nothing could be further from Mulligan's mind just now, as he and Eager retire to a full side's easy blowing with no thought of doing anything special with their two lead-horn instrumentation. The result is like Lester Young played by students: an honest reflection of the great tenor man's style but with nothing new added, certainly nothing of their own. The cut also shows that for Mulligan to devise something new for just two horns, a more disciplined structure would be needed. In all their subsequent repertoire, the Mulligan-Baker quartet never turned out a loose-blowing side like "Mulligan's Too"; indeed, their unique baritone-trumpet sound is unimaginable without the tight, almost constricting format of the subtly voiced melodies and interweaving, mutually supporting solos characteristic of the California quartet, each number accomplished within just a few minutes. "Mulligan's Too" shows that Gerry Mulligan had a great deal of growing yet to do, with many more innovations along the way, even though his work with Winding's groups and the New York tentette provided a solid base for his coming sextet.

- **Stan Kenton and His Orchestra:** "All the Things You Are," "Swing House," "Young Blood," and "Walking Shoes," from *Kenton '56: The Concepts Era*, Artistry AR-103, 5 November 1956. Gerry Mulligan: arrangements; Ed Leddy, Dennis Grillo, Lee Katzman, Phil Gilbert, Billy Catalano: trumpets; Bob Fitzpatrick, Kent Larsen, Jim Amlotte, Kenny Schroyer (bass): trombones; Jay McAllister: tuba; Irving Rosenthal, Erik Kessler: French horns; Lennie Niehaus (alto), Bill Perkins, Richie Kamuca (tenor), Pepper Adams (baritone): saxophones; Stan Kenton; piano and leader; Ralph Blaze: guitar; Don Bagley: bass; Mel Lewis; drums.

Early in 1952 Gerry Mulligan left New York. His final years there, despite the last two sessions with Miles Davis and his tentette's album from Prestige, had not been as productive as they might have been—a problem with drugs had developed that would trouble the young musician for another year. He spent several months hitchhiking to California, living out the plot of that most typical novel of the rebellious times, Jack Kerouac's *On the Road*. Following stopovers in Reading and Albuquerque, he settled into Los Angeles and met Stan Kenton, becoming for that leader another stereotype of the age: the rebel without a cause. For a brief and rocky period Mulligan worked as his arranger. It was obvious to all that the pair never got along, although of the two, Kenton was the more generous in acknowledging the other's talent. Drugs may have been part of it: Kenton had no tolerance for abusers and kept them away from his band's personnel, while for Mulligan's part his struggles with narcotics may have contributed to his volatility. There were public shoutdowns of Kenton and protestations that the young arranger felt he had more musical ability in his little finger. Mulligan said Kenton had the drums play too loud and overloaded the band's ten brass instruments to the detriment of good dynamics; Kenton responded that if he'd let Gerry have his way, the result would not have sounded like the Kenton band at all. At their worse level, Kenton had Mulligan assigned to writing just the dance numbers, asking Bill Russo to modify the young man's concert charts. But at their best, Mulligan and Kenton worked well enough together to add a new sax-oriented dimension to the

band and to soften its sometimes overbearing approach to fast-tempo
swing.

During the summer and fall of 1952 the Kenton band was at one of
its heights, being featured on an NBC radio series as it barnstormed
across the United States before taking off for a triumphant tour of
Britain and the Continent. Considering that another young arranger,
Bill Holman, was being brought on board and would prove to be one
of Kenton's personal favorites, it is a tribute to Mulligan's art that his
arrangements remained part of the band's book as long as they did.
Kenton '56: The Concepts Era, an album recovered from a club date
taped that year, features the wide range of Mulligan's writing for the
band, including his originals "Young Blood," "Walking Shoes," and
"Swing House," plus the Kern and Hammerstein standard, "All the
Things You Are" (his other frequently played composition, "Limelight," appears on *Contemporary Concepts* [Creative World ST-
1003]. "Young Blood" is the Kenton chart for which Mulligan is
remembered, and it stands out among the band's material for is effortlessly flowing sax line that becomes deftly absorbed by the brass
for a strong thematic finish. The piece is obviously a blowing vehicle
for the first and second trumpets, which flank an alto solo originally
slotted for Lee Konitz and played on the 1956 date by Lennie Niehaus, plus a tenor sax solo done here by the band's top swinger,
Richie Kamuca. All this cooking leads naturally to a slam-bang out
chorus, complete with a high-screeching trumpet bridge and some
wild drum work. "Limelight" shows that Mulligan could handle a
solid brass lead with sax fills, part of the Gene Krupa jump Kenton
may have remembered when hiring the young arranger. Its trombone
solo is punctured with sharp fills from the drummer, who is featured
at the chart's conclusion in a manner reminiscent indeed of Mulligan's
work for Krupa. "Swing House" presents itself in a more subtle manner, with soft, high saxes playing over an understated brass background; but soon a sharp trumpet-led theme emerges, leading to
some unobstructed solos helped along with extremely deft fills from
the band. For its commanding sense of swing, this number is nevertheless a refreshing change from the heavy-handed Kenton manner
and gives more than a hint of the conflict in visions between leader
and arranger.

Mulligan's own hand is more evident, however, in "Walking
Shoes," one of his classic compositions here unveiled with Kenton. Its
theme is stated by unison trumpets and trombones, joined at the end
by sweetly harmonizing saxes, with a neatly phrased trumpet bridge
in the middle. Its loping melody sounds like a classic Gerry Mulligan

solo—it is by far the most personally characteristic song he has ever written. The relaxed tempo and nonharmonic fills (themselves a big-band innovation) coax the Kenton soloists out of their thundering-elephants mood and allow them to exploit their instruments' pure sound rather than just flood the stage with notes. Richie Kamuca shows especially well in this context, as does the suddenly more melodic Lennie Niehaus. The piece ends with an inventive new out chorus, implying that with this tempo and these chords Mulligan could go on generating melodies forever. When it comes to a standard, Mulligan lets the band play pretty, putting trumpeter Ed Leddy in the spotlight for some extremely expressive playing on "All the Things You Are." His horn is allowed to hang out over the soft, abstract section sounds that are sustained over the tune's slow tempo in the Claude Thornhill manner, a reminder that, as with the later Lawrence jump numbers, Mulligan was more interested in drawing talents out of his bag of experience than devising entirely new strategies.

He did have new plans for jazz in mind, but they would develop in a catch-as-catch-can manner, predicated on two factors encountered in Los Angeles: a tiny club with no room for a piano, and a breathy-toned, lyrical young trumpet star named Chet Baker, who was willing to accompany Mulligan into a strange new world of two horns supported by just bass and drums. Together they formed the Gerry Mulligan Quartet, which far more than his stormy and sometimes frustrating work for Kenton justified the trip west.

CHAPTER THREE

CALIFORNIA CONCEPTS

It is no small tribute to Gerry Mulligan's impish imagination, his ability to improvise with facts, and his appealing talent for self-promotion that the theoretical justification for his headline-making pianoless quartet may have been devised after the fact. But such was one of the first lessons the young New Yorker learned about California: here was a new state of mind, a wealth of possibilities, where the lack of confining traditions made it easy to quite literally invent oneself. As inventive as his new quartet with Chet Baker may have been, the circumstances of its formation, its rise to fame, and the elaborate explanation Mulligan devised for its structure are just as remarkable.

Why a small group of just four musicians, the smallest Mulligan had ever worked with? True, the size of his groups had been shrinking steadily, a sign of the musical times as big-band swing faded and bebop and then progressive cool emerged, a strategy the young arranger had been consciously pursuing. But even though it seemed to be a steady course from the big bands of Krupa, Lawrence, and Thornhill to the Davis nonet and then the Winding septet and sextet, there remains the fact that the first work Mulligan sought on the West Coast was writing for the biggest band he'd yet encountered, the mammoth twenty-piece organization of Stan Kenton. In addition, even after the quartet had been packing them in, helping launch a record label, and being reported in *Time* magazine, Mulligan added six musicians and recorded an LP for Gene Norman and Capitol with a new version of his 1951 New York tentette. As the future would reveal, Mulligan's heart was always in big-band writing, and although those bands would take on increasingly innovative forms (climaxing with the Concert Jazz Band in 1960) the 1952 quartet appears as more of an aberration than a logical point in Mulligan's development.

So the immediate answer lies amid more mundane concerns. Unlike New York City, the club scene in Los Angeles did not allow for large bands in big rooms; the two places Mulligan found work were at the Lighthouse in Hermosa Beach and the Haig, a tiny club (seating just eighty-five patrons) on Wilshire Boulevard. As small as this latter place was, its turnover barely allowed a leader to pay his men union scale—and at that, just to three or four of them. Low pay cost Mulligan his first drummer, Chico Hamilton, who felt obliged to support his family by taking a better job with Lena Horne.

As for dropping the piano, there's a simple explanation for that as well. Mulligan had been working in Monday-night jam sessions at the Haig, which is how he met Chet Baker and, over four or five weeks' playing, discovered that they shared enough musical ideas upon which to form a small group. Just then the club hired the Red Norvo Trio as its regular weekly attraction; because Mulligan had learned by accident that his big horn could carry the day without piano (when Jimmy Rowles had failed to show for a recording date the month before, Gerry cut three numbers without him, the baritone sax making it with just bass and drums), he assured the club owner that some extra space could be created (and more income generated) by storing the piano and hiring Mulligan's quickly devised pianoless quartet as a Monday-night fill-in for Norvo. And so was born the structure of the Gerry Mulligan Quartet, which *Time* would breathlessly report as the latest mind-bending innovation in modern progressive jazz.

The group's recording history is similarly accidental. The Haig's publicist was a former artist and repertory man named Richard Bock, and it was he, impressed with Mulligan's off-night jamming, who suggested Gerry tape some numbers at engineer Phil Turetsky's tiny bungalow in Laurel Canyon. It was for the first of these sessions, on 10 June 1952, before Mulligan had met Chet Baker, that pianist Jimmy Rowles missed the date and the idea of going pianoless was born. That afternoon Mulligan, bassist Red Mitchell, and drummer Chico Hamilton produced "Get Happy," " 'S Wonderful," and "Godchild," an interesting mix of standards and a bop original in a style one month later hailed as the unique Baker-Mulligan approach to small-group jazz. The small taste of piano comes from Mulligan himself, a talent he would employ in many subsequent groups. Next week, at the Haig's Monday session, Mulligan and Baker met, and on 9 July

another taping date was scheduled with Turetsky. Chet Baker's trumpet here made its recording debut with Mulligan's baritone sax on
"Haig and Haig" (the version developed from "Dinah") and "She
Didn't Say Yes, She Didn't Say No," creating the two-horn counterpoint that added the one missing touch. But it was still not the classic
quartet format, for this group boasts a piano and no drums. Not until
16 August did Mulligan get his personnel stabilized, and with "Bernie's Tune," "Lullaby of the Leaves," and a brief version of the set-
ending signature theme, "Utter Chaos," the patented sound of the
Gerry Mulligan Quartet was first captured for posterity.

- *The Gerry Mulligan Quartet:* "Lullaby of the Leaves" and "Bernie's Tune," from *The Complete Pacific Jazz and Capitol Recordings of the Original Gerry Mulligan Quartet and Tentette
  with Chet Baker*, Mosaic MR5-102, 16 August 1952. Chet Baker:
  trumpet; Gerry Mulligan: baritone saxophone; Bob Whitlock:
  bass; Chico Hamilton: drums.

With a 78-rpm single carrying the bebop original "Bernie's Tune"
plus the old standard "Lullaby of the Leaves" the quartet was marketed to a growing audience by Richard Bock's new record label
created for the purpose, Pacific Jazz (later World Pacific Records, a
pioneer of the West Coast style of jazz). By early fall the Haig was
packed, often more people waiting outside than the tiny room could
hold. Chet Baker's surly James Dean looks and Mulligan's mischievous wit made them stars of sorts, and Gerry's elaborately propounded theories for launching a small group without piano were a
natural complement of intellectual adventure and southern California
innovation for daring's sake. His arguments made sense, even if after
the fact. The piano is an orchestra, he explained, and especially in a
small-group format tends to limit the horn-player's options by virtue
of the chordal structures it selects. Far better to rely on the string
bass, music's natural basis for both rhythm and sound (Gerry was no
fan of overstrenuous drumming, as he'd made clear with Kenton and
stressed again by choosing percussionists like Chico Hamilton and
Larry Bunker, who were famous for their brush work and light touch).

"Bernie's Tune" and "Lullaby of the Leaves" are not only the quartet's initial releases but among its most representative, defining the
group's strengths and setting a standard for its subsequent work. Like
the economics of the Los Angeles entertainment scene that set the
rules for its formation, the specific factors of putting a four-piece,
two-horn, pianoless group on record make a major contribution to the

format. The records, as far as singles, were still 78s, which meant an average playing time of three minutes per side. This necessitated short solos, perhaps one chorus each for baritone sax and trumpet, because the absence of piano demanded that the two horns spend time creating harmonic effects between themselves as compensation. The three-minute format was a bit old fashioned; but, as it happened, Mulligan was basing part of his new group's appeal on applying its unique instrumentation to familiar old standards—which, of course, were well known to the public in their original three-minute dimensions. To fill out the sound, one horn would play a simple figure in the background, occasionally reaching in for some serendipitous harmony. With the pretty-playing interplay of sax and trumpet for the opening and closing themes, one instrument taking the lead at the beginning with the roles reversing for the end, the quartet was producing precious miniatures, every note of which seemed carefully selected to yield, from minimum resources, a maximum effect. Even the up-tempo songs had to be played softly, creating a novel experience for listeners accustomed to hearing the brisker numbers in jazz played with great gusto. For Mulligan and Baker, however, understatement was the key, almost as if too much exuberance would break their fragile form. Yet record buyers and club audiences were entranced, for almost every aspect of the quartet's performance was something new, treating jazz in a way never before suggested. Whether planned or improvised, the effect was certainly innovative.

"Bernie's Tune" is the initial choice for an up-tempo bop number, a song the Kenton band had performed during Mulligan's tenure as arranger. The somewhat arresting theme is stated by the trumpet with baritone sax in close harmony; the song's rhythmic pauses allow drummer Chico Hamilton to contribute almost melodically with brush work. A trumpet bridge by Chet Baker is played in straightforward fashion over some smoother brushes, then the band returns to the main theme. Mulligan's solo is equally direct; for both it and Baker's following performance, Bob Whitlock's bass line is especially noticeable (in a way that the piano would necessarily efface) as it sets both melody and rhythm upon which the horns play. For Baker's solo Mulligan stays in, playing much more softly but almost constantly behind the trumpet's line. This configuration leads to a foregrounded interplay between the two horns for a full sixteen bars, their polyphony creating a fugue effect with what traces of the original melody remain, until the bridge is given over to the drums alone; then another eight bars of polyphony bring the horns back to where they can comfortably state the theme once more before ending just short of the tune's bridge

(which would have brought back the trumpet alone, something un-
wanted after the nice contrast established between the horns playing
together both loosely and then more cozily to end).

As a familiar standard with both theme and words known by listeners, "Lullaby of the Leaves" invites Mulligan to prepare some
self-consciously compositional effects. To his credit, they work bril-
liantly, allowing the two horns, bass, and barely evident drums to
offer as broad a range of effects as some much larger bands. To emphasize this range, he starts the number minimally, with just his
baritone sax announcing the theme above the bass. He's joined in
midstatement by the trumpet, whose supporting line emerges from a
harmonized note; their two lines interweave until the bridge is given
over to a trumpet lead with gentle sax harmony, an effect much like
program music in which Baker's trumpet mimics the falling, swirling
leaves while Mulligan's deeper horn takes the part of a cold November wind. After the melody is repeated, Baker steps forth for an
exceptionally soft and breathy solo. Soon Mulligan's bari slips into the
background for some whispers of support before taking the lead voice
for both bridge and out chorus. At this point Mulligan plays arranger,
cranking up the quartet for some double-tempo work with the horns
in close harmony, then shifting back to conventional time for the end
of the phrase played by baritone sax alone. Trumpet and bari harmonize at the tops of their reaches for the bridge to this section, after
which the number ends with Mulligan stating the theme, all of which
ends with a rallentando played at the absolute bottom of his and
Baker's horns.

Between 10 June 1952, with his prototypical session without piano
at Phil Turetsky's house beyond the Hollywood Hills, and exactly the
same date one year later, again at Turetsky's, Gerry Mulligan recorded an astounding seventy-seven numbers—most of them for
Richard Bock's fledgling Pacific Jazz label, but also a tentette and
then a quartet session for Gene Norman, plus nine quartet cuts for
critic Ralph J. Gleason's Fantasy Records in San Francisco (the result
of a successful engagement at the Blackhawk, rave reviews in the
Chronicle by Gleason himself, and a strong recommendation from
Dave Brubeck). Classics that they are, these sides have remained in
almost perpetual reissue and form a key part of even the smallest jazz
library. The strongest cuts for Richard Bock were reissued as *Gerry
Mulligan Quartet* (World Pacific PJ-1207), while a broader range of
lesser-known material fills *The Genius of Gerry Mulligan* (PJ-8); the
full book of Mulligan's work for Pacific Jazz, plus the California tentette sessions, are available in a five-record compilation made by

Mosaic Records, *The Complete Pacific Jazz and Capitol Recordings of the Original Gerry Mulligan Quartet and Tentette with Chet Baker* (MR5-102), with additional sources for the larger group being *Gerry Mulligan Tentette* (Capitol Jazz Classics Volume 4, M-11029) and *Gerry Mulligan Tentette and Quartet* (Quintessence Jazz, QJ-25321). The sets of tunes for Ralph J. Gleason are on the first side of Fantasy 3-220, *The Gerry Mulligan Quartet/The Paul Desmond Quintet*, and (together with the tentette recordings) are reissued on Prestige 24016, *Gerry Mulligan and Chet Baker*. The quartet's work for Gene Norman appears on *Gerry Mulligan with Chet Baker (Special Added Attraction: Buddy DeFranco and His Quartet with Voices)*, the Gene Norman Presents album GNPS 56.

Of these seventy-seven numbers—as thorough as any small group has ever been recorded, and astounding considering that the quartet would play together for just a year—a few look forward to the soon-to-follow sextet of 1955–1956, but most pieces remain unique to the quartet. In a few cases there are numbers resurrected from earlier groups with which Mulligan had been associated—Kai Winding's, the Miles Davis Nonet and even a few from the big bands of Elliot Lawrence and Stan Kenton. But in most cases the quartet's versions come across as radically different from those of the earlier organizations. What this reveals is that in his compositional sense Mulligan took special care to select just the right material for his odd new orchestral format. Whereas there had been an easy crossover of material from the big bands to Winding's septet and sextet and even to Davis's *Birth of the Cool* ensemble, the new quartet had to search long and carefully for a perfect fit in the numbers it would play.

● **Gerry Mulligan** "Godchild," from *The Complete Pacific Jazz and Capitol Recordings of the Original Gerry Mulligan Quartet and Tentette with Chet Baker*, Mosaic MR5-102, 9 July 1952. Gerry Mulligan: piano; Red Mitchell: bass; Chico Hamilton: drums.

A preview of what Mulligan had in mind for his new group is offered in the treatment accorded "Godchild" as recorded in the trio session on 9 July 1952. This was the date pianist Jimmy Rowles missed, but after recording two numbers with baritone, bass, and drums, Mulligan sat down at the keyboard himself for a structurally new rendition of this number he'd recorded with both Miles Davis and Kai Winding just three years before. For the Davis nonet Mulligan's arrangement had emphasized the arhythmic, lower-pitched nature of Wallington's tune, while for Winding's group these features were smoothed over to create a more swinging, spirited blowing vehicle. Each arrangement had been tailored to the particular leader, to the group's orchestration, and most of all to the occasion's dominant idea: adapting the intellectual complexities of bebop to a larger-group format for Davis, more lyrical swinging for Winding and company. "Godchild" had shown the adaptability Mulligan surely was seeking now at this bold new stage of his career.

What he does with this number sets the terms for much of what would transpire with his subsequent quartet. First to be established is the melodic role and occasional solo status for the string bass. In this new prominent role Red Mitchell opens the song by playing not its main theme but rather the variation upon it Mulligan used in his arrangement for the inaugural *Birth of the Cool* session with Miles Davis, and which just half a year later he'd rewrite into his own piece for the tentette, titled "Ontet" (on which he again plays piano). The melodic figure in question is used as a section fill midway through the Davis version and again as part of the out chorus. The faster tempo that Kai Winding's group takes for "Wallington's Godchild" a few months after the Miles Davis date makes this more complex melody inappropriate for that particular arrangement, but the figure remained in Mulligan's head long enough for it to reemerge at Turetsky's home three years later. On this date the "Ontet" theme precedes Wallington's, which is played by the piano's bass notes. For Davis, this low-pitched theme kept the arrangement close to the ground until the "Ontet" variation lifted up the section work and kicked the soloists along. Here, because Mitchell's bass has sung out the Mulligan theme so lyrically, the piano statement of George Wallington's own melody works as more of an interlude than as a style setter. That Mulligan has something else than Wallington's mood in mind is signaled when he plays only the first four bars, and then instead of proceeding with the melody he repeats that first snatch of melody one chromatic step higher, making a deliberate effort to raise the tune's consciousness.

And that he does, providing some lyrical yet percussive piano playing on a song that no longer needs to drag along in the bass clef. The implied melody Mulligan follows sounds more like "Ontet" than "Godchild," and the entire context becomes so developed that the tentette's eventual appropriation of this song as Gerry's own seems inevitable.

• **The Gerry Mulligan Quartet:** "Jeru" and "Five Brothers," from *The Complete Pacific Jazz and Capitol Recordings of the Orig-*

inal Gerry Mulligan Quartet and Tentette with Chet Baker, Mosaic MR5-102, 27 April and 20 May 1953. Chet Baker: trumpet; Gerry Mulligan: baritone saxophone; Carson Smith: bass; Larry Bunker: drums.

As for horn work, two more 1949 numbers show the new route Mulligan's thinking and playing were taking. "Jeru," of course, is one of the most typical cuts from the *Birth of the Cool* repertoire, its ethereal theme and airy structure sounding just the notes Miles Davis wanted for his ensemble approach to bop (a direct borrowing from Mulligan's work for the Claude Thornhill Orchestra, which had also performed this number). When Mulligan and Baker take the song in hand during their 27 April 1953 session for Richard Bock in Los Angeles, the Thornhill band's echoing unison and the Davis group's tight stack of horns (from tuba and French horn through Gerry's baritone sax to the alto sax and trumpet on top) give way to some snappy, up-tempo blowing more reminiscent of Mulligan's "Five Brothers" as written for Stan Getz's sax ensemble in 1949, itself a reflection of the Woody Herman style of big-band swing. The theme of "Jeru" remains the same, but the brisker tempo makes it more progressive and less self-consciously "cool" than the Davis-era number. Baritone and trumpet play in close unison, snapping off the notes in a manner that emphasizes percussive impact above instrumental sound. The horns' timbres show off in the bridge, where Mulligan and Baker harmonize, but they return for a pell-mell repetition of the out chorus before a solo from the bari. Here Mulligan makes a strongly melodic line, its structure emphasized by rhythmic groupings; for once he is able to play lots of notes, as the tempo demands, but without losing sense of the tune's direction (as happened on several of the sides with Kai Winding's groups). When Baker's time comes, the bari remains in the background for support and subtle harmony, its whole notes a nice contrast to the trumpet's breathy flurry. Then come sixteen bars of polyphonic improvisation, the two horns interweaving for the baroque effect by now identified as one of the quartet's most typical features; there's a bass bridge, then some high harmonic variations as one version of a possible out chorus, before the horns settle down to their opening unison for one more pass at the theme.

"Five Brothers," as performed by Getz and by Thornhill, had been one of Mulligan's more catchy melodies, yet a song that remained trapped in its Thundering Herd style of dedicated, up-tempo swing. The quartet's version, however, as recorded live at the Haig on 20

May 1953, when the group was most self-confident, shows how in this new format Mulligan could devise an orchestral form as pertly appealing as its melody. For Getz's and Thornhill's saxes, Mulligan had the end notes of each phrase extended, as an integrated sax section is most likely to do (in a tradition dating back to Glenn Miller's famous "String of Pearls"). Now, for baritone sax and trumpet, the song takes on a snappier quality, the notes softly popped (thanks to deft tonguing) rather than slurred at the end; unison playing emphasizes this clear attack, with each note clearly enunciated. The solos show themselves in contrast to this manner, with Mulligan's loping bari ambling along in front of Baker's soft, quarter-note backgrounding (a subtle emphasis of beat as well as harmony). When Baker solos, Mulligan takes just the opposite approach to gain the same rhythmic effect, punching out a jerky series of notes on each beat. As usual for the quartet, the solos are followed by some sharp polyphony, then by a slower, simpler bridge, and then by the full structure of the melodic treatment winding down into a predictable but nice-sounding rallentando.

Some numbers from the Gerry Mulligan songbook stay relatively the same, but those are the ones the quartet can play without having to make special adaptations for its unique format. "Turnstile" is one of them. For the Brew Moore-Kai Winding group Mulligan had framed it as a straight-ahead but not overly rushed swinger, the tempo at which he himself could construct a fast but unjumbled solo. That speed remains to his liking for the quartet's 3 January 1953 date with Fantasy Records, on which the tune is delivered intact from its 1949 days with the Winding septet. If anything, Mulligan and Baker so enjoy its dimensions that they expand them in kind, forgoing their customary penultimate polyphony to riff out a high-harmony variation on the infectious melody; this figure, which Mulligan has sounded at the beginning of his own solo, prompts sax and trumpet to trade fours (something rare on a quartet number), and for a second chorus they invite the drums to answer. Much the same happens with the compositions Mulligan had sold to Stan Kenton: "Limelight," "Swing House," and "Walkin' Shoes." Since its Kenton days the latter has seen its final G elided, but otherwise it is basically the same number as performed by the Kenton band, a marvelous downsizing of orchestration from twenty pieces to four. In the case of "Walkin' Shoes," it had meant keeping the larger aggregation under stricter control than its leader usually exercised; an exercise in dynamics, Mulligan's arrangement matches easy blowing to its gentle, relaxed tempo, such that Kenton's players have ample breathing space for solos in the loping Mulligan manner. Only at the end does Gerry open things up for some rousing section work, but despite its volume the easy pace remains unaffected. When the quartet plays this song, however, it seems as though its melody was written with Mulligan's bari and Baker's trumpet in mind, as their respective sounds form a natural unison highlighted by the smallest bit of harmony at the figure's end. The one difference is that, with only four pieces, there's no need to hold dynamics in check; instead, the horns blow naturally, a bit less subdued on their solos, but again quieting down to the lower registers of their horns for the move towards an out chorus. "Limelight" and "Swing House" are likewise easy adaptations, perhaps because Mulligan had written them at the same time he formed his quartet. The former comes across with more brassy echo for Kenton, but that could be a case of engineering. "Swing House" has its compositional effect switched around for the quartet, which is instrumentally incapable of playing both theme and variation at the same time, as happens with Kenton. But separating the parts serves to clarify their almost classical beauty of form—nothing coldly mathematical here in the permutations Mulligan draws from the melody, which he makes sing, swing, rock, and whisper in its various forms.

The small size and limited resources of the quartet, together with the three-minute limitation for success as a 78-rpm single, reinforce each other and help create the most appealing features of Mulligan's new sound. The relative paucity of lead parts—just sax and trumpet— plus the new melodic role for the bass made each song a minimal affair. But rather than seeming sterile and empty, this forced understatement gives the listener more to do: creating the implied orchestral and harmonic effects otherwise provided by piano, filling in the other four or five notes the two horns simply implied, and generally fleshing out the bare bones that Mulligan's quartet provided. Like abstract expressionist painting in the hands of Jackson Pollock or Franz Kline, Mulligan's conceptions and executions allow the listener to participate in the song's creation, carrying forth what the musicians imply and taking what is in fact a lovely miniature and expanding its dimensions to a full-performance mode. Yet space enough remained for Mulligan and Baker to play together in complementary heterophony, each with a fully complex line that the openness of the pianoless format never allowed to become cluttered. As for their individual strengths as soloists, Mulligan made a quantum leap in his apparent mastery of the big horn; and while Baker's playing was praised at the time as being equal to that of Miles Davis, his subsequent thinness leads some critics to believe that it was Mulligan's clever fills behind his work that made it seem so much better at the time. In sum, the emphasis on clear melodic line, the improvised polyphony and mutual support for solos, the tuneful role for string bass (such as an earlier age's tuba might have had), the ability for a drummer to take solos without pounding the house down, and the identity of individually sounded lines (even when playing together) restored a sense of individual and group inventiveness that had been absent from jazz for two decades, having been steamrollered under the crush of big-band music.

And of course there were the tunes themselves. Although the California tentette would do Mulligan's own material, about half of the quartet's repertoire consisted of old standards. Many of them are handled in gentle, loving fashion: "Moonlight in Vermont" is a natural vehicle for Baker's soft and breathy trumpet, as is the song that became his signature piece, "My Funny Valentine." In these numbers and others like them ("Lullaby of the Leaves," "The Nearness of You") Mulligan orchestrates his tiny miniatures with subtle tact, knowing just when to draw on sweet harmony and when to lay out completely, letting one horn (or perhaps just the bass) play the song's notes in their singular purity. Other standards, however, spark his wit, giving listeners the playful lower-register pumping of "I'm Beginning to See the Light" and the jaunty, deliberately sing-song rhythm exploited in "Aren't You Glad You're You." Sometimes where a tune was traditionally played in an extraverted manner, the quartet handled it in just the opposite way, as in its softly understated treatment of "Makin' Whoopee" or the relaxed mode for "Cherry" (building to high, swinging harmony at the end, another exercise in the remarkable range of dynamics that could be drawn on from such a small group). Wittiest of all is Mulligan's rendition of "Tea for Two," where, as he'd done for Gene Krupa so many years before with similar camp standards, he virtually rewrites the melody—not as a boppish exercise but as a way of revealing hidden dimensions of whimsy within the original tune. All in all, Mulligan's handling of these familiar numbers contributes vastly to the quartet's range; without them, it's doubtful the group would have had such wide appeal or been able to show off its radical techniques to ears not acquainted with its bases for innovation.

Of the numbers Mulligan wrote specifically for the quartet, "Nights at the Turntable" shows how his compositional sense was suited to the format of two horns, bass, and drums. Each element contributes equally to the tune's effect, from the slight variations of unison and polyphony, plainsong and harmony between the trumpet and sax to the rhythmic role bass and drums take in adding their little emphases to the melody. The melody itself has lots of notes, punched out softly; the bridge has relatively few, and those are played smoothly. The interplay continues right into Mulligan's apparent solo, with Baker's background fills easing forth now and then for rhythmic and harmonic contributions; when he takes the lead for the bridge, it is an almost seamless transition. For the final chorus the harmonic parts from the beginning are reversed, giving things a slightly different timbre for the song's end. The melody itself has ended with a catchy little Dixieland flourish, one more reminder of Mulligan's coolness-be-damned attitude toward using what he wanted in his music.

Within its remarkably productive year of operation, the quartet underwent two temporary metamorphoses, into a tentette (with some modifications of Mulligan's ten-piece New York ensemble) for eight numbers recorded in late January 1953 and as a quintet when Lee Konitz sat in for a June 1953 session at the Haig followed by some taping at Phil Turetsky's home. For each, the quartet remained the basis for Mulligan's work. He explained the larger group as an outlet for his writing, basically the present quartet plus the orchestration of Miles Davis's *Birth of the Cool* nonet, hence the two trumpets (Pete Candoli joining Baker) and the Davis-style tuba and French horn supplementing the New York tentette's second baritone sax (the other changes restore the alto sax, here played by Bud Shank, in place of Allen Eager's tenor, plus dropping maracas and piano except when Gerry would double on keyboard). Although the orchestration is much closer to the nonet than to the 1951 tentette, just one number makes it clear that for this new group Mulligan had something different in mind—certainly different from the more predictably structured nine-piece group (plus vocalist) led by Shorty Rogers with which Gerry had recorded in November 1952.

● *The Gerry Mulligan Tentette:* "Westwood Walk," "Walkin' Shoes," "Rocker," "A Ballad," "Taking a Chance on Love," "Simbah," "Flash," and "Ontet," from *The Complete Pacific Jazz and Capitol Recordings of the Original Gerry Mulligan Quartet and Tentette with Chet Baker*, Mosaic MR5-102, 29 January (first four numbers) and 31 January 1953. Chet Baker, Pete Candoli: trumpets; Bud Shank (alto), Gerry Mulligan, Don Davidson (baritone): saxophones; Bob Enevoldsen: valve trombone;

John Graas: French horn; Ray Siegel: tuba; Joe Mondragon: bass; Chico Hamilton (replaced by Larry Bunker for 31 January cuts): drums.

"Westwood Walk" (his own composition, as seven of the eight numbers would be, complemented by the old standard "Takin' a Chance on Love") opens with a tightly voiced but lightly enunciated ensemble showing no trace of the ethereal high trumpet and alto sound so characteristic of the *Birth of the Cool* arrangements. Having altoist Bud Shank instead of Lee Konitz may be part of the reason, but the substitution of valve trombone (played by Bob Enevoldsen) for slide trombone does more to articulate and lighten the sound (plus anticipates Bob Brookmeyer's work with the future sextet). Without a piano, the solos sound more like those of the quartet, particularly Mulligan's opening performance as played against the bass line. What ensemble backing there is follows the quieter pattern used by a single horn in the quartet, and when the whole group takes on melodic phrasing Mulligan starts them with two or three different lines, which from their initial unison sound soon weave together to form a full harmony—the listener can actually hear the harmonic parts coming together.

There is even more of the quartet sound to "Walkin' Shoes," a number it had recorded just ten weeks before. The initial line is played by both big saxes, but not in the forceful manner of the New York Tentette. Here Mulligan and Don Davidson hold back to play softly, as befits the song's strolling nature. The brass comes in after a bit to create a counter line, but as far as a characteristic ensemble sound, the baritone sax keeps its distinctive (but not overplayed) voice out front throughout the tune, stamping everything about it as a Gerry Mulligan performance. "Rocker" benefits from this same richness of orchestral palette; the horns provide a sound richer than even in the Elliot Lawrence arrangement, and there is none of the icy thinness engineered for Miles Davis with the nonet and Charlie Parker at Carnegie Hall. Mulligan achieves this effect by letting the instruments play a bit looser, both in their section work and in their individual attack (a broader embouchure for the brass and a bit looser tonguing for the reeds). As will happen with the sextet, Mulligan stacks the parts at broad-enough intervals so that one can hear the individual horns—in the ensemble chorus for "Rocker" the trumpet and trombone can be heard clearly on top, while the bari is evident filling in the bottom with a slightly different phraseology. For "Takin' a Chance on Love," which features Mulligan in a piano solo inside the number, the ensemble sounds even more like the future sextet, with the distinct individual presence of bari, alto (tenor in the later group), trumpet, and trombone, yet creating a solidly integral ensemble effect. The sound is at once compact and yet multiform, another quartet feature now writ large.

As with the Miles Davis sessions, Mulligan uses his tentette to stretch out his writing ability. In the quieter Claude Thornhill-Gil Evans mode is "A Ballad," in which the veiled, almost foggy ensemble sound is itself played like a piano, another example of Mulligan following the Duke Ellington practice of playing his orchestra like a keyboard. This control allows his solo horn to slip in and out of its orchestral frame like a figure in the mist. There is also a faster yet more abstract number—here more solidly in the *Birth of the Cool* tradition—"Simbah," in which an unmemorable melody and minimal voicings nevertheless carry the tune through its complement of solos and ensemble work. "Flash" is in this sense one of the session's more original charts, for it opens with Mulligan playing the melody on piano; an ensemble treatment is not heard until the ending's out chorus, where the piano's percussive brilliance is recalled as the odd mix of horns (from tuba and French horn through valve trombone, trumpets, and saxes) strives to match its attack.

The tentette's masterpiece, however, may well be "Ontet." Credited as a Mulligan original, it is in fact an ensemble variation on George Wallington's "Godchild" as scored in Mulligan's arrangement for the Davis group. What makes it a deserving Mulligan composition is the way it thoroughly overhauls the Wallington number *and* transforms the original tune's weaknesses into strengths. Again, the inspiration comes from Mulligan's casting about for ideas and formats for what would become his quartet, for it was at the initial Turetsky session with bass, drums, and Mulligan's baritone set aside for piano that his arrangement, still credited as "Godchild," took shape. In the tentette format it remains a quiet, unobstrusive tune, with little evidence that there are ten instruments in the room. The piece begins with Mulligan's piano playing the theme, which leads directly (with overlapping notes) into Chet Baker's trumpet solo. This solo is deftly backed by some level ensemble playing, after which the lead is passed back to piano. Mulligan's sound on the keyboard is percussive and bright, each note struck clearly and resoundingly. After him, there's one more solo, this time from valve trombone, before the ensemble makes its first thematic appearance, playing the notes Mulligan had first orchestrated on the piano. Along the way parts have been passed back and forth between soloist and ensemble players without any flourish, fanfare, or interruption of the song's easy beat—a major philosophical change from the big-band strategy of announcing each transition. Mulligan's piano solo gets the same laid-back support from the brass as does Baker's trumpet, and after Bob Enevoldsen's solo the ensemble comes back for the theme with no more to-do than when it stepped in behind Chet Baker for those unastonishing fills. The effect is compellingly original, as the bass line's melodic rhythm keeps the melody moving along through various solo and ensemble variations and the piano, trumpet, and valve trombone slipping in and out at equal volume and with equal presence to the brass-led ensemble. It's a format that completely integrates solo and ensemble playing, giving neither a major claim to the arrangement and depending equally on both. With no hierarchal distinction between melody and improvisation, "Ontet" is delivered as a seamless whole, the most significant contribution the original quartet had made with its similar approach to the three-minute song.

The Miles Davis Nonet's version of "Godchild" had put the tuba in the lead, creating a novel but rather bottom-heavy sound. In orchestrating his New York tentette in 1951 Mulligan had made his own gesture toward depth by replacing tuba and French horn with a second baritone sax. For his California ensemble he has it both ways, keeping the second bari but calling back the tuba and French horn from *Birth of the Cool* days. The result is an exceptional range for scoring—almost four full octaves—with a multiplicity of effects for sound, depending on whether Mulligan wishes to cross-voice the baritone with tuba at the bottom of their registers or with the French horn, alto sax, and trumpet at the top. The contrasts with the New York group are obvious, but the difference with Miles Davis's group is just as pronounced. In the former case it derives from the added range, but compared to the Davis nonet Mulligan's new ensemble sound benefits from a looser, brighter quality, the result of bringing tuba and bari sax up while keeping alto and trumpet from straining too high.

That the California tentette recorded only eight numbers is regrettable and was surely as disappointing to Mulligan as was the Miles Davis ensemble's failure to catch on with anyone except a tiny in-group of musicians. In New York the problem had been with clubs and recording labels, neither of which were interested in promoting this oddly packaged new product. In California the times were more ripe, and the band had stronger personnel than the New York tentette and a more even distribution of talent than the Davis nonet. This time the problem came with Gerry's recording contract for the large group, which he'd signed with promoter Gene Norman. At the time, Norman did not hold a recording license from the American Federation of Musicians and so had to route the Mulligan sessions through Capitol Records. Had Capitol run the show itself, it might have sustained the group through subsequent recordings; but Norman's resources allowed only a one-shot affair, and so all we have today of the tentette are eight numbers crammed into two recording sessions within a breathless three-day period of 29 and 31 January 1953. By the time Gene Norman had his license and his own label, Gene Norman Presents/Crescendo Records, there was just time to do five sides with the quartet on 7 May ("Varsity Drag," "Speak Low," "Half Nelson," "Love Me or Leave Me," and a second version of "Swing House"). By now Mulligan's interests were pointing elsewhere, and the quartet itself was within a few months of dissolving.

There was, however, one last modification of its form, a change that had great implications for Mulligan's subsequent work in the fifties. In town between tours with Stan Kenton, altoist Lee Konitz took advantage of his old friend's invitation to sit in at the Haig. Richard Bock had his tape recorder in the house, and even though the numbers were improvised (giving Konitz the lead while Mulligan and Baker provided minimal cushion, mostly softly played whole notes in the background), the results were good enough to schedule some further, more formally organized sessions. Discographers debate whether the Konitz sides were cut in January or June 1953; a Kenton road trip during the latter month argues for January, but at that time it seems Mulligan would have used Konitz on the tentette dates, if he'd been available, rather than newcomer Bud Shank. Moreover, the concluding session at Turetsky's home took place in June, making it even more unlikely that Mulligan would have allowed five months to elapse between the project's inception and completion. Mulligan's and Baker's playing on the Konitz numbers are at once more self-assured yet abstract, a style the two had been developing in the final quartet recordings in late May (when Bock also had his Ampex on hand), and so it is possible that this Konitz material could represent, at least in theory, the last phase of the original quartet's experiments.

- **Lee Konitz with the Gerry Mulligan Quartet:** "Too Marvelous for Words," "Lover Man," "I'll Remember April," "These Foolish Things," "All the Things You Are," "I Can't Believe That You're in Love with Me," "Broadway," "Almost Like Being in Love," "Sextet," and "Lady Be Good," from *Lee Konitz Plays with the Gerry Mulligan Quartet*, World Pacific PJM-406, Jan-

uary or June 1953. Chet Baker: trumpet; Lee Konitz (alto),
Gerry Mulligan (baritone): saxophones; Carson Smith or Joe
Mondragon: bass; Larry Bunker: drums.

Of this group's material, the Mosaic package of Pacific Jazz and
Capitol recordings offers the addition of "Bernie's Tune" and some
alternate takes, but understanding Lee Konitz's contribution is easi-
est with the analytical format of the original World Pacific album,
where the side A features the fully integrated pieces while on side B
one finds the live set on which Konitz takes the lead while the quartet
improvises a supporting arrangement. To get a sense of Mulligan's
own development, side B should be played first, as in historical order, for here we have Konitz coming in as himself, playing the style
of alto familiar from Claude Thornhill and Miles Davis days, and
therefore having little impact on the quartet's nature (nor it on his
own style). But the advantages of planning and the more organized
context of a studio date allow Mulligan to take both Konitz's ensemble
and solo playing and integrate it with the quartet's format and sound—
leading, as one might suppose, to a prototype for the next great step
Gerry would take, to the four-horn-lead sextet of 1955–1956.

For both sides, the songs selected are, with the sole exception of
Mulligan's freshly composed "Sextet," old standards. Some are up-
tempo, like the bouncy "I Can't Believe That You're in Love with
Me" and the perennial "Broadway," while others are soft and slow.
On one occasion Mulligan overplays the old "Tea for Two" trick and
through innovative voicing and phrasing completely transforms "Lady
Be Good" into a barely recognizable bebop turn. What these treatments have in common, however, are features that would in just
more than two years distinguish the Gerry Mulligan Sextet: an ensemble in which each horn's distinctive voice was placed within a
range allowing it at once to be itself and contribute to a solid sound,
a rousing sense of melody at beginning and end (in the Dixieland
strut tradition), plus the even more characteristic Dixieland technique of spontaneous polyphony among the horns as a way of induc-
ing a bit of comic disorder before gathering the twisting and turning
marchers for a more uniform direction at the end.

The five standards Konitz plays on the Haig date (where the audience seems unusually quiet and attentive to his fragile solos, with the
quartet barely evident) are all wistful love songs: "Too Marvelous for
Words," "Lover Man," "I'll Remember April," "These Foolish
Things," and "All the Things You Are." As opposed to Mulligan's
prankish habit of turning a familiar song against itself, Konitz prefers

to make a bittersweet song even sadder and to let a morose lament virtually disappear into its own played-out rhythm. In all the pieces Mulligan and Baker play softly but usually with thematic counterpoint in mind, for where Lee sounds a distinct lead melody on "Too Marvelous" Chet and Gerry hang back abstractly, while the alto's tendency to get lost in intellectual abstraction very near the start of "These Foolish Things" prompts the bari and trumpet to come in with cushioning that restores a sense of tunefulness. This latter playing leads to some fortuitous harmonies between lead and supporting horns and surely prompted Mulligan to think of the ensemble effects he could achieve if given time just to sketch a head arrangement. The need for such writing is evident on "I'll Remember April"; halfway through their set, Mulligan must have realized how morbid things were becoming, and so this otherwise wistful standard is perked up with a Latin rhythm. But even though the rhythm support and trumpet lead follow orders and give it a Mexicali flavor, the Konitz effect soon causes the number to drift into airy dreamings. By the time "All the Things You Are" comes around, the group has surrendered to this ethereal mood, allowing Konitz to hang back himself for a few bars while just the bass line gets things going, the absolute minimum in reductive effects; when it does come in, the alto is more abstract than ever. Of these live cuts, only "Bernie's Tune" (not part of the released material but present in the Mosaic collection) achieves an ensemble effect, and that because Konitz simply adds a fifth part to a standing quartet arrangement, adding in the process some exceptionally eerie color in the manner of Claude Thornhill's and Gil Evans's writing for French horn (an obvious consequence of all the normal-sounding parts already being taken).

The five ensemble-based numbers gracing the issued album's A side show Mulligan at his arranger's best, making the crucial step from the formality of the tentette sessions at the year's beginning to a hint of what the sextet would sound like in future years. The key is Mulligan's sense of just how much spontaneity to set loose, from the polyphony of penultimate choruses to a somewhat broader and more personal attack in the straight ensemble work. Once again he exploits a great variety of sounds, from the deliberately ragged handling of "I Can't Believe That You're in Love with Me" (prepared for by the introductory jerkiness between the bass line and the drummer's brush work) to the exceptional smoothness of "Broadway" (another case of Konitz taking an existing set of harmonies and creating a rather surprising niche for his own line). None of these five numbers sounds alike; in "Almost Like Being in Love" Mulligan learns that just because there are three horns present he needn't write all of them into the ensemble, and so Konitz's alto doesn't appear until the melody is stated and it's time to help Gerry create a soft cushion for solo trumpet. This variety would come to characterize the sextet, where for different numbers Mulligan would put a different horn in the lead or stack the ensemble combinations in various shades of color. Closest to the sextet's sound is the prospectively titled "Sextet"; even though the fourth horn is implied, the breadth of timbre among alto, trumpet, and baritone fills the ear much as would the larger group's sound. When the sextet did get underway in 1955, its instrumentation would substitute tenor sax and valve trombone for alto, giving a much wider range of choices; but for "Sextet" listeners could intuit what the later group would sound like, at least when Zoot Sims and Bob Brookmeyer were playing in their higher registers.

The original Gerry Mulligan Quartet was at its apex of fame when circumstances conspired to fragment its parts forever. A narcotics bust put Mulligan on the "sheriff's honor farm" for an at times arduous ninety days, part of it spent in solitary confinement, and the legal rigmarole kept him out of circulation (and off his horn) for a full six months. On his release, Mulligan was met by Chet Baker's demand for what seemed like an extraordinary raise in pay, something the beleaguered Mulligan felt he couldn't manage at this time of getting his own affairs back on track (for the record, Mulligan's top personal earnings at the Haig were $200 per week; his report was that Baker asked for $400 per week, while the trumpeter's version is $300). One would prefer to think, however, that Mulligan's choice not to re-form the original quartet was a forward-looking decision, based on the new moves he'd been making near the end with Lee Konitz's participation. In declining Chet's offer Mulligan found himself heading back East to his natural base in New York City and picking up new musicians along the way—including bassist Bill Crow, drummer Dave Bailey, and valve trombonist Bob Brookmeyer, all of whom would be with him throughout the next decade as his groups took various forms and his own development proceeded. The California concept of the pianoless quartet would have one more edition, with Brookmeyer in Baker's place, but then things would expand, until by the decade's end Mulligan was prepared once again to launch a new era in jazz.

CHAPTER FOUR

NEW YORK, NEW YORK

Replacing Chet Baker with Bob Brookmeyer was not at first the innovation it later turned out to be. Less sure of himself as an instrumentalist and uncertain of Mulligan's own direction, Brookmeyer spent his first dates with the quartet not only sticking to the trumpet parts in the old 1952–1953 arrangements but even playing Baker's recorded solos note for note. But gradually the new group devised its own charts and found a new, appropriate sound—a bit lower and certainly more gritty than the original version and also more swinging. Where the Mulligan-Baker duo had framed its work in miniature, handling each note as if it were a precious diamond, the Mulligan-Brookmeyer team burst out with a more rau- cous exuberance, part of Bob's own Kansas City heritage. Humor became part of their routine—not the intellectualism of playing "Tea for Two" like a Chinese opera, but rather the happy swinging of "Love Me or Leave Me" and the ability to take a torch song like "Laura" and perk it up into a medium-tempo number capable of rocking to an almost flagwaving conclusion. Both arrangements drew on the quartet's deeper voice, with Brookmeyer's induced raspiness adding a textural quality to Mulligan's increasingly vocal way of sounding out the baritone's full reaches. In their hands, the familiar "Bernie's Tune" was no longer the hesitant, somewhat timid number Baker had played but rather an excuse to play wide and open with its intentionally abrasive melody and interruptions of rhythm. Above all, Brookmeyer's lusty trombone style made "Walkin' Shoes" sound more Mulliganesque than ever before; it and

"Open Country" characterize the new quartet's ability to swing in a manner much looser than imagined during its previous California incarnation.

Between 1954 and 1957 the chronologies of Mulligan's groups overlap, but that's because in the weeks preceding the second quartet's debut Gerry was experimenting with various instrumental combinations, this time in pursuit of his eventual sextet. The Brookmeyer repertoire is preserved in the 1–7 June recordings from the Paris Jazz Festival of 1954. Its introductory edition of eight tunes (plus set-ending renditions of "Utter Chaos") appeared on the LP titled *Gerry Mulligan Quartet: Paris Concert* (Pacific Jazz PJ-1210); a later Pacific Jazz reissue in the days when the label was owned by Liberty Records, with the same title but cataloged as PJ-10102, drops "The Lady Is a Tramp" but adds "Makin' Whoopee," "Soft Shoe," and "Motel"; the double-album compilation prepared by Vogue (K18P-6755/6) in 1984, *The Fabulous Gerry Mulligan Quartet: Paris Concert 1954*, omits "Soft Shoe" (the number so labeled is in fact "Motel") but adds to those songs already on PJ-10102 "Lullaby of the Leaves," "Gold Rush," "Limelight," "I May Be Wrong," "The Nearness of You," and "Bark for Barksdale." Before getting to the *Gerry Mulligan Quartet: Recorded Live in Boston at Storyville* (Pacific Jazz PJ-1228) from sets on 1–6 Deember 1956 with Brookmeyer, Crow, and Bailey, one encounters the transitional *California Concerts* (World Pacific PJ-1201), on which the version of the quartet with Jon Eardley on trumpet plays four numbers at a late fall concert before being augmented by Zoot Sims and Bob Brookmeyer for the first released performances of the sextet in December 1954, recorded two years before the quartet's Storyville dates. Yet to be marketed was the sextet's album cut on 21 September 1955 for Mercury Records in New York, and so any strict reading of the calendar yields less analytical data than a consideration of how, in Brookmeyer's company, Mulligan's quartet was growing to include six musicians who'd do the best yet in translating his ideas into sound and providing the context for his own most successful playing.

- *The Gerry Mulligan Quartet:* "I May Be Wrong," "The Nearness of You," "Moonlight in Vermont," "Makin' Whoopee," "Lullaby of the Leaves," "The Lady Is a Tramp," "Love Me or Leave Me," "Walkin' Shoes," "Five Brothers," "Laura," and "Come Out Wherever You Are," from *The Fabulous Gerry Mulligan Quartet: Paris Concert 1954*, Vogue Jazz Series K18P-

6755/6, 1–7 June 1954. Bob Brookmeyer: valve trombone; Gerry Mulligan: baritone saxophone; Red Mitchell: bass; Frank Isola: drums.

The two-and-a-half years from Paris to Storyville cover several changes in Mulligan's own work but also show how it would take some time before Brookmeyer could make his presence felt in the quartet and start influencing Gerry's direction. Of the seventeen numbers preserved from Paris, a staggering fifteen are covers of Mulligan-Baker material—the heart of the original quartet's repertoire, with only the trumpeter's most personal work missing. For Bob Brookmeyer, the inhibiting factor must have been considerable, although the real importance lies with Mulligan, for whom the six months out of circulation and off his horn proved to be a considerable hold in development. The material he presents in June 1954 is a virtual reprise of his musical situation of a year before when he was busted. The painfulness of Brookmeyer's timidity and Mulligan's own arrested growth is most evident in the formerly delicate, miniaturized show-case numbers of the first quartet, where Baker's formerly breathy yet dominant lead fades away in Brookmeyer's hands to an uncertain whisper. "I May Be Wrong" shows this the most—the parts are distributed identically but to Brookmeyer's loss, for although his horn is present it is less forceful than Mulligan's supporting bari (which eventually takes over the song). When the tempo retards for "The Nearness of You," the valve trombone again defers its assigned lead voice until it comes time for soloing, when Brookmeyer finally emerges with some presence. More promise is shown on "Moonlight in Vermont," where both horns are at their best balance for any of the soft and slow pieces. Where there are chances for humor, as in "Makin' Whoopee," or room for variation, as in "Lullaby of the Leaves," the Brookmeyer-Mulligan tandem plays better, surely giving the leader a cue toward future planning.

Significantly, humor and spirited variation were to be hallmarks of the sextet, and in several Paris numbers Mulligan and Brookmeyer start cooking in this direction. Their version of "The Lady Is a Tramp" lies squarely between the sextet's coming romp with this same tune and the Mulligan-Baker treatment from 1953, which in comparison sounds cautious and almost fragile. "Love Me or Leave Me," when compared with the earlier quartet's version, sounds written with Bob Brookmeyer's horn in mind, its raspy growl an obvious substitute for Chet Baker's breathy intonation but soon becoming a trademark natural to the interweaving bari-trombone sound. Where the two seem made for each other is on "Walkin' Shoes" and "Five Brothers." The various effects of unison and contrapuntal harmony are given full treatment as the players move back and forth between each in a smooth, natural fashion, either one making a solo bridge seem appropriate. "Walkin' Shoes" adds what will be the sextet's most apparent feature, spontaneous polyphony, here in a manner that highlights the echoing sonority of these two deep horns harmonizing near the top of their range. This format invites Mulligan to solo in his most vocal manner, while Brookmeyer's linearity makes a nice contrast. Each player writes memorable melodies within his improvisation, and as a result the listener is never lost in mere doodling (a danger in some of the last tapes of the Mulligan-Baker affair).

The two numbers original to the Brookmeyer era, "Come Out Wherever You Are" and especially "Laura," show this edition of the quartet's true brilliance. "Come Out" is swift and snappy yet provides a good blend of the two horns' deep, rich sound, here balancing their forces perfectly. The solos clip along atop the rhythm, and all seems happy and bright. "Laura," a Frank Sinatra torch song if there ever was one, has none of that morose mellowness in Mulligan's and Brookmeyer's hands, thanks to their decision to forgo the familiar languid tempo in favor of a more loping swing. Playing squarely on Red Mitchell's bass line, the two horns almost boom out what would otherwise be a quieter melody and then swing into their solos with true song-making relish, creating new tunes rather than just fooling with the standard's chords. Both the valve trombone and baritone sax reach from top to bottom, often swinging from extremes to produce an easy, loping pace. The horns express a mutual feel for each other, playing in and around one's featured line and then the other's, but always in a way that emphasizes the beat.

● *The Gerry Mulligan Quartet:* "Bweebida Bwobbida," "Birth of the Blues," "Baubles, Bangles, and Beads," "Rustic Hop," "Open Country," "Storyville Story," "That Old Feeling," and "Bike Up the Strand," from *Gerry Mulligan Quartet: Recorded Live in Boston at Storyville*, Pacific Jazz PJ-1228, 1–6 December 1956. Bob Brookmeyer: valve trombone; Gerry Mulligan: baritone saxophone (piano on "Storyville Story"); Bill Crow: bass; Dave Bailey: drums.

This sense of the rhythm emerging from Mulligan's and Brookmeyer's horns is the most apparent feature of their Storyville album taped in the first week of December 1956. In the meantime Mulligan had played quartet dates with trumpeter Jon Eardley and, more significantly, expanded the group to include Zoot Sims on tenor with Brookmeyer brought back on valve trombone, forming the sextet that premiered on the *California Concerts* album almost a year before recording three more for Mercury. But it is helpful to consider the Boston club date material here because it indicates how the quartet developed after Paris, slowly shedding its Chet Baker influence and allowing Brookmeyer both to emerge as a soloist and begin contributing his own compositions to the group's repertoire. The rhythmic swing of "Laura," it turns out, is what the quartet would explore and exploit, thanks to Brookmeyer's sound and manner of playing.

Of the eight numbers on the Boston LP, none are from the Baker-era quartet, an amazing reversal of field from the Paris-concert catalog, which was almost entirely a reprise of the trumpeter's image and influence. His jail sentence and drug troubles now years behind him, Mulligan was once again growing and creating, no longer needing to lean on this earlier material that had brought him his first national fame. But these eight pieces, on which the valve trombone is consistently strong, are most notable for Brookmeyer's influence, taking the quartet in a direction notably different from its California days.

In the mode of the surprisingly swinging "Laura" from the Paris concert are "Birth of the Blues" and "That Old Feeling." As a standard, the latter shows the innovative rhythm most emphatically, and it turns out that this depth of swing is all that it takes for the lower-pitched horns to forge their own identity. Once again both ensemble parts and solos take foothold by playing solidly on the beat, having only to add a half beat here and subtract another half there in order to make the tune swing as widely as a gradeschool playground at noon recess. Mulligan's favorite way of playing and composing mimicked his habit of easy, free walking, as codified in "Walkin' Shoes," so the tempo of "That Old Feeling" seems a natural choice. Even more so, because it was composed in that manner, "Birth of the Blues" invites both horns to swing through their registers. Some bands, notably in Dixieland, use the trombone to reinforce the bass line, and that's how Brookmeyer plays here, using the explosive attack of his large-belled horn to sound out the rhythm as his solos come down heavily on the first and third beats of each measure. In contrast, Mulligan's approach seems even more loping, as he tends to slide around the rhythm, pausing now and then for measures that stress the first beat over all the others, giving a more pronounced gait to Brookmeyer's left-right march. Although Brookmeyer takes the lead, Mulligan stays with him for much counterpointing that blends in and out of harmonized passages, giving just a hint of the polyphony that in other numbers gets a chorus of its own. The trombone solo is especially strong and melodic, with more than a cushion of support from bari (at times, two lines emerge to cross and blend).

Brookmeyer's originals, "Rustic Hop" and "Open Country," come at a slightly faster but not at all rushed tempo. Although the two share the same design of brisk swing and pert melodizing in and around the beat, the latter is by far the strongest in its wholehearted embrace of Bob's hometown Kansas City roots in honky-tonk raucousness. Of course that temptation toward rowdiness is controlled here as the horns start out with a bit of underplaying, but as the trombone comes down solidly on each one and three the number soon heats up. Mulligan uses his solo space to write a new song with his extremely organized, melodic playing, but for his part Brookmeyer prefers to interweave snatches of his original tune. When the time comes for spontaneous polyphony, both horns feel inspired to contribute some of their best interactive playing. The feeling of Dixieland exuberance builds as this jamming leads into a last-of-the-whorehouse harmonizing within a newly devised phrase, itself a rousing variation on the song's theme, which after the original bridge is stated one more time to end the piece. All told, "Open Country" is probably Brookmeyer's most successful number with the quartet.

Complementing the loping swing and up-tempo numbers is the set's slow piece, "Baubles, Bangles, and Beads." Here the horns play sweetly but not in the breathy Chet Baker manner, his softness yielding to a diaphragm-deep resonance of bari and trombone. The precious jewel in this number is harmony, handled lovingly and passed back and forth not just as an object of admiration but as a vehicle for the exchange of lead voice. Sealing the difference is the $\frac{3}{4}$ time, which Mulligan at times plays over, but which Brookmeyer exploits to its waltz-time ultimate. Rounding things out are Mulligan's bluesy piano on "Storyville Story" (where Brookmeyer falls in with some spirited blowing beyond the ken of Chet Baker's fragile style), the humorous "Bike Up the Strand" (recalled from its days as a novelty number for Elliot Lawrence), and Mulligan's familiar "Bweebida Bwobbida" (here with its second *w* for the moment restored). This last tune, which had always been somewhat of an awkward vehicle, now finds its ideal instrumentation and pace as the horns pause for the stops and starts of its jerky melody but then at once rip into some unfettered swinging solos.

On 17 May 1957, Swedish radio presented a valuable portrait of the fully realized quartet with Brookmeyer, and it is pleasing to see both the balance of material presented and the musicians' mastery of it. Collected as *Gerry Mulligan in Sweden* (Jazz Information CAH-4003/ 4), this double album contains thirteen tracks plus a three-minute interview with Gerry conducted by producer Olle Helander. Nearly all numbers are introduced with brief commentary by Mulligan as well, offering a revealing glimpse of how the leader himself viewed his repertoire at the time.

Since the Paris concert of 1954, a third version of the quartet had intervened: the edition with trumpeter Jon Eardley captured on the *California Concerts* LP. But the Bob Brookmeyer version remained, in Gerry's words, the "new" group; introducing "Yardbird Suite," Mulligan starts out calling it "old" material, but corrects himself and qualifies it as being from a "middle" period. This middle serves as a fulcrum between the tunes dating back to Chet Baker's days with the quartet and Bob Brookmeyer's more recent additions—indeed, the balance is almost exactly fifty-fifty between old and new, with the scales tipped slightly to the present by virtue of the fresh treatment given several of the older compositions.

What the Stockholm concert audience hears on *Gerry Mulligan in Sweden* is a survey of Mulligan's work in the 1950s, reaching back to songs and arrangements done with Chet Baker and the California tentette and gathering in more recent trends within the polyphony (in the matter of the sextet) added to "Walkin' Shoes." Brookmeyer himself seems anxious to break new ground even beyond Storyville, for his opening solo on the concert's introductory "Birth of the Blues" rushes somewhat awkwardly through a busy, bop-styled line that Mulligan picks up for half a chorus but almost immediately drops in favor of the tune's more customary loping swing. Gerry shows new thinking on "I Can't Get Started," one of his rare non-blues piano performances (in which he sounds a bit like Al Haig), and experiments with a remarkably new style of soloing on "Baubles, Bangles, and Beads." Some of this may be posturing for an appreciative audience, as most likely explains the lavish piano introduction to an otherwise customary "Blue at the Roots." But for every familiar piece, such as the classic quartet renditions of "Moonlight in Vermont" and "My Funny Valentine," there is something new, from Brookmeyer's radical personalization of the older "Frenesi" to the pervasive retailorings of the horns' interplay to accommodate the raspier sound of valve trombone. Above all, Mulligan and Brookmeyer seem extremely comfortable with each other. Unlike parts of the Paris concert, nothing sounds warmed over from the Chet Baker days, for by now the new quartet has played this material long enough to make it their own.

Storyville and Stockholm, then, reestablish a second front-line voice for Gerry Mulligan's music. For the next five years he would use both instrumentations alternately, moving from trumpet and bari to valve trombone and bari and then back again for quartet dates, even as his studio recordings would consist of "meetings" with other famous players and eventually the work of the Concert Jazz Band. The irony is that despite such a wealth of concert material with Bob Brookmeyer, including a set at Newport taped just seven weeks later, this version of the quartet would not enter a studio until 1962. Instead, the four-piece group recorded by Columbia at the decade's end featured trumpeter Art Farmer. The archive for 1954–1957, therefore, consists of club dates and concerts, including the interesting interlude with trumpeter Jon Eardley in December 1954, just as a prototype of the sextet was taking shape. For an appearance at Stockton High School Auditorium on 3 December, Mulligan fronted a West Coast version of the current quartet, with himself and Eardley joining the old veterans Red Mitchell and Chico Hamilton (the resulting album, *California Concerts*, on World Pacific PJ-1201, gives the date as 12 November, but elsewhere both producer Richard Bock and discographer Jorgen Grunnet Jepsen agree on the December occasion). Some of the Paris, Boston, and Stockholm ambience is evident here, from the appreciative crowd noise to the set-ending rendition of Gerry's theme, "Utter Chaos." But on the whole, the Mulligan-Eardley combination lacks the Brookmeyer edition's punch, even though there are several distinct innovations from Baker's days with this same instrumentation and rhythm section.

● *Gerry Mulligan:* "Blues Going Up," "Little Girl Blue," "Piano Blues," "Yardbird Suite," "Blues for Tiny," "Soft Shoe," "Makin' Whoopee," "Darn That Dream," "Ontet," "A Bark for Barksdale," "Nights at the Turntable," "Frenesi," "Limelight," "People Will Say We're in Love," "Western Reunion," "I Know, Don't Know How," "The Red Door," "Polka Dots and Moonbeams," "I'll Remember April," "There Will Never Be Another You," "It Don't Mean a Thing (If It Ain't Got That Swing)," and "In a Sentimental Mood / Flamingo / Moon Mist," from *California Concerts, Volumes 1 and 2*, Pacific Jazz / Capitol compact discs CDP-7-46860-2 and CDP-7-46864-2, 3 and 14 December

1954. Jon Eardley: trumpet; Bob Brookmeyer: valve trombone
and piano; Zoot Sims: tenor saxophone; Gerry Mulligan: baritone saxophone and piano; Red Mitchell: bass; Chico Hamilton
or Larry Bunker: drums.

Part of the Stockton concert's problem is its start. Booked to
follow Dave Brubeck after an intermission, Mulligan's group is
announced to a round of applause; but we then hear Gerry announcing, in comic confusion, "Thank you very much, ladies and
gentlemen. [Pause.] I think maybe I'll play some blues while you
get seated." The resulting number, obviously improvised and somewhat out of balance as the set was to include a loosely organized
blues piece (on piano) anyway, is not as strong as an opener should
be. Neither Mulligan nor Eardley plays outspokenly, and Jon
quickly reveals that he's not the type of player to blend into polyphony and support blowing easily, preferring to close his ears and
drive on straight ahead, oblivious to every line but his own. Mitchell and especially Hamilton with his favored brush work play less
forcefully than Bill Crow and Dave Bailey, and as a result the quartet seems lost up there on the oversized high school stage better
suited to pep rallies and orchestra programs than a four-piece group
not that accustomed to playing for a sitdown audience.

In terms of dynamics and pacing, things stay at the same level for
Eardley's showcase number, "Little Girl Blue." It then becomes Mulligan's job as pianist to heat things up with "Piano Blues," but the
result is nearly as pallid as its name. As a tossed-together arrangement, it anticipates "Storyville Story" but lacks that number's brightness. For his spotlight piece and in this looser format as well, Eardley
proves that a more solid-sounding trumpet could adapt itself to the
Mulligan quartet. His playing has absolutely none of Chet Baker's
breathy intonation and bops along in a more East Coast style of
punching out notes. Yet when it comes to the obvious format for this
approach, Charlie Parker's "Yardbird Suite" (which in his album notes
Mulligan identifies as one of his favorite Parker compositions), the
ensemble work reverts to the Baker-era's softer understatement while
the trumpet solo comes across as slightly confused. Where the horns
should be mixing a bit of polyphony behind Red Mitchell's bass solo,
their attempts peter out into almost nothing at all, while the straight-
ahead jamming that follows never takes direction. Worst of all, the
transition from polyphony to final chorus is anything but seamless,
the shift to much softer dynamics coming about with no identifiable
cause.

Ironically, the best material from the quartet's days with Jon Eardley comes from two anthologies, *Jazz West Coast* (World Pacific K18P
9258) which includes a solid performance of "Soft Shoe," and *The
Genius of Gerry Mulligan* (Pacific Jazz PJ-8) where the group shines
on "Blues for Tiny," a far stronger number than either of the blues
pieces included on *California Concerts*. "Soft Shoe," a canonical item
from both the Baker and Brookmeyer editions of the quartet, provides a better mix of lines, giving Eardley an assigned place in the
format; as a result, the song is delivered with a much stronger sound
yet without the trumpet wandering afar on its own disinterested track.
The truly impressive group impact, however, is achieved on "Blues
for Tiny," thanks to some intriguing unison and harmony blends between bari and trumpet plus the second-phrase structure that allows
bassist Red Mitchell (the song's composer) to lay down a solo line
answered by the horns. As happened during the Brookmeyer days,
both horns respond to this strong start with some of their best soloing
from this date, both in terms of melodically inventive phrasing and
command of delivery. In terms of presence, "Blues for Tiny" out-
classes everything else this version of the quartet preserved on
record.

Just eleven days later, on 14 December 1954, Mulligan brought
along Zoot Sims and Bob Brookmeyer to unveil the first sextet (which,
with the alternation of Jon Eardley and Don Ferrara, on trumpet,
would be the group's front line of horns throughout its 1955 and 1956
recordings). The occasion was another concert, this time at Hoover
High School in San Diego. Larry Bunker was now on drums, a
stronger presence in terms of driving the larger group than Chico
Hamilton might be expected to provide; Red Mitchell remained on
bass. Within the sextet, Eardley's trumpet sounded more at home
and less inclined to ignore the group's direction. On baritone sax,
Mulligan glows with obvious pleasure, incubating what would prove
to be the happiest small ensemble so far.

The four horns announce themselves in a bright, bold clarion call at
the start of "Western Reunion," an up-tempo, straight-ahead swinging number that gives everyone a chance to blow. The ensemble work
is extremely simple but strong, even brassy, although for the polyphony that develops during the bass solo everyone plays down, the best
riffing emerging from the bari and trombone's low-register nudging.
Things are slowed down to a pleasant stroll for another Mulligan
original, "I Know, Don't Know How," which would remain a favorite
through the next decade. The song's melody is, in fact, bifurcated,
allowing equal emphasis to the tenor-sax lead and the valve trom-

bone's contrapuntal answer. Behind them, low-playing trumpet and baritone sax provide a soft, warm cushion. The full effect is built on two complementary features: the most characteristically individual voices of the players (Sims's breathy but extremely clear tone, Brookmeyer's raspy burr, plus Mulligan's ability to provide low and rich support) and the timbres of each horn. These would be two distinguishing factors of the sextet's work on its three Mercury LPs, where for both ensembles and polyphony Mulligan would make sure that listeners not only were noticing exactly where each instrument was at all times but who (even in the most tightly stacked ensemble) was playing it. Realizing how many different effects four horns could produce is part of the effect, and on "I Know" Gerry pulls things together for the bridge and then redivides the parts for the following chorus. At the number's end, following the organized backing for solos, the horns take the first chorus a bit more loosely, varying their counterlines, but then come together at end, much as the initial run-through of the theme was highlighted by a tight ensemble coda.

A compact-disc issue from 1988, *California Concerts Volume 2* (Pacific Jazz/Capitol CDP-7-46864-2), picks up five additional quartet numbers from the Stockton date plus four more sextet numbers. For the quartet the material consists of covers of Chet Baker-era pieces, while two of the larger combo's cuts—"I'll Remember April" and "There Will Never Be Another You"—place Brookmeyer on piano to accompany Mulligan and then Mulligan on piano to back up Zoot Sims. But significant for what they reveal about the great range Mulligan was already drawing from the sextet are "It Don't Mean a Thing (If It Ain't Got That Swing)" and the medley "In a Sentimental Mood/ Flamingo/Moon Mist." Both are Ellington numbers, anticipating Gerry's own expansion of vision toward the eventual Concert Jazz Band, where Ellington tonality and orchestral shadings would be a similarly broadening talent. As a pair, the two are handled as differently as can be, "It Don't Mean a Thing" contrasting an opening unison phrase with a fully harmonized answer (plus much polyphony in the later phrases), the medley featuring some extremely fine writing. "In a Sentimental Mood" gives Mulligan the lead; like its subsequent recording on the sextet's final Mercury album, the emphasis is on the tune's haunting loveliness as Gerry's lead is fully cushioned by the tenor, valve trombone, and trumpet playing in soft, breathy fashion. "Flamingo," which the 1956 sextet omits, is here a showcase for Zoot Sims, whose tenor line is backed by Mulligan on piano. Gerry grabs his horn, however, in time for the opening notes of "Moon Mist," an exceedingly delicate handling of this already fragile song.

For the full sextet, these numbers are the extent of its premiere. Mulligan fills things out with various breakdowns of the larger group, he and Sims complementing each other's playing with "Red Door" (on *California Concerts*) with Brookmeyer on piano and Eardley sitting out, while Mulligan's horn is featured by itself on a cut from *The Genius of Gerry Mulligan*—"Polka Dots and Moonbeams," where both tenor and trumpet have retired in favor of a Brookmeyer-led piano trio in support of Gerry. Numbers highlighting the baritone sax and in which the other horns would be reduced to orchestral framing would become a small but regular part of the sextet's work in coming years, and the practice would continue with the Concert Jazz Band in the sixties. As for "Red Door," the happy combination of these sax-playing friends generates as much excitement as the full complement of horns; their solid, tight ensemble sets the tone for their soft yet strong presences in their solos, which devolve into traded phrases such as sextet numbers like "Mainstream" would exploit. All told, the four cuts from December 1954 give an accurate forecast of what the Gerry Mulligan Sextet would be doing in the next couple years.

Veteran sidemen from this group describe it retrospectively as their leader's happiest group by far. Mulligan had fun with it, they explain, because its size was easy to manage ("It can sometimes take Gerry all day to get one or two things done," Bill Crow has observed) while its dimensions of sound allowed for both individual and rousing ensemble effects. The tightness of its ensemble, while still letting the individuality of the horns (and their players' approaches) be heard, is the sextet's most distinguishing feature. It was above all a live-performance group, though after the San Diego session of December 1954 it was recorded only in the studio. Memories of its live shows, however, are stunning, as the four horns are described as spreading out across the stage or bandstand as far as one hundred feet, broadcasting their sound to all quarters and laying down a formidable harmonic screen, even as Mulligan's ensemble stacking kept them together as an integral unit.

The Gerry Mulligan Sextet recorded nineteen different numbers plus a number of alternate takes, one of which, a variation of "Blue at the Roots," was issued on its third album, following the master take on album two. This healthy chunk of work was accomplished in five recording sessions—21 and 22 September and 31 October 1955, and 25 January and 26 September 1956—with a largely stable personnel (Mulligan on bari, Zoot Sims on tenor, Bob Brookmeyer on trombone, either Jon Eardley or Don Ferrara on trumpet, Peck Morrison or Bill Crow on bass, and Dave Bailey on drums). The repertoire was almost immediately issued in its entirety on three LPs from Mercury Records: *Presenting the Gerry Mulligan Sextet* (EmArcy MG-36056), *Mainstream* (EmArcy MG-36101), and *A Profile of Gerry Mulligan* (Mercury MG-20453), with the same material plus alternate takes reissued on Japanese pressings in 1984 as *Mainstream: Gerry Mulligan Sextet*, Volumes 1, 2, and 3 (EmArcy 195J-34, 35, and 36). The group's work is consistent from start to finish, vouching for the six months Mulligan took off following the quartet's disbanding in order to develop and perfect the sextet's instrumentation and orchestral approach.

Its strength is in no small part due to its musicians. Gerry had been working closely with Bob Brookmeyer for several years and had selected Bill Crow and Dave Bailey as his rhythm section of choice, depending only on their other previous commitments. Zoot Sims had been a jam-session partner since the late 1940s in New York, and now that Mulligan was based on the East Coast once more he could count on the tenor man's services. As if Chet Baker's departure had put a curse on that slot for Mulligan, although more appropriately because Baker's distinctive style left such a discernible wake, trumpet would not be a completely satisfactory instrument for Mulligan's groups until 1959, when Art Farmer reintroduced the breathy style to the reformed quartet. But good writing and the disciplining effect of the other three horns around them kept Jon Eardley and later Don Ferrara in their roles, to the extent that their equally bright manners of playing could lend that Dixieland-lead touch Mulligan was seeking. The key soloists, however, remained Brookmeyer, Sims, and Mulligan himself, who was playing these days at the top of his form. In later years these three would form the nucleus of solo work for the Concert Jazz Band, giving that orchestra some of the sextet's flavor and reminding listeners how crucial were the individual sounds of Sims's sharp yet breathy tenor, Brookmeyer's gutty trombone, and of course Mulligan's increasingly vocal bari.

●   *The Gerry Mulligan Sextet:* "Mud Bug," "Igloo," "Broadway," "Ain't It the Truth," "The Lady Is a Tramp," and "Elevation," from *Presenting the Gerry Mulligan Sextet,* EmArcy MG-36056, 21 September and 31 October 1955, from *Mainstream,* EmArcy MG-36101, 25 January and 26 September 1956, and from *A Profile of Gerry Mulligan,* Mercury MG-20453, 26 September 1956. John Eardley or Don Ferrara: trumpet; Bob Brookmeyer:

valve trombone; Zoot Sims (tenor) and Gerry Mulligan (baritone): saxophones; Peck Morrison or Bill Crow: bass; Dave Bailey: drums.

How much Gerry Mulligan's approach to four-horn ensemble writing had grown during the early 1950s is clear when one compares
several of the sextet's renditions with their originals from the Kai
Winding dates back in 1949. That the sound needn't always be different is apparent from how Jerry [Hurwitz] Lloyd's composition
"Mud Bug" is played in 1955 virtually identical to its 1949 arrangement for Kai Winding's group. That Mulligan could still fancy this
less-dimensional sound for a four-horn ensemble is proved by his use
of another Lloyd number, "Igloo," for which Gerry scored the parts
in the same manner. Lloyd's writing calls for straight-ahead swing,
and as the horns punch things out there is little leeway for the richer
voicings and contrapuntal lines Mulligan would use in other tunes to
broaden the texture. A definite reminder of the Stan Kenton band's
orchestration carries over in "Bernie's Tune," the sextet's first recorded number; and for "Makin' Whoopee" the original quartet's
arrangement is kept intact, right to the exchange of leads between the
song's opening phrase and close.

But the far-greater majority of the sextet's numbers are reorchestrated and restructured for effect. The new group's signature sound is
written into the new ensemble voicing and rhythmic support on
"Broadway." Where the Winding version was decidedly metallic,
Mulligan's sextet boasts a more broadly distributed balance, one that
doesn't let any single instrument or register dominate the ensemble's
tonal texture; yet all four instruments can be heard (something the
Winding septet could not boast), including Zoot Sims's sharp breathiness, Jon Eardley's bright attack (which Sims's more aerated sound
helps to soften), Bob Brookmeyer's buzzing rasp, which at once adds
rich color and slightly abrasive texture, and of course Gerry Mulligan's own bottom richness, which not only provides a vocal substruc-
ture but takes over some of the bass drum's fills from the 1949 version
with Kai Winding. Like Buster Harding's 1940 composition for the
Count Basie band, "Ain't It the Truth," "Broadway" is a pre-bop
swing number that nevertheless helped introduce the forward-looking
lyricism of tenorist Lester Young, and Mulligan keeps this tradition in
mind when he opens up the scoring kept in line for the Jerry Lloyd
numbers. Both of these old Basie tunes enjoy a looser, more lyrical
sense of swinging; "Ain't It the Truth" boasts a sweetly rich ensemble, which Mulligan lays on as rich as spun honey but with none of the

cloying sentiment that might slow things down—as mellow as the notes are, everyone's attack remains crisp and precise. "Broadway" itself remains a classic, both as recalled from Lester Young's days and as encapsuled as the singly most representative number the Mulligan sextet would do. The dimensions added beyond the chart written for and executed by the Kai Winding group are stunning: not only is the thematic statement painted more richly by the ensemble, but the horns flirt with polyphony during their solid but restrained support of the soloists, who in turn mix it back and forth with the background riffs as they develop engagingly melodic lines. Such interaction adds rhythm to each solo's songlike effect and contributes to the rousing out-chorus variation Mulligan adds as the last key ingredient missing from the 1949 version.

The sextet's power derives from its position, as much in Mulligan's head as in simple numbers of instrumentation, midway between his small-group and big-band work. True, the Miles Davis Nonet and the New York and California tentettes were closer in size to the Krupa and Lawrence orchestras, plus the presence of tuba and French horn evoked memories of Thornhill, but for those ensembles Mulligan chose compositional effect and the elegance of integrating soloists with orchestral support rather than flat-out swinging, such as he'd done many times with charts for Krupa and Lawrence. With the 1955–1956 sextet, he arranges things so that there is much more lyrical drive than in the nine- and ten-piece groups—a bow to Lester Young rather than to Charlie Parker and the other beboppers whose intellectualization colors so many of the *Birth of the Cool* scores. True, the sextet benefits from rich orchestration, but the solidly swinging stack of trumpet, tenor, trombone, and bari yields a sound trimmed for swinging rather than for pondering moody effects (even though a haunting orchestral voicing of Gil Evans' transcription from Debussy could be produced for "La Plus Que Lente" during the sextet's last recording session in the fall of 1956).

What type of number seems the sextet's favorite? Most likely "The Lady Is a Tramp," a tune that, in its quartet days with Chet Baker, seemed to cry for looser and broader treatment, an approach Mulligan can be seen reaching for as he starts adapting the number when Bob Brookmeyer takes over brass duties in the four-piece group. Although the sextet's rendition maintains the same tempo and rhythmic feel, Mulligan adds a new dimension by planning a steady accretion of lines—first the baritone, then the trombone, and finally the trumpet and tenor slipping in to take the bari's lower line so it can reach much higher for a counterstatement against what has now become a supporting ensemble. This M. C. Escher-like exchange of roles, in which one horn seamlessly changes parts with two others and the lead melody suddenly turns into the background, makes "The Lady Is a Tramp" reflect the structural reversal of its title right within the song itself, a musical oxymoron that sets the mood for the interplay to follow. The solos and their background accompaniment conspire to create a joyful polyphony of genuine group effort, making obvious the fun Mulligan and his close friends were having with the sextet.

In the sextet's hands, earlier numbers that once seemed pro-forma exercises in musicianship and composition theory now come across with the feel of good-time blowing, yet they are still admirable for integrity of purpose and coherence of structure. Consider how the Elliot Lawrence band played "Elevation" and "The Swinging Door": the former was somewhat of a rush-through job for the trumpets, anxious to get to the ensemble-introduced solos, while the Zoot Sims number, later properly credited and retitled as "Red Door," showed how the big band's flourishes could become a retarding gesture, slowing things down to some rather predictable gesturing by the sweetly harmonizing sax section. It was during the new group's prototypical late 1954 concert in San Diego that Mulligan discovered what sizing down "Red Door" could accomplish, clearing away the grand orchestral business so that his baritone and Zoot's tenor could clip along in an unobstructed monotone whose briskness revealed the tune's ability for driving swing. For the sextet's version of "Elevation," a number dating from Gerry's teens, the headlong rush of Elliot Lawrence's trumpet section is discarded in favor of a diversion of lines reminiscent of "The Lady Is a Tramp" recorded eleven months earlier. For the first phrase, baritone and trombone play in sharply tongued unison, their swift attack keeping the mood crisp and bright while allowing the tempo to back off quite a bit from its previous manic pace. Then for the second time through trumpet and tenor sax join in for a full ensemble, the effect adding much color after the opening low unison. The solos maintain this enriching feel, with Mulligan's singularly vocal line creating new melodies in interplay with the other supporting horns, reaching above and below them, sometimes playing with their established rhythm and sometimes against it. The subsequent solos are given to Brookmeyer, Sims, and Ferrara, replicating the order of their appearance in the tune's ensemble section. Then come a few phrases of improvised riffs and spontaneous polyphony, some of the latter played with great effect against Bill Crow's bass solo, all before a reprise of the full ensemble that so convincingly got things underway. It's the pattern from "Ain't It the Truth" and "Broadway," but one that the sextet never lets go stale.

That the sextet had a broader range is clear from its several less-than-typical numbers, all of which seem written as showcase vehicles for Mulligan's own playing. The touchingly handled "Everything Happens to Me" repeats the *California Concerts* format of putting Brookmeyer on piano to support an especially lovely solo by the leader, bringing in trumpet and tenor only for a closing chorus; Brook-meyer's piano solo is an odd footnote, sounding like he'd just been listening to Thelonious Monk. "Blue at the Roots," in contrast, puts Mulligan at the keyboard for some barrelhouse piano playing that inspires a series of strong solos from the horns. Most remarkable, however, are the Duke Ellington medley recorded at the sextet's first Mercury session and "La Plus Que Lente" from its final date almost exactly a year later. For the "Moon Mist" section of the medley, Mulligan scores a rich, trombone-led phrase that resounds with El-lington tonality, against which the bari forms its solo; "In a Sentimen-tal Mood" follows with Mulligan taking the lead against some equally rich orchestral support. "La Plus Que Lente" is virtually sui generis; probably the only Claude Debussy composition to be performed by a jazz group in the 1950s (or perhaps ever), Gil Evans's transcription of its haunting melody gives Mulligan a framework for creating espe-cially odd-timbred voicings for the horns, almost as if he has called in the tuba and French horn from his days with Thornhill, Miles Davis, and the California tentette. As has been his wont, Gerry plays in and out of the ensemble support, which here seems less improvised than studiously compositional. Most remarkable, and something not at-tempted since its momentary appearance with the Davis nonet per-formance of "Jeru," is the alternation between various measures of time. As the number progresses, Mulligan does this more and more until he can begin soloing with assurance through these romantically disconcerting changes. Happily, he uses each to highlight harmonic effects as he interacts with the supporting horns, making it all seem like a natural blend. Unlike other jazz renditions of the classics, Evans and Mulligan's handling of Debussy maintains the feeling of the orig-inal composition, actually drawing new effects from the jazz group rather than sacrificing the French master to a run-it-through-the-mill jazztime rendition.

With the 26 September 1956 session that produced "La Plus Que Lente" and four other numbers, the Gerry Mulligan Sextet came to an end. Later that year Mulligan would take his quartet with Bob

Brookmeyer up to Storyville in Boston for his last Pacific Jazz LP, but
his sights were set elsewhere for the future. Two factors contributed
to this new direction and especially its interim phase during 1957,
1958, and 1959: his desire to form a big band—not just a nine- or
ten-piece ensemble, but a complete jazz orchestra—and the need to
finance this venture. The financing was done by Mulligan himself,
through facilities provided by Norman Granz's Verve label, which, as
the 1950s concluded, was proving itself to be the recording company
at the center of mainstream jazz. Granz would not only record the Concert Jazz Band beginning in 1960, but in the three preceding years he
would produce a series of one-on-one sessions in which Mulligan
would meet a wide range of other performers, most of which he'd never
performed with (Paul Desmond, Stan Getz, Johnny Hodges, and Ben
Webster), while other labels would bring him together with Thelonious Monk and with vocalists Annie Ross and Jimmy Witherspoon—
as wide a range of jazz talent the times might provide. As low-
overhead undertakings, these dates allowed Mulligan to earn money
without having to foot the bill for his own group, which was allowed
to go into limbo during these years that Gerry marshalled resources
for the future Concert Jazz Band. The band itself had a false start,
taking conventional form for a brief session with Columbia (released
twenty years later on *Gerry Mulligan: The Arranger*), and there was
a *Reunion with Chet Baker* album done for World Pacific and a brief
but extremely successful re-formation of the quartet, this time with
Art Farmer on trumpet.

The legacy of the 1957–1959 years, however, is more than just
money for the CJB. The experience of playing small-group sessions
with talents as diverse as Webster and Desmond, Hodges and Monk,
and Ross and Witherspoon put a greater emphasis on Gerry's solo
work than ever before. The romping success of the sextet had fired up
his playing; delicately edged with Chet Baker, his work with Bob
Brookmeyer and then with the other horn players, especially his close
friend Zoot Sims, unleashed a more confident sense of improvising,
and by 1956 his solos were strongly vocal, often new songs in themselves, plus his approach now showed a compositional bent, especially as he'd interacted with the polyphony behind him. Playing with
such legends as Hodges and Webster and contemporary giants including Desmond, Getz, and especially Monk, whose style was eons
away from his own, caused him to listen even more closely. The result
is most apparent on the quartet's 1959 album featuring Art Farmer,
What Is There to Say?, where Mulligan's playing is as well crafted as
anything from the Chet Baker days yet immensely more vital and

convincingly complex. It would be this style of baritone sax work around with the Concert Jazz Band was built.

- ● ***Manny Albam and the Jazz Giants:*** "Am I Blue?" from *Leonard Feather Presents: An Encyclopedia of Jazz on Records, Volume 5*, MCA2-4063, 2 April 1957. Manny Albam: leader; Nick Travis, Art Farmer: trumpets; Bob Brookmeyer: valve trombone; Phil Woods (alto), Zoot Sims (tenor), Al Cohn (tenor and baritone), Gerry Mulligan (baritone): saxophones; Hank Jones: piano; Milt Hinton: bass; Osie Johnson: drums.

Interesting hints of where Mulligan's orchestral sound would and would not be going are found in two unusual recording gigs from April 1957. The first involves the baritonist's work on one of arranger Manny Albam's "Jazz Giants" projects, *Manny Albam and the Jazz Greats of Our Time* (Coral CRL-57173). For sessions on 2, 3, and 4 April, Albam put together a light and airy yet energetic ten-piece group with Nick Travis and Art Farmer on trumpets, Bob Brookmeyer on valve trombone, a sax section of Phil Woods (alto), Zoot Sims and Al Cohn (tenors, with Cohn doubling on baritone), and Gerry Mulligan (bari), plus a rhythm section of Hank Jones, Milt Hinton, and Osie Johnson. This particular aggregation departs from Albam's customary personnel and larger sections in order to recruit players more commonly associated with Mulligan and present them in a format in striking anticipation of the CJB. And although Art Farmer did not continue with Mulligan's big band, this session does stand as his first recorded work with Gerry (over a year before his part in the new quartet would take shape), and his collaboration with Bob Brookmeyer looks forward to their presence in the 1963 Mulligan sextet. Brookmeyer, Sims, and Mulligan would be the featured soloists in the Concert Jazz Band, and Albam's charts actually look past Gerry's writing for his own abortive big band two weeks later and sound much more like the CJB than anything Mulligan was to do himself until 1960.

Unless, that is, Gerry had a hand in the scoring for the Albam sessions, which is a distinct possibility. The clearest aural evidence for such comes on a track not included on the original album but added to Coral's release in England (LVA-9089) and preserved on *Leonard Feather Presents: An Encyclopedia of Jazz on Records, Vol. 5* (MCA2-4063), "Am I Blue?" From start to finish, the song's full presentation is unmistakably Mulliganesque, due either to Gerry's penning of the score or to Albam's gifted ear responding to the essence of Mulligan's orchestral art. The piece begins with a solo bari line—not just the melody, but as a counter figure to Phil Woods's alto sax, which rolls high and easy in response to a loping bass line set down by Gerry's big horn. Then, much as the quartet had done and the CJB would do, the bridge is given over to Bob Brookmeyer's valve trombone; it takes this middle part alone but then continues into the close of the chorus with an intermix of brass support. Then comes the featured soloists—Sims, Woods, and Mulligan—all playing in an open, relaxed, kicked-back manner with minimal orchestral interference. Sims shapes his solo with an ear cocked toward the casual fills from open brass, while Woods's higher, clearer horn benefits from having the trumpets muted. What comes across as pure Mulligan, however, is the format for Gerry's own solo, most of which is undertaken with just bass and drums in accompaniment, the band hanging out until the end of each phrase when there's a chance for a complimentary ensemble figure. This balance of equals between solo horn and sections would be a hallmark of the CJB, a concerto grosso technique Mulligan and those writing for him would exploit to the fullest.

Following Mulligan's centerpiece solo, which overlaps its first structural run-through into the second phrase, comes a muted bridge by Art Farmer (with bari-led chords emerging from an Ellingtonian background, something else the CJB would do) before Al Cohn, Hank Jones, and Milt Hinton divide up the remaining solo space. But there's still time for section work, here letting the ensemble play a more complex variation of the opening bari and alto figures. Then, as a reminder of how Mulligan's horn work had transformed this all-too-common show-tune melody into a walking bass line, Gerry and Phil repeat the opening phrase to end things.

● ***Gerry Mulligan and His Orchestra:*** "Thruway," "All the Things You Are," "Mullenium," and "Motel," from *Gerry Mulligan: The Arranger*, Columbia JC-34803, 19 and 20 April 1957. Gerry Mulligan: arrangements, leader, and piano; Don Ferrara, Don Joseph, Jerry Lloyd, Phil Sunkel: trumpets; Bob Brookmeyer (valve), Jim Dahl, Frank Rehak: trombones; Lee Konitz, Hal McKusick (alto), Charlie Rouse, Zoot Sims (tenor), Gene Allen, Gerry Mulligan (baritone): saxophones; Joe Benjamin: bass; Dave Bailey: drums.

Two weeks after the sessions with Manny Albam, something quite different transpires under Mulligan's ascribed direction. The fifteen-piece band he took into the Columbia studios on 19 and 20 April 1957 produced some fine music, but listening to its four cuts in light of what Gerry had done with Albam earlier that month and especially with a mind toward what the Concert Jazz Band would yield three years later shows why Mulligan must have felt compelled to take a new direction, perhaps to let the effects of his more experimental work with the Albam ensemble settle in; like the six-month hiatus between the quartet and sextet, some time away from leading and maintaining a group (always an exhausting drain) would be necessary to get his new ideas in order, for the April 1957 material was nothing new at all.

The band was half again as big as Manny Albam's Jazz Giants and more than twice as heavy. Its instrumentation—four trumpets, three trombones, five saxes (plus Mulligan in a featured role, as Woody Herman sometimes fronted his Herd on alto), and rhythm—looked back to the standard format in place since Fletcher Henderson's work in the early 1930s. This was a structure that led inevitably to scoring in sections rather than intermixing a trumpet with two of the saxes as had brightened up the attack so considerably on Albam's "Am I Blue?" As with the Jazz Giants sessions, several friends were in the band— Jerry [Hurwitz] Lloyd from the 1949 Kai Winding Septet, Bob Brookmeyer and Zoot Sims from the sextet, and even Lee Konitz from the Thornhill orchestra and then the quartet-plus-Konitz dates of 1953— but in all cases their presence evoked Mulligan's past associations much more than implying what the future might bring. "Thruway," the session's major number and the only one of the four released (as an alternate) before the decade had elapsed (on the 1962 Columbia sampler, *Who's Who in the Swinging Sixties*, CL 1765/CS 8565), is essentially an enlarged and extended sextet number, the various sections taking the roles assigned to individual (and more interesting) instruments from the smaller group. Mulligan's fifteen-piece aggregation is simply too large to handle the tune's appealingly light melody, and when it comes to showcasing the soloists they seem to be in a different world entirely—the band either hangs out to make things sound like the trio at Turetsky's house in 1952 or else overplays their fills to the soloist's discomfort (as happens noticeably with Jerry Lloyd and to some extent Bob Brookmeyer, who finally ignores them). When things do sound better at the end, it is because the writing calls up the sextet's format for some polyphony and distinctive voicings.

"All the Things You Are" pulls the band's massive resources back to feature the bari by itself and then with Konitz's also interweaving, but when it makes its inevitable appearance the orchestra seems confused, certainly no tribute to Mulligan's writing. "Mullenium," which had swung along with both Elliot Lawrence's band and the New York tentette, here puts Mulligan's featured horn in the position of walking on thin ice, while the band drags with the tempo designed for the solo rather than ensemble effect. Mulligan finally surrenders the final cut, "Motel," to the sextet's conception. It is a nice number by itself, but the decision not to employ the larger band such as was done for Thornhill and would happen again with CJB is regrettable.

When Columbia finally released this material on its retrospective album, *Gerry Mulligan: The Arranger* (JC-34803) in 1977, its appeal was decidedly historical, combined as it was with cuts from Elliot Lawrence and Gene Krupa sessions of the late 1940s. There remains some controversy about the label's treatment of Mulligan; to interviewers he expressed confusion and dismay at how his producers sat on the tapes and declined further support of his big band, while to others he complained that this group's particular format did not allow him to express the ideas now germinating in anticipation of the CJB. A clearer sense of direction would be obvious in his and Bob Brookmeyer's work with cornetist Phil Sunkel six months later on an album entitled *Jazz Concerto Grosso* (ABC Paramount ABC-225). Many of the personnel span the earlier band and the CJB, but its structure was radically different from the April 1957 affair. Now the trombone section was reduced to one conventional horn and a bass trombone, the third chair being taken by tubaist Don Butterfield. But more important, the sections themselves do not play in a traditional exchanging-of-riffs fashion but rather function as an integrated ensemble (their voices stacked in variations drawn from Miles Davis, Claude Thornhill, and Gil Evans). The purpose of this ensemble is to support and interact with three players up front—Mulligan, Brookmeyer, and Sunkel—in a concerto grosso manner. This approach would be one of the essential keys to Mulligan's work with the CJB, and the fact that it is nowhere in evidence for the Columbia recordings suggests that it was his own somewhat late-developing plans rather than the label's lack of support that prevented more from happening. Listening to Sunkel's title track plus the two other numbers performed by a smaller, seven-piece group, makes one realize that the Concert Jazz Band was now definitely on the horizon; this October 1957 session produces a much more innovative sound, drawing on resources unsuspected just six months earlier. The writing itself is much more adventurous, with a plethora of lines intersecting in a style Mulligan, with his love of spontaneous polyphony, would surely appreciate. Like the best of the CJB cuts, "Jazz Concerto Grosso" begins with a solitary line (one whose odd melodic cast is enhanced by its rhythmic structure and voicing with the tuba and bass trombone), which is run through almost every conceivable variation as the three lead horns move in and out of the supporting ensemble. Just as the April recordings look backward to the sextet, this October work almost fully anticipates the CJB of nearly three years later.

Whether motivated by external or internal pressures, however, Mulligan did abandon the big-band format for the coming years in favor of a wide range of performances, from the one-on-one sessions to movie work and another brief version of the quartet. All would make their contribution to the radical new vehicle the Concert Jazz Band would prove itself to be on its debut in 1960.

Working with Norman Granz subjected Mulligan to the odd dimensions of this producer's style, allowing the classic *Gerry Mulligan Meets* . . . recordings but also dropping him into the grab-bag assortment of the jam-session album, *Jazz Giants '58*, a 31 July 1957 get-together for Verve (MGV-8248) reminiscent of Granz's less-than-disciplined Jazz at the Philharmonic performances. Here Mulligan joined Stan Getz, Harry Edison, Oscar Peterson, Herb Ellis, Ray Brown, and Louis Bellson for some playing based on no better or more apparent idea than that they all happened to be under contract to Norman Granz. Although the liner notes report that Mulligan supplied head arrangements for the set's four blowing numbers plus a "Ballade" medley featuring himself, Edison, Brown, and Getz in turn, the charts seem little more than notes for the order of solos, as neither side provides any ensemble parts. Oscar Peterson's piano actually holds the material together, introducing most tunes and framing the interpolations for the four ballads. Mulligan's playing is itself relaxed and enjoyable but most certainly marks a resting period between the impasse with his big band and the coming head-to-head sets.

- *The Gerry Mulligan-Paul Desmond Quartet:* "Blues Intime," "Body and Soul," "Wintersong," "Standstill," "Line for Lyons," "Battle Hymn of the Republican," and "Fall Out," from *The Gerry Mulligan-Paul Desmond Quartet,* Verve MGV-8246, 1 and 27 August 1957. Paul Desmond (alto) and Gerry Mulligan (baritone): saxophones; Joe Benjamin: bass; Dave Bailey: drums.

The first of his *Gerry Mulligan Meets* . . . occasions comes right after the Peterson jam session. Mulligan had been maintaining his reputation by taking the quartet (with Bob Brookmeyer) to Newport, where he also sat in with Teddy Wilson's group for a run-through of "Sweet Georgia Brown." It was there that Paul Desmond brought up the idea of an album together, and so when Gerry returned from Los Angeles and a quartet date at the Hollywood Bowl, he quickly arranged to follow the Granz session with a 2 A.M. meeting with Desmond in the same studio—hence their first three cuts, dated 1 August 1957, followed after the clock passed midnight during the 31 July engagement with Norman Granz's all-stars.

The proximity of these two sessions is important, for it shows how ready Mulligan was for the Desmond meeting. Their first cut, "Body and Soul," suits the languid tempo of the late hour; but that venerable old standard merely served to get their reeds wet. With Desmond's "Blues Intime" the swinging gets underway, Gerry laying down a fuguish line that Paul immediately takes up to introduce the song's continual structure of interplay. The vast differences in register and timbre between the alto and bari are at once effaced by the two players' obvious enjoyment of each other's company, anticipating the title song Desmond would write for their 1962 reunion, *Two of a Mind*. While Mulligan begins the tune in a restrained manner reminiscent of Desmond's work with Dave Brubeck, the altoist quickly shows that he's shed any inhibitions and is ready to blow with an expanded sense of rhythm and range. The absence of a piano allows Desmond to meet Mulligan within his own boppy yet loping style, and the number's break-time pauses allow each player to exploit the range of his horn.

Throughout these numbers these two soloists build songs based on an awareness of each other's presence, interacting almost simultaneously rather than just interweaving lines, a quality achieved in the Mulligan canon only a year and a half before, when Gerry and Zoot romped through each other's tracks on the sextet's honky-tonk "Mainstream." Thus is created a truly spontaneous polyphony, the denseness of which is clarified by the purity of what Mulligan and Desmond are playing. Their mutual feel is most apparent on Desmond's "Wintersong," where his baroque styled, Bach-like phrasing (a carryover from the Brubeck quartet's "Brandenburg Gate") prompts Gerry to respond in kind, remarkably transforming his usual mode of playing. Two sessions produced this album, the second session waiting until 27 August, following a date with Thelonious Monk; some of Monk's influence can be heard on the latter set of tunes. If the initial cuts were dense, the last three show the solid yet fluid beauty of a Jackson Pollock canvas during the height of his drip period, Mulligan's and Desmond's spiny lines doing with musical notes what Pollock's paint accomplishes on canvas.

- **Thelonious Monk–Gerry Mulligan:** "Rhythm-a-ning," "Straight, No Chaser," "I Mean You," " 'Round Midnight," "Sweet and Lovely," and "Decidedly," from *Mulligan Meets Monk*, Riverside RLP-1106, 12 and 13 August 1957. Gerry Mulligan: baritone saxophone; Thelonious Monk: piano; Wilbur Ware: bass; Shadow Wilson: drums.

The Gerry Mulligan-Paul Desmond album is the first of the *Mulligan Meets . . .* for Norman Granz; that the formulaic title would be picked up for later sessions indicates that the tradition was not yet consciously underway. But when Orrin Keepnews of Riverside Records, Granz's closest thing to an equal rival in jazz production, penciled in 12 and 13 August for the taping of *Mulligan Meets Monk*, the multilabel series was definitely underway. Gerry had sat in with the pianist at least once before, in an informal session following the first of his Paris concerts in June 1954; observers note that for the first phrase Mulligan had seemed confused but soon adjusted and swung right into Monk's radically unconventional style of playing, enjoying himself and delighting others until Gerry's wife rather bossily announced it was time to go home. In 1957 the turf was still Monk's, as the two were recording on Monk's label and with the nucleus of his group from the Five Spot (Wilbur Ware and Shadow Wilson), with Mulligan in the unlikely position of sitting in for John Coltrane. Initial plans called for one day's blowing with the small group, then a larger band session to follow. But both principals were so pleased with the three tracks layed down on 12 August that they urged Keepnews to forget the big band and let them come in next day for another small session, which is how the album was completed.

In a good-humored fashion, Monk does a fair amount of leading Mulligan around. Especially on the Milestone Records reissue, which includes several alternate takes (*Thelonious Monk/Gerry Mulligan— 'Round Midnight*, M-47067), the pianist can be heard giving his little bleeplike signals now and then through the sax solos as a way of keeping Gerry on course, especially when the bari neglects Monk's odd structures and wanders off into conventional doodling on a simplified set of chords. But on such classics as " 'Round Midnight" and "Straight, No Chaser" Mulligan does more than justice to Monk's music, not only departing from the way John Coltrane was handling these numbers at the time but actually anticipating how Monk's horn man of the sixties, Charlie Rouse, would play the tunes. On both tunes Mulligan matches Monk's tonality and emerges from his sound. The soloing shows less of a tendency to lope around the chords than to explore them in a more angular way, something present in his other work but here especially complementary to Monk's style. Monk himself remains a master of odd harmonics plus arhythmic stops and stutters; what's remarkable is that Mulligan is able to cushion in behind him, lending the kind of support Chet Baker might have expected in the quartet days but that proves adaptable to Monk's playing.

Although the majority of the album's numbers are material associated with Monk, Mulligan brings in one of his own tunes (written for the occasion) and places his stamp on several others. "Decidedly" resurrects the bebop practice of inverting both the melody and the title of an old standard to form an "original"; here the model is the Charlie Shavers trumpet classic, "Undecided." Although the melody is pure Mulligan, Monk immediately flavors it by adding distinctly Monkish fills. As if to prove that the song remains his own, Gerry then takes his most melodic and swinging solo of the set—or at least starts out that way, because before it proceeds too far Monk brings him back into a more subtle appreciation of the day's transformed tonality and rhythms. The alternate take on the Milestone reissue shows this even more so, but both versions reveal how after making their individual statements both men wind up supporting each other and even producing some genuine polyphony before the number's out chorus. "Sweet and Lovely" provides a good chance for blending talents because it is a number from both of their repertoires. Here Mulligan's backing proves especially enhancing, again anticipating how tenorist Charlie Rouse would handle the tune five years later. The finest collaboration, however, remains "I Mean You," a Monk classic to be sure, but now one written, it seems, with Mulligan's horn and his style of playing it in mind.

- **Stan Getz–Gerry Mulligan:** "Let's Fall in Love," "Anything Goes," "Too Close for Comfort," "That Old Feeling," "This Can't Be Love," and "Ballad," from *Getz Meets Mulligan in Hi-Fi,* Verve MGV-8249, 22 October 1957. Stan Getz: tenor saxophone; Gerry Mulligan: baritone saxophone (Getz and Mulligan exchange instruments for the first three numbers); Lou Levy: piano; Ray Brown: bass; Stan Levey: drums.

Gerry's next meeting, on 22 October 1957 with Stan Getz, would promise to be less confrontational than the session with Monk.

But thanks to several little twists this meeting makes its own contribution to Mulligan's development, implying things that would come to fruition in the period immediately following the Concert Jazz Band. The major factor was that, in Norman Granz's scheme of things, Mulligan was not the headliner. Although Gerry's name had preceded Desmond's and Monk's (the latter circumstance reversed for the Monk reissue), this new undertaking was titled *Getz Meets Mulligan in Hi-Fi*, an album followed soon after with two additional tracks from the same session released as side one of *Stan Getz and Gerry Mulligan / Stan Getz and the Oscar Peterson Trio* (Verve MGV-8348). Getz's leadership shows at once in two ways: choice of materials and choice of personnel, including format. Only one tune is from Mulligan's songbook, the "Ballad," which seems as if crafted for Getz's sweet and airy style of tenor; the other numbers consist of old standards from Getz's big-band years of the 1940s and Charlie Parker's "Scrapple from the Apple" on the second LP. The conventionality of this material is enhanced by the instrumentation Getz brought along: piano, bass, and drums, in particular pianist Lou Levy's light but thoroughly systematic style of fills (the bane of Mulligan's pianoless quartet) and bassist Ray Brown's strongly melodic playing. This would be Mulligan's first-ever small-group session with a conventional rhythm section (Monk's idiosyncratic playing hardly qualifies as conventional), and to throw things wittily and mischievously off kilter he persuades Getz to swap horns for three numbers, giving the session a most unusual sound.

Switching horns turns out to be just what it takes to turn familiar tunes like "Let's Fall in Love," "Too Close for Comfort," and "Anything Goes" into fresh new interpretations. As early as his first arrangements for Elliot Lawrence and Gene Krupa Mulligan had shown his comic approach to the songs of both Harold Arlen and Cole Porter, and putting Getz on bari fits right into the goofy melodic twistings and interchange of orchestral parts that had distinguished such early charts as "Between the Devil and the Deep Blue Sea" and "Begin the Beguine." On "Let's Fall in Love" and "Too Close for Comfort" Getz and Mulligan find the ideal tempo for soloing on their new horns, Stan coaxing new lyricism from the big instrument while Mulligan lopes along in a tenor style reminiscent of Brew Moore. For thematic statements, their lines alternately blend and cross, giving the slightest hint of polyphony but principally stressing harmonic effect (the bari and tenor finding a new common timbre in being blown by players more accustomed to their sax's respectively higher and lower pitches). For the brisker "Anything Goes" Mulligan creates a sense of busy-ness by adding several notes to the melody and pulling the horns out of their quick unison for some harmonic stretches near the end of each phrase, followed by a boppish cascade of further extraneous notes to make things seem more hurried than ever. When the guys get back on their own instruments for side B, the effect is smoother than ever, both solos and thematic statements showing the high polish each brings to his chosen horn. Fittingly, the numbers show off Gerry's and Stan's range of playing, from the gentle interweaving and exchanging of lead on "Ballad" to the happy, relaxed swinging of "That Old Feeling." To prove that they can cook with the best, the two propel their way through an up-tempo "This Can't Be Love," in which Getz pulls out his "Four Brothers" style of full-speed-ahead improvisation while Mulligan bops along as is his wont.

Getz Meets Mulligan adds to Gerry's repertoire a renewed sense of humor, from the orchestrated collisions of "Anything Goes" (with Getz particularly enjoying the baritone's explosive effects on its bottom notes and Mulligan taking full advantage of the tenor's sharper attack) to the expansive swinging evident in "Too Close for Comfort" (where the harmonies are drawn out in almost barbershop-quartet fashion). This ability to create new moods with old standards, plus the chance to showcase pretty-playing horns as in "Ballad," show up again in the CJB. But there's also Lou Levy's piano to deal with. Rather than inhibiting Mulligan, Levy's piano gives him a more confident sense for his solos, which are impelled forward rather than pausing too often to explore modalities (a penchant that Thelonious Monk's little kicks from the piano had corrected). That Mulligan appreciated what such a supportive yet not-too-obtrusive piano could do became evident in one of his first recordings after the CJB was disbanded, "*Jeru*," where his horn is supported by the piano of Tommy Flanagan (plus the expanded rhythm of bass, drums, and congas).

• *Gerry Mulligan–Chet Baker:* "Reunion," "My Heart Belongs to Daddy," "When Your Lover Has Gone," "Stardust," "Jersey Bounce," "Surrey with the Fringe on Top," "Travelin' Light," and "Ornithology," from *Reunion with Chet Baker*, World Pacific PJ-1241, 3 and 11 December 1957. Chet Baker: trumpet; Gerry Mulligan: baritone saxophone; Henry Grimes: bass; Dave Bailey: drums.

Mulligan's next meeting was with his past, yielding the World Pacific LP *Reunion with Chet Baker*. Produced by Richard Bock in New York in two sessions during December 1957, the album picks up virtually where Mulligan and Baker left off in the summer of 1953. The selections reflect the original quartet's taste, including a pertly swinging, infectiously tuneful original by Gerry ("Reunion"), a conventionally handled standard ("When Your Lover Has Gone"), some excuses for extremely pretty playing ("Stardust" and the nicely crafted "Travelin' Light"), outright whimsy ("My Heart Belongs to Daddy" and "The Surrey with the Fringe on Top"), softly stated swinging ("Jersey Bounce"), and, to round things out, Charlie Parker's "Ornithology." Both horns play in their familiar manner, Mulligan reining in some of his free blowing as developed with the sextet in order to recapture the masterpiece-in-miniature effect of 1952–1953; Baker seems to have aged a bit, playing in a more understated manner and in a few places seemingly dry of inspiration, yet there are plenty of occasions where he rescales the lyrical heights established years before. At their best, Mulligan and Baker remind listeners of what drew them together in the first place: a sympathy for each other's atypical sound, a willingness to step back now and then to offer subtle, cushioning support for each other's solos, and most of all a desire to listen to the other's lines and shape one's own work out of it. The seamlessness of their treatment of "Stardust," their ability to bounce as lightly as the title of "Jersey Bounce," and both horns' achievement of a totally integrated sound for "Travelin' Light" makes it clear that, had they wished, the two instrumentalists could have revived the quartet and played on as long as they wished, albeit in an early-fifties manner.

For Mulligan this was the last thing imaginable. Always complaining about his fears of going stagnant, his reunion with Chet Baker revealed how comfortable things could be if he would let them. Throughout the album's material runs an appealing but, one might suppose for Mulligan, frightening tendency to lay back; even the album's up-tempo numbers show the soloists tending to relax, while the pretty-sounding pieces rely more on sound itself than on how the players shape it. If the quartet were to take shape again, it would have to be with some element of difference.

- *Annie Ross–Gerry Mulligan:* "I Feel Pretty," "Give Me the Simple Life," and "Let There Be Love," from *Annie Ross Sings a Song with Mulligan!*, World Pacific WP-1253, 11 and 17 December 1957. Art Farmer (Chet Baker on "Let There Be Love"): trumpet; Gerry Mulligan: baritone saxophone; Bill Crow (Henry Grimes on "Let There Be Love"): bass; Dave Bailey: drums; Annie Ross: vocal.

Because of his desire for something different, it is not surprising to see Mulligan invite singer Annie Ross to the last session with Chet Baker for the first of several studio dates that first had her working with the quartet and then with just baritone sax, bass, and drums, taking the role of the group's second voice. The effect on Mulligan is immediate, restoring his playing to its strengths and exuberance as displayed on the sextet's albums. Mulligan's solos are more dynamic, forceful, and of greater range, while his support for Ross draws on much more polyphony than he dared risk behind Baker just an hour before.

Obviously pleased with this session's results, Mulligan booked two more recording dates with Annie Ross, both in Los Angeles: on 11 February 1958, with Chet Baker rejoining on trumpet, and on 25 August of that same year, with the trumpeter Mulligan had chosen for his new quartet now rehearsing, Art Farmer (Michael Cuscuna locates these sessions in New York during December 1957). "The Lady's in Love with You" was not issued until the Pacific Jazz sampler, *The Genius of Gerry Mulligan*, but the ten numbers with Ross originally listed from February and August appeared on *Annie Ross Sings a Song with Mulligan!* (World Pacific WP-1253). Elements of the original quartet's thinking are evident here, including the delicate treatment of standards, the desire to swing some faster tunes with the best of them, and, as in "I Feel Pretty," a fair dose of Mulligan's mischievous whimsy. Especially with Art Farmer involved, the group's arrangements integrate themselves with the singer's voice, making "Give Me the Simple Life" not just a standard jazz-backed refrain but rather a genuine encapsulation of what Gerry Mulligan sounds like with words. Ross's voice is responsive to the quartet's sound, and vice versa, building on the format's reputation for enunciating and articulating notes with the precision of a human voice. On "I Feel Pretty" voice and trumpet harmonize a tag line while baritone sax supports with counterpoint; "Let There Be Love" puts an especially sweet voice over the horn fills, their backing taking on enough character for Ross to sing in harmony. What was developing from these vocal sessions was a more richly expressive quartet, one in which Mulligan could do much more than showcase miniature effects. That original form had been dictated by Pacific Jazz's three-minute 78 rpm singles, but now it was the day of the LP record, where three or four cuts could fill an entire side, making the optimum tune twice as long or more.

The quartet Mulligan was envisioning took most of 1958 to develop. Its progress came in stages, each of which would contribute its effect to the single album the quartet would record in December 1958 and January 1959, *What Is There to Say?* Art Farmer's style of trumpet was the significant addition, although the presence of Mulligan's favorite bassist and drummer, Bill Crow and Dave Bailey, made this group more rhythmically forceful than the original quartet had been in its Chico Hamilton days. But as with the sessions with Annie Ross, which broadened the already vocal tendency in Mulligan's playing to include such effects for scoring as well, the grab bag of activities filling out 1958 had their impact on Mulligan's vision.

● ***Billie Holiday–Count Basie–Gerry Mulligan:*** "Fast and Happy Blues" and "Dickie's Dream," from *The Real Sound of Jazz*, Pumpkin 116, 8 December 1957. Roy Eldridge, Joe Newman, Joe Wilder, Doc Cheatham, Emmett Berry: trumpets; Vic Dickenson, Dickie Wells, Benny Morton: trombones; Earle Warren (alto), Ben Webster, Coleman Hawkins (tenor), Gerry Mulligan (baritone): saxophones; Count Basie: piano; Freddie Green: guitar; Eddie Jones: bass; Jo Jones: drums. "Fine and Mellow," from same program. Roy Eldridge, Doc Cheatham: trumpets; Vic Dickenson: trombone; Coleman Hawkins, Ben Webster, Lester Young (tenor), Gerry Mulligan (baritone): saxophones; Mal Waldron: piano; Danny Barker: guitar; Milt Hinton: bass; Osie Johnson: drums; Billie Holiday: vocal.

During these years Gerry Mulligan was being recognized as an all-star, and several television-show and jazz-festival samplers find him playing with an extremely wide range of major jazz figures, from Louis Armstrong, Duke Ellington (whose orchestra spotlighted Mulligan in a duet with fellow baritone saxophonist Harry Carney, the century's only other true giant on that horn), and Pete Johnson to Teddy Wilson and his own sideman, Bob Brookmeyer. Of greatest historical and creative interest, however, is Mulligan's presence on an album eventually released as *The Real Sound of Jazz*, a transcription of the historic CBS Television broadcast of 8 December 1957. Mulligan appears on three cuts, two with the Count Basie All Stars ("Fast and Happy Blues," "Dickie's Dream") and one accompanying Billie Holiday on "Fine and Mellow." The Basie numbers show Gerry holding more than his own above the roaring big band and in the company of fellow soloists Coleman Hawkins, Ben Webster, Dickie Wells, and Joe Newman, all of whom had built careers within this style of music that Mulligan could only appreciate as a student. Yet his solos hold up, each showing great facility in not only covering its own line but interacting for rhythmic effect with the riffing sections behind him. On "Fine and Mellow," however, he finds himself in a smaller group and at a much slower tempo; these quieter surroundings highlight Billie Holiday's exceptional voice and inflection and also showcase one of Lester Young's finest performances. Mulligan's own solo pays homage to Young, their mutual lyricism and softly swinging style bridging both generations and epochs in jazz styling. In these sets Mulligan is integrating himself with the living history of jazz, much of which would pass from the scene within just a few years (with the deaths of Holiday and Young, the First Lady and President of American music for the past quarter of a century). On the bandstand, the much younger Mulligan proves himself an able section player with Hawkins, Webster, and Earle Warren; the entire experience immensely deepened Mulligan's sense of representing the mainstream of jazz.

- **Gerry Mulligan and the Sax Section:** "Four and One Moore," "Crazy Day," "Turnstile," "Sextet," "Disc Jockey Jump," "Venus de Milo," and "Revelation," from *The Gerry Mulligan Songbook, Vol. 1*, World Pacific PJ-1237, 4 and 5 December 1957. Lee Konitz (alto), Zoot Sims, Allen Eager (alto and tenor), Al Cohn (tenor and baritone), Gerry Mulligan (baritone): saxophones; Freddie Green: guitar; Henry Grimes: bass; Dave Bailey: drums.

Odd influences on both the Art Farmer edition of the quartet and the Concert Jazz Band are found in two intermediate-sized ensembles Mulligan led during this transitional period. In New York on 4–5 December, as Gerry was getting his reunion with Chet Baker underway, World Pacific Records commissioned arranger Bill Holman to prepare half a dozen Mulligan originals for five-piece sax section plus guitar, bass, and drums; Mulligan himself wrote and scored "Crazy Day" for the session that produced *The Gerry Mulligan Songbook, Vol. 1*. No subsequent volumes ever appeared, but the December set serves as a good reminder of how lyrical Mulligan's compositions are. Five-and-a-half months later Gerry found himself in Los Angeles, fronting a septet of West Coast-style musicians with Art Farmer and himself representing the East, playing six Johnny Mandel compositions and arrangements for the film *I Want to Live!* Here the manner of the day was sound and dynamics, complementing the solid swinging of the sax-section cuts in New York. Together, the sessions anticipate the range and effect of both the new quartet and the CJB,

First pianoless quartet with Chet Baker, The Haig, Los Angeles, 1952. © William Claxton.

The Haig, Los Angeles, 1952. © William Claxton.

Lee Konitz joins Mulligan and Baker at The Haig, 1953. © William Claxton.

Lee Konitz records with Mulligan and Baker at engineer Phil Turetsky's home, Hollywood Hills (Laurel Canyon), 1953. © William Claxton.

Second pianoless quartet with Chet Baker, Carson Smith, and Larry Bunker at Gold Star Studios, Hollywood, 1953. © William Claxton.

William Claxton's montage for a proposed LP cover, 1953. © William Claxton.

Gerry Mulligan Quartet and Sextet in San Diego, 1954. © William Claxton.

Quartet in San Diego, 1954
(with Jon Eardley, Red Mitchell, and Chico Hamilton).
© William Claxton.

Sextet in San Diego, 1954 (with Jon Eardley, Bob Brookmeyer, Zoot Sims, and Red Mitchell—not visible is drummer Larry Bunker). © William Claxton.

Backstage at San Diego, 1954. © William Claxton.

Quartet with Bob Brookmeyer, Bill Crow, and Dave Bailey in Boston, 1956.
© William Claxton.

With Father Norman O'Connor and Richard Bock, Boston, 1956.
© William Claxton.

At the tailor shop in Cambridge,
Massachusetts,
1956. © William Claxton.

With Ben Webster, Hollywood, 1959.
© William Claxton.

Hollywood, 1959. © William Claxton.

With Judy Holliday, Hollywood and Beverly Hills, 1960. © William Claxton.

The Concert Jazz Band, Newport Jazz Festival, 1960. © William Claxton.

Concerto Grosso: Mulligan, Bob Brookmeyer, and Zoot Sims supported by the Concert Jazz Band, Newport Jazz Festival, 1960. © William Claxton.

In the early 1960s in the trademarked checked jacket.
Institute of Jazz Studies, Rutgers University.

Circa early 1970s. The Bettmann Archive.

Recording soundtrack for *La Menace*, 1982.
Courtesy of DRG Records.

With Zubin Mehta at the New York Philharmonic, December 1989.
Photo: Bert Bial, courtesy of Gerry Mulligan Productions, Inc.

New York, 1989. Courtesy of Gerry Mulligan Productions, Inc.

contributing to the wide variety of projects Mulligan was undertaking during these years and stretching his talents to a new point of creative elasticity.

The *Songbook*'s ensemble shows how many different effects can be achieved from such apparently limited orchestration, and Mulligan fashions his original for the date, "Crazy Day," with these potentialities in mind. Mulligan of course leads on baritone; Lee Konitz provides the logical complement to Gerry's rich, deep sound, but to provide the arranger a broad palette of sound the other three horn men double: Zoot Sims on alto and tenor, Allen Eager doing the same, and Al Cohn extending his deeper-voiced style of tenor-sax playing by covering the baritone as well. Holman often divides Mulligan's lines in two, playing the higher horns against the lower, bringing them together for Mulliganesque touches of both polyphony and harmony. Gerry shows his approval be designing "Crazy Day," a sing-song refrain type of tune in the manner of "Mainstream" from the sextet, in a similar mode, the Konitz-led altos setting a high part that is counterpointed by his and Cohn's horn playing at their bottom, with Allen Eager's tenor in between. All of these sounds are present in a conventional big band's sax section but are usually stacked together for a sectionlike effect. Taking them apart effectively deconstructs the sound and shows how much more a band can do when its constituent parts are recognized. If forced mechanically to replicate the three sections of a full band, as Holman scores "Disc Jockey Jump," the result is less rich, but such original voicings as "Four and One Moore" (written originally for saxes) and of course "Crazy Day" have the horns both cover parts and be themselves at the same time. "Venus de Milo," despite its *Birth of the Cool* familiarity, is another reminder of how essentially sax-oriented Mulligan's creations are.

● *Gerry Mulligan's Jazz Combo:* "Black Nightgown," "Theme from *I Want to Live!*," "Night Watch," "Frisco Club," "Barbara's Theme," and "Life's a Funny Thing," from *Gerry Mulligan: The Jazz Combo from "I Want to Live!*," United Artists UAL-4006, 24 May 1958. Art Farmer: trumpet; Frank Rosolino: trombone; Bud Shank (alto and flute), Gerry Mulligan (baritone): saxophones; Pete Jolly: piano; Red Mitchell: bass; Shelly Manne: drums; Johnny Mandel: arrangements.

However strong the orientation toward saxophone, brass still retains an important role in the particular genius of Gerry Mulligan— sometimes as a foil for the strongly contrasting baritone but more often as a cutting edge. Without any trumpets on the *Songbook* session, Holman and Mulligan found it necessary to add guitarist Freddie Green to the rhythm section, adding a crispness to the beat that otherwise might have melted beneath the saxes' sweetness. But for the *I Want to Live!* combo, Art Farmer's trumpet provides a more than adequate bite, while Frank Rosolino's trombone both deepens and enriches the ensemble. Although the scoring is Mandel's and rides along on a classically West Coast sound enunciated by Bud Shank's alto sax, there is a strong presence of the emerging quartet in these numbers, especially in the introductory "Black Nightgown," which has Mulligan and Farmer snapping off little honky-tonk tag lines in the Dixieland manner that seemed more of an intellectual posture in the Chet Baker days.

I Want to Live! is the first Mulligan project (short of the Concert Jazz Band, which would debut in a year and a half) to display such a broad range of sounds and dynamics, all the more remarkable when coming from just a seven-piece group with only one player doubling (Bud Shank on alto and flute). "Black Nightgown" puts all the horns up front for some classic toe-tapping, but on its heels comes the spooky title song on which Shank's flute and Mulligan's bari interweave in a counterpoint of contrasts, supported by brief echoing fills from muted brass. Other tunes offer straight-ahead swinging and rousing ensemble effects, all of which would be exploited six months later by Mulligan and Farmer in the new quartet. Farmer's presence anticipates that group, but Mandel's forever-active interplay of lines will be recalled as well, in addition to the movie combo's biting attack. Both the new quartet and CJB would show more range and dynamics than Mulligan's earlier groups, and his involvement in this film work may well have been an influence. Mandel's writing reveals a heavy Mulligan presence, with the snappy "Life's a Funny Thing" sounding like it could have been penned by Gerry himself; as it is, the song's division of lines and pauses for effect sound not only like a Mulligan composition from earlier years but imply the treatments given such songs by the Concert Jazz Band a few years hence.

- *The Gerry Mulligan Quartet:* "Blueport," "My Funny Valentine," "Utter Chaos," "As Catch Can," "Just in Time," "What Is There to Say?" "Festive Minor," and "News from Blueport," from *What Is There to Say?*, Columbia CL-1307, 17, 18, and 23 December 1958 and 15 January 1959. Art Farmer: trumpet; Gerry Mulligan: baritone saxophone; Bill Crow: bass; Dave Bailey: drums.

It's a pity that the "new" Gerry Mulligan Quartet, including Art Farmer plus old hands Bill Crow and Dave Bailey, did not stay together longer than the year it did, because its single album, *What Is There to Say?*, showed it could do everything from the original quartet and more. On the other hand, its very success indicates Mulligan's restlessness for new work and strong desire to form a larger ensemble for his writing—it was the Concert Jazz Band forming and rehearsing for its debut in 1960 that brought this edition of the quartet to its close. Considering himself a small-combo player, Art Farmer declined to join the larger band, and when Mulligan recorded again with a four-piece group in 1962 the brass part was given to Bob Brookmeyer. As it is, this one album must suffice as the example of how Mulligan's classic small-group format, the vehicle that had brought him national fame in the decade's earlier years, had developed into something even more accomplished during this remarkable decade of diverse experience and growth.

The album's title song announces the new group's intentions. A soft and delicate old classic, it fits the mold of standards Mulligan liked choosing back in 1952–1963 as a way of showing how his big, oxy horn could handle such tunes with care and as a vehicle for the minimalistic, pianoless format that demanded that the listener be either musically sharp enough or sufficiently familiar with the material to fill in the obvious gaps. But on 15 January 1959 (following earlier sessions in December 1958), the quartet rises to a whole new level of performance and interpretation, Mulligan's bari and Farmer's trumpet playing an extended, interweaving duet over Crow's rhythmless bass bowing—a lovely pas de deux whose elegance sets a tone much more ambitious than simply the miniaturistic effect so favored by the Baker-era quartet. The trumpet's first notes are almost at once echoed by Mulligan's baritone sax, welcoming it as it were into the group, the occasion for which is made more solemn by Bill Crow's unaccustomed bowing. With a thematic statement from the trumpet the song itself begins in conventional rhythm, but in a rhythm that will never remain constant, at times retarding and then, for the first section of solos, perking up. This changeable rhythm is another signature of this particular quartet, being present on nearly every one of the album's cuts, most noticeably on the aptly chosen "Just in Time" but also on several other tunes where it figures in the number's compositional structure.

Rhythmic variation and showcasing of sound underscores how Mulligan was enriching the basics for this group. Although it had the same instrumentation and some of the same repertoire as the original 1952 combo, this quartet wished to add more to the shock value of having no piano by doing more of virtually everything else possible. Among the album's eight numbers there is no repetition, and within each song Mulligan creates obvious differences between beginning, middle, and concluding parts—it is the only quartet album where he credits himself for arrangements (a back-cover photo from the studio shows the men playing off music stands). Two numbers from Chet Baker days, including the trumpeter's signature piece, show how broader this quartet's treatment could be. Purists might consider it a scandal that Art Farmer's debut with Mulligan should include a rendition of "My Funny Valentine" in the same form as Baker's 1952 performance, but external shape is all that remains the same; there's extra harmonic and especially rhythmic interplay between sax and trumpet here, and Farmer plays much more warmly and interpretively, actually using more breathiness than Baker (whose self-consciously showcased, spotlighted tone for this song had been more solid, even venturing toward vibrato). "Festive Minor" is the most obvious contrast. When recording the tune with Chet Baker, Mulligan took the entire first half by himself, with the song itself cast in a familiar loping rhythm. When Baker comes in, it is with an open horn, and none of the tune's intriguing interplay occurs until the final chorus, during most of which Mulligan leans back in favor of random doodling. With Art Farmer, "Festive Minor" assumes its classic style among Mulligan's more unusual works, the trumpet muted and the baritone sax interweaving with oblique harmonies. Most important, the time signature changes almost every eight bars, from the Turkish effect of the theme to straight time for some of the solos, with several variations in between. As a result, both horns get a chance to show off something other than routine blowing, while the composition itself sticks in the mind as an especially well-crafted achievement in musical pleasure.

Such rich pleasure is the new quartet's hallmark, and that richness includes some much more aggressive playing than in Chet Baker's days with Mulligan. Nothing from the 1952–1953 category matches Bill Crow's "News from Blueport" or Art Farmer's "Blueport" (both of which are credited to Mulligan on the album to win ASCAP royalties); the former tune is centered on a bass figure, recurring several times in the song as part of its rhythmic variation, but both tunes rely on exceptionally loud blowing and strong harmonies (usually thirds) between the two horns, all of which is supported by more forceful drumming than any edition of the quartet would customarily feature. Such constant variation adds to each tune's dimensions, especially the imposition of $\frac{4}{4}$ time over the standard $\frac{6}{8}$ signature in "News from Blueport." If André Hodeir had been impressed by Mulligan's brief time-signature changes in his *Birth of the Cool* work, the regular use of irregular time on this album should qualify as an innovation. Combined with the drummer's lead voice on Crow's and Farmer's numbers, this practice enlarges the quartet's presence as much as any of the devices used in the group's original format six years before.

● **Ben Webster–Gerry Mulligan:** "Chelsea Bridge," "Who's Got Rhythm," "Go Home," "The Cat Walk," "Sunday," and "Tell Me When," from *Gerry Mulligan Meets Ben Webster*, Verve MGV-8343, 3 November and 2 December 1959. Ben Webster (tenor) and Gerry Mulligan (baritone): saxophones; Jimmy Rowles: piano; Leroy Vinnegar: bass; Mel Lewis: drums.

Having worked so well on television with musicians of a generation or two older, Gerry Mulligan surprises no one by turning out fine meetings with Ben Webster and Johnny Hodges. This television work—together with more movie work—rounds out his 1950s and sets the stage for his Concert Jazz Band. Both older horn men were master stylists, their very tones on tenor and alto sax being unmistakable from almost the first note played. The same could now be said for Mulligan's presence on baritone saxophone, and so the encounters are among the richest in the full series.

The Webster session is notable not so much for its four upbeat, innocuous little tunes on which Mulligan proves his usual witty self, but for the two slow numbers, "Tell Me When" and "Chelsea Bridge." The latter, of course, is remembered as Webster's classic solo piece with the Ellington orchestra, but for this occasion Mulligan himself takes on the role of a supporting ensemble by creating an oddly appealing wavelike effect behind the tenor's melody and by soloing in a manner that reveals how much of his own style, always attributed to the bari's deep richness, is actually influenced by Ben Webster's approach to tenor saxophone. "Tell Me When" continues this Ellington mood, with Gerry offering such sympathetic and fully integrated support that the song is over before one notices that he's never taken a solo, having showcased Webster's tenor throughout. Like "Chelsea Bridge," "Tell Me When" recalls the style of Ellington's 1940–1941 band, and one has to look at the credits to see whether it was composed by the Duke himself or by Billy Strayhorn, whose arrangements were contributing so much to this era of music; the utter surprise is that the song was written by Mulligan himself.

The Webster meeting has its Basie moments as well, including another Mulligan original, "The Cat Walk," written in Basie's manner. The Count's influence looks back to Mulligan's writing for and playing with his sextet, while his more characteristic work with Webster (and again with Johnny Hodges) speaks for the strong Ellington influence brought to bear on the Concert Jazz Band. But Webster's bluesy growling and broadly rhythmic playing suggests a dimension of Gerry Mulligan's playing evident much further in the future: blues-oriented sets with Jay McShann and T-Bone Walker during the 1970s. Listeners need not wait two decades, however, because with the close of their second session Webster would bring his colleague to just such an occasion that same night.

● *Jimmy Witherspoon–Ben Webster–Gerry Mulligan:* "Time's Gettin' Tougher Than Tough," "How Long," "Corina-Corina," "C. C. Rider," "Roll 'Em Pete," "Every Day," "Outskirts of Town," "Goin' to Kansas City," "Trouble in Mind," and "St. Louis Blues," from *At the Renaissance,* HiFi Jazz J-426, 2 December 1959. Same personnel as above, plus Jimmy Witherspoon (vocals).

A chance encounter with blues singer Jimmy Witherspoon on the evening of 2 December 1959, following the second session with Ben Webster, brought Mulligan into contact with a style of blues singing untouched among his earlier dealings with Basie-style material. Invited by Webster to accompany him to the live session being taped at Los Angeles's Renaissance Club by Witherspoon's label, Mulligan found himself improvising head arrangements and taking solos not only in support of the vocalist but in the company of Webster's tenor, Jimmy Rowles's piano (both of which take lead roles), plus Leroy Vinnegar's bass work and Mel Lewis's drumming. Gerry's playing, under such carefully arranged wraps for the Verve session earlier that day, loosens up for the club sets with Witherspoon and the band, but the most interesting feature of Mulligan's work is that he does not overdo his enthusiasm. On "C. C. Rider" he solos in the blues idiom but without sacrificing the complexity of jazz; for "How Long" he derives his featured part from the supporting work done with Webster behind Witherspoon's opening choruses; while for "Outskirts of Town" he distinguishes himself in a supporting role alone, playing a soft but solid bottom underneath Webster's already low tenor. There's some fooling around this night, such as taking double-time solos on a couple tunes, but he and Webster also concoct some remarkably effective polyphony behind Witherspoon on the classic "St. Louis Blues."

- *Johnny Hodges–Gerry Mulligan:* "Bunny," "What's the Rush," "Back Beat," "What's It All About," "Eighteen Carrots for Rabbit," and "Shady Side," from *Gerry Mulligan Meets Johnny Hodges*, Verve MGV-8367, 17 November 1959. Johnny Hodges (alto), Gerry Mulligan (baritone): saxophones; Claude Williamson: piano; Buddy Clark: bass; Mel Lewis: drums.

Between his sessions with Ben Webster, Mulligan paused for his meeting with Johnny Hodges. As with the Ben Webster album, *Gerry Mulligan Meets Johnny Hodges* shows both how much Mulligan admired the Ellington tradition and how much of his own playing was influenced by that orchestra's sax section—oddly enough, far more by Ben Webster and Johnny Hodges than by baritonist Harry Carney, whose deep vibrato was at once more traditional and removed from the future Mulligan envisioned for the big horn. The Hodges set is special, however, because of Gerry's approach to it, not so much showing off his own playing or even paying homage to Rabbit as providing a format for the altoist's special talents. The album's six numbers are equally divided between Mulligan's and Hodges's compositions, though in Mulligan's case the writing favors his colleague more than himself. Tunes like "Bunny" and "Eighteen Carrots for Rabbit" could be considered the usual Mulligan session fare, except that the soft treatment (abetted by a gentler style of support from Claude Williamson and Buddy Clark, who handle piano and bass more softly than could be expected from Rowles and Vinnegar on the Webster dates) puts the ball in Hodges's court, where his instrument's timbre and range are much more comfortable than Mulligan's. All six numbers are suited to alto sax in general and to Johnny Hodges in particular, and Mulligan does his best playing when, as on Hodges's characteristically easy swing for "Back Beat," he adjusts his baritone playing to the laid-back blues style Hodges establishes in his own solo. Some critics might call this a chameleon effect, as Mulligan adopts Hodges's phrasing and habit of shuffling around the beat; but on its own terms Mulligan's solo hangs together and does justice to his own style, even though its angularity and witty exuberance are held in check by his fear of overplaying after Hodges.

The session's most special moments come with the ballad Gerry brought along, a composition titled "What's the Rush" he'd written with his new companion, actress Judy Holliday. The song is a special

one he'd record with Judy a year and a half later; the poignancy of its
title is underscored by the fact that there was a rush in their relationship, for Ms. Holliday was dying of cancer. It is significant that
this song's debut and only other performance is with Hodges. His
unique tone and style give the number a feminine touch, with his
richness more than compensating for the extremely retarded tempo.
With its words still a year away from public performance, "What's the
Rush" nevertheless speaks of time and loss in a tenderly loving way,
thanks to Johnny Hodges's sympathetic interpretation. Most significant of all, Mulligan stays out of the performance, giving the number
entirely to his colleague from the history of jazz.

●   *André Previn–Gerry Mulligan:* Soundtrack from *The Subterra-
    neans*, MGM Records E-3812ST, late 1959. "Why Are We
    Afraid," "A Rose and the End," "Analyst," and "Two by Two":
    André Previn conducting a large orchestra with featured parts
    by Gerry Mulligan (baritone saxophone), Art Pepper (alto sax-
    ophone), Jack Sheldon (trumpet), Bob Enevoldsen (valve trom-
    bone), André Previn (piano), Red Mitchell (bass), and Shelly
    Manne (drums). "Bread and Wine," "Things Are Looking
    Down": Art Farmer: trumpet; Bob Enevoldsen: valve trombone;
    Art Pepper (alto), Bill Perkins (tenor), Gerry Mulligan (bari-
    tone): saxophones; Russ Freeman: piano; Buddy Clark: bass;
    Dave Bailey: drums.

In 1960, just as the Concert Jazz Band was getting under way,
Gerry Mulligan found himself winding up his remarkably diversified
decade's work by appearing in movies. Two were minor acting roles:
with Judy Holliday in *The Bells Are Ringing* (as her blind date) and
as Tony Curtis's bandleader on a cruise-ship interlude featured in *The
Rat Race* (where he appears playing an out chorus on tenor to Curtis's
baritone and then advising the young man to mix with the customers
instead of writing love letters to Debbie Reynolds back in New York).
But in the film version of Jack Kerouac's *The Subterraneans* Mulligan
is featured both playing André Previn's music and acting in the role
of a beatnik priest (who uses jazz music in the service of evangelism).
Previn's score is immensely more Hollywoodish than Johnny Mandel's for *I Want to Live!*, with lushly orchestrated strings intruding far
too often for a truly jazz theme (whether on record or on the screen).
Yet the personnel is impeccable, including recent Mulligan alumni
Art Farmer, Red Mitchell, and Dave Bailey, plus horn men Art
Pepper, Bill Perkins, Bob Enevoldsen, and Jack Sheldon, comple-

mented by an equally California rhythm section of Previn, Buddy Clark, and Shelly Manne. Mulligan plays on six of the album's twelve cuts and is billed second only to Previn—plus an artistically effective sketch of him playing baritone (etched on a cinder-block wall) graces the jacket cover. The entire production, issued on MGM Records, is much more the generic movie score than the *I Want to Live!* soundtrack. For that earlier film, Johnny Mandel had used the same combo throughout; and even though their playing ranged through a wide variety of material, its consistency of format and the persistence of the major soloists' musical personalities kept things as unified as any album issued by a California-based septet—a group quite similar to the ones Mulligan had been playing with since his Kai Winding days in 1949. In *The Subterraneans* Previn fields no less than four distinct groups, from his piano trio and Mulligan's combo to an orchestra backing Carmen McRae and a richly scored string section. It's the last ensemble that makes the score sound so Hollywoodish, with too many of its effects coming down to the classic *film noir* cliché of violins swelling up and then receding as a bluesy alto sax wails. Art Pepper does plenty of that on the movie's "love theme" and other numbers, and it probably counts as an innovation that Mulligan's baritone is sometimes placed in the same role. But his combo is given the chance to approach Mandel's standard only twice: on the simple blues arrangement for "Things Are Looking Down" and again with the up-tempo number associated with Gerry's acting role, "Bread and Wine." It's on this latter number that Previn throws in too many self-consciously minor changes as a way of signaling the "way out beatnik style," but thankfully Mulligan is able to draw on his strongly vocal style of playing as a way of working around this awkwardness.

Playing an underground bohemian priest in *The Subterraneans* may have seemed an odd business for Gerry Mulligan to be undertaking as 1960 began, particularly in terms of the staggering achievement he'd made as a jazz musician and leader over the previous ten years. Yet the very self-consciousness of Jack Kerouac's demimonde was a good reminder of how far the saxophonist had come. The late forties had seen him shoot from his teens in Philadelphia to the top of the modern jazz world, an intimate of Charlie Parker and a trusted associate of Miles Davis, plus emerging as a soloist while maintaining his bread-and-butter occupation as the era's most sought-after big-band jazz arranger. The early months of 1950, however, had shown him beginning the decade with a discouraging zero level of production. Jazz commentators have ascribed that fallow year to his troubles with narcotics, a problem that would ensnare him again three years later and threaten, to nip his emerging fame in the bud. As it happened, the California bust put an end to his revolutionary quartet before it could peak—meaning before it could reach a plateau and threaten to bore its leader, a weakness that plagued him far more than his brush with drug use.

Mulligan's three months on the detention farm drove him out of California as well, which, hindsight shows, helped set his course through the immensely productive 1950s. The greater balance of that decade was spent in New York, where East Coast musicians such as Bob Brookmeyer, Zoot Sims, Jon Eardley, Art Farmer, Bill Crow, and Dave Bailey would prove more suitable to his evolving style than the overly cool California style being developed by Art Pepper, Bud Shank, and their crowd of players with whom Mulligan would occasionally record but would never sound as natural. It's inconceivable that the Concert Jazz Band could have developed in Los Angeles, where studio work kept the best musicians on a steady payroll but also too busy for the hundreds of hours of rehearsal time an organization like the CJB would demand. Also, the most serious elements of the jazz-music press were in New York City, where critical acclaim (plus the appreciation of informed, hip audiences such as those found at the Village Vanguard) would pave the way for the band's subsequent performances and recordings.

Gerry Mulligan's first successes had been in New York, and the city surely remained his image of "making it big." Los Angeles had money and talent, to be sure, but its ambience could too easily lead to nightclub audiences demanding one more cover of "My Funny Valentine" rather than being receptive to something new, while the immense musical talents and unlimited amounts of cash provided by Hollywood could labor at great length only to produce something like *The Subterraneans*. And so 28 May 1960 found the man in New York, counting the cadence and signaling the producer to roll the tapes for his first cuts with the Concert Jazz Band.

CHAPTER FIVE

THE CONCERT JAZZ BAND

Its first number begins with the band's most minimal and yet most basic element, a walking bass line, with some brush-on-cymbals work coming a beat or two after the drums. The tune itself is an old standard, the Warren-Dubin oldie, "Sweet and Slow." And what the bass line figures, the melody delivers: an easy, loping-with-the-rhythm, harmonized duet between baritone sax and trumpet, floating with the song's theme as easily as a pleasure boat down a lazy stream. Though a light-playing sax section comes in for the bridge, the first impressions listeners get of Gerry Mulligan's new big band are reincarnations of his earlier combos, from the Chet Baker and Art Farmer versions of trumpet and bari pairings to the valve trombone and sax edition with Bob Brookmeyer, interspersed with the sextet's lead sound of baritone, tenor, trumpet, and valve trombone up front. When the orchestra itself enters, it is in unique form—a clarinet harmonizing atop the saxes to repeat and somewhat exaggerate a comic phrase the lead horns had played, or the trumpets with their wa-wa mutes deliberately overstating the bridge. When not foregrounding the arrangement's deft humor, the orchestral ensembles remain in the background, the saxes especially light and airy, the brass subdued and supporting. Solos are restricted to the spotlighted players, Mulligan on baritone sax and Brookmeyer on valve trombone, each interacting with the background in a way that exploits their most characteristic styles, from Mulligan's strongly melodic way of vocalizing a solo to Brookmeyer's brash and vulgar sound effects. When the trumpet section gets center stage, it's to play a section-scored solo phrased with admirable restraint, creating a contrast between the paucity of line and the immensity of potential force delivering it.

There's a proper musical term for this approach to scoring, *concerto grosso*, indicating a style in which a small group is framed by the larger orchestra, with the listener's attention being passed back and forth. It serves as a perfect choice for the first cut on the Concert Jazz Band's first LP and sets a standard the band would maintain for its subsequent recordings and concert performances. Mulligan's course had been set on the CJB ever since he left the Kenton band, in disgust at its monolithic approach to jazz writing, in 1952. In the meantime he'd explored the full range of jazz combos, from his pianoless quartet and tentette of California days, through the powerfully swinging sextet of 1955–1956, to his extended series of meetings with a diverse range of instrumental stylists. At each point his own playing and writing took on new broadness and depth—indeed, from 1952 through 1959 he was experiencing the full history of jazz, from club dates with Jimmy Witherspoon to soloing with Billie Holiday and Lester Young, jamming with Johnny Hodges, and handling bari in a sax section of 1930s' all-stars. This enrichment came on the heels of an equally remarkable late forties period that had found Mulligan at the center of both Gene Krupa's big-band swing and Miles Davis's late bebop ensemble and writing for and playing in Kai Winding's smaller group. In 1960 no single figure could claim such wide experience and expertise. And so when the Concert Jazz Band debuted as the *ne plus ultra* of Mulligan's career, it was to an especially high sense of anticipation.

A great deal was expected from the CJB, and in retrospect it's remarkable how much the band was able to deliver. Its recorded output totals five major albums plus a collection of outtakes—not a great deal of material, but not at all thin considering that initially the organization could be held together only for a year and a month, almost exactly the tenure of Mulligan's original quartet (whose easier logistics had yielded in excess of sixty numbers). In its first stretch the CJB cut twenty-five tunes and did covers of "Come Rain or Come Shine" and "Go Home" with different soloists being featured. Although the French collection of unissued tapings, *Gerry Mulligan: New York December 1960* (Musidisc Europe Jazz Anthology JA-5236/ MU-213), contains the additional "Everything Happens to Me," it is not the CJB but a 1955 air take from the Steve Allen TV show, featuring Gerry but with little prominence for the band, suggesting that for its first nineteen months the large group's catalog scarcely exceeded two dozen tunes.

And yet these twenty-five numbers form an impressive canon by themselves and also add much to the range of big-band jazz as well as to Mulligan's own repertoire. After so much jumping around from project to odd project in the fifties, Mulligan poured almost solid concentration into the band, interrupting its recording and performing schedule only for his work with Judy Holliday. The five major albums were themselves packaged in a most distinguished manner, the first in the style of a formally engraved invitation and backed with an elegant Fabian Bachrach photo portrait (other poses would be used on subsequent albums, climaxing with a full-color shot for the cover of the CJB's fifth). In 1962 the organization began to waver economically under the financial pressures needed to keep it going, and Mulligan re-formed the quartet with Brookmeyer and took on other gigs as well. But in sessions on 19 and 21 December 1962, the Concert Jazz Band made its farewell album, in which it would fulfill its promise as a vehicle for the most ambitious and exploratory big-band writing within the jazz idiom. These last eight numbers (four of them actually constituting two-part movements of larger pieces) do more than raise the CJB's score to thirty-three tunes; they expand the possibilities for jazz writing as exceeded only by the classic Ellington bands and provide an exceptional vehicle for Mulligan's playing. Although the CJB was planned as a laboratory and performance vehicle for his own composing and arranging, its progress took a somewhat different course. While Gerry himself found that supporting and directing the band took so much time that he was unable to do as much of the writing as he'd hoped, the commissioning of charts from the best young arrangers served not only to expand the orchestra's dimensions but place Mulligan in distinctively new solo opportunities. Together with the Bachrach portrait, two of the CJB's albums featured its logo, an expressively drawn baritone sax. That horn's special sound, as developed by Gerry over the previous fifteen years and now showcased in an especially fine jazz context, established his stylistic trademark in indelible fashion.

The Concert Jazz Band's five albums, supplemented by the set of outtakes from its Birdland broadcasts issued on Musidisc Europe, show the band growing at a steady pace, taking progressive advantage of its rich orchestral format while never becoming so complex that the structure collapses under its own weight—although at the very end, after being out of the studios for almost a year and a half, its ambitious undertaking of multisectioned scores flirts with that risk. Many of the same musicians were carried over from the abortive 1957 band, although there were four crucial differences: the CJB was smaller, with one less trumpet and sax; the trombone section remained at three, but its tonal range was extended by having one each of slide trombone, valve trombone, and bass trombone; there were now four saxes in the section instead of five, Dick Meldonian doubling on tenor and alto rather than having the section stacked conventionally with two of each plus baritone (Mulligan's own horn was an additional instrument for solos and concerto grosso effects); and also saxophonist Gene Quill was often found on clarinet. The orchestral sound and flexibility were important considerations, and for the initial album's notes (*Gerry Mulligan: The Concert Jazz Band,* Verve MGV-8388) the leader enumerated his criteria for achieving the same clear sound and interweaving lines that had characterized the quartet, sextet, and tentette: a clarinet among the reeds (not to lead, as in Glenn Miller fashion, but to add to the section's sound) plus most of the solo work going to a few key players (whose musical personalities would become familiar to listeners). Mulligan's audience was already well acquainted with these favorites, and so recognition would not be a problem. In addition to presenting Gerry's own baritone sax and Zoot Sim's tenor, Bob Brookmeyer's valve trombone became one of the CJB's most distinguishing features. Indeed, it is a combination of a concerto grosso effect between the quartet and the larger ensemble with Brookmeyer's loose and lively approach to his horn that sets the band's initial style. It is surely Bob's version of the quartet, reminiscent of its happy and sometimes boisterous Storyville album from 1956, and not the preciousness of the Chet Baker-California group that Gerry has in mind for this first Concert Jazz Band album.

• *Gerry Mulligan and the Concert Jazz Band:* "I'm Gonna Go Fishin'," "Sweet and Slow," "Bweebida Bobbida," "Manoir des mes Rêves (D'Jango's Castle)," "You Took Advantage of Me," "Out of This World," "My Funny Valentine," and "Broadway," from *The Concert Jazz Band,* Verve MGV-8388, 28 and 29 May, 1960 (first number) and 25, 26, and 27 July 1960. First number: Danny Stiles, Don Ferrara, Phil Sunkel: trumpets; Bob Brookmeyer (valve), Wayne Andre (slide), and Alan Raph (bass): trombones; Gene Quill (alto and clarinet), Dick Meldonian (alto), Jim Reider (tenor), Gene Allen, Gerry Mulligan (baritone): saxophones; Bill Takas: bass; Dave Bailey: drums. Other numbers: Nick Travis, Don Ferrara, Conte Candoli: trumpets; Bob Brookmeyer (valve), Wayne Andre (slide), Alan Raph (bass): trombones; Gene Quill (alto and clarinet), Dick Meldonian (alto), Zoot Sims (tenor), Gene Allen, Gerry Mulligan (baritone): saxophones; Buddy Clark: bass; Mel Lewis: drums.

Gerry Mulligan's first album with the Concert Jazz Band dates from an initial New York session producing "I'm Gonna Go Fishin' " (also released as a single for the jukebox trade), followed by seven more numbers cut two months later in Los Angeles, during the same late July 1960 trip that yielded the Johnny Hodges album. Although "I'm Gonna Go Fishin' " is the only one of these first numbers that is heavily devoted to big-band writing, Mulligan and producer Norman Granz save it for the album's final slot, preferring to build up through a wide range of more subtle effects. The first of them is the concerto grosso notion introduced with "Sweet and Slow," in which additional instruments and then orchestral sections join in one by one, supplementing the sweet harmony of baritone sax and trumpet, which chime in with the initial walking bass line. Then comes one of Mulligan's compositions from Elliot Lawrence days, "Bweebida Bobbida," but scored more like its classic form from the quartet with Brookmeyer than in its swing-band version—a matter of somewhat slower tempo and inverted rhythms as well as orchestral scope. Putting baritone and trombone out front starts the tune with a level of flexibility the section writing is challenged to maintain, and does. The background fills on this number are exceptionally deft, their tightness allowing a fair amount of complexity while never taking the focus away from the two star horns plus rhythm. Concluding side A is another style of tune Mulligan would make a regular feature, "Manoir des mes Rêves (D'Jango's Castle)," which sustains a Mulligan solo throughout, backed by the band's soft whole notes (in the manner of Claude Thornhill's orchestra) while the bari gradually emerges in rhythmic breaks and then reintegrates itself as a lead voice slightly above the sections, plus the enjoyable romp of "You Took Advantage of Me," another loose and loping number in which the band is given more opportunities to step in with its support. As an introduction to the Concert Jazz Band, this first side is impeccable, showing how a reincarnation of the Storyville quartet could infect the spirit of an entire orchestra (as the sections capably adopt the two original horn's roles for the final ensemble of "Bweebida Bobbida"), while the resources of the band itself could draw forth the best from Mulligan and Brookmeyer out front.

On the B side of *Gerry Mulligan: The Concert Jazz Band* Mulligan shows his new aggregation's range, dynamics, and variety of orchestral effects. Whereas bari and valve trombone had carried side A, now the CJB itself sets forward as an integral unit, making its claim on a musical heritage reaching back to Ellington. "Out of This World" is presented in a mood befitting its title, as the baritone sax alone sets the tune's bolero tempo, to be joined by Brookmeyer's trombone before some rich orchestral support eventually drives the rhythm into a straight driving four. The arrangement is best characterized as a matter of voice, reaching from the exotic interplay of baritone and bolero-styled bass to the full band's dynamics, which take delight in intoning the "out of this world" mood and then shifting gears into more solid swing for both the soloists and a concluding trumpet-section line played over the high-reaching trombones.

"My Funny Valentine" resurrects the quartet's original Chet Baker arrangement and proves that its melodic effects are transcribable for a baritone sax lead and orchestral support, another classical music effect akin to rescoring a violin piece for flute, or vice versa, a process that often reveals new facets of a supposedly familiar number. As in "Manoir des mes Rêves," Mulligan's horn plays throughout, the background alternately swelling and receding and toward the end sustaining pretty notes that Mulligan encircles at the top of his register, using those side-key high notes that sound especially emotional on the big horn. Contrasting with this delicate work is "Broadway," a favorite from septet days with Kai Winding and Mulligan's own sextet. Here the concerto grosso opportunities are passed over in favor of a tribute to Mulligan's late-forties style of big-band jazz, producing a smartly swinging number that lets listeners experience what it would have been like for Gerry to have been one of the Four Brothers and for Bob Brookmeyer to have soloed in front of the Woody Herman Herd, plus a reminder of Zoot Sims's own playing with that band. The supporting section work riffs along with the beat, inviting the horns to reach above and dive below its steady line. It was from this tradition that the Lester Young style of lyrical improvisation adapted by the sextet was born, and the arrangement's debts to both the Basie and Herman bands are obvious, yet there's still enough of the Krupa and Lawrence spirits to stamp it as Mulligan's work.

The Concert Jazz Band's inaugural album ends with a major production, Bill Holman's arrangement of "I'm Gonna Go Fishin'," a rock-and-rollish romp in $\frac{6}{8}$ time. It not only contains the most writing for the band so far but cranks it up several notches above anything else on the LP. Its sixties focus is all the more evident coming on the heels of the late-forties style "Broadway," with the drumming making the biggest shift—from Woody Herman smoothness to a more rhythmically aggressive attack in the manner of other early anticipations of fusion with rock music such as Cannonball Adderley's "This Here" and "Sack of Woe." Like the Adderley numbers, "I'm Gonna Go Fishin' " makes a small compromise by shifting from the rock beat and waltz time for an occasional imposition of $\frac{4}{4}$ to introduce the solos. But Mulligan's chart makes these shifts extremely brief, inviting the players to enjoy the rocking beat that $\frac{6}{8}$ provides. Bob Brookmeyer especially has fun with this rhythm, drawing on his horn's full guttiness for a solo that never seems ofay in the least. Following the solos comes some section work by the trumpets, playing a line as driving and improvisatory as anything the individual horns did. The gesture toward fusion, the variety of distribution in the parts, the strong rhythmic emphasis, and most of all the good time everyone obviously has with the number makes "I'm Gonna Go Fishin' " look forward from the CJB (whose repertoire would have nothing else similar to it) to Mulligan's band of the seventies and eighties, where fusion stars such as Tom Scott and Howard Roberts would establish an even stronger bond with rock.

●   *Gerry Mulligan and the Concert Jazz Band:* "Go Home," "Barbara's Theme," "Apple Core," "Theme from *I Want to Live!*," "The Red Door," "Come Rain or Come Shine," and "Go Home (second version)," from *Gerry Mulligan and the Concert Jazz Band On Tour*, Verve V/V6-8438, November and December 1960. Same personnel as 25–27 July above, except trombonist Willie Dennis replaces Andre, alto saxophonist Bob Donovan replaces Meldonian, tenor saxophonist Jim Reider is added to take Sims's section parts, baritone saxophonist Gene Allen doubles on bass clarinet, and baritone saxophonist Gerry Mulligan doubles on piano.

If the first album made its mark by placing the Brookmeyer edition of Mulligan's quartet in a concerto grosso format, encouraging strong interaction between spotlighted horns (especially Brookmeyer's lusty valve trombone) and a supporting ensemble, the CJB's next effort kept the band waiting a bit while Gerry and his old friend Zoot Sims stepped forward for some limelight playing in the company of unobtrusive orchestral support. The occasion was a tour, and although the album itself wasn't released until 1962, with the Village Vanguard session already on the market, *Gerry Mulligan and the Concert Jazz Band on Tour: Guest Soloist, Zoot Sims*, featuring performances from

November 1960—in Santa Monica, Berlin, and Milan—reveals how solidly knit the organization was becoming. The support for Mulligan and Sims is impeccable, and the band's range is extended with Gene Quill playing clarinet more often than not, plus Gene Allen doubling on bass clarinet (another instrument of the times, which was just now being added to the small-group repertoire of Eric Dolphy). The exotic sound of Allen's instrument is used to good effect on the two pieces from Johnny Mandel's film score, "Barbara's Theme" and "Theme from *I Want to Live!*" These are the movie's slow numbers, and Mulligan takes no small risk playing them in back-to-back slots on the album's first side, after the almost equally slow "Go Home." But whereas "Go Home" recalled the easy but free blowing of the Ben Webster meeting—it's Webster's composition, here arranged by Bill Holman as a tribute to one of Webster's logical successors on the tenor sax, Zoot Sims—these numbers from the film score demand subtle tonal shadings, which Mandel had accomplished with all the studio devices of echo and dynamics. That the CJB is able to pull off these numbers on stage, and on European stages at that—in Milan and Berlin, where fans prove more exuberant than anywhere at home except the Newport Jazz Festival on cheap beer night—is no small tribute to the band's organizational strength.

The second side of this tour album starts with an up-tempo jump number, but the band itself hangs out while Gerry and Zoot plus a rhythm section led by Bob Brookmeyer on piano re-create the quintet that played "The Red Door" six years earlier at San Diego for the *California Concerts* LP. Here in Santa Monica the effect is pure nostalgia, as is the later track of "Apple Core" (Mulligan's original from Elliot Lawrence days), which Bill Holman arranges in a Stan Kenton manner that reduces the CJB to giving emphatically conventional fills and phrasings. Yet the B side's structure actually serves to frame the band's most original number, "Come Rain or Come Shine," in a rendition that anticipates the Village Vanguard taping a month later where Mulligan would take the lead himself. Here the focus is on Zoot Sims, who plays all the way through with delicate orchestral support that distinguishes the band as much as himself. Ending side B is another version of "Go Home," which Mulligan advises has been added to show how much a song can change from night to night, but which in fact exhibits how spontaneous the CJB could be, for not only are the solos put in a different mood, but the band itself comes up with different fills and riffs and a fully alternative structure for the song itself. Although a Ben Webster composition, Mulligan seems to be using it here as one of his standard piano blues numbers, with the horns improvising behind his keyboard lead. Such a format was easy enough for the quartet and sextet, but for a twelve-piece band (plus two featured soloists, Mulligan and Sims) to keep it together under such circumstances is remarkable, no less that it was accomplished on stage.

- **Gerry Mulligan and the Concert Jazz Band:** "Blueport," "Body and Soul," "Black Nightgown," "Come Rain or Come Shine," "Lady Chatterly's Mother," and "Let My People Be," from *Live at the Village Vanguard*, Verve V-8396, 10 December 1960. Same personnel as November and December above, except trumpeter Clark Terry replaces Conte Candoli, bassist Bill Crow replaces Buddy Clark, and tenor saxophone soloist Zoot Sims is omitted.

A month later the Concert Jazz Band was performing at the Village Vanguard in New York, the first time such a large group had been booked into the room that conventionally hosted four- or five-piece combos. The booking and its recording were political moves, part of Mulligan's two-edged campaign that a large jazz band need not be considered a dance band and that the complexities and opportunities for the type of jazz to which one usually listened (as opposed to danced) should not be restricted to a small number of players in a head-arrangement format. Although the CJB had been recording for only six months, the December 1960 sessions make a quantum leap in artistry. There are links to the first two albums, of course: "Blueport" serves as another concerto grosso number, this time recalling Art Farmer's role in the quartet; there's an extended solo piece, "Body and Soul"; Mulligan's fancy for the Johnny Mandel score of *I Want to Live!* is evident in the CJB doing a third selection, "Black Nightgown"; and there's one piano blues tune, "Let My People Be" (this time with a set of traditional calls from the sections). But the two showcase prizes are "Come Rain and Come Shine," on which Mulligan does even more interacting with the orchestra than Zoot Sims attempted on tour, and "Lady Chatterly's Mother," the first of a set of originals for the band commissioned from the era's brightest arrangers. Here it is Al Cohn, but on subsequent albums the gates would be open to talents as diverse as Johnny Carisi, George Russell, and Gary McFarland.

Of all the material on *Gerry Mulligan and the Concert Jazz Band: Live at the Village Vanguard*, it is Al Cohn's original that indicates best where the band was going. His adaptation of "Blueport" had

employed busily complex yet unobtrusive figures among the supporting sections as Mulligan and Clark Terry re-created the two-horn
interplay of Art Farmer's composition; of all the CJB's concerto grosso
treatments, it is the one that most consistently maintains the quartet's
feeling—which is quite ironic, as Cohn has the band playing almost
throughout, and some very involved playing at that. His key is the
band's tightness; the writing is so close and the players remain so
integral that a great deal of notes, rhythmic variation, and textures of
sounds can be offered in support of the trumpet and bari without
getting in their way or without even distracting the listener. It is this
style of arrangement, on which one has to stop and recall how active
the band has been, that characterizes Cohn's written-from-the-top
original, "Lady Chatterly's Mother." The original sax-section line is at
once punctuated by brass section fanfares (which do not obstruct the
forward swing); parts and character are exchanged for the intro to the
bridge, and then the sections return to the main theme for an even
smoother treatment. The chart's brilliance, however, is in its structuring of the solos and section work. The same backing figure—an
extremely complex one among the saxes—is used for all three solos,
creating an evenness among the complexity. But most crucial is
Cohn's ear for the soloist's horns, having the saxes come a bit more
forward with their high parts when backing Brookmeyer's trombone
work, then holding back a little when Clark Terry's solo approaches
their register. Mulligan can be counted on to have fun with all this
business in the background, and like the other featured horns he
plays in and out of the riffs and fills. The climax, however, comes with
the sax ensemble, which, after the trombone, trumpet, and baritone,
steps forward to play an intricate yet expressive line in the manner of
a deftly phrased saxophone solo, all of their background figures now
taking shape as a new lead voice. Like the section work on "Blueport," Cohn writes these parts with both rhythm and melody in mind,
giving drummer Mel Lewis plenty of chances to add little breaks to
the beat (which is solid enough to bear occasional interruption).
Despite—or rather because of—all this well-integrated complexity,
"Lady Chatterly's Mother" ranks as the hardest-swinging number the
CJB ever recorded.

On the Sunday afternoon's program from which Mulligan drew this
album, the band was surely cooking; its Basie-like rendition of a
simple head arrangement like "Let My People Be," ostensibly just
another run-through of Mulligan's standard head arrangement for
piano and band, comes close to Cohn's piece in rocking along. Two
other notes distinguish the band's accomplishment and nature. "Black

Nightgown" is the first faster-tempoed number that the CJB plays from Johnny Mandel's score; whereas the slower tunes had benefited from the band's depth, especially its use of haunting bass clarinet, this somewhat more swinging piece demands a light and bright treatment, right down to the honky-tonk tag line Mandel fancied as an announcement that the final chorus was at hand. The Concert Jazz Band's treatment is equally deft, getting the same sharp sound and light handling that Mandel's seven-piece combo displayed, even though almost twice that number of instruments—thirteen—are all playing here. The album's tonal achievement, however, is its performance of "Come Rain or Come Shine." On tour the month before, this number had been a showcase for Zoot Sims's tenor; now baritone sax takes the lead, proving at once how the CJB was orchestrated to complement the lower horns, for Mulligan's baritone—combined with his melodically vocal style of playing—blends much better with the band's supporting ensemble than did Zoot's tenor, as pretty as it was. As a rule, the best-sounding CJB solos come from baritone sax and valve trombone.

In his comments to Nat Hentoff for the album's liner notes, Mulligan admits that critics have faulted him for not giving the CJB more adventurous arrangements, but he replies that too many avant-gardists write for the page or for themselves instead of for a group of musicians who must above all enjoy playing together. The band and not its material should come first, he explains. Before taking another step, his musicians would have to develop a sense of mutual comfort. The Village Vanguard issue indicates that this sense is close at hand.

- *Gerry Mulligan and the Concert Jazz Band:* "All about Rosie," "Weep," "I Know, Don't Know How," "Chuggin'," "Summer's Over," and "Israel," from *Gerry Mulligan Presents a Concert in Jazz*, Verve V-8415, 10 and 11 July 1961. Same personnel as 10 December above, except trumpeter Doc Severinsen replaces Clark Terry and alto saxophonist Bob Donovan doubles on flute.

The big step toward more innovative arrangements comes with a new album recorded seven months later. Here the arrangements span three decades of jazz, from Johnny Carisi and George Russell through Bob Brookmeyer to a young Gary McFarland. The structure of the songs they work with also becomes more involved, running ten and one-half minutes in the case of "All about Rosie," which boasted a three-part organization as well. This number plus Gary McFarland's "Weep" (six minutes, but seeming longer, and with its own component sections built in) fill the album's first side, delivering on Mulligan's promise to present the CJB in a concert format. Even though the B side switches back to more conventional lengths (four numbers running between three and five minutes each), the total effect is of a concert, with an emphasis on effects arranged for listening—a style that would carry over to the band's next (and last) LP a year and a half later.

George Russell's "All about Rosie" is the Concert Jazz Band's most ambitious project to date and indicates why the band was winning popular and critical polls alike. While not avant-gardist, the composition and its performance have their cerebral moments, particularly in the first section where a childlike solo trumpet figure is progressively developed into orchestral complexity and depth. But throughout this first section the band maintains a sense of swinging and of complicating things, and after a few minutes the movement ends, replaced with a slow and sultry sax-based figure in which alto and baritone at different times play the main theme, while instead of complicating things the orchestra offers a wide-ranging collection of quiet effects (at one point putting bass trombone below flute for some surprisingly successful support). Here the result of increasing dynamics and cumulative addition yields not busyness but rather an enhanced feeling of swing, particularly that loping sense of coming down on the beat after sliding around in between that has proven to be one of Mulligan's favorite rhythmic configurations. The third section begins with the drummer's figure, which is taken up in turn by all three sections. In contrast to the second movement's use of exotic sounds, such as clarinet and bass clarinet together, the trumpets, saxes, and trombones here reassert their traditional section-based identity, allowing the first set of solos in Russell's piece. Despite the diverse nature of the three sections, the performance holds together, thanks as much to the CJB's command of its materials as to Russell's compositional integrity, based as it is on the three major variations of that initial trumpet theme.

Gary McFarland's "Weep," while much shorter, is almost as complex as Russell's number, for the young arranger exploits every resource of the CJB in order to cast Mulligan's baritone in an interesting context. There is the sonorous support reminiscent of "Come Rain or Come Shine" from the Village Vanguard album but also an innovative use of trumpets, which from the very start propose their own slightly sharper sound to the lead voice of Mulligan's baritone. Gerry's sax here is subtly deepened by unison playing with Gene Allen's baritone sax and, alternately, by close harmony with Bob Brookmeyer's valve trombone, each of them bearing a tradition from Mulligan's earlier groups (the New York tentette and the quartet with Brookmeyer respectively, not to mention the voicings favored in the sextet).

The tune's melody is immediately given a compositional cast, as its smooth flow nevertheless puts the baritone sax's main line in counterpoint with the bell-like tolling of the trumpets, a background figure repeated during Gerry's solo and developed through various permutations with the saxes and trombones. Meanwhile, Mulligan's horn pays back the band for its support by blowing softly in the spaces behind their section line a phrase later. When it comes time for a Harmon-muted trumpet solo, the background is given to clarinet and bass clarinet as a way of preparing for the number's soft ending—not a repeat of the main theme but rather a winding down with a repeated figure from the bridge. From the melody to the solos and their backing, and especially considering the number's general framework with its subtle emphasis on differing shades of sound from component parts, McFarland's "Weep" is decidedly compositional—a style the CJB, with its confident control of tone and dynamics, could handle especially well.

A Concert in Jazz's B side takes the band back to its style of the first three albums: shorter numbers, yet sufficiently long for work by the featured soloists (which was more and more coming down to Mulligan and Brookmeyer), all of which draw on the interplay between either a single horn and the full orchestra or a front line from one of Gerry's earlier groups passing the lead back and forth with the band. Brookmeyer's arrangement of a Mulligan composition recorded by the *California Concerts* sextet, "I Know, Don't Know How," captures the essence of the Mulligan-Brookmeyer spirit. The following year, with the CJB hung up in financial limbo, Gerry and Bob would record a rousing quartet version of this number. Here Mulligan's lead is answered by the orchestra's interplay rather than the valve trombone's, although Brookmeyer distinguishes himself with a strong solo and with some polyphony near the end (one of the Concert Jazz Band's unique talents was making room for such playing while never seeming sloppy or busy). For the side's second cut, Gary McFarland supplies another piece, "Chuggin,' " which is even more compositional in effect than his first number. Mulligan's piano begins things with a student-in-the-studio type figure (a natural for his rudimentary style of keyboard playing); this figure is picked up by Willie Dennis's trombone, followed by a regular accretion of orchestral elements until the full band is playing along. Everything remains as light as the piano introduction, however, to the point that Gene Allen can take a convincing solo on bass clarinet, an instrument demanding plenty of space in which to be heard. Thanks to this, the baritone sound remains present throughout the tune, and when Mulligan himself solos, McFarland backs him with some deep, echoing trumpets. When the sax section plays, it is in a voicing with clarinet in place of alto, allowing the baritone again to take a more apparent part in the saxophone choir.

"Summer's Over," a Mulligan-Judy Holliday composition (here without the words) and Johnny Carisi's "Israel" conclude the side, moving from the combo effect of the first two numbers to a soloist-with-orchestra treatment. Carisi's tune was featured on the *Birth of the Cool* session of 22 April 1949, and while it's a disappointment that his arrangement of his number for the CJB is virtually identical to his chart for the Miles Davis Nonet, it shows how the Mulligan band was closer in concept to the Davis ensemble than to a conventional big band. If anything, Carisi's adaptation leans toward the swing-band mode for its backing of Mulligan's soloists, making it the most conventional piece by far. "Summer's Over" tells a different story, that of soft orchestral elements coalescing to form a virtually seamless compositional whole. The arrangement is Brookmeyer's, but its Thornhill-Evans sound and the baritone sax's initial lead and subsequent interaction with the band, keeping the horn squarely before the listener throughout, stamp it as a classic Mulligan number, Brookmeyer simply adapting techniques Gerry had used for the past one-and-a-half decades.

After its *Concert in Jazz* LP in July 1961, the CJB did not record for nearly eighteen months, while its leader moved through a variety of other, smaller projects to support himself and reestablish a financial basis for the band. For most of the CJB's existence, Mulligan himself, not a producer or record company, had met its payroll. Albums could not be spun off as easily or quickly as in a smaller group; bookings were not as plentiful, the logistics of travel were staggering, and such a finely tuned unit had to be kept in an almost constant state of rehearsal, something doubly difficult because its personnel consisted of top players who could command a good income elsewhere. Yet between 18 and 21 December 1962, the Concert Jazz Band managed to record its most ambitious album, the forward-looking title ('63) belying the band's impending economic fate.

- *Gerry Mulligan and the Concert Jazz Band:* "Little Rock Getaway," "Ballad," "Big City Life," "Big City Blues," "My Kind of Love," "Pretty Little Gypsy," "Bridgehampton South," and

"Bridgehampton Strut," from *Gerry Mulligan '63: The Concert Jazz Band*, Verve V/V6-8515, 18–21 December 1962. Clark Terry (doubling on fluegelhorn), Nick Travis, Don Ferrara, and Doc Severinsen: trumpets; Bob Brookmeyer (valve), Willie Dennis (slide), Tony Studd (bass): trombones; Gene Quill (clarinet and alto), Eddie Caine (flute and alto), Jim Reider (tenor), Gene Allen (bass clarinet and baritone), Gerry Mulligan (clarinet and baritone): saxophones; Bob Brookmeyer, Gerry Mulligan: piano; Jim Hall: guitar; Bill Crow: bass; Gus Johnson: drums.

For this affair there were both continuities and changes. Its eight tunes were in the manner of Russell's "All about Rosie" and McFarland's "Weep"—long on orchestral treatment and given to reflective parts, four of the numbers being parallel compositions with sequential titles. There were new voices: Clark Terry's fluegelhorn, Jim Hall on guitar (as a solo rather than simply rhythmic instrument), and Mulligan on clarinet. Brookmeyer's piano playing also had a featured role, and to both deepen and brighten the brass attack a fourth trumpet was added to the section, making this final version of the CJB its biggest, with a roster of fifteen. This combination of new elements gives the last edition of the Concert Jazz Band more presence and punch at the same time that it creates opportunities for even broader dynamics (which the two-sided compositions by Brookmeyer and Gary McFarland would exploit). And even though this album marks the end of the Concert Jazz Band, two of the new instruments—guitar and fluegelhorn—would be the distinguishing factors in the new sextet Mulligan would organize in 1963.

Of all the CJB albums, this last contains the most concert material and the fewest conventional tunes. Of the latter there are only two—Mulligan's "Ballad" and an up-tempo "Little Rock Getaway"—and both benefit from more studied orchestrations. True, "Ballad" had sounded much the same with the California tentette nearly a decade before, but its treatment here is not so much retrospective as it confirms how Mulligan was developing toward the CJB's ensemble sound earlier, at least for a slow piece (the tentette's brisker numbers anticipated the livelier combo mood of the sextet). What distinguishes Mulligan's "Ballad" this time through is both the depth gained from the additional instrumentation and the sharpness added by Jim Hall's guitar joining the lead, complementing the bari's fuller sound. Though a much faster and immensely brighter piece, "Little Rock Getaway" draws on special characteristics of sound as well, from its bari-led sax ensemble to the pertness of exchanges with the brass. How well the number propels itself is apparent not just from Mulligan's strong solo (bari always having a harder time on the faster tunes) but from Jim Hall's guitar solo carrying itself in front of the full band.

Transitional in nature is "My Kind of Love," which on earlier albums might have relied on a concerto grosso effect but here calls for an easy, relaxed orchestral statement for its theme, setting the style for (rather than responding to) the baritone sax and valve trombone interplay that had become a CJB feature. On earlier numbers Mulligan and Brookmeyer had simply regenerated their exuberance from the Storyville quartet, to the extent that the listener could easily forget there was a band in support. No such invitation is offered here, for the CJB's presence reflects rather than just passively supports their easy counterpoint.

Central to the album, and indicative that the Concert Jazz Band had reached its height, are the special compositions Mulligan's favorite arrangers brought to its book. On Gary McFarland's "Pretty Little Gypsy" Mulligan takes out his clarinet for a recording debut (beginning a trend that would soon find him doing serious work on alto and soprano sax). As with his piano playing, simplicity is the rule, a style that fits McFarland's plan of proceeding with compositional increments and increasing dynamics, from the solo clarinet supported by light rhythm all the way to a faster tempo and full brass support. Bob Brookmeyer, by now grown from scoring Gerry's favorite Thornhill-Evans techniques to finding an orchestral voice of his own, uses a similar plan for his two-part number, "Big City Life" and "Big City Blues," which fills half of the album's first side. Here the introductory solo voice is his own, on piano; a quiet duet develops with the orchestra, enhanced by the tune's slow tempo; figures from trumpet and flute are introduced, until the rhythm builds to support a cup-muted solo by Clark Terry, before the piano takes things out with some extremely slow and delicate afterwords with the orchestra.

Present throughout "Big City Life," Brookmeyer's piano starts off "Big City Blues" with some chordal explorations before sounding out a bass line that establishes both tempo (medium swing) and structure (twelve-bar blues). Here Jim Hall's guitar, playing a rhythmic cadence, establishes the link to Mulligan's solo clarinet, which in turn leads to brass and sax-section statements solidly in the Ellington mold. Brookmeyer's arrangement, again like an Ellington piece, calls for a great deal of dynamics and structural variation, from a full-blowing band to just the drums, bass, and rhythm guitar backing up a trumpet solo. In its final three phrases the piece winds down in stages, from the full ensemble to soft saxes and finally just the clarinet and bass, which take things out much as they began.

Even more Ellingtonian, and stamping the Concert Jazz Band with that memory as it disappears into the history of American music, are Gary McFarland's "Bridgehampton South" and "Bridgehampton Strut." Following the young arranger's "Pretty Little Gypsy" and filling the balance of side B, these complementary numbers both draw on the tonal shadings that distinguished the Duke Ellington Orchestra in its classic 1940–1941 period. Clarinet and fluegelhorn, with their distinctive coloration and timbre, contribute an angularity to the ensemble playing that earlier editions of the CJB had only hinted at (but that were within the Mulligan repertoire as early as the first sextet performance onstage at San Diego in December 1954, playing "In a Sentimental Mood" and "Moon Mist"). Although the first piece features Clark Terry's fluegelhorn, Mulligan's baritone sax shows that it can handle the same colorings and rhythmic supports. It is with "Bridgehampton Strut" that the Concert Jazz Band marches from the limelight with a mood comprising the same mix of the funereal and joyful as those Dixieland bands to which Mulligan's spirit has always been so responsive. The tempo is much more brisk, of course, because numbers such as Ellington's "Harlem Air Shaft" have intervened and lent their own sense of multicultural and multidimensional joy to the history of jazz. The band's two clarinets add much to the reed section's odd tonality, plus the trombones (with Ellington's same configuration of valve, slide, and bass instruments) do a good job of finding those harmonies that distinguished Duke's 1940–1941 band. For its final chorus, all of these elements come together, and with a good-humored blat from the bass trombone the CJB makes its last statement and vanishes from the scene forever.

While criticized for not being sufficiently avant-garde, Mulligan's Concert Jazz Band did make a considerable contribution toward the redirection of American music. Up to 1960, no big jazz band had made a decisive break with the three-section orientation that had distinguished the genre since Fletcher Henderson's strategies of the early 1930s; perhaps because of the dominance of Stan Kenton on the one hand and Woody Herman on the other (not to mention the nostalgia-generating reincarnations of bands bearing the names of the great prewar leaders, plus the living presence of Benny Goodman himself), something "new" was most likely to take the forms of being only louder, higher, and more frantic, such as Maynard Ferguson's band. With Mulligan's shifts in orchestration and strategy, plus his idiosyncratic and personal choice of materials, there begins a genuine new wave of big-band music, albeit all imported—Dizzy Gillespie bringing arranger and pianist Lalo Schifrin from South America and any number of producers drawing on the talents of Michel Legrand from Europe, all as a way of introducing a more exotic sound and innovative structure, two things Mulligan's band had already achieved, although now it was begging for support.

Such a fate was not Mulligan's alone, for while literary critics of these same years were praising similar imports in fiction from Argentina and France (Jorge Luis Borges, Julio Cortázar, Samuel Beckett), American innovators such as Robert Coover, Steve Katz, and Ronald Sukenick were being cold-shouldered out of their own country. For a time these writers left for abroad, to return with more success (and the European stamp of expatriate approval) a decade later. Mulligan himself remained in the United States, producing new jazz albums any way he could. The results were as various as his broad range of work during the late 1950s but not as evenly successful. Within three years the former leader of the Concert Jazz Band and one-time intimate of Charlie Parker and Miles Davis was fronting a small combo playing "King of the Road" and "A Hard Day's Night" in an exceedingly popularized manner. The CJB had died, and so had the love of Gerry's life, Judy Holliday. Not that the middle 1960s would constitute a dark night of the soul. But these years would once again take him through experiences never shared by other jazz musicians, and the music that resulted bears its own interest and makes a contribution to the better days that would follow.

CHAPTER SIX

BRIGHT LIGHTS, NIGHT LIGHTS

Part of the apparent directionlessness of Gerry Mulligan's work through the 1960s, in the wake of the Concert Jazz Band's dissolution, can be traced to his almost overwhelming presence as a major jazz musician. In its hunger to consume more and more of the already digested, America tends to demand what it considers the most typical performances from its artists while denying them opportunities to develop and grow. Only such a cultural disposition can explain why Mulligan was pulled on stage for every imaginable occasion and invited to record with obviously redundant piano trios during the same years that his CJB begged for the financial support being spent so carelessly on contrived "festival" performances.

A festival mentality was a major part of the problem. While certain choices proved strokes of brilliance, such as placing Mulligan in a sax section of 1930s veterans and backing up Lester Young and Billie Holliday for the CBS Television spectacular "The Sound of Jazz," other occasions spoke less to Mulligan's influential roots and more to the all-star grab-bag mentality that shamed the times—from the witless mayhem of what the Newport Jazz Festival degenerated into to the absurdity of the *Playboy* Jazz Poll's vision of such superstar combos as Mulligan on baritone, Boots Randolph on tenor, Jonah Jones on trumpet, and a vocal trio of Crosby, Stills, and Nash. Such ridiculous combinations never played together, of course; but *Playboy*, faithful to its readers' majority vote, would have an artist depict them assembled on stage nevertheless, while toward its end the same "people's voice" mentality dictated the happenings at Newport. The fact that these people voicing their opinions were simply responding to the indiscriminate maw of mass-market advertising, or were (in the case of some festivals) drunk to the point of falling down, never mattered to those promoters anxious to take their dollars.

Thankfully, most of Mulligan's performances from this era survive with some dignity. His Newport appearances show up on two albums, *The Teddy Wilson Trio and Gerry Mulligan Quartet with Bob Brookmeyer at Newport* (Verve MGV-8235) from 6 July 1957, and *Duke Ellington and His Orchestra: Newport 1958* (Columbia CL 1245/CS 8072) recorded 3 July 1958. For the 1957 festival Mulligan's quartet plays "My Funny Valentine" and a full version of its theme, "Utter Chaos," both in the manner established from the Paris concerts of 1954 onward; the album begins, however, with Mulligan being "prevailed upon" to join the Teddy Wilson Trio for "Sweet Georgia Brown," which Mulligan tackles in a straightforward blues style. A year later he was expecting to do an easy jam on "Perdido" with the Ellington band, simply as a way of satisfying all those *Playboy* pollsters who yearned to see and hear the half-century's two masters of the baritone sax play together (regardless of how different and perhaps incompatible their approaches were). Ellington himself saved the occasion by bringing along a composition, "Prima Bara Dubla," that created a context for each player's strengths. But as the sixties began, Mulligan's festival appearances became either insipidly routine (appearing with an almost stock trio of Claude Williamson, Buddy Clark, and Mel Lewis, laying down awkwardly inappropriate treatments of numbers that demanded an entirely different format, such as "Jeru," or haphazardly organized (including that scourge of jazz festivals, the "jam session," which in Mulligan's case tossed him together with such diverse talents as Ruby Braff, Bud Freeman, and Buddy Rich). These performances are available today on odd reissues, such as the Europa Jazz (EJ-1024) *Europa Jazz: Dizzy Gillespie, Gerry Mulligan* and the Nippon Columbia compact disc (33C38-7682) *Mulligan*. But even here there are little treasures, such as the Europa Jazz's cut of a 1966 reincarnation of the Woody Herman Herd playing "Four Brothers" with a featured sax section of Stan Getz, Zoot Sims, Al Cohn, and Gerry Mulligan (on which each has a sixteen-bar solo).

- *Judy Holliday–Gerry Mulligan:* "What's the Rush," "Loving You," "Lazy," "It Must Be Christmas," "The Party's Over," "It's Bad for Me," "Supper Time," "Pass That Peace Pipe," "I've Got a Right to Sing the Blues," "Summer's Over," and "Blue Prelude," from *Holliday with Mulligan*, DRG Records SL-5191, 10–17 April 1961. Judy Holliday: vocals. Nick Travis, Don Ferrara, Al DeRisi: trumpets; Bob Brookmeyer (valve), Alan Raph (bass): trombones; Gunther Schuller, Earl Chapin, Fred Klein: French horns; Walter Levinsky (alto and clarinet), Al Klink (tenor and flute), Don Asworth (tenor and oboe), Gene Allen (baritone and bass clarinet), Gerry Mulligan (baritone): saxophones; Bernie Leighton: piano; Bill Crow: bass; Dave Bailey: drums.

Fame can work both ways, and for at least one occasion in the 1960s it allowed Mulligan to produce something especially personal: an album's worth of songs with Judy Holliday, four of which they coauthored themselves. Although not issued until 1980 (by DRG Records), the recordings done originally for MGM in April 1961 reveal an important side of Mulligan's art, here expressed in the most personal way imaginable, for Judy Holliday's cancer had been diagnosed less than a year before. Gerry's close relationship with her almost exactly parallels her struggles with the disease, and biographer Gary Cary testifies to the immense amount of support Mulligan provided, even after their time together had ended (Judy Holliday died in 1965, and Mulligan escorted her children to the funeral). The four songs they wrote together—Mulligan and Holliday collaborating on the lyrics, with Gerry supplying the melody—begin as testimonies to their mutual love and how, given space to develop, it promises to transform the world. But there's an inescapable dose of realism in the album's penultimate number, their "Summer's Over," both the sound and lyrics of which speak to the transiency as compelling as any romantic poet's view of this passing world.

Musically, the arrangements (by Mulligan plus Bob Brookmeyer, Al Cohn, Ralph Burns, and Bill Finegan) and Gerry's own compositions reveal a dimension beyond that even of the Concert Jazz Band, at the time in its heyday. Because so many of the tunes are subdued, there are key changes in the band's orchestration: three trumpets, but only two trombones (bass and valve), with the brass section now supplemented by three French horns; the four reeds are similarly colored by having each sax player double, on clarinet, flute, oboe, and bass clarinet respectively; the rhythm section includes piano (with apparent doubling on celeste), and Mulligan's baritone remains the featured solo instrument, although there's also a more limited role for Bob Brookmeyer, Gerry's musical soul mate in even this most intimate of occasions.

This patented stamp of the Mulligan-Brookmeyer quartet, which by the 1960s had eclipsed the Chet Baker version in its contributions to both Gerry's songbook and sound, appears on the Irving Berlin number, "Lazy," on which the valve trombone takes a solo supported all the way by baritone sax, the two horns coming together for a concluding harmonic phrase just as they had established a decade before in Paris and at Boston's Storyville. Mulligan himself is careful to create a larger role for his horn than simply playing out in front of the band, although there's some of that to get the album underway. At times he blends with Brookmeyer as in the old quartet days; then on "I've Got a Right to Sing the Blues" he plays a virtually counter-pointed duet with Judy, his always vocal baritone sax answering her lyrics. For the Cole Porter tune "It's Bad for Me" he pares the band's sound down to a more combolike feeling, while for "Blue Prelude" he re-creates the sextet's presence with a trumpet-and-bari figure that gets repeated by the trombones and other scaled down sections later to produce a genuine motif throughout the arrangement. Oddly enough, his most straight-out jazz solo is on the novelty tune, "Pass That Peace Pipe," almost as if to leave the comedy element to Ms. Holliday, which was of course her forte. Another number closely associated with her career was "The Party's Over" (from her show and movie *Bells Are Ringing*); even though Gerry has a cameo role in that film, he gives the song to Judy herself, keeping his horn and all but the clearly supportive elements of the band out of her way.

Although it is never forced or contrived, there is a steady interplay between Mulligan and Holliday on this album. It is most pronounced in the songs they wrote together, their roles as instrumentalist and vocalist working at complementary poles. "What's the Rush" begins at a loping tempo with Mulligan out in front of the band, only to be called to a slightly more retarded tempo by the song's first words, cautioning not to rush so much. For the more pertly up-tempo "Loving You" Gerry uses an ensemble effect to counterpoint Judy's creatively optimistic theme. For the unhappiness expressed of a holiday season alone in "It Must Be Christmas," he mirrors the sadness in Judy's voice by taking his baritone solo in its upper register against the equally high-reaching French horns, re-creating that sense of strain developed by Claude Thornhill and Gil Evans so many years before; for this number as well as in "The Party's Over" and his and Judy Holliday's own "Summer's Over," the scoring makes full use of the reed section's more classical instruments. Although the bari has interwoven itself with Holliday's voice and drifted in and out of the ensemble playing at times, Mulligan makes a crucial choice in "The Party's Over" by having Judy sing wordlessly what would otherwise be an obvious horn solo. His absence is implied in the presence of her voice, an ironic twist on what fate would bring.

There's a natural symbiosis between this album's two voices: Mulligan's baritone sax, which, in his manner of playing, reaches toward the horn's higher range, while Holliday's vocal is, with her illness, shaded toward more somber colors. In a subtle and unpatronizing way, the two are reaching toward the characteristics of that other saxophonist-vocalist couple in the history of jazz, Lester Young and Billie Holiday. Mulligan's playing had been showing this influence since the late 1940s, when a whole school of bright young players—Brew Moore, Zoot Sims, Stan Getz, and Warne Marsh among them—were following Young's postwar lead in lyricizing this possibly overbearing instrument. Those other players were, like Young, tenor saxophonists; Mulligan's originality was to apply Prez's style to the upper register and more vocal ranges of the larger bari. The distance between Holiday and Holliday had been closing for reasons that were as much Billie's as Judy's, with Billie's voice deepening with age and abuse even as she moved toward material more commonly associated with her close namesake. The treatment Judy accords her material was almost certainly undertaken with *Lady in Satin: Billie Holiday with Ray Ellis and His Orchestra*, one of Billie's last full albums, in mind.

Yet *Holliday with Mulligan* is surely Judy and Gerry's own occasion, from the blending of their respective voices to the choice of material and shaping of arrangements. The album has a thematic cast, moving from the need for (and joy of) love, to its eventual, inevitable loss, to the ravages of time and fate. In this sense the Gordon Jenkins number that concludes their effort, "Blue Prelude," is a fitting signature piece for their collaboration. The song's thematic message, that love is but a prelude to sorrow, codifies their own relationship, and in making this statement Judy Holliday's voice is at its saddest. Yet Gerry Mulligan has his own statement to make, and in doing so "Blue Prelude" becomes the number on which he is most consistently and confidently present, not only through his upbeat solo but by means of a constantly repeated background figure, a lingering reminder that despite the retarding character of Holliday's lyric, life itself goes on.

How much he drew from their relationship is evident on subsequent instrumental albums—almost enough, in fact, to propel him beyond the disappointment of the Concert Jazz Band's demise. His next half-dozen albums are all strong efforts, ranging from comic exuberance to a new depth and seriousness eclipsing even the more studied efforts of the CJB. Working with Judy Holliday—specifically, working with her voice—added a new sense of lyricism to his music, and for the next three years his small-group recordings would speak even more completely than his earlier quartet and sextet efforts.

- *Paul Desmond–Gerry Mulligan:* "The Way You Look Tonight," "Blight of the Fumble Bee," "All the Things You Are," "Stardust," "Two of a Mind," and "Out of Nowhere," from *Two of a Mind,* RCA Victor LPM/LSP-2624), 26 June (first two numbers), 3 July (third and fourth numbers), and 13 August 1962 (last two numbers). Paul Desmond (alto), Gerry Mulligan (baritone): saxophones; John Beal (26 June), Wendell Marshall (3 July), or Joe Benjamin (13 August): bass; Connie Kay or Mel Lewis (13 August): drums.

The first evidence of Mulligan's new range and potency is his second meeting with Paul Desmond, titled *Two of a Mind.* Recorded over three sessions between June and August 1962, its six tunes reflect Judy Holliday's spirit. She was present in the control room and, according to producer George Avakian's liner notes, renamed one of Gerry's originals to more accurately catch its spirit. His choice of material for all three dates shows Holliday's influence as well, a mix of standards, show tunes, and originals that allow himself and Desmond a wide range of effects that nevertheless play to their strengths.

Mulligan's special contribution to these sessions is a penchant to go toward the abstract. In their first meeting five years earlier—before Judy Holliday and before the Concert Jazz Band—Desmond had been swept up in Mulligan's more forcefully swinging style, but for *Two of a Mind* Gerry holds back from his own exuberant manner and allows Desmond's more intellectual and occasionally abstruse nature to take over. The album's title is misleading, for rather than sharing an approach with the alto saxophonist Mulligan is, as in his work with Holliday, adapting his own style to Desmond's, discovering what hidden resources the Dave Brubeck Quartet alumnus can draw out.

One resource is pure tonality. Paul Desmond's work with Brubeck was distinguished by his alto's sound: a breathy yet clear texture that made him as distinguishable as Johnny Hodges on an instrument whose more limited range too often leads its players to sound much the same. This tonality is featured from the start on "All the Things You Are," where the linear melody is compressed into bell-like ringing tones from the alto and bari, reducing a series of notes into one and replacing a full thematic phrase with just its high points. The result is abstract and concrete at the same time, not so much dispensing with the familiar theme as distilling it to an essential gesture. A complementary use of abstraction takes place on the two other well-known standards, "Stardust" and "The Way You Look Tonight." In each the tune's melody is either elided or completely effaced by the horns' improvisation within the song's chord structure, making the effect that of a Willem de Kooning "Woman" or one of William Baziotes's biomorphic figures—the original object is present only in the trace of an artist's gesture, whether that movement be made with paintbrush or musical instrument. That Mulligan and Desmond were up to such intentions is clear from the way they handled their numbers from the first and third session: "The Way You Look Tonight" is minimally figurative and thematic but much more so than "Two of a Mind," credited as a Paul Desmond composition but actually a run-through of "Look for the Silver Lining" with no implication of the standard's melody whatsoever; rounding out their work is "Out of Nowhere," the odd changes and twisting melody of which force the soloists to stay closer to the composer's intentions, thus allowing the session to run the full gamut of musical responses to the thematic object.

Unlike the 1957 Mulligan-Desmond meeting, this occasion is an especially quiet one—another example of the softer touch Gerry was favoring in the wake of his recordings with Judy Holliday. Of all his encounters with other famous horn men, the two albums with Paul Desmond are the only ones to go without piano, but this second time around the effect is even more subdued, the two horns almost whispering to each other at times. On the other hand, Desmond uses the space vacated by piano to make his own playing more fluid, even adding a third horn track on "The Way You Look Tonight" to create more interesting polyphony (both with the baritone sax and his own line).

- **Tommy Flanagan–Gerry Mulligan:** "Capricious," "Here I'll Stay," "Inside Impromptu," "You've Come Home," "Get Out of Town," "Blue Boy," and "Lonely Town," from *"Jeru,"* Columbia CL-1932/CS-8732, 30 June 1962. Gerry Mulligan: baritone saxophone; Tommy Flanagan: piano; Ben Tucker: bass; Alec Dorsey: congas; Dave Bailey: drums.

Mulligan's other major achievement from the summer of 1962, in the midst of the year-and-a-half-long hiatus of the CJB, was to record a thoroughly new album with a rhythm section including piano and conga drums. This Latin touch would be sustained through later albums of the 1960s, but for this first effort the results are especially interesting. From the start of his career, not only as a soloist but as an arranger, Mulligan's distinctive contribution had been the suppression of harmony in favor of both a clearer melodic line and a chance for more complex yet swinging polyphony. The distinctive contribution of *"Jeru"* is showing how Mulligan's devotion to line, especially as a musical gesture akin to the painterly abstraction he was expressing with Paul Desmond during these same summer months, could be enhanced by the addition of a bossa nova rhythm from the congas (played by Alec Dorsey) and piano (Tommy Flanagan). Indeed, the album's concept is rhythmic, conceived and produced by drummer Dave Bailey, who through his long association with Mulligan's smaller groups doubtlessly saw his leader's potential for dealing with increased and more various rhythm. Tommy Flanagan's playing is especially helpful here, for rather than getting in the way of the horn's use of chordal possibilities it restricts itself to a rhythmic role with its fills; when Flanagan plays a melodic line, as in the harmonized out chorus of the opening cut, "Capricious," it is with the light phrasing and delicacy of touch that characterizes Paul Desmond's playing on the sessions that surround the *"Jeru"* date (30 June 1962). The rhythm itself proves more various than a simple bossa nova effect, for the congas lope right along with Mulligan at his favorite pace of relaxed swinging on "Inside Impromptu" and never get in the way of his solos when he wants them to be straight-ahead expressions; on the other hand, Mulligan himself is eager to adapt his own phrasings and rhythms to the bossa nova beat, which results in the happy brightness of "Capricious."

Material chosen for the *"Jeru"* cuts reflects Mulligan's new interest in show tunes and in the work of Kurt Weill. His playing on "You've Come Home"is strongly reminiscent of Judy Holliday's approach to similar tunes on *Holliday with Mulligan*, while Gerry uses his own upbeat style of swinging to cheer up the otherwise pessimistic tones of "Lonely Town" and "Here I'll Stay." Yet the most representative numbers from *"Jeru"* are the bouncy ones—particularly "Capricious" and "Inside Impromptu," both written by pop jazzman Billy Taylor (part of the entertainment-society crowd Mulligan was meeting courtesy of Judy Holliday)—for here the baritone sax work is particularly light, thanks to its integration with the lively but never overbearing bossa nova rhythms. Although he had been working with piano trios since the "meetings" began five years before with those instrumentalists who might not play that smoothly without keyboard support,

Mulligan now for the first time fits himself in with the full rhythm section. Not only is he more comfortable with the piano, drawing from it rather than worrying around its chordal limitations, but he proves able to let his drummer (in this case drummers) play more obviously and constructively, a far cry from Chico Hamilton's work exclusively with brushes on the first quartet sides a decade earlier.

● *The Gerry Mulligan Quartet:* "I Know, Don't Know How," "I'm Getting Sentimental over You," "Piano Train," "Lost in the Stars," "I Believe in You," and "Love in New Orleans," from *The Gerry Mulligan Quartet*, Verve V/V6-8466, 25 February (first number) and 14–15 May 1962. "Jive at Five," "Four for Three," "Seventeen-Mile Drive," "Subterranean Blues," "Spring Is Sprung," and "Open Country," from *Spring Is Sprung*, Phillips PHM-200-077, 11–12 December 1962. Bob Brookmeyer: valve trombone and piano; Gerry Mulligan: baritone saxophone and piano; Bill Crow: bass; Gus Johnson: drums.

Elements from *"Jeru"* carry forward to Mulligan's next groups, the first of which involves reorganizing the pre-CJB quartet. Its two LPs cut in 1962 represent the style of work Gerry was doing in between dates with the Concert Jazz Band, and the first (especially the live cut from the Village Vanguard, "I Know, Don't Know How") harks back to the sessions with Bob Brookmeyer at Storyville in 1956. The mood is one of lusty self-confidence, and whether fast or slow the numbers all speak for the collective sense of enjoyment these veterans feel in playing together. Their spirit transforms "I'm Getting Sentimental over You" from a sweet dance-band-era signature tune into a happy romp, the two horns interweaving and blending in perfect consciousness of each other yet never sacrificing an ounce of their own natural strength. "I Believe in You" seems as if written with Mulligan and Brookmeyer in mind, and each draws on the song's structure for his most typical effects, from the baritone's deeply vocal resonance and angularity of lines to the valve trombone's flurry of notes interspersed with rhythmic grunts and growls. "I Know, Don't Know How" is here taken back from the CJB to become a combo piece once again, as it had begun in the prototype of the sextet as early as December 1954. From his association with Judy Holliday comes Mulligan's now-familiar interest in show tunes, including his own subtly evocative "Love in New Orleans" (which he wrote for a television production) and, most rewardingly, Kurt Weill's "Lost in the Stars," in which the compositional elements of the Concert Jazz Band are transposed to the quartet, the two horns almost always playing lines together and rarely stepping back from the melody, yet always producing an immense variety of sound.

Spring Is Sprung, Mulligan's first album produced after the Concert Jazz Band had made its final recording, is a less exuberant affair than the Verve sets, even though the Storyville mood is sustained with two piano blues numbers (one with Mulligan on piano, the other with Brookmeyer) and a closing out with "Open Country" from the 1956 engagement. Mulligan's own "Four for Three" looks forward to his writing, eight years later, for the *Age of Steam* fusion session, both in its use of $\frac{3}{4}$ time and more forceful theme. The album is best remembered for its opening cut, a treatment of Count Basie and Harry Edison's "Jive at Five" that refines the key elements of the Mulligan-Brookmeyer collaboration, from their counterpointed lines to their interpolated passages in unison. The tune is handled in a restrained, soft-touch manner—a good reminder that the two horns always sound best when holding back a bit and playing around rather than squarely on the beat.

- **Gerry Mulligan:** "Night Lights," "Wee Small Hours," "Festive Minor," "Morning of the Carnival from *Black Orpheus*," "Prelude in E Minor," and "Tell Me When," from *Night Lights*, Phillips PHM-200-108, July or September and 3 October 1963. "The Ant Hill," "Crazy Day," "Old Devil Moon," "Butterfly with Hiccups," "You'd Be So Nice to Come Home To," "Theme for Jobim," "Blues for Lynda," and "Line for Lyons," from *Butterfly with Hiccups*, Limelight LM-82004, July or September and October 1963 and 25 June 1964. Art Farmer: trumpet and fluegelhorn; Bob Brookmeyer: valve trombone; Gerry Mulligan: baritone saxophone and piano; Jim Hall: guitar; Bill Crow: bass; Dave Bailey: drums. Hall and Farmer are omitted on last four numbers.

Mulligan's key advance during these years results from augmenting the quartet with two instruments added to the final sessions of the Concert Jazz Band, fluegelhorn and guitar. Introduced by Clark Terry to the CJB (and via his own combo with Bob Brookmeyer), the fluegelhorn shares the same modified tonality as does Jim Hall's guitar, which is tuned four steps higher than conventionally. Both instruments are softer than usual and speak with the sense of high straining that the Claude Thornhill band achieved by having the French horns, trombones, and tubas play at the tops of their ranges.

Mulligan takes these properties of sound and expression and shapes the new sextet's first album around them. The balance of instruments is so different from his 1955–1956 sextet that the term hardly seems appropriate for the second group; rather than a hard-blowing and polyphonically interacting front line of four horns, this new group has the valve trombone and bari each playing softer in order to blend with the subtler shadings of Art Farmer's fluegelhorn, while Jim Hall's guitar has the ability to play in either the figuratively melodic or rhythmically supportive dimensions. On their first of two albums, *Night Lights*, all six numbers are soft and quiet, with an emphasis on solo statements rather than extensive ensemble scoring, though what orchestration there is plays a gently supportive role. The arrangements for five of the pieces are structured the same way: an individual horn takes the lead for an initial chorus, supported by a softly playing guitar; where the rhythm is to have a bossa nova beat, the drums and bass will make this Latin statement all the more apparent for the softness of background and presence of just the trumpet (or fluegelhorn), trombone, or baritone sax; then, after a series of solos, the ensemble will come together for a restrained reprise of the theme.

The one exception to this rule is the first (and title) track, Mulligan's slow-paced and duskily atmospheric "Night Lights," on which he plays piano throughout. Piano takes the lead, with Dave Bailey moving his brushes across a quiet snare, Bill Crow limiting his bass to one firm note per measure, and Jim Hall using his tightly strung guitar to sound a tight, high chord strum that sounds almost as if it could come from a celeste. The strategy is to hold off the brass until the mood has been established, which takes just two phrases; then trumpet comes in for a melodic bridge and improvised melody, followed by a two-phrase solo by trombone, a piano bridge on the melody (the first time Mulligan plays this figure, for the trumpet has taken it first time through), and then the tune's geometric completion with piano repeating the melodic statement that began things just one full run-through before. The strategy of letting the soloists divide up the melodic phrases and bridge, plus having the piano turn over the first bridge to solo trumpet but then, second time through, taking it back from the trombone, makes the number complex and simple all at once and gives the impression of a much longer and more complete performance than its 4:50 time would indicate.

For the subsequent numbers, Mulligan places either his own bari or Brookmeyer's or Farmer's horn out front for the first phrase of each. In this manner the fragile yet ideal form of each melody is spotlighted at the start, with the particular rhythmic support undistracted by any possible business with a second voice—indeed, subtle as it is, the rhythm is in this way established as the tune's second line. The technique brings back memories of the original quartet from its Chet Baker days, especially with Art Farmer playing as breathily as ever on trumpet and succumbing to the natural softness of the more open-bored fluegelhorn. But instead of the preciousness of the quartet's work in miniature, complemented by a spare hardness within the rhythm, the new sextet uses understatement to create a mood of quiet withdrawal—above all, the six numbers on *Night Lights* are contemplative pieces.

Comparisons with Mulligan's earlier small groups are invited by his choice of materials. The link with the earlier Art Farmer edition is made by "Festive Minor," for the first phrase of which the bari hands over its counterpoint to guitar, with the result that Art Farmer's trumpet assumes even more prominence on the tune than it had on the *What Is There to Say?* LP. On the other hand, Bob Brookmeyer has plenty of work on this new album but no real occasions for his gutty style of playfulness that had characterized his influence on Mulligan's groups through the Storyville album, the sextet days, and the quartet albums recorded in the year-and-a-half preceding this September 1963 session. His loosest playing, in fact, is reserved for "Festive Minor"—Art Farmer's spotlight—in which it figures as a momentary high between the number's initial softness and its more even ensemble effect at the end. Mulligan's playing is itself at its clearest; with the album's tempos ranging from slow and quiet to a medium swing, he's in his most comfortable element, and as on the *"Jeru"* album his adventuresomeness and wit find an outlet not in polyphonic effects but in the enhancement of rhythm, the most extreme example of which here involves playing Chopin's "Prelude in E Minor" to a bossa nova beat.

The key instrument for *Night Lights* is guitar—and not just the generic instrument itself, but Jim Hall's guitar, strung four steps tighter and played in an exceedingly soft manner. Present on all numbers, it shows its best effect on the last, "Tell Me When" (brought over from Mulligan's meeting with Ben Webster), where it creates an atmosphere from which Brookmeyer's solo statement can emerge like a figure from the misty shadows. But even on the other tunes, where it takes the place of one horn's counterpoint while the other makes a thematic statement, the guitar distinguishes itself as the major factor that both colors the new sextet's sound and structures its arrangements.

Perhaps to prevent confusion with the radically different 1955–

1956 group, this new assemblage of six musicians was never called a "sextet"; the album cover simply reads "Gerry Mulligan" as a credit for the combo. The same style of attribution graces the group's next and last LP, *Butterfly with Hiccups*, a compilation of the upbeat material not previously used from the 1963 sessions plus several pieces from the quartet (with Bob Brookmeyer) that Gerry was presenting as a club combo in 1964 and 1965. Like *Night Lights*, this new record is something of a concept album, for most of its material is happy and bright—even, like the title cut, idiosyncratically amusing, as Mulligan's jerky piano style makes a thematic statement about inebriated lepidopteran behavior. Both the jauntier style of these numbers plus the presence of the quartet cuts make the entire production sound less exotic than the *Night Lights* session and much more like the old fashioned, good-time, and good-humored playing for which Mulligan and Brookmeyer were famous. Yet even here Jim Hall's guitar makes its presence felt, for the group's approach to "That Old Devil Moon" is both colored and structured by the arrangement based on the guitar's rhythmically stated minor chords. Hall's gesture of muting his strings sets the style for what follows, giving the song its exotic yet upbeat quality.

"Butterfly with Hiccups" and "That Old Devil Moon" both follow the format used on most of the *Night Lights* tunes, with a solo voice stating the melody at the beginning, followed by the other soloists taking their improvisations, and then an ensemble chorus at the end. But the two other numbers done by the sextet prove too upbeat for this, particularly because the jauntiness of their themes demands an ensemble opening as well as close: "The Ant Hill," which starts side B in a manner similar to the piano contortions of the title track, and Mulligan's honky-tonk theme from the *Songbook* album of 1957, "Crazy Day." In this latter number there is a bit of backing off from the instrumental concept developed on the sextet's previous numbers, here in favor of playing some straightforward ensemble work in the manner of the 1955–1956 six-piece group. That the new version was not to be sustained is clear from half of this album's material— four of eight numbers—being played by the quartet with Brookmeyer. Yet even in these pieces there is evidence of Mulligan's new trends, for its "You'd Be So Nice to Come Home To" is played to a somewhat more complicated beat—not exactly bossa nova in the manner of the *"Jeru"* cuts but certainly more involved than anything Dave Bailey had done on previous recordings with Mulligan and Brookmeyer. "Line for Lyons," which dates back to the original quartet with Chet Baker, is here treated with rhythmic pauses within its melodic phrase (which had been played in straight time in its previous recordings with Baker and then Paul Desmond). The greatest dimensional change takes place on the two quartet numbers featuring Mulligan on piano. His "Theme for Jobim" begins with a Chopin-like statement, out of which Brookmeyer's valve-trombone line emerges naturally yet with an unmistakable jazz flavor, all sufficiently integrated so that the arrangement can return to its much slower classical theme at the end with no confusion. But even the piano blues, "Blues for Lynda," benefits from $\frac{3}{4}$ time, allowing bassist Bill Crow an especially melodic solo, against which Brookmeyer pits the guttiest features of his own instrument.

- **Gerry Mulligan:** "King of the Road," "A Hard Day's Night," "I Know a Place," "Can't Buy Me Love," and "Downtown," from *If You Can't Beat 'Em, Join 'Em,* Limelight LM-82021, 22 and 26–28 July 1965. "Night Lights," "Please Don't Talk about Me When I'm Gone" and "Love Is the Sweetest Thing," from *Feelin' Good,* Limelight LM-82030, 20–22 October 1965. Gerry Mulligan: clarinet (on "Night Lights") and baritone saxophone; Johnny Gray: guitar; Pete Jolly: piano; Jimmy Bond: bass; Hal Blaine; drums; unidentified ten-piece string section conducted by Harry Bluestone on last three numbers.

From *Night Lights* to *Butterfly with Hiccups* there is a definite easing off of the cutting edge of jazz but nothing to prepare listeners for the step towards popularization Mulligan would take with his next two LPs, recorded in July and October 1965: *If You Can't Beat 'Em, Join 'Em* and *Feelin' Good.* Most surprising is the choice of material, including pop songs by Roger Miller, Petula Clark, and the Beatles, but of equal musical import is the instrumentation and personnel Mulligan selects for these cuts: jazz pianist and bassist Pete Jolly and Jimmy Bond, but also rock studio-session professionals Johnny Gray on Fender guitar and drummer Hal Blaine. The second album adds a ten-piece string section to flesh out the film numbers and lusher show tunes. Among the numbers from both albums there is nothing with an inherent jazz feel. On the contrary, all are popular tunes so driven into popular consciousness by AM radio that it is nearly impossible to imagine them apart from their Top 40 context. And so the result is much more a transposition of Mulligan into the world of pop rock than it is a jazzification of such material.

Even within these terms, there are relative successes and failures on the *If You Can't Beat 'Em* album. Mulligan himself is obviously attracted to these tunes' melodic lines—appreciably so, for their catchy melodies are what have insinuated them into popular consciousness. In the liner notes he confesses to admiring just this property in Roger Miller's songs, and when he chooses material from the Beatles (as opposed to more rhythmically based rock groups such as the Rolling Stones) he's responding to the same quality of melodic invention. But playing the melody alone doesn't make for a good jazz adaptation or jazz-pop synthesis. The key is having the supporting instruments make their own contribution in kind, which happens with Pete Jolly's easily swinging piano rhythm on "I Know a Place" and "A Hard Day's Night"; here the effect is one of rhythmic transposition to accompany the shock of hearing a pop line played on such a distinctive jazz instrument as Mulligan's baritone sax, for the pianist exaggerates the syncopation to give each song a feel of roundhouse swing. For "Can't Buy Me Love" Mulligan and his rhythmic support stick to the tune's original driving beat, but here their transpositional device is to exaggerate its rocklike qualities by giving the guitar more prominence than in any other number. And in stark contrast to Jim Hall's style of muting, Johnny Gray plays his Fender in twangy, open-stringed fashion, almost as a parody of rock-and-roll fretwork. Even where the approach fails, as in the rushed tempo and piling up of notes in "Downtown," Mulligan's love for the number's angularity of line is obvious. As a result, this first attempt at jazz-pop fusion is far from being the compromise or sellout it might have been, thanks to Mulligan's commitment to melodic line and moments of brightness in devising complementary rhythmic strategies to present his style of playing in a pop context.

Any charges of sellout are more applicable to the results produced on *Feelin' Good*. Ostensibly an occasion for introducing Mulligan to strings, the performances are much more akin to "easy listening" than to such more jazz-based experiments as Charlie Parker's work with strings one-and-a-half decades before. Since both the jazz and rock camps have equal disdain for such efforts, Mulligan's performance on this album struggles to find any definable listener allegiance. That he plays clarinet on quite a few of the numbers is even more suspect, since instead of the interesting approach taken to the instrument on the last of the Concert Jazz Band LPs, his reed work here, pillowed as it is in the rich and even syrupy string accompaniment, sounds more like Acker Bilk (especially on "Night Lights," here alternately titled "The Lonely Night") than that of other sax players (such as Art Pepper) who were doing an occasional number on clarinet at this time. Rather than tight and even boppish as with the CJB, Mulligan here plays in a broad and breathy tone, pandering to the strings rather than rising above them. His lines, however, bear a strong resemblance to his work on baritone, and from cut to cut there is an almost seamless quality to his work on the two radically different instruments. The fairest judgment of the *Feelin' Good* album is that Mulligan plays best—on "Please Don't Talk about Me When I'm Gone" and "Love Is the Sweetest Thing"—when the song's melodic line is strongest and, consequently, the strings need to be least in evidence.

- **Zoot Sims–Gerry Mulligan:** "Davenport Blues," "Sometime Ago," "Take Tea and See," "Spring Is Sprung," "New Orleans," and "Decidedly," from *Something Borrowed, Something Blue*, Limelight LS-86040/LM-82040, 19 July 1966. Zoot Sims (tenor), Gerry Mulligan (alto and baritone): saxophones; Warren Bernhardt: piano; Eddie Gomez; bass; Dave Bailey: drums.

   The last of Gerry Mulligan's involvements with the Phillips-Limelight label, which had taken him from the subtle heights of *Night Lights* through a steady deterioration of musical elements to the two popularizations just described, ends at least on a more even note with his Zoot Sims collaboration, *Something Borrowed, Something Blue*. The album's six numbers are arranged in the style of Mulligan's meetings from the late 1950s, and as a result Sims is given as much prominence as was accorded to Stan Getz, Ben Webster, Thelonious Monk, Paul Desmond, and Johnny Hodges on those earlier LPs. For those sessions, Mulligan had adapted his own playing to emphasize his partners' strengths. For this meeting with Sims, who'd been an integral part of Mulligan's own group style for more than a decade, altering his approach need not be a factor; instead, Mulligan takes a more radical step in highlighting Sims's tenor (and his light, breathy way of playing it) by setting aside his own baritone on four of the six numbers in favor of alto sax, recording on this horn for the first time. As a result, there is even more of the eminently compatible interplay between the two horn men than ever before. On the two bari numbers, Mulligan plays high, as always, but on alto he favors that instrument's lower reaches, and so in each case his tonality reaches toward Sims's on tenor sax.

   The salient qualities of this 1966 meeting with Sims are the two horns' eager interplay within a softer and mellower context than allowed on their harder-swinging sextet recordings a decade earlier. A lazily paced and sweetly harmonized version of Bix Beiderbecke's

"Davenport Blues" begins the set—certainly different from Mulligan playing counterpoint with a twangy Fender guitar on "King of the Road," but equally referential to a particular school of music, here the river-based Dixieland of Beiderbecke's 1920s. Although the other five numbers from this album move on toward more conventional playing, there is still a lingering suspicion that Mulligan has been filling these awkward years of the middle 1960s—in the wake of the Concert Jazz Band's inability to maintain itself economically and in the face of Judy Holliday's death—with gimmicks of one sort or another. The "something blue" of this album's title is fulfilled by the Beiderbecke number, while the borrowings date from earlier albums ("Decidedly" from the Monk meeting, "Spring Is Sprung" from the quartet's 1963 album of that title) and from whoever lent Mulligan an alto sax for the date. The occasion's deliberately soft touch carries over to the other number Gerry does on baritone, "Sometime Ago," which is played in a waltzing $\frac{3}{4}$ rhythm that almost allows the horn lines literally to dance with each other in high-register harmony. "Spring Is Sprung," with Mulligan on alto, is handled in a much smoother fashion than on the Brookmeyer album; here, as on "Decidedly," the horns adopt the smoothness and occasional unison quality of the initial Mulligan-Desmond meeting, while "Take Tea and See" is performed in the manner of those spiny abstract lines that characterized *Two of a Mind*. On these and the album's other numbers there is a great deal of trading fours between Mulligan and Sims, a notable characteristic of their earlier sextet work. Indeed, almost every feature of *Something Borrowed, Something Blue* recalls an earlier facet of Mulligan's work, from the piano trio backing (as on nearly all of the *Mulligan Meets . . .* LPs) to the way each tune is structured.

● **Gerry Mulligan:** *The Fortune Cookie*, the soundtrack album, United Artists UAL-4145, 1966, and *Luv*, the RCA/Columbia Pictures Home Video VHS cassette, 1967. Gerry Mulligan: baritone saxophone, with studio orchestra unidentified; orchestrations by Bill Holman.

Judy Holliday's influence not only remains present in Gerry Mulligan's combo work of the 1960s but put him even more directly in the role of playing and writing music for films. Although his horn work was prominent in *I Want to Live!* and *The Subterraneans*, it is in coauthorship with Ms. Holliday that he earns his first screen composer's credit, for the title song of the 1965 movie *A Thousand Clowns*. From here two more film assignments followed: playing

André Previn's score for *The Fortune Cookie* (1966), and both composing and performing the music for the Hollywood version of *Luv*
(1967). These were Jack Lemmon pictures, and since Lemmon's film
work with Judy Holliday dated back to the early 1950s, the connec-
tion was complete.

The two soundtracks reveal a side of Mulligan that at once fits easily
into the commercial entertainment mainstream while retaining the
essence of his own sound and style. Indeed, both films make an
appreciable advance over *I Want to Live!*, which used Gerry simply
in a conventional-sounding West Coast combo, and *The Subterraneans*, where the few combo tracks were less central than the film-
noir touch of having the soulful bari wail over lushly supportive
strings. In *The Fortune Cookie* composer Previn voices Mulligan's
horn and especially his style of playing as an element in both plot and
characterization. Within the movie's scheme of comic intrigue, Gerry's playing becomes a motif associated with "The Bad Guys," as one
of his tracks is titled, while a trombone section and an alto-sax line
signal the alternative role of "The Nice Guys." As such, Mulligan's
role establishes the theme of intrigue right at the beginning and then
figures prominently in its resolution near the end, where the elements his horn introduced are melodically and tonally reprised.

André Previn's writing is itself derivative, in the best sense of
Hollywood acknowledging that nothing succeeds like success. The
model here is Henry Mancini's theme from *The Pink Panther*; significantly, it is Mulligan's horn style that adds a touch of originality and
lifts the score from predictability into respectable jazz excitement.
From Mancini's *Pink Panther* tune Previn takes the "creeping-up-on-
you" rhythm (sounded by the steel strings of electric bass and guitar)
and subversively haunting melody breathed so low and seductively
by an alto flute. But transforming it all is Mulligan's baritone sax
played in Gerry's patented manner of making a melodic line sound as
if it were conceived as a figure for walking bass. The horn, of course,
sounds atypical and serves as an unmistakable calling card for the
film's bumbling heavies. In contrast with the flutes, it both quotes
and modifies Mancini's immensely popular theme. In terms of dynamics and structure, Mulligan's voice modulates among three musical roles: subversive in announcing the melody, lyrical in singing it
through the middle parts, and percussively aggressive when it joins
the brass to punch out the ensemble's statement. Later on, the initial
effect of mystery is a helpful reminder in the reprise of this and
several other subthemes, "One Million Dollars." Played against the
bottom string of electric guitar, Mulligan's line shares this sense of

interweaving bass- and treble-clef effects. Finally, when in "The Detectives" the entire orchestra passes around what was initially the bari's theme, one realizes how richly suggestive it has been, playing an important role in extending and deepening the film's narrative.

For the film version of *Luv* (not issued as an LP record but available on video cassette from RCA/Columbia Pictures Home Video) Mulligan inherits Previn's role of composer and shows himself capable of much more originality in using the suggestiveness of jazz. With creative control of the score itself, Gerry uses not just the distinctive sound of his chosen instrument (and style of playing it) but what he learned in writing for the Concert Jazz Band. Thus, the film's title cut employs two distinct techniques for announcing the narrative theme: an initial, classically performed violin and piano duet (suggesting romantic love in its most conventional form), which soon dissolves into the $\frac{6}{8}$ time rompings of a full jazz orchestra, plus a freewheeling melody sung out by baritone and alto saxes playing in third-interval harmony (a structure that signals the disruptive pairings of unlikely lovers as the plot expounds how love turns into "luv"). This title music is the only fully individual song in the film's score, which is most likely why there was no soundtrack album issued. But Mulligan remains busy during the film's ninety-six minutes. Much of what's offered is incidental music, but all of it plays an important role in identifying characters and announcing developments in the plot. Throughout, Gerry employs a broad palette of effects, from Sousa-style band music to accordion and mandolin love songs, including a leitmotif of classic Dixieland (on which Mulligan can be heard playing baritone) signaling each appearance of the lissome Linda. Mulligan's music, in fact, is one of the production's few redeeming values, for in the hands of screenwriter Elliott Baker, playwright Murray Schisgal's charmingly offbeat Broadway hit becomes an awkwardly forced vehicle for unmotivated, disconnected attempts at wackiness—a situation holding Jack Lemmon, Elaine May, and Peter Falk as hostages to their most embarrassing performances.

Although not all of his mid-sixties activities are as creditable to the progress of jazz as had been his previous work, Mulligan's accomplishments of these years bear a certain notoriety. No jazz fan can imagine any other member of the *Birth of the Cool* nonet scoring a Jack Lemmon movie, much less showing up sixteen years later with an armful of Roger Miller and Petula Clark tunes to record; the image of Miles Davis or Lee Konitz doing so is staggering. Yet Mulligan did it without embarrassing himself and managed to establish a sympathy of melodic line between pop music and what was now mainstream

jazz, an avenue Miles Davis eventually did explore in the late 1980s
(on his *Tutu* album and others). Perhaps his fate was to attempt to
fuse his interests with rock music before fusion itself became an identifiable school; when jazz-rock collaborations did become more ac-
ceptable (and also better) in the 1970s, Mulligan was there with his
Age of Steam ensemble, the momentum for which might be traced to
these early experiments. The most obvious lessons from this experience, however, are the same ones that can be drawn from any other
transition or development in Mulligan's career: a fear of going stagnant and, even more so, a fear of letting his style of jazz drift too far
from the American popular mainstream. One must always consider
Mulligan's roots, which were not in the brainy avant-garde of bebop
but in the swing bands of Gene Krupa and Elliot Lawrence. His first
major contribution to the history of jazz had been a fusion of sorts,
taking certain musicians and specific ideas from the Claude Thornhill
band over to Miles Davis's ensemble and helping set jazz on a "cool"
but listenable course that prevailed for nearly two decades.

Mulligan's dedication to jazz involved making it swing, despite occasional pressures to the contrary. Perhaps his efforts of the mid-1960s
are best seen in this light, given the disappointments he had to face in
his earlier work at the beginning of the decade. Closing the decade and
making a transition to the 1970s would find him joining forces with
another musician whose most familiar vehicle of expression, virtually
the signature by which he had been known for almost twenty years,
had just disbanded. The Dave Brubeck Quartet, featuring Paul Desmond on alto sax, had been a mainstay throughout the 1950s and 1960s,
virtually identifying itself with the sound of jazz for many borderline
listeners while maintaining its integrity with hardcore fans. Mulligan
had already done significant work with Desmond—the only one of his
"meetings" partners to return for a second engagement—and so the
new partnership with Brubeck was by no means an extreme or exceptional act. But there remained enough distance between their styles
and approaches to make the move significant, especially since Brubeck
himself was at the end of one trail and the beginning of another as was
Mulligan. Their association produced just five albums, but over its
four-year duration both artists would benefit from its bridge into a new
age of music.

CHAPTER SEVEN

COMPADRES WITH
BRUBECK

The spring of 1968 found Gerry Mulligan and Dave Brubeck in parallel situations at similar points in their musical careers. Although a few years older than the baritone saxophonist, Brubeck had risen to prominence almost simultaneously with Mulligan. Their two quartets helped set the tone for fifties jazz, and into the sixties both players continued to develop in styles building on the principles of "white" jazz music—that is, with techniques drawing more on the classical European approach than on African or black American influences. As American society was itself transformed in the years surrounding 1968, this orientation became more critical, for while broad segments of the culture were turning to a more rhythm-and-blues-based music, Mulligan sought pop roots in the Beatles and Roger Miller, while the Brubeck quartet's hiply intellectual penchant for tweaking the nose of pop culture with such projects as *Dave Digs Disney* (which actually made successful jazz renditions of such tunes as "Heigh Ho" and "Some Day My Prince Will Come") continued unabated with such albums as *Gone with the Wind* (which included "Camptown Races") and *Anything Goes! The Dave Brubeck Quartet Plays Cole Porter*. For the general public, Brubeck's quartet had meant "jazz" for seventeen years, and its readily identifiable sound and stylistic approach guaranteed the success of these otherwise novel projects.

This strong indentifiability, however, could easily turn into a rut, making other styles of expression unlikely or impossible. And so in 1967 Brubeck disbanded his quartet, which had featured Paul Desmond, Gene Wright, and Joe Morello for so many years that their collective presence had become a virtual trademark of mainstream jazz, and turned instead to several classically based individual projects. His situation, then, matched Mulligan's, though for different reasons. Gerry's Concert Jazz Band did not record after December 1962, but not for reasons such as its leader's wish to explore new frontiers, unfettered by his previous style. Instead, economic demands had nipped the CJB almost in the bud, just as cancer had taken Judy Holliday's life before she and Gerry could collaborate on more than half-a-dozen recorded songs and one produced album featuring their material and others'. Nevertheless, Brubeck and Mulligan found themselves suddenly alone in 1968, uninvolved in ongoing groups and gigs for the first time in their professional lives.

Yet they were still Dave Brubeck and Gerry Mulligan, and by spring the country's leading jazz promoter, George Wein, was approaching Brubeck to collect on a promise to appear at the Mexican version of Wein's Newport Jazz Festival. Because a similar package celebrating the 1968 Olympics in Mexico City soon expanded the commitment to four additional appearances, Brubeck decided to forgo touring as a single and assemble a group instead. Bassist Jack Six had worked with him on his classical performances, and George Wein suggested drummer Alan Dawson. Because Mulligan was already being included on the tour as a featured attraction, Brubeck elected to meld the two acts as "The Dave Brubeck Trio Featuring Gerry Mulligan." With two warm-up concerts in Charlotte and New Orleans, the four players set out for Mexico and the album that would appear as *Compadres: The Dave Brubeck Trio Featuring Gerry Mulligan* (Columbia CS-9704).

Brubeck's and Mulligan's histories had intersected at several previous points, but their unison was still surprising—and, to the anticipation of some ears, potentially jarring. Their respective groups had shared concert stages many times before, dating back to the *California Concerts* program of 1954 when the Brubeck quartet would play the evening's first half followed by Mulligan's combo after the intermission. And of course Mulligan and Desmond had recorded two full albums together. There had even been an occasion, when Desmond was temporarily out of action with dental work, in which Mulligan took his place within the Brubeck quartet and its repertoire. Yet Mulligan meeting Brubeck would be an affair entirely different from a blowing session with Paul Desmond, for it had been in affiliation with the classically trained pianist that found Desmond at his abstract brainiest. Mulligan had made his first claim to fame by publicly re-nouncing the piano and its supposedly inhibiting effect; now he was to work in tandem with one of the era's most distinctive and imposing keyboard figures—not a light-fingered session man willing to add the minimum of rhythmic fills but a self-described heavy-handed and chordally inclined master, whose voice and presence in the quartet had been even more forceful than the group's horn. Mulligan himself took pride in the commanding presence and distinctive voice of his own solo playing, plus he was bringing three compositions to fill out nearly half of this first album's program. The possibilities for a collision were certainly present.

- **Dave Brubeck-Gerry Mulligan:** "Jumping Bean," "Adios, Mariquita Linda," "Indian Song," "Tender Woman," "Amapola," "Lullaby de Mexico," "Sapito," and "Recuerdo," from *Compadres*, Columbia CS-9704, May 1968. Gerry Mulligan: baritone saxophone; Dave Brubeck: piano; Jack Six: bass; Alan Dawson: drums.

Although the two players never did collide, towering strengths makes *Compadres* and the four other American albums (recorded through 1972) successful. Their debut number, Mulligan's own "Jumping Bean," depends upon it for effect. No easy *Mulligan Meets Brubeck* tune in the style of the simple little ditties composed to get a blowing session underway, this piece is rhythmically complex and hard hitting in the sharp attack it demands from both lead instruments, creating a situation in which both the piano and baritone sax must play in a percussive manner. For this attack to work, neither player can back off in favor of the other; like a synchronized combat team, each must slug it out ahead with an implicit trust that the other will be in place. Mulligan's solo in particular sustains this mood; where he might be expected to drift, he takes direction from the song's emphatic rhythm, a stutter-and-clash affair that precludes lots of lazily flowing notes and demands that he approach his horn like its bass clef cousins in the bottom reaches of the orchestra. Between Brubeck's solid left hand and Jack Six's determined playing, the only style open for Mulligan's work is within their rhythmic structures. But rather than feeling confined, his solo assumes direction and functions as the equivalent of Brubeck's pounding piano.

Good pacing of a concert demands contrasting material, and in structuring the album's first side Mulligan and Brubeck turn to the slower, smoothly swinging (over a Latin rhythm) "Adios, Mariquita Linda." Its melody is a strong and familiar one, coming directly from the Mexican culture to which the two composers refer in the originals they've brought along. Partially for this reason, Mulligan keeps his solo very close to the melody; but his faithful reflection of the song's melodic nature is also a sign that he likes it, and much like his playing on the Beatles and Roger Miller tunes from a few albums back his confident playing of the song's original line confirms that there has been something in it akin to his own way of handling a score. How Mulligan handles a song that invites more inventive soloing is made clear on the next number, Brubeck's "Indian Song," which returns to the harshly percussive style with which the album began, here augmented by the drummer's imposition of a $\frac{6}{8}$ time signature. Within this radically different context Mulligan takes pains to construct a definite, clear melodic line of his own, for in its rhythmic busyness this is just what the song itself lacks. Thanks to Mulligan's strong solo, Brubeck can take a more contemplative turn himself, exploring a set of classical exercises that the number never could have borne without Gerry's self-invented melody intervening.

The balance of *Compadres* benefits from this complementarity. When the number demands it, the two men can play together forcefully, their two instruments creating as much drive and presence as a much larger ensemble. Such is the effect in "Amapola," the closest they come to straight out blowing on this first LP. More often, the two support each other's more subtle work, especially on an older Mulligan composition that had been waiting for just such an appropriate premiere: "Lullaby de Mexico," a delicate composition in the manner of Brubeck's own "Tender Woman" from the first side. In both cases the numbers' careful construction and almost fragile structure demand that the two players work in almost duet form, each offering a gentle cushion to the other's gestures toward a melody that would collapse if overstated. Mulligan's clear lead distinguishes both pieces, and his solos sustain the compositional mood throughout. His own "Lullaby" asks bari and piano to play together at the end, and their gentleness is all the more remarkable in view of the immense power unleashed in earlier numbers.

If *Compadres* has a weak link, it is Mulligan's "Sapito," which comes across as a novelty piece; moreover, its faster pace and plethora of notes force the bari to struggle a bit, hardly a situation that flatters its composer. But this solitary lapse is more than compensated by the beauty of "Recuerdo," Brubeck's tonally haunting and rhythmically complex ballad. Though piano and sax begin the piece together, the two players soon divide for their own approaches—Mulligan taking a strongly melodic solo, Brubeck relying on his personal, classical style both for thematic and rhythmic improvisation.

From the perspective of two decades, the material chosen for *Compadres* might seem a bit patronizing; although George Wein made much of Brubeck's reputation in Mexico, that country's audiences were not treated to the master playing his own famous material but rather horsing around with supposedly nativistic songs, which to some ears could sound like a vaudevillian parody of Hispanic rhythms and themes. To their credit, neither Brubeck nor Mulligan let their solos be overdirected by this Mexicali impulse, but that fact makes it even more evident that the Spanish flavor of their tunes is mere window dressing. Only on Brubeck's "Indian Song" and Mulligan's "Lullaby de Mexico" is their playing strongly influenced by the song itself, and in both cases these compositions predate the tour's occasion. And so, even as Mulligan makes a decided turn away from the 1960s promotional style that had threatened to compromise his work, the festival influence lingers as a pressure to slant material and performances to a show-biz impression of what audiences want and expect.

● **Dave Brubeck–Gerry Mulligan:** "Limehouse Blues," "Journey," "Cross Ties," "Broke Blues," "Things Ain't What They Used to Be" "Movin' Out," and "Blues Roots," from *Blues Roots*, Columbia CS-9749, 1969. Same personnel as May 1968 above.

Of the five American-issued Brubeck-Mulligan albums, four are concert or festival performances (three of them abroad, where the pressures to conform to supposed audience expectations are even stronger). Hence their single LP done in the studio, *Blues Roots*, takes on a strongly different character from the others, since for once the two giants are immediately responsible only to themselves. The result is by far their most idiosyncratic album and perhaps Mulligan's most avant-gardist project to date, for the seven cuts push the blues structure to its most abstract limits. Each number chooses one facet—rhythm, melody, the chromatic nature of chord changes—and explores it with a thoroughness usually not found outside of the classical conservatory. Such a mode comes naturally to the formally trained Brubeck, a student of Darius Milhaud, but for Mulligan—who learned his theory in the bands of Tommy Tucker and Johnny Warrington—the undertakings of *Blues Roots* make for a radically new experience. On his Jimmy Witherspoon album Mulligan had explored the blues from its roots in popular culture, but now more abstract and theoretical questions were being brought to the table.

For the opener, "Limehouse Blues," the percussive aspect of the idiom gets major, almost exclusive emphasis. Brubeck takes the first phrase by literally pounding out a single chord in place of the song's melodic line, at the same time that Mulligan reduces his own instrument to its most basic function, sustaining a bottom-of-his-horn low note throughout. As the piece develops, the two players augment rather than develop their roles, Brubeck's piano taking on a syncopated striking of two chords while Mulligan's bari hits on just the opposite beat to create a solid wall of sound, nearly all of which is percussive in nature. The effect is intentionally jarring, not at all what listeners have come to expect from this classic at the center of jazz's most traditional canon, but appropriate nevertheless as a distillation of the song's key element—much like an infrared photograph that highlights the most prominent features of a topography, or an expressionistic canvas capturing the more extreme reaction of a painter's subconscious feelings.

How important that percussive effect is becomes clear with the second number, Mulligan's own "Journey," which forgoes all except the most casual rhythmic support in order to emphasize the lyrical bluesiness of his horn. Here his playing is relaxed and more characteristically simple, which yields an interesting result: at this pace, with the rhythm flowing smoothly instead of percussively forceful, Mulligan's songwriting capabilities carry his own solo through to its lyric completion, while in these circumstances Brubeck, forced to a lighter touch, relies on the conservatory approach of chordal permutations and rhythmic symmetry. Yet Brubeck proves himself equally abstract, albeit in a more modernistic way, on his own composition, "Cross Ties." Played in a brisk $\frac{3}{4}$ (which yields the rhythmic feeling of $\frac{6}{8}$, even though the solos and melody take a three-to-the-bar cast), the piano begins by playing on top of the rhythm but gradually drifting away from it into stutters and spurts of percussively phrased lines. Mulligan takes these at face value and adds his own spice to the potpourri, much as Paul Desmond delighted in doing on the *Two of a Mind* LP. Mulligan goes to the extent of adopting Desmond's practice of double-tracking a third melodic line (at which point the rhythm backs off to allow the piano line and the two baris to create an atonal, partially arhythmic effect). When the bass joins them with a fourth line, while the drums introduce various other rhythms to which the piano responds, the blues structure is stretched almost beyond recognizable form.

This peak of abstraction is sustained through Teo Macero's "Broke Blues," a five-minute exercise in which Brubeck (apparently on harpsichord) sets a classical mode within which Mulligan plays a baroque line, much like the Bach-inspired numbers from the Brubeck quartet's earlier *Jazz Impressions of Eurasia* LP. What anchors the Age of Enlightenment approach is the fact that all four instruments play constantly throughout the piece, with no apparent solos by any one instrument. Rather, in the Bach tradition, all four solo simultaneously, the interweavings of their lines taking complementary paths thanks to the composition's rationalistic design.

With the album's second canonical blues, "Things Ain't What They Used to Be," Brubeck and Mulligan take on the challenge of another piece whose traditionality almost defies any further distillation. Johnny Hodges's composition does survive almost to the end, when after some legitimate swinging by both Brubeck and Mulligan the piano starts wandering away from the tune's loping pace in favor of some random-sounding phrases that, try as they might, fail to deconstruct the song. A faster pace keeps things moving beyond such temptations in Brubeck's "Movin' Out," where Mulligan's horn stretches the outer limits of each four-bar change without ever sounding intellectually dense. By comparison, Mulligan's experiments with the chromatic structure of "Things Ain't What They Used to Be" are more extreme, yet when the piano and bari get together for some polyphony toward the end of Brubeck's song the tonality once again begins to wander. It makes sense, therefore, that the album concludes with Mulligan's "Blues Roots," the solid wailing of which prompts Brubeck to lay copper strips across his instrument's strings to make it sound like a thumbtacked honky-tonk piano. Mulligan's playing emphasizes the four-to-the-bar beat, enhanced by piano, bass, and drums hitting the rhythmic roots while his sax does a minimal amount of sliding around in between.

As on the *Compadres* album, *Blues Roots* distinguishes itself as anything but a traditional horn and piano-trio album. Once again, Brubeck's instrument has spotlighted itself as much as Mulligan's; within the catalog of Gerry's work, only his meeting with Thelonious Monk carries the same impression, for in terms of relative dominance he might as well have been playing with another horn.

- ● *Dave Brubeck–Gerry Mulligan:* "Things Ain't What They Used to Be," "The Sermon on the Mount," "Indian Song," "Limehouse Blues," and "Lullaby de Mexico," from *Live at the Berlin Philharmonic*, Columbia KC-32143, 7 November 1970. Same personnel as May 1968 above.

The distillation factor yields especially good results on the next Brubeck-Mulligan album, taken from performances during the Berlin

Jazz days in 1970. With one exception, the selections are drawn from
Compadres and *Blues Roots,* but qualities of each previous album
cross-fertilize each other and produce a synthesis of solid performative jazz. "Things Ain't What They Used to Be" and especially "Limehouse Blues" lose some of their avant-garde abstraction in favor of the
Mexican album's more exuberant sense of swing, while "Indian Song"
is redistilled to emphasize its rhythmic properties, and "Lullaby de
Mexico" is explored in terms of dynamics and tonalities, its compositional parts being dissembled before the audience's ears.

Like the *Compadres* effort, *Live at the Berlin Philharmonic* is solidly presentational. The emphasis is on maintaining a sense of swing
throughout, and any tendencies to tamper with structure serve only
to energize further the "live" nature of this performance. As if to
emphasize the roundly swinging nature of "Things Ain't What They
Used to Be," Mulligan jumps right into the first phrase with a super-
imposition of the Ellington band's other rolling number, "Don't Get
Around Much Any More"; both his and Brubeck's solos maintain this
expansive sense of swing until just before the end, when some sax-
piano polyphony threatens to get abstract, until the out chorus brings
things back to the solid Johnny Hodges idiom. Brubeck's "Indian
Song," one of the more successful pieces from *Compadres,* is here
presented with an even greater emphasis on rhythm, to the extent
that Alan Dawson's long drum solo fits in naturally with its presentation. In both numbers Brubeck's tendencies toward the percussive aspects of piano do not become a matter in themselves but are
instead enlisted in support of the song's rhythm—swinging in the
first, staccato in the second. It is a sure sign of the new quartet
beginning to gel.

There may be some slackening of avant-gardist effort in this fresh
synthesis, but not too much. The cacophonous pounding that made
"Limehouse Blues" such a jarring affair on *Blues Roots* is now limited
to just the first few bars, after which Brubeck settles back into such a
traditional treatment that the festival audience can applaud in recognition of its familiar theme; what gestures there are toward an abstract
understanding of the song's percussive and tonal elements are reserved for occasional interpolations with the baritone, a much less
dogmatic approach than taken on *Blues Roots.* When Brubeck and
Mulligan wish to highlight a special effect, it becomes the quality of
sound itself; "Lullaby de Mexico" is reshaped for this performance to
emphasize its dynamics and phraseology, while Brubeck's original
(and the album's one new piece) "The Sermon on the Mount" forgoes
any developing rhythmic and melodic structure in favor of spotlight-

ing the stirring beauty of Mulligan's deep-voiced horn, the playing of which comes closest to creating something out of nothing.

● **Dave Brubeck–Gerry Mulligan:** "Blues for Newport," "Take Five," and "Open the Gates," from *The Last Set at Newport*, Atlantic SD-1607, 3 July 1971. Same personnel as May 1968 above.

Following their 1970 Berlin appearance, Mulligan and Brubeck collaborated on two more albums, each of them taped at festival appearances: *The Last Set at Newport* from 3 July 1971, and the reunion with Paul Desmond given the apt title *We're All Together Again for the First Time*, a collection of takes from late October and early November 1972 in Berlin, Paris, and Rotterdam. On these LPs Mulligan's direction is clear, taking less of a creative role in the Brubeck combo while showing evidence of writing for his own new group, which had recorded the *Age of Steam* album in the months preceding Newport. Because of the dominance of Brubeck's own material and his strong playing on the first LP and the presence of Desmond on the second, these productions fit more squarely in the canon of the Dave Brubeck Quartet than they do in Mulligan's—for once the group's formal name, "The Dave Brubeck Quartet Featuring Gerry Mulligan," seems appropriate.

The Newport material is a combination of Brubeck's past, present, and future, with no role for Mulligan other than to respond to it. If *Compadres* had been fashioned in this mold, it's doubtful that anything more sustained would have resulted from the Brubeck-Mulligan meeting. As it is, the group had been together long enough to approach this music without sacrificing its own personality, but while Mulligan maintains a commanding presence as a soloist, it is obvious that his own creative efforts are heading elsewhere. Comprising just three numbers, *The Last Set at Newport* is definitely Brubeck's affair, from the retrospective look at "Take Five" (the first time Mulligan would be asked to play an old Brubeck classic, and a Paul Desmond composition at that) through the opening "Blues for Newport" (a blues credited to Brubeck) to the leader's symphonically based "Open the Gates (Out of the Way of the People)," which complements his "Sermon on the Mount" from the Berlin festival.

The blues piece is the album's most impressive contribution, one of those rare performances in which creativity has been stimulated rather than complicated by the festival context. Bill Chase's electronically dominant fusion group had preceded the quartet on the bill, and Dave confessed to organizer George Wein that he feared he couldn't compete with its sound level. Advised to go out there and wail, Brubeck and Mulligan deliver their most energetic playing in the service of an extremely percussive, heavy-handed blues that despite its heavy beat never gives up on swinging. Brubeck's playing can even be said to rock, while Mulligan throws the pianist's playing into even higher contrast by taking the better part of his own solo in several variations of rhythmic stop-time.

"Take Five," in its fame as a virtual identifier of the Brubeck quartet at its peak, is the greatest challenge to Mulligan's playing. He exerts his own personality almost at once, slurring and swinging the bridge more than Paul Desmond did on the quartet's hit record, but then backing off for the rest of the tune, playing his own riffs in response to the time signature instead of constructing a careful melodic line as had his predecessor. That the term "predecessor" itself comes into play shows how the innovative aspects of the Mulligan-Brubeck collaboration were beginning to run their course, with the future remaining more solidly in Brubeck's hands as the baritone sax player's creative genius begins looking elsewhere. This disposition is no more apparent than on Brubeck's "Open the Gates," where Mulligan doesn't really solo at all, his role being reserved for the symphonic duty of joining in with the leader's piano at its peak to create the number's orchestral height.

● **Dave Brubeck–Paul Desmond–Gerry Mulligan:** "Truth," "Unfinished Woman," "Take Five," and "Rotterdam Blues," from *We're All Together Again for the First Time*, Atlantic SD-1641, 28 October and 4 November 1972. Same personnel as May 1968 above, with the addition of alto saxophonist Paul Desmond.

The European reunion album with Paul Desmond is just that, an occasion for bringing together the key elements of Brubeck's 1950–1967 and 1968–1972 periods with an eye toward his and Mulligan's futures. That those futures were heading in remarkably different directions is clear from the album's two new numbers, "Truth" and "Unfinished Woman." The former is a Brubeck oratorio, subtitled "Planets Are Spinning," and of all the quasi-classical pieces Brubeck had brought to his collaboration this one is by far the least jazz oriented. Mulligan and Desmond attempt conventional enough solos, but Brubeck's performance speaks of the modernist conservatory throughout. Its back-to-back position with Mulligan's new composition makes for an especially strong contrast, for while Brubeck was heading in a classical direction, Mulligan's piece was one of the first numbers written for his Ark/Orchestra, a fusion group that would propel its leader through the 1970s and 1980s. The number, based on the repetition in two chords of a simple riff, outlines Mulligan's new goals, which include a fresh emphasis on rhythm and a greater interest in sustaining sounds (as opposed to constructing elaborate melodies). His solo builds on these new influences, holding single notes much longer and limiting his phrasing to the major chord, not shifting the direction of his line until the chord structure itself changes.

The balance of *We're All Together* consists of the original Brubeck quartet (without Mulligan) doing a reprise of one of their more famous numbers, "Koto Song," plus Gerry joining in for a fresh version of "Take Five," in which a softer approach brings new attention to the melody. "Rotterdam Blues" is an improvised encore, as is "Sweet Georgia Brown," the latter lasting just one minute. The blues piece is good-humored barrelhouse playing, in which some of Mulligan's favorite licks from the *Meeting* sessions of a decade and a half before resurface. But with Brubeck's sixty-second solo curtain call, the lights come down on this period of collaboration—a workshop exercise of sorts that not only sustained the two great musicians through a difficult transitional period but allowed them both to refine key aspects of their playing, reaffirming their jazz roots no matter what the nature of the group's material.

CHAPTER EIGHT

THE AGE OF STEAM

When Gerry Mulligan took to the A & M Studios in Hollywood between February and July 1971 to record *The Age of Steam* (A & M SP-3036), he was leading his own group through some explicitly jazz material for the first time in over five years. The collaborations with Brubeck had monopolized his festival appearances since 1968, but the impact of those rock-music and easy-listening LPs for Limelight in the middle 1960s had now made it clear that as a creative force Mulligan was in deep need of new direction. Following the dispersal of his Concert Jazz Band in 1963, he had turned to the six-piece group for exploring some of the CJB's softer innovations, many of them inspired by his work with Judy Holliday; yet as Judy's death from cancer drew near, the sextet withdrew back into Mulligan's familiar quartet with Bob Brookmeyer, and after Judy's death not even that group continued to record—all listeners had were the unusual pop efforts with studio rock musicians and strings and the single reunion album with Zoot Sims (which found Mulligan playing the majority of its material on alto sax). The Brubeck years had been secure in terms of adulation and reinforcing key skills, not to speak of being exposed at close range to the work of an equal genius. But as Mulligan's role in the Brubeck quartet receded, evidence of his own new ideas began popping up, most noticeably in his fresh composition performed on the final album with Brubeck, "Unfinished Woman." Although this piece would not have a concert recording under Mulligan's leadership until 1974 and wouldn't be done in the studio until September 1980, its original elements—so evident in the performance with Brubeck—give obvious clues to Mulligan's new plans.

Rhythm would be one step in this direction: as Alan Dawson proved on the collaborations with Brubeck, there was a lot more a drummer could do than simply swish brushes or ride a cymbal; their rendition of "Unfinished Woman," though simpler than Gerry's later versions, emphasized this new rhythmic center, with Dawson setting a mood as well as signaling the beat—and the beat itself was a more intricate one, offering four notes to an older style's one or two, with a stronger role for syncopation within each beat. The supporting rhythm would now float rather than drive, filling in as a comping piano used to, thus freeing the keyboard (which would in the future be electric as often as not) for work at once more melodic and percussive. The songs themselves would draw on this rhythmic richness and in consequence find that there was not as much need for flashy melodic devices—the horns could wail on one chord much longer, given all the interesting things the rhythm section was now free to do. As a result, Mulligan's own solo voice could now make do with one note for a measure or two or three and actually support the chord changes rather than expecting them to make way for him. Always a relaxed and loping player, Gerry would find this new style complementary to his horn's deep-throated ability to sing, and therefore the more vocal elements of his playing come into deeper focus. In the process, his *Age of Steam* aggregation would produce some of his prettiest and strongest baritone sax work.

- *Paul Beaver–Bernard L. Krause–Gerry Mulligan:* "Gandharva," "By Your Grace," "Good Places," "Short Film for David," and "Bright Shadows," from *Gandharva,* Warner Brothers WS-1909, 10–11 February 1971. Bud Shank: flute and alto saxophone; Gerry Mulligan: baritone saxophone; Gail Laughton: harp; Howard Roberts: guitar; Paul Beaver: pipe organ; Bernard L. Krause: Moog synthesizer.

Fusion's contribution to Mulligan's style takes this first and most decisive step on a recording date with the organ-synthesizer duo Beaver and Krause on 10–11 February 1971, just when the half-year's worth of sessions that yielded *The Age of Steam* was beginning. Three players overlap—Bud Shank on alto and flute, guitarist Howard Roberts, and Mulligan himself—but the comparisons between the Beaver and Krause *Gandharva* album and Mulligan's own first fusion LP are more subtle than obvious. In fact, the piece he wrote for Paul Beaver (playing the massive pipe organ in San Francisco's cavernous Grace

Cathedral), Bernard L. Krause (on Moog synthesizer), Bud Shank (flute), Gail Laughton (two harps), and Howard Roberts (electric guitar), titled "By Your Grace," is the starting point for his longer and much grander "Entente for Baritone Sax and Orchestra" recorded with the Houston Symphony almost exactly sixteen years later in 1987. In this embryonic version Mulligan responds to both pipe organ and to the cathedral itself (whose 150-foot-long and 90-foot-high dimensions provide a seven-second decay time for both the organ's and baritone sax's rolling sound), and as a result "By Your Grace" promotes the long notes and echoing sonority that Gerry would find ideal for sailing above the electronic action and busy, complex rhythms of his more rock-and-rollish *Age of Steam* band. The piece begins with a Bach-styled organ chord, which Mulligan's bari joins as if it is another mid-range pipe. The cathedral's deeply sonorous dimensions fit right in with the composition's lofty, churchlike sound, a quality Mulligan is able to exploit in contrast by playing a melodic variation in a much lighter, chamber-music fashion over a deftly plucked harp. Before the end there's time for some more antiphonal interaction in the manner of J. S. Bach, another reminder that Mulligan's first work in jazz-rock fusion has shown that there is much more to the style than simply bringing along electric bass and guitar.

The rock elements of *Gandharva* are slow to emerge but are definitely there—part of Beaver and Krause's belief that contemporary rock music was something deep and complex. Mulligan's "By Your Grace" is actually the second movement in the side-long performance, which has begun with the one-minute title track consisting of sound effects from Moog and pipe organ (actually produced to show off the cathedral's acoustics, which will couch the subsequent numbers). Gerry's horn playing reveals three distinct styles as it reacts with pipe organ, harp, flute, and then a more active pipe effect before the theme is restated. Beaver and Krause's own "Good Places" follows the similar tactic of introducing Mulligan's baritone within the pipe organ's chordal mass, where it sounds like a pedal stop before assuming melodic shape to play a slow, gently winding tune soon joined by Bud Shank's sweeter alto. This smaller horn from jazz music serves as the more obvious contrast, putting Mulligan more firmly in the classical camp. But only until "Short Film for David," the Beaver and Krause composition that opens the door to full three-part fusion among classical, rock, and jazz. The opening notes are from Howard Roberts, whose electric guitar can pluck out a few folkish notes and have them reverberate naturally through the great cathedral with an effect unmatched by the most sophisticated Fender amp. Soon the organ's deepest pipe is laying down a solid bottom to answer; the guitar begins a quiet rhythmic strum, which bari and alto quickly take up for some traded fours. Now and then the deep organ note will roll in like a foghorn or the fog itself, and the quality of *The Age of Steam's* first number is born: the single-chord, rhythmically pulsing, deep-trombone-anchored drone of "One to Ten in Ohio" that will clearly announce Mulligan's induction into the fusion era. Concluding *Gand-harva* is "Bright Shadows," the duo's eeriest venture into postmodern music, in which Mulligan's horn works against the harp and flute until it can pave the way for full synthesizer sound, something kept in check since the side's first hint of what the Moog can do.

● ***Gerry Mulligan and the Age of Steam Band:*** "One to Ten in Ohio," "K-4 Pacific," "Grand Tour," "Over the Hill and Out of the Woods," "Country Beaver," "A Weed Grows in Disneyland," "Golden Notebooks," and "Maytag," from *The Age of Steam,* A & M Records, SP-3036, February–July 1971. Harry Edison: trumpet; Bob Brookmeyer: valve trombone; Bud Shank (alto and flute), Tom Scott (tenor and soprano), Gerry Mulligan (baritone and soprano): saxophones; Roger Kellaway, Gerry Mulligan: piano; Howard Roberts: guitar; Chuck Domanico: bass; John Guerin, Joe Porcaro: drums; Joe Porcaro, Emil Richards: additional percussion; Ernie Watts, Kenny Schroyer, Jimmy Cleveland, Roger Bobo; additional horns.

From *Gandharva* Mulligan moves directly to an album whose title makes a political statement, for as younger players were turning to electronic aids and devices—including the technologies exploited by Tom Scott, the first fusion player Mulligan recruited—the older saxophonist reasserts just what conventional wind instruments could do in these new surroundings of electrified sax, piano, guitar, bass, and even drums. The clear voice of his conventionally miked baritone sailing above the electronic ensemble is a hallmark of this *Age of Steam* LP and signals just how contemporary his horn could sound while still under its own power, a clear legacy of his work with Bernard L. Krause's Moog and Paul Beaver's cathedral organ. Augmented by the familiarity of Bob Brookmeyer's valve trombone, Mulligan's horn bridges the gap between modern jazz and fusion by drawing on qualities from each. This is just how Gerry approaches the first number, "One to Ten in Ohio"—like the album's other seven tunes his own composition, fulfilling the never-completely-kept promise with the CJB to form an ensemble for his own writing, this time with a more rhythmic push.

Push along is what "One to Ten" does; having no clear, obvious chord changes, and consequently no dominant melody, the song makes its mark with rhythm, beginning with figures from electric piano and guitar that set both tone and tempo. Into this especially active conflux of sounds, radically new to the Mulligan repertoire, he drops a hostage from the old days, Bob Brookmeyer, whose valve trombone is of all the conventional instruments most suited to responding with rhythmic puffs of breath. By now electric bass, congas, and tambourine are ready to join the bells that have begun sounding behind Brookmeyer's emerging melodic line, but not before Mulligan himself comes in to take the lead for eight bars and then falls back for some rhythmic counterpoint. This counterpointing opens the way for the rhythm section's augmentation and also sets the stage for the first outright fusion soloist in the person of Tom Scott, whose initial squeaks and honks on the tenor establish themselves as one last addition to the building rhythm before he takes an R & B-style King Curtis solo, followed at once by Mulligan's only slightly more lyrical work on baritone sax. After this, the piece recedes into its rhythmic conformation, fading out with the subtlest of wails from the guitar. As Mulligan's introduction to fusion, "One to Ten" is an ideal vehicle, for neither side has had to sacrifice or compromise, yet the final result is as contemporary as any jazz-rock group was doing at the time and actually anticipates some of Tom Scott's most representative work on his own.

The other cuts on *The Age of Steam* share several characteristics with "One to Ten," emphasizing rhythm over melody, blocks of sound over chordal progressions, and a dedication to mixing the more percussive aspects of blowing with a steady but busy and deep rhythm section (this last point developed from the Latin rhythms of the *"Jeru"* album almost a decade before). "K-4 Pacific" uses a mix of electric piano, guitar, and flute to create a railroad sound, the feeling of which is sustained by the soloists playing in a stop-time rendition of wheels clicking across the rail joints. These features of rhythm plus solos eventually yield to the album's most conventional ensemble work, in which the new ten-piece group approaches the Concert Jazz Band yet benefiting from the stronger sense of drive produced by having as many as five players in the rhythm section (piano, bass, and guitar—all electric—plus drums and congas) backing up baritone, trombone, tenor, alto (Bud Shank, doubling on flute), and trumpet (Harry Edison).

The compositional aspects of Mulligan's work on *The Age of Steam* support his commitments to a new playing style. Even the three-part "Over the Hill and Out of the Woods," which features his piano throughout, is built on drawing the most from a simple riff figure in which the conventional keyboard interweaves with a growing ensemble, then retards for a flowing legato passage, and finally cranks up the tempo for a spate of solos in almost roaring big-band fashion—yet with no more melodic complexity than the simple opening phrase. Strongly rhythmic concoctions dictate the approach for "A Weed Grows in Disneyland" and "Maytag" (the latter inspired by memories of his mother's noisy washing machine), while "Grand Tour" and "Golden Notebooks" float on clouds of sound generated by bari and alto in the former and Mulligan's light-touch electric piano in the latter. Roger Kellaway's driving conventional piano on "Country Beaver" sets a percussive approach that Mulligan matches with a tightly voiced, sharply attacking ensemble, in which the horns perform much like a banging, two-fisted piano player (such as he had been working with in the Brubeck group!). In all instances, the material on *The Age of Steam* signals as great a leap in Mulligan's style as can be found at any point in his career.

- *Chet Baker–Gerry Mulligan:* "Line for Lyons," "Song for an Unfinished Woman," "My Funny Valentine," "Song for Strayhorn," "It's Sandy at the Beach," "Bernie's Tune," "K-4 Pacific," and "There Will Never Be Another You," from *Carnegie Hall Concert, Volumes 1 and 2*, CTI Records CTI-6054 and 6055-S1, 24 November 1974. Chet Baker: trumpet; Gerry Mulligan: baritone saxophone; Bob James: piano; John Scofield: guitar; Ron Carter: bass; Dave Samuels: vibraphone and percussion; Harvey Mason; drums. On the last number Gerry Mulligan is omitted, trombonist Ed Byrne is added, and trumpeter Chet Baker also sings.

This new style is sustained through four additional albums with the same general instrumentational approach and in meetings in Italy with Enrico Intra and Astor Piazzolla. But the initial test of Mulligan's new vision would come on his next recordings (following his Newport and European appearances with Brubeck), a two-album Carnegie Hall reunion with Chet Baker. Here was an easy chance to fall back into retrospective playing, for the affair was booked as part of the "living legends of jazz" mystique then dominating jazz. Baker himself preferred to approach the date in this manner, suggesting the quar-

tet's well-worn "Line for Lyons" and his own signature piece from
California days with Gerry, "My Funny Valentine," as his featured
contributions. Mulligan's playing had undergone a transformation
with his new group, showing less tendency to rephrase melodies and
more affinity for building on rhythm. The original Gerry Mulligan-
Chet Baker quartet had been founded on just the opposite principles,
and it is interesting to see how the Baker-Mulligan reunion transpires
under the new conditions. To forestall any lapse into sterile nostalgia,
Mulligan brought something with him besides his horn: the five-piece
electric rhythm section whose instrumentation had configured his
Age of Steam band, with the roles here filled by young fusion musicians Bob James (piano and electric piano), Ron Carter (bass), Harvey
Mason (drums), Dave Samuels (vibes and percussion), and John
Scofield (guitar).

This rhythm section, combined with Mulligan's new writing and
his fresh sense of playing, would transform the Carnegie Hall event
from a piece of retrospection to another deliberate forward step.
Even though Chet Baker's vote was for the older material he had
been playing in local clubs as he rebuilt his career after years of drug
addiction and illness, his playing is carried along by Mulligan's new
emphasis. Both "Line for Lyons" and "My Funny Valentine" begin in
the traditional quartet manner, with all but the bass, drums, and
Mulligan's horn hanging out until the very end of his solos; but as the
lead is passed to Mulligan, the other instruments join in, augmenting
his new style of playing. On "Line" Bob James decides not to offer
traditional fills but instead supplies a melodic line that creates some
effective polyphony with the big horn, another advantage of the electric piano (with its clearer, sharper, and more penetrating voice).
"Valentine" finds James comping in the traditional manner but in a
way that encourages Mulligan to rely on his rhythmic encouragement, giving the number a faster and more swinging character than
its old quartet versions. The rhythm section makes its strongest contribution on "Bernie's Tune," where the song's natural rhythmic complexity encourages the drums to take a far greater role than in any
previous Mulligan treatment of this piece, even to the extent of taking
a solo at the end. Throughout these older pieces, Gerry's playing is
especially strong, often riding on the rhythmic elements in order to
weave and sing a new melody as solid as the original's. The only time
Mulligan's influence is not exerted is on Baker's vocal, "There Will
Never Be Another You," where he stays out altogether and trombonist Ed Byrne takes the role of the second horn.

The four newer numbers Mulligan brings to Carnegie Hall, all of which draw on the full rhythmic and electronic resources of his younger sidemen, are in a direct line with his writing and playing introduced on *The Age of Steam* three years before. Where there were significant ensemble parts on the 1971 versions, the baritone sax now carries it alone, indicating how augmented rhythm and a less melodic style of composition were the key elements all along. Although John Scofield's guitar playing is more in the style of Jim Hall and less like the rock-influenced playing of Howard Roberts on the earlier album, his work blends well with the lighter touch of Bob James on electric piano. Ron Carter's strong electric bass and the enlarged percussion session also create an especially busy and complex base for Mulligan's composing and playing, both of which count less on melody than earlier in his career.

Repeated from *The Age of Steam* is "K-4 Pacific," while "Song for an Unfinished Woman" is given a more contemporary treatment than for its debut almost exactly two years earlier with Dave Brubeck. Now sax and guitar (for the first) and sax and piano (on the second) take over the more exotic interplays, giving "Woman" an especially lighter and gentler feel. The unveiling of "Song for Strayhorn," not given full orchestral treatment until 1980, shows how steadily Mulligan's new catalog was growing—and how his writing was taking on an especially moving lyricism, dedicated as it was to persons close to his inspiration. Many of the *Age of Steam* compositions made thematic reference back to the early years of his childhood when his family had moved from New York City to Ohio; now he was using the poetic style of his playing to evoke musical memories as well, the Strayhorn references being made especially touching by his own playing in the style of a bowed bass over Bob James's electric piano adjusted to sound like a harp. "It's Sandy at the Beach" is dedicated to the new woman in his life, actress Sandy Dennis; a solidly driving song, it reaffirms Mulligan's new commitment to fewer chord changes and more sustained playing on one basic tone, with complexity being supplied by the five-person rhythm section. On this number Chet Baker joins in, taking a solo that could have been played by Miles Davis,who was himself adopting fusion elements during these same years. For the other new Mulligan numbers, Baker stays out, not venturing a new voice for this material that precludes his older style of playing.

The Carnegie Hall concert might be considered a political statement, announcing to a nostalgia-inclined audience that Gerry Mulligan had no intentions of riding on an old reputation. His new styles of composing and performing were underscored at this reunion, but

in the following year another dimension of his work appeared, drawing on the influence of European jazz.

Since his Paris concerts with Bob Brookmeyer in June 1954, Mulligan had made Europe a regular part of his itinerary, playing in every
venue from classical concert halls to circus rings. Although some
Continental promoters preferred to book attractions along the lines of
"the living legends of jazz," Mulligan had steadfastly refused this
approach, at each stage of his career using his European tours to
introduce his newest developments in jazz, from the reformed quartet with Brookmeyer to the innovations he and Dave Brubeck were
preparing in the early 1970s. But by the mid-seventies Mulligan was
learning that these trips to Europe could be a two-way street. He was
not only bringing his own music and musicians across the Atlantic to
delight European audiences, but European jazz musicians were making an impression on him, to the extent that he wished to work with
them at length. And just as Mulligan was bringing over a taste of
America, the sharp flavors of Europe were appealing to him, to the
extent that beginning in 1974 he would elect to spend a considerable
part of each year in his favorite country abroad, Italy—particularly
the hillside environs of northern Italy outside Milan, where he eventually found a wife and home. Associations with Enrico Intra and
Astor Piazzolla soon emerged as an important aspect of this part-time
relocation.

- **Enrico Intra–Gerry Mulligan:** "Nuova Civilta," "Fertile Land,"
  "Rio One," and "Champoluc," from *Gerry Mulligan Meets Enrico Intra*, Pausa PR-7010, 16–17 October 1975. Gerry Mulligan: baritone and soprano saxophones; Giancarlo Barigozzi:
  soprano saxophone and flute; Enrico Intra: piano; Sergio Farina:
  guitar; Pino Prestipino: bassoon; Tulio de Piscopo: percussion.

Though bearing an old-time *Gerry Mulligan Meets . . .* title, this
opportunity to work with Enrico Intra derives from a conception that
differed entirely from his blowing-session meetings with Stan Getz,
Johnny Hodges, Ben Webster, and the others from that much different period in Mulligan's career. With Intra the emphasis is on composition; the entire first side is given to a suitelike piece, composed
by the Italian pianist, with no less than six distinct movements, plus
additional shifts in dynamics and tempos within these subdivisions.
The flip side offers three shorter pieces, including Mulligan's own
"Rio One," but none of them are styled like the head arrangements of

Getz Meets Mulligan and the like. "Rio One" is closest to a conventional song, but even here Mulligan follows his only recently introduced practice of sounding out an easy melody that draws its strength from complementing the busy machine of the group's Latin rhythm. Intra's long and shorter pieces draw on the session's unique instrumentation, in which to his piano and Mulligan's baritone sax (with doubling on curved soprano brought over from the *Age of Steam* sessions) were added guitar, bass, and drums and such exotic choices as bassoon and a second reed man doubling on flute and straight soprano sax. In this context melodies and rhythms are never set in distinct patterns but rather benefit from a fluid grace that remains constantly interactive and redirective; several pieces demand extremely involved drumming, and the art is never to let Mulligan's horn overplay itself in trying to keep up with the action. Instead, the baritone sings with confident presence and deep emotion. In his liner-note comments to critic Nat Hentoff, Mulligan admits his displeasure with the artificial nature of so much recent extended "free form" blowing and suggests that his work with Intra has been an attempt to reformulate such avant-garde tendencies so that new jazz can still swing within an identifiable context yet remain free of needlessly constraining structures. Such compositions as "Nuova Civilta" and "Champoluc" do just that by emphasizing originality of performance over prescription of particular melodic lines. Indeed, it is difficult without a score to know just how much of each performance is written and how much improvised, other than the obvious cues for dynamics and tempo that make each piece such a varied experience.

In this respect the achievement of the side-long "Nuova Civilta" is remarkable, for it not only shows the range of Mulligan's playing but reveals how much can be accomplished by the baritone sax, both alone and paired with other instruments from Intra's ensemble. The baritone's opening figure is played, of course, as a melody, but it is in fact establishing the first movement's rhythm. When the piano joins in, it is to make this rhythmic function clear, but at the same time the horn's lower register is being complemented by Giancarlo Barigozzi's especially fragile flute line. This combination is not forgotten, for at key moments in later movements the flute will reappear to augment whatever new aspect of the bari is being introduced, be it the atonality picked up from Intra's piano work or the complexities offered by the extremely active rhythm section.

- ***Astor Piazzolla–Gerry Mulligan:*** "Twenty Years Ago," "Close Your Eyes and Listen," "Years of Solitude," "Deus Xango,"

"Twenty Years After," "Aire de Buenos Aires," "Reminiscence," and "Summit," from *Summit (Tango Nuevo)*, Atlantic ATL-50168), 24–26 September and 1–4 October 1974. Gerry Mulligan: baritone saxophone; Astor Piazzolla: bandoneon; Angel "Pocho" Gatti: piano, electric piano, organ; Fillipo Dacco, Bruno de Filippi: guitars; Giuseppe Prestipino: bass; Tulio de Piscopo: drums and percussion; Alberto Baldan, Gianni Ziliolo: marimbas; Umberto Benedetti Michelangeli: first violin; Renato Riccio: first viola; Ennio Miori: first cello.

Concept figures even more centrally in *Summit (Tango Nuevo)*, the album on which Mulligan and Astor Piazzolla interface their respective instruments (baritone sax and bandoneon) as dancers in that most studied and yet elemental meeting of cultures, hemispheres, and ages: the tango. All eight cuts are cued to similar rhythms and melodic variations, even the single composition Mulligan interpolates with Piazzolla's material. The tone is somewhat like Gato Barbieri's score for the Bernardo Bertolucci film, *Last Tango in Paris* (1972), itself an index of Western European morals and manners in the years following the events of May 1968—a period when sex and behavior had been liberated but hopes of political and a deeper cultural liberation disappointed, leaving an aftermath of purely carnal sensation. Throughout, Mulligan and Piazzolla are just like dance partners, exchanging the lead and venturing apart, only to return to a tightly choreographed interplay, much like the tango itself.

It is, however, a new tango, one that loosens up the form via changes in dynamics and tempo only to return to the dance's elemental strictness and even harshness—like Bertolucci's film, another comment on the way emotions had been jerked around by postmodern times until all that remained were the physical sensations of that jerking. Hence the easy floating style of "Twenty Years Ago," on which baritone and bandoneon alternately cushion each other for their respective leads, invites the even gentler and sweeter approach of "Close Your Eyes and Listen," only to have the mood broken by the harsh striking in "Years of Solitude," in which the initial percussion survives a legato passage to end the tune as a march. Yet as if this were not harsh enough, "Deus Xango" follows with the most emphatic division yet between horn and keyboard synthesizer, restoring the rhythm of a classic tango with melody played stiffly by bandoneon until the baritone is compelled to join right in with this established manner. From here, the players experiment with even jerkier rhythms and more dissonant harmonies, but with happier effect: both

Piazzolla's "Twenty Years After" and Mulligan's "Aire de Buenos Aires" move from this initial cacophony into some of the album's sweetest playing, a reminder that contrast is the essence of tango form. In Mulligan's piece, structure is cleverly employed to make this point, as it is the bridge of his tune, in distinction to the harsher melodic sections, that sounds all the prettier and eventually establishes itself as the major movement.

The album's last two numbers, "Reminiscence" and "Summit," offer the only extended horn solos, but even here the emphasis is on the two instruments' passages into and out of unison playing. Throughout the album Piazzolla has played a game, drawing the most European sounds possible from his broadly ranging instrument, only to have Mulligan at first mimic them (from canals of Venice legato to a banks-of-the-Seine concertina style) and then transform them to thoroughly American jazz—all by insinuating his horn's sound and style of play within Piazzolla's music before making it his own. Once again, by moving into a radically different realm, Mulligan has not only avoided predictability and boredom but has come back to his own style in a completely re-created and rejuvenated manner.

Gerry Mulligan's European work, however, is only one part of his broad range of projects following his years with Brubeck and the inauguration of the *Age of Steam* band. The late 1970s and early 1980s would find him recording with such diverse and unique talents as Lionel Hampton and Charles Mingus, plus scoring a French film and adding his instrumental voice to two of pop singer Barry Manilow's jazz-influenced albums. Yet amid these productions, which are admittedly ancillary to Mulligan's career, can be found the major developments in his own writing and playing, both of which follow in a direct line from the *Age of Steam* and *Carnegie Hall* albums. Recorded in November 1976, September 1980, and during 1983 respectively, Mulligan's three major LPs show him running his own compositions through three sizes of groups, from the tightly organized sextet of *Idol Gossip* (Chiaroscuro CR-155) through the full-sized jazz band of *Walk on the Water* (DRG SL-5194) to the essential quartet (augmented on two of the six cuts by a six-piece horn section) captured on the Grammy Award-winning *Little Big Horn* (GRP Records GRP-A-1003). The changing instrumentation gives each album its own sound, but there is such a strong coherency of development, particularly along lines contrasting with Mulligan's work in the middle 1960s, that the years since 1971 constitute as strong a phase as any such identifiable period in his five-decade career.

● **Gerry Mulligan's New Sextet:** "Idol Gossip," "Strayhorn Two,"
   "Walk on the Water," "Waltzing Mathilda," "Out Back of the
   Barn," "North Atlantic Run," and "Taurus Moon," from *Idol
   Gossip*, Chiaroscuro CR-155, 27 November 1976. Gerry Mulligan: soprano and baritone saxophones; Dave Samuels: vibraphone; Mike Santiago: guitar; Tom Fay: piano; George Duvivier:
   bass; Bob Rosengarden: drums.

The *Idol Gossip* sextet is virtually the setup Mulligan premiered
at Carnegie Hall two years before and became the group with
which he toured Europe in December 1976. Although piano, vibes,
and guitar all take their share of solos and contribute to the ensemble effects, they are basically rhythm section instruments, joining the bass and drums (here played by jazz veterans George
Duvivier and Bob Rosengarden) as a support element for the clear
line of Mulligan's solo bari (and, on two cuts, the sweet and almost
cuddly curved soprano sax—unlike the more conventionally used
straight soprano a notoriously difficult instrument to keep in tune
with itself and therefore as idiosyncratic a choice and as equal a
challenge as the cumbersome baritone).
    This album opens with a rephrasing of an old Mulligan quartet
classic, "Bernie's Tune," initiating a practice Gerry would follow on
subsequent albums, taking a once familiar melodic phrase and re-
shaping it as the bridge to a new tune, or vice versa. Here the retitled
piece is the album's namesake, "Idol Gossip," in which the presence
of just one horn allows a smoother mix of ingredients than when Chet
Baker's or Bob Brookmeyer's brass line contributed to the original's
contrapuntal maelstrom. For "Idol Gossip" the initial lead lines are
taken by baritone sax and guitar; following Mulligan's solo, the clarity
of his supporting instruments allows three overlapping lines to develop among his horn, Mike Santiago's guitar (again in the tight Jim
Hall tradition), and Dave Samuel's vibraphone. Finally, in the new
tradition of simple beginnings progressively multiplied into busy and
complex constructions, Tom Fay's piano adds a fourth melody, until
the four voices are playing as if in a round, each just two bars behind
the other, yielding an effect immensely more involved than the original "Bernie's Tune," the jarring complexity of which Mulligan's new
tune at first seemed to have left behind.
    Idol Gossip's other six cuts touch on the various aspects of Mulli-
gan's writing and playing in evidence since the *Age of Steam* recordings in 1971. There is the new emphasis on rhythmic push in "North
Atlantic Run," the baritone's sharp staccato compensating for the lack

of many chord changes (which are in fact reserved for the contrasting smoother bridge), just as the swinging $\frac{3}{4}$ time and mellow effect of the curved soprano provide the more interesting features of "Walk on the Water." This unique tone contributes to "Taurus Moon" as well, almost as if John Coltrane's introduction of this highest pitched of the saxes on "My Favorite Things" had forever stamped it as a waltz-time vehicle. Dave Grusin shares credit for the revamping of a recent Mulligan composition now called "Strayhorn Two," in which the structure of "Song for Strayhorn" (premiered at Carnegie Hall two years earlier) is chordally deepened and its highly emotional edges rounded off. For tradition's sake there is Mulligan's favored style of an easy loping line on "Out Back of the Barn," a tune that lets him comfortably slide around the bari's great range, all the time propelled by a good-time backbeat. Joining these six Mulligan compositions is one of Gerry's characteristically offbeat choices that nevertheless reveals the roots of his musical fancy: the Australian anthem "Waltzing Mathilda," which he plays in the manner of *If You Can't Beat 'Em, Join 'Em*, with his horn emphasizing the song's appealing melody first in a lead line played over the rhythm section, and then in a solo that, through several chromatic rises, remains very close to the theme. In terms of new contributions, *Idol Gossip* finds Mulligan interacting more closely than ever with the percussively clear sound of the vibes, particularly on his curved soprano, which he plays with a particularly sharp attack that its built-in mellow sound allows without becoming brittle. As a result, his playing is more strongly rhythmic than ever.

- *Gerry Mulligan and His Orchestra:* "For an Unfinished Woman," "Song for Strayhorn," "42nd & Broadway," "Angelica," "Walk on the Water," "Across the Track Blues," and "I'm Getting Sentimental Over You," from *Walk on the Water*, DRG Records SL-5194, September 1980. Laurie Frink, Barry Ries, Tom Harrell, Mike Davis, Danny Hayes: trumpets; Keith O'Quinn, Dave Glenn (slide), Alan Raph (bass): trombones; Gerry Niewood (alto), Ken Hitchcock (alto and tenor), Gary Keller (tenor), Ralph Olson, Seth Broedy, Eric Turkel (soprano), Gerry Mulligan (baritone and soprano), Joe Temperly (baritone): saxophones; Mitchel Forman: piano; Jay Leonhart, Mike Bocchicchio: bass; Richie DeRosa: drums

Walk on the Water expands these new factors in Mulligan's art to their largest dimension, a full-size band equal to the abortive 1957 group that had proven too unwieldy for the sound Gerry wanted at

the time (and that came three years later with the CJB). What's
different now is that both Mulligan's playing and writing have
changed, lightening up quite a bit in terms of chordal density and
letting the horns hang back in favor of attention to the rhythm section. As a result, there is even more open space than in his very first
big-band arrangements of the late forties, which had been noted for
their airiness. The *Walk on the Water* charts have the least section
work of any of his big-band albums; most often, Mulligan's horn is out
in front of just the rhythm players, with plenty of room for other
soloists to come in before the theme is restated at the end by the
ensemble.

This new approach is apparent on the opening selection, Mulligan's
already familiar new composition "For an Unfinished Woman." For
the opening theme, handled before by piano, Gerry employs not the
full band but just the trumpets, muted for further reduction (and to
make their attack more like the high keys of the piano). This new
format allows an even deeper-sounding voice for his counterpointing
bari playing beneath. After this, his solo parts demand only occasional
interpolations from the orchestra, their parts leading in and out of
each other in concerto grosso fashion, another touch from the CJB. It
is only for the final chorus that the brass blows with open bells,
emphasizing their choir effect. The same structure prevails on another previously recorded yet relatively new number, "Song for
Strayhorn," except that the full brass is called on earlier to create a
rich cushion for the baritone, which has returned to Mulligan's original strong sentiment. For the initial bridge and out chorus, these
fully voiced trumpets take on the tonality of a Broadway pit orchestra,
clearing the way for some solos unencumbered by anything other
than an almost subliminal trombone riff. To end the piece Mulligan
gives the brass section a variation on his theme and then takes the out
chorus himself, an inverse reflection of the song's beginning.

Mulligan's fun with the curved soprano sax continues on "42nd and
Broadway," the third of his four compositions and six arrangements
on this album of seven tunes. A deceptively simple line, its repetition
shows how much can be accomplished with so little, given the resources at hand; here the new band plays in 1940s-1950s fashion,
doing much exchanging between the riffing sections, all of which get
to play their appropriate variation of their leader's tune. The same
tiny horn takes a featured role on the title cut, "Walk on the Water,"
where it now functions as a section instrument, leading the other
saxes (one of which is a straight soprano, the harsher tonality of which
makes for an interesting voicing that runs right down through the

altos and tenors). In the company of pianist Mitchel Forman's "Angelica," a tune apparently written with Mulligan's bari style in mind, the album concludes with two tributes to Gerry's predecessors in big-band jazz: Duke Ellington and Tommy Dorsey. For Ellington it's a literal transcription (and tonal re-creation) of "Across the Track Blues," in which that orchestra's classic sounds are faithfully reproduced, from the overly sweet harmonizing trombones and sax section led at its top range by a pair of screeching clarinets, to Mulligan's baritone itself, which is played in deep vibrato as a bow to Harry Carney, both in its solo and section-leading guises. That Mulligan can imitate this style is remarkable, given his own idiosyncratic approach to the big horn. But his arranger's pen is just as graceful for Dorsey's old theme, which is here taken upbeat via some inventive orchestral fills behind the soloists, two of which (tenor and alto) are able to use this formerly staid vehicle for some spirited trading of fours.

Walk on the Water paints its effects with a broad brush, but never one that obstructs the clarity of Mulligan's new style. The orchestral effects are rich when present, yet never overused; instead, theirs is such a rare sweetness that each occasion of their playing is a treat. Unlike earlier big-band albums, Mulligan keeps his own horn out front as often as it would be in a smaller group; the great constant among the *Idol Gossip*, *Walk on the Water*, and *Little Big Horn* LPs is the regular presence of his most characteristic playing, highlighted in its lead function whether his supporting group be an aggregation of four, six, or fifteen pieces.

- *Gerry Mulligan:* "Little Big Horn" and "Another Kind of Sunday," from *Little Big Horn*, GRP Records GRP-A-1003, 1983. Marvin Stamm, Alan Rubin: trumpets; Keith O'Quinn: trombone; Lou Marini (alto), Michael Brecker (tenor), Gerry Mulligan (baritone): saxophones; Dave Grusin: keyboards; Anthony Jackson; bass; Buddy Williams: drums. "Under a Star": Gerry Mulligan: baritone saxophone; Dave Grusin: piano and OBX synthesizer; Jay Leonhart: bass; Buddy Williams: drums. "Bright Angel Falls": Gerry Mulligan: baritone saxophone; Dave Grusin: electric piano; Richard Tee: acoustic piano; Anthony Jackson: bass; Buddy Williams: drums. "Sun on Stairs" and "I Never Was a Young Man": Gerry Mulligan: baritone saxophone (and vocal on last number); Dave Grusin: piano; Jay Leonhart: bass; Butch Miles (replaced by Buddy Miles on last number): drums.

On *Little Big Horn* itself, Mulligan found the format so effective in supporting his well-known musical voice that the album won a

Grammy Award. There are sufficient contemporary elements in this production to make it sound attractive to commercial ears, such as synthesizer and electric piano on several numbers, plus an impeccably staffed horn section (Marvin Stamm and Alan Rubin, trumpets; Keith O'Quinn, trombone; Lou Marini, alto sax; Michael Brecker, tenor; plus Mulligan himself taking the section's bari line, a reminder that these cuts were multitracked). All of the tunes are Mulligan's own, though pianist Dave Grusin shares credit for helping with the arrangements (most of which draw heavily on his acoustic piano, Fender Rhodes, and OBX synthesizer). Gerry's own presence, especially in these award-winning circumstances, helps explain his attractiveness to a pop artist such as Barry Manilow, who would almost at once engage Mulligan's services on the first of two jazz-influenced albums employing the saxophonist's distinctive stylings and sound. American music tends to glamorize the celebrityhood of such sound, be it Frank Sinatra's voice or Louis Armstrong's brightly cutting trumpet. It is a tribute to Gerry Mulligan's integrity that he has been able to play this game and—with the Grammy Award and the Manilow sessions—win, all witout pandering to simplified tastes or even taking an edge off what remain the essentials of his style.

That style carries the six cuts of *Little Big Horn*. The title track is one of two that uses the six-piece horn section, but only following the theme's introduction by the core of baritone, piano (Fender Rhodes here), bass, and drums; the tail end of the theme and the bridge are supported by some tight riffs that continue through the initial out chorus. Mulligan keeps the lead to himself right into his solo, which is played in the same driving manner, inviting the horns in for some support near the end. Rhythmic push and a busier-than-usual drummer are by now a familiar element in the new Mulligan style, and Grusin's solo playing augments this feel by using the electric piano for left-hand chords while his melodic line is taken on the acoustic instrument. For the last time through Mulligan double tracks the bari line as a way of integrating himself with the section, whose fills on the out chorus therefore take more prominence.

By contrast, "Under a Star" is a slow and rich synthesizer piece within which Mulligan's horn can play its lyrically sweetest. As befits its ballad nature, the song features Mulligan for all but the first and second phrases of the last chorus, where Grusin takes a fitting interlude before the bari restates its theme with even fuller sentiment. For a slow number like this, the synthesizer offers the impression of a full orchestral treatment, which prepares for the contrast of the next cut, a fully acoustic quartet treatment of an old-style Mulligan composition titled "Sun on Stairs." The piece draws on the perkiness of the Brookmeyer years and the sharp intonation and miniaturization effect of the original quartet with Chet Baker; Mulligan's pert line is answered by the piano in the manner of Baker's 1952 trumpet, while the bridge makes a further bow to the past by rephrasing the thematic line from "Venus de Milo." The selection's placement is another of Mulligan's political statements: that he can still write appealing tunes in the manner he'd perfected three decades before and—more important—that such material could now be played in the context of studio horn sections and synthesizers and sound just as attractive and just as integral to his overall approach.

The album's highlight is the cut beginning side B, "Another Kind of Sunday." The composition is pure Mulligan, an easily syncopated swing in the manner of "Walking Shoes," but its treatment is greatly enriched by the freshest elements of his recent approaches to both writing and playing. Like so many of his new numbers, it is built on an exceedingly simple line whose repetition is enhanced by contributions from the rhythm section and from orchestral voicings. The theme itself is briefly introduced by acoustic piano, just long enough for its funky percussive character to take hold with the listener so that when it is taken up by the horns the feeling remains one of a strutting backbeat keyboard. Throughout the piece Mulligan lopes around with the feel of a walking bass, his playing not only closely responding to the rhythm but taking on a strongly rhythmic character itself. Dave Grusin doubles on both electric and acoustic piano, giving the bari the same style of sharp-punched support his own soloing showed on "Little Big Horn" a side before. Moving in and around the horn riff that's repeated throughout the tune, Mulligan has the enjoyable time of his life with this composition, reaching to the point of $\frac{6}{8}$ triplets as the trumpet-led section struts out of the piece in classic Dixieland fashion. Given the exceptionally creative interplay Mulligan's horn creates among the number's melodic, rhythmic, and ensemble work, the piece demands to be choreographed.

This "get up and dance" feeling is sustained on "Bright Angel Falls," in which Grusin's Fender Rhodes is joined by Richard Tee's acoustic piano to recreate the funky feeling of Tee's contemporaneous "Saturday Night Live" studio band, Stuff. Mulligan writes the piece so as to emphasize the contrast between an opening legato passage and the song's interior rocking beat, a way of playing with the somewhat classical style of theme and variation he'd been using in his scoring for the film *La Menace*. On the more rhythmic parts his sax playing approaches the style Tom Scott had used on "One to

Ten in Ohio" from *The Age of Steam* (Scott's style is itself a tribute
to the Junior Walker-King Curtis approach to funky tenor). When
the two pianos go at each other in a simultaneous solo, Mulligan's
sense of spontaneous polyphony is reborn in a thoroughly contemporary setting.

"I Never Was a Young Man," which concludes *Little Big Horn,*
begins with the piano tinkling out the familiar style of a classic Mulligan ditty, which one expects to find picked up by Gerry's saxophone. Instead, we hear the man himself singing a line about the
relative merits of youth and age, in an exceptionally innocent-
sounding voice that belies his current appearance as a grey and shaggy
guru. It is the same sharp Irish tenor, full of spunk and brightness,
that joshed the late-arriving audience for the *California Concerts*
about playing some blues while they got seated. Here the message is
again comically sharp, advising that he'd never been a young man
even when he was a young man, since professional goals always had
him chasing that mountain called Downtown. Having sacrificed the
joys of youth, he now intends to be an old man—a really, really old
man—who will enjoy the pleasurable irascibility of advanced age
while caring not a lick about getting to that next goal, Heaven, since
that place is more than likely just to have another mountain waiting,
of which he's had plenty already. The song's lightness makes it a
pleasantly upbeat ending to the album, but its message serves as a
good explanation of how the extremely healthy accomplishments of
his own groups' last three albums have been achieved.

As always, Mulligan has spent this recent phase of his career taking
on various other assignments, none having deflected from his development reaching from *The Age of Steam* through *Little Big Horn* but
most of which reflects passing interest at best—a case of fulfilling his
duties as a major and now senior spokesman for the traditions of jazz
in our time. On 4 February 1972 this role found him working with a
stage full of all-star musicians welcoming the return to work of Charles
Mingus. With two dozen players participating, the results are less
than a clear-cut interpretation of and collaboration with Mingus, but
the double album's worth of material preserved on *Mingus and
Friends in Concert* (Columbia KG-31614) indicates how jazz itself was
becoming a bit funkier and bluesier under the impact of the same
fusion trend Mulligan had been following in his own work. Although
there are no rock elements in the concert, the central presence of
tenor saxophonist Gene Ammons moves the affair quite prominently
in the direction of blues roots (another interest of Mulligan's, to-

gether with Dave Brubeck). Although Gerry solos on just three cuts ("E's Flat, Ah's Flat Too," "Little Royal Suite," and "E.S.P."), his bari can be heard as an important element in most of the numbers. Noteworthy is master-of-ceremonies Bill Cosby's comic conducting of "Honeysuckle Rose," in which the ensemble reacts to the man's frantic wavings and gesturings with a series of melodic and rhythmic variations and free jazz improvisings suggesting barrelhouse disorder courting the edge of structural chaos and atonal cacophony. Throughout this piece Mulligan's horn can be heard among the initial responses to change, just as on the scat-sung "Ool-ya-koo" he suggests the figures used to fill behind Cosby and Dizzy Gillespie's vocals. The classic Mulligan voice is most apparent in the ensemble work on "Us Is Two," where his horn's cellolike tonality both deepens Mingus's line and keeps the band swinging through the tune's changes.

Later in the decade Lionel Hampton would produce and play on a series of albums hosting such luminaries as Teddy Wilson, Dexter Gordon, Earl Hines, and Buddy Rich—plus Mulligan on his own featured album and in the company of Charles Mingus on another. For *Lionel Hampton Presents: Gerry Mulligan* (Who's Who in Jazz WWLP-21007) Hampton is the functional leader, even though four of the six numbers are Mulligan's own. The instrumentation is virtually the same as Gerry's *Idol Gossip* group, with a basic core of sax, vibes, and guitar, plus a rhythm section of piano, bass, and drums that is here augmented by congas, another recent Mulliganesque feature. But Hampton's strong presence casts the sound in entirely different terms, harking back to the swing-age feel of Hamp's work with the Benny Goodman Sextet. It is interesting to hear tunes like "Apple Core" and "Line for Lyons" played in this style, another reminder of how strong are Mulligan's roots in the swing era. Though his own solos are in character, the larger context remains Hampton's, all the way to recasting "Line for Lyons" as a medium-swing shuffle for which Gerry dutifully adapts his melody but then solos in a manner having little to do with his original writing of the song. If the album can be said to make a contribution to the serious Mulligan canon, it would be the introduction of a new ballad, "Song for Johnny Hodges," the flowing smoothness of which proves a natural vehicle for both Gerry's horn and Hamp's active but easy vibes.

Lionel Hampton was again the moving force that brought Mulligan into the studio with an ailing Charles Mingus eight days later. This 6 November 1977 session yielded *Lionel Hampton Presents: The Music of Charles Mingus* (Who's Who in Jazz WWLP-21005), in which Mulligan serves as part of Mingus's familiar ten-piece ensemble and

also solos on each number. For the most part, Gerry's playing adapts
itself to the dominant Mingus format, which even catches Hampton
up in its heavily idiosyncratic style. For his solos, Mulligan appears to
relish the bass player's odd chord changes, which enhance rather than
confuse his own characteristic sense of angularity in bending an improvised melody. On a classic such as "Slop," Mulligan's horn fits as
naturally as would any of Mingus's stable of performers, and the
deeply encompassing sweep of his bari playing lends an added dimension to "Fables of Faubus." The ten numbers from the Mingus
catalog, about equally divided between well-known and less familiar
pieces, keep Mulligan on his toes, leaving no space for him to slack off
into festival jam session blowing; the only time he appears lazily
comfortable is on the slow-paced "Caroline Keikki Mingus," when he
spends half a phrase playing a familiar whole-note backing line behind
Woody Shaw's trumpet solo. The session's true accomplishment,
however, is obvious when compared to Mulligan's recordings with
Thelonious Monk twenty years earlier. There the pianist's sui generis
style had at times confused Mulligan's playing, with Monk calling
Gerry off any time the bari threatened to sound like West Coast jazz.
Here there is no such danger, perhaps because of the presence of a
fair-sized ensemble and distinctive charts to guide it, but at least
partly thanks to Mulligan's immensely broader experience. One must
not forget that for the *Mulligan Meets Monk* session Gerry had less
than a decade's experience playing in small groups, with over half
such work being within the distinctive confines of his pianoless quartet. Now, by 1977, he had carried his horn through sessions with most
of the world's major jazz musicians and had deepened and developed
his own style through the extensive series of meetings following the
Monk date, his Concert Jazz Band and work with Judy Holliday, the
sextet with guitarist Jim Hall, the years of collaboration with Brubeck,
and the first six years of his fusion work beginning with *The Age of
Steam*. Coming into a studio and creating the functional bridge between such diverse talents as Lionel Hampton and Charles Mingus
was something he was almost uniquely equipped to do.

• **Mel Tormé–Gerry Mulligan:** "Real Thing" and "Medley: Line
  for Lyons, Venus de Milo, Walking Shoes," from *Mel Tormé and
  Friends Recorded at Marty's in New York City*, Finesse W2X-
  37484, May 1981. Mel Tormé: vocal; Gerry Mulligan: baritone
  saxophone; Mike Renzi: piano; Jay Leonhart: bass; Donny Osborn: drums.

Other dates would reaffirm Mulligan's more personal qualities, from the nature of his quartet work in the early 1950s to his collaboration with Judy Holliday a decade later. Both factors figure prominently in the partial set contributed to the *Mel Tormé and Friends* album recorded live in 1981. For this occasion Tormé introduces Mulligan for the premiere of their words-and-music collaboration, "The Real Thing." Though conceived verbally with Tormé's new wife in mind, the tune's nature recalls almost uncannily the nature of the Mulligan-Holliday projects collected on *Holliday with Mulligan*. Mel's lyrics grow naturally from Gerry's music, and when the bari comes in for some background accompaniment for the bridge it's as if Mulligan is meeting himself within his own art. His quiet support is a reminder of the old quartet format of one horn backing the other's lead line; as with the Judy Holliday numbers twenty years before, Gerry displays a quiet yet compelling sense of genius in knowing just how much to offer in complement to Tormé's voice. His sax solo is similarly restrained, keeping close to the melody that is this song's true lyric statement. For the last phrase, voice and horn are almost equally prominent—not because Gerry plays more or louder but because the two voices reach toward each other from their respective poles to find a commonly human meeting ground. Yet, as with Judy Holliday, such collaborations demand a comparable amount of genius on both parts. With Mel Tormé, vocalist and lyricist talents manage to hold their own with Gerry's sense of composition and improvising. A few years later, singer Barry Manilow would draw on both men's contributions, but with less success.

But first there's a three-part medley in which Mulligan and Tormé reveal an enduring quality of Gerry's work. The piece is introduced to the audience at Marty's as an encore, but the material is obviously rehearsed and in part specially written. The tunes are three of Gerry's oldest: "Line for Lyons," "Venus de Milo," and "Walking Shoes," representing in turn his first quartet, his writing for and playing in the Miles Davis *Birth of the Cool* sessions, and the contribution of his California tentette. These were three diverse enterprises, but in performance with Tormé, Mulligan reminds listeners of their essential compositional and performative integrity. For the first, Mel takes Chet Baker's lead line, with just enough breathiness to recall the trumpeter's hallmark style. Gerry reprises his own part on this number, playing a counter line in and around, above and below the Baker-Tormé melody, and as with the ending of "The Real Thing" we're reminded of how instrumental Mel's voice can sound when he wishes, just as Gerry's horn sings with an unmistakably human quality. Following his solo, Mulligan completes the picture by backing Tormé's scat singing in his patented quartet manner. "Venus de Milo," with its somewhat more ethereal melody having been crafted by Miles Davis's and Lee Konitz's high-reaching horns, takes Tormé to the upper reaches of his range, while Mulligan proves how much of the accompanying orchestral line, which back in 1949 had included trombone, French horn, and tuba in addition to Gerry's horn, is conceivable for bari alone. Finally, for "Walking Shoes" Tormé reveals more collaborative talent by giving over the first two songs' scatting for some original words matching both the melody and title-implied theme of Mulligan's song from nearly thirty years before. The lyrics are especially well-turned, their assonance, alliteration, and rhyme matching the recurrent motifs in the melody. The brisker pace, however, transforms its execution into a more standard thirty-two-bar vehicle, to which Gerry reacts with an atypical, boppish solo, complete with strings of thirty-second notes in Charlie Parker fashion—no space for easy loping here.

Answering pop singer Barry Manilow's call for work on two jazz-flavored commercial LPs, *2:00 AM Paradise Café* (Arista AL8-8254) in 1984 and *Swing Street* (Arista AL-8527) in 1987, Mulligan was asked to lend his fame and credibility to a project also drawing on the strengths of Mel Tormé, Sarah Vaughan, and veteran jazz sidemen Shelly Manne, George Duvivier, Mundell Lowe, and Bill Mays. The fact that nearly all the material is Manilow's own prevents these albums from being true jazz works, nor is Manilow anywhere near the artist Tormé is; hence there's little of the mutually creditable interplay that distinguished the latter's work with Mulligan. Moreover, these newer albums' highly produced nature allows little chance for playing away from the score, and for the second LP, where Mulligan works on just a single cut, his part is tracked separately at a second recording studio a continent away. The *Paradise Café* cuts, which actually brought the key players together in a Los Angeles studio, stand a better chance of drawing out the true qualities of Mulligan's work, and on "What Am I Doin' Here" he devises some attractive interplaying with Manilow's voice, much as he had weaved around the trumpet leads of another putative vocalist, Chet Baker, so many years before. Other times Mulligan creates some quasi-ensemble effects with Manilow's piano, but the slow pace of the entire complement of numbers gives Gerry little chance for solo expertise beyond sounding his horn's distinctive voice—which is, after all, why Manilow hired him. That Mulligan can sound so natural in these circumstances, yet without playing a note that compromises his jazz ethic, shows not only how broad is the range of his playing but how what was, back in 1946, the unlikeliest of saxophones to accompany a torch singer can now handle the job as well as tenor or alto, another tribute to Gerry's lyricism.

● ***Quincy Jones–Gerry Mulligan:*** "Main Title Track," "Seldom Seen Sam," "Parole Party," "Miasmo," "Sahara Stone," "Slam City," "Listen to the Melody/Dixie Tag," and "End Title," from *The Hot Rock,* Prophesy SD-6055, 1972. Quincy Jones: leader and composer; Clark Terry: trumpet; Jerome Richardson (clarinet, soprano, and tenor), Gerry Mulligan (baritone): saxophones; Frank Rosolino: trombone; Clare Fisher: piano; Ray Brown, Chuck Rainey, Carol Kaye: bass; Grady Tate: drums; Victor Feldman, Emil Richards: vibraphone and percussion; Dennis Budimir: guitar; Mike Melvoin: synthesizer; Tommy Tedesco, Bobbi Porter, Milt Holland: percussion.

At points between the extremes of playing in Charles Mingus's ensembles and integrating himself with Barry Manilow's voice and piano are Mulligan's film and symphonic work of the 1970s and 1980s. Yet with each can be found specific elements of performing and writing that had been developing since the *Age of Steam* LP in 1971— elements that in turn build on strengths in his playing and composing traceable as far back as his initial work for big bands in the 1940s. The year after *The Age of Steam* finds Gerry taking important solo leads in Quincy Jones's score for a Robert Redford film, *The Hot Rock.* Mulligan's horn work figures prominently on seven of the soundtrack album's twelve cuts, functioning as a motif element but also making strong jazz statements on its own. The picture's theme song, "Listen to the Melody," pits a tuneful figure against an ominously impending snare-drum effect and an organ line that alternates between eeriness and the carnivalesque. When Gerry makes his first appearance within the "Main Title Track," it is to restate this lyric theme but in a way that can sound radically different depending on its context, whether played against calliope organ or more haunting orchestral ponderings. His freest playing comes in a minor character's signature piece, "Seldom Seen Sam." Here baritone sax takes the lead over some odd, heartbeat style rhythm that grows in intensity and complexity as a way of directing the tune, a reminder of what percussion had been invited to do on *The Age of Steam.* Eventually such flexibility leads to some interesting free-form lines exchanged between Mulligan and

Clark Terry, a style that segues directly into the linear busyness of "Parole Party," where thirty-second-note runs tumble amid high-speed bongo drums until the competing waves of sound resolve themselves into an anticipation of New Age space music.

Mulligan's most distinctive work, however, takes place in the film's second half, where the bari figures in all of the score's thematic and atmospheric statements. "Miasmo" places the big horn among a haunting wind ensemble that slowly gives way to a line picked up by trombone and muted trumpet, again supported by bongos and other complex rhythm, while "Sahara Stone" shows how the tonal qualities of a Middle Eastern theme can blend logically with some bari figures played against a conventional Western orchestra, another reminder of thematic elements of *The Hot Rock*'s story line. The tense climax of this cops-and-robbers narrative is sounded by the bari's weird voice on "Slam City"; what André Previn had used in an almost comic sense for *The Fortune Cookie* is here employed by Quincy Jones for stunning dramatic effect. But the most surprising touch recalls Mulligan's own scoring for *Luv*, where old-fashioned Dixieland could not only cue a character but invite the soundtrack musicians to stretch out on their horns. This is precisely what Quincy Jones asks for in the film's last two cuts, "Listen to the Melody/Dixie Tag" and "End Title." On both the familiar theme is stated by baritone sax and the other horns, only to have the musicians break out of its somewhat commercial, rinky-dink rhythm to blow the tune and its changes through some exuberant, kicked-back Dixie polyphony. For the first track, the tempo is fast and celebratory, while in the second it is more relaxed and loping, being passed back and forth with a more customary rendering of the film's theme. Structurally, the Dixieland tracks serve to end things on an upbeat note, reminding the audience how these good-time, free-spirited elements have been latent in the music all along. In terms of Mulligan's work alone, it is a joy to hear him blowing so easily and naturally in a Dixieland session traditional enough to satisfy any purist.

Gerry Mulligan's film work has always seemed coincidental with other aspects of his writing and performing. The fact that he wrote and played the score for *Luv* relates to his work for André Previn on a similar Jack Lemmon movie the year before, *The Fortune Cookie*, which in turn connects to his association with Previn years before during the filming of *The Subterraneans*. A similar trail takes him into the company of those involved with a 1973 British film, *The Final Programme*, released in the United States as *The Last Days of Man on Earth* (Embassy Home Entertainment video cassette, VHS-4033). Two years before, Gerry's growing interests in both jazz-rock fusion and contemporary symphonic music had drawn him to two San Francisco musicians with similar interests, Paul Beaver and Bernard L. Krause—a project that yielded the *Gandharva* album plus inspiration for Gerry's tune "Country Beaver" on *The Age of Steam.* Now Beaver and Krause were doing the score for this Robert Fuest cinematic adaptation of Michael Moorcock's science fiction novel; remembering Mulligan's haunting baritone sound on the *Gandharva* tracks, many of which are reflected in the score for this film, the two drafted an important musical part for him and made sure Gerry was available to play it.

The part itself does not appear until relatively late in the film, when the hero finally kills his antagonist, and the way is cleared toward resolving the plot. For this number, Beaver and Krause lay down a deep pipe-organ background reminiscent of Mulligan's "By Your Grace," adding harp as used on several *Gandharva* tracks, and bringing in the baritone sax for a slow lead statement. Much more so than did Quincy Jones, Beaver and Krause draw on Mulligan's smoothly flowing yet full-voiced resonance, using pipe organ and harp to showcase Gerry's way of playing the horn more like a cello than the umppa-pa instrument its inventor had in mind. For the film's end credits, Mulligan repeats this number with full orchestral accompaniment and as such it becomes one of his more noteworthy performances of the early 1970s, especially in the way it highlights his ability to sail his big horn's vocallike line over the supporting instruments with no sense of clutter at all. This strong but effortless voice would become his seventies trademark, a clear step beyond both his polyphonous combo style of the 1950s and his spotlight soloing in concerto grosso manner with the Concert Jazz Band.

- *Sergio Mendes–Gerry Mulligan:* "Meu Mundo é Uma Bola (My Life Is a Ball)," "Voltando a Baurú (Back to Baurú)," "A Tristeza do Adeus (The Sadness of Goodbye)" [two versions], "Amor e Agressão (Love and Aggression)," and "Meu Mundo é Bola (My Life Is a Ball)" [second version], from *Pelé,* Atlantic SD-18231, 1977. Sergio Mendes: leader and composer; Gerry Mulligan: soprano and baritone saxophones; Pelé, Oscar Castro Neves: guitars; Chico Spider: keyboards; Bill Dickinson: bass; Jimmy Keltner: drums; Steve Forman, Laudir de Oliveira, Chacal: percussion; Pelé, Gracinha Leporace, Carol Rogers: vocals.

Such playing and writing demand an awareness of rhythm that in the 1960s had been new to jazz. While not exclusively Latin, such multifaceted activeness made an obvious impression on bossa nova music, with which Mulligan had been toying as early as the *"Jeru"* album of 1962. It would be another film gig, this time under the leadership of Sergio Mendes (whose Brasil '66 group had parlayed such South American rhythms into pop fame), that brought Gerry solidly into the tradition. The occasion is a film directed by François Reichenbach and produced in Mexico during 1977, *Pelé*. A documentary honoring the retirement of the great Brazilian soccer star, the film boasts a soundtrack that invites Mulligan to collaborate with not just young American studio fusion rockers but such Brazilian percussionists as Laudir de Oliveira and the legendary Chacal. As with his *Age of Steam* group, he plays both baritone and soprano saxes and shows the same ability to spin a melodic line that at once complements and draws energy from the extremely busy rhythm supporting it.

The *Pelé* soundtrack album (Atlantic SD-18231) reveals how Mulligan's horn work is integrated with all aspects of the evolving score. The film's main theme is "Meu Mundo é Uma Bola (My Life Is a Ball)," composed and sung by Pelé himself. For this softly voiced, lilting melody the rhythm is steady and easy, taking its cue from Pelé's guitar strumming. For the second phrase, however, Mulligan's baritone sax joins in with an equally melodic fill, answering the vocal part with a similar statement taking some of its shape from the rhythmic support evident at the start. Following some incidental tracks is the active and lively "Voltando a Baurú (Back to Baurú)," where Gerry's toylike curved soprano proves an ideal voice for skipping around the fast, tight rhythm as it enjoys a truly Latin melody with none of the patronizing gestures that at times detracted from the material on *Compadres* a decade before. "A Tristeza do Adeus (The Sadness of Goodbye)" is the score's first deeply serious movement, and for it Mendes uses the bari in two different ways: first, as the number is played slowly by synthesizers and various keyboards, Gerry's horn fills in very softly in the background; then as the rhythm reshapes the piece as a samba, the baritone moves from supporting fills to a gently played, almost wispy enunciation of the theme, emphasizing the instrument's reediness rather than its deep-voiced timbre. In dancelike fashion Gerry moves both with and around rhythm and keyboard, weaving the tune's chord changes a different way each time, sometimes favoring a third or fifth, other times bending along right with the melody's basic note. For the up-tempo "Amor e

Agressão (Love and Aggression)" the baritone begins in unison with the singer's voices, then stands alone to carry the theme; as occasions for solos develop, Mulligan alternately floats above and engages the very busy rhythm taking shape around him, another *Age of Steam* hallmark in his style. Yet even here Gerry is careful to let the rhythm section lead the way rather than trying to bend it overly much to his purpose; from the start there have been two elements to draw on— the drums' fast action and the keyboard's slow tolling of percussive chords—and from these two examples Mulligan is able to fashion a universe of rhythmic variations for his own solo lines. Similar inter- action with voice characterizes the baritone's role on a reprise of the main theme, which ends the film. Gerry's horn introduces them, comes back for a solo, then rejoins them for the same melodic fill used at the movie's beginning. As credits role, Mulligan plays on in a style of strong, compositional improvisation, shaping new songs within the confines of this now familiar tune. Yet even here there's time for a surprise, as for the fadeout he quickly shifts to soprano sax for an even more lyric goodbye.

- *Gerry Mulligan:* "Dance of the Truck," "Introspect," "Watching and Waiting," "Trucking Again," "New Wine," "The Trap," "Theme," "Vines of Bordeaux," "The House They'll Never Live In," "Watching and Waiting" (reprise), "The Pantomimist," "In- trospect" (reprise), "Vines of Bordeaux" (reprise), from *"La Menace" Original Motion Picture Soundtrack*, DRG Records MRS-506, film released in 1977, this recording made in 1982. Gerry Mulligan: soprano and baritone saxophones, clarinet, key- boards, composer, and leader; Dave Grusin, Derek Smith, Tom Fay: keyboards; Peter Levin: Moog synthesizer; Edward Walsh: Oberheim synthesizer; Jack Six, Jay Leonhart: bass; Bob Rosen- garden, Michael Di Pasqua: drums.

In 1977 Mulligan not only performed on the *Pelé* soundtrack but wrote his most important film score, the intricate set of compositions serving as the music for French director Alain Corneau's *La Menace*. The recorded version employs a ten-piece group, the most prominent features of which, besides Mulligan's horn, are the acoustic and elec- tric pianos and two styles of synthesizers, Moog and Oberheim. All ten never play together, for there is much substituting from track to track, with bassists Jack Six and Jay Leonhart and pianists Dave Grusin and Tom Fay (both of whom have arranged with Mulligan) sharing duties on those instruments. Most important to the album's concept, there is no other horn, although Mulligan occasionally dubs a second track on soprano; the feeling is that of *Idol Gossip,* albeit with a heavy dose of electronic effects from the synthesizers. The key is that Mulligan relies more and more on his single line out in front of an increasingly busy rhythm section, an aspect of his style that can be traced as far back as the *"Jeru"* album in 1962.

Rhythmic variations behind Gerry's often legato line makes the *La Menace* score, which dates from the 1977 filming but was not produced as a Mulligan-led album until five years later, as rich and varied as anything on his *Idol Gossip, Walk on the Water,* and *Little Big Horn* LPs. Because the numbers are thematically integrated, as a film score should be, his work here serves as an album-length coda to his compositional and playing styles from those three projects and also directs attention to the effects he would achieve in his symphonic works premiered just two years later. The score's technique of rephrasing an initial line through various tempos, time signatures, and orchestral settings gives the work a unified feeling, much like an extended classical piece; Mulligan's devotion to melody, through as many variations as possible on such a minimal element, creates a self-consciously compositional feel. Among the work's ten numbers (and three reprises) there is only one departure, the cameolike appearance of "The Pantomimist," in which Mulligan's clarinet playing recreates the Hal Kemp sound of that reed instrument played within a megaphone, a style Gerry may well have drawn on first for his teenage work with the Tommy Tucker society band. All other aspects of the score are exquisitely balanced, including several pieces running a minute or less, in contrast to the usual length of three to five minutes.

- **Gerry Mulligan–Houston Symphony Orchestra:** "Entente for Baritone Sax and Orchestra," "The Sax Chronicles," "Song for Strayhorn," "K-4 Pacific," from *Symphonic Dreams,* Pro Acoustic Digital Recordings PAD-703, 6–7 February 1987. Gerry Mulligan: baritone saxophone, with the Houston Symphony Orchestra conducted by Erich Kunzel; Bill Mays: piano; Dean Johnson: bass; Rich DeRosa: drums (piano, bass, and drums join Mulligan and the symphony for the last two numbers).

The main theme from *La Menace* has a distinct Beethoven cast to it, a style Mulligan finds natural to the deep baritone sax and closely accompanying piano, particularly when the two instruments engage in counterpointed interplay. His interest in developing a catalog of

symphonic works for baritone sax dates back at least to his performance of Bill Holman's "Music for Baritone Saxophone and Orchestra" with the Los Angeles Neophonic Orchestra in 1966, of which no
commercial recording exists. A wealth of such material graces *Symphonic Dreams*, a 6–7 February 1987 recording with the Houston
Symphony Orchestra (directed by Erich Kunzel) assembling works
Mulligan had been performing since 1984 with symphonies in the
United States and Europe. There are three varieties of the classical
Mulligan here: his twelve-minute composition, "Entente for Baritone"; the five-piece "Sax Chronicles," in which Harry Freedman
adapts several of Gerry's tunes to historically classical settings; and
concerto grosso performances of "Song for Strayhorn" and "K-4 Pacific." These last numbers work a two-way street, showing how a
symphony orchestra can play honest jazz and revealing the rich properties of Mulligan's playing and writing. "Strayhorn" is performed
with the same scoring pianist Tom Fay used in adapting Mulligan's
arrangement to the *Walk on the Water* big-band context, although
Gerry's additional writing for the strings shows that he has a great
command of that section's voice. It's "K-4 Pacific," in an arrangement
entirely Mulligan's own, that fully integrates his quartet's performance with the symphony orchestra's; there are strong supporting
elements for his own strong solo plus segments by piano, bass, and
even drums, but the piece's major accomplishment is its revelation of
the classical elements within Mulligan's original composition, a matter of counterpointing rhythm and melody that jazz and symphonic
music have in common.

There are two approaches to classical music itself among the album's more complex works. Mulligan's "Entente for Baritone" features a slow baritone line over the strings, followed by punctuations
from the brass, after which the string section's line grows into a part
for woodwinds; finally, the brass is given a chance for some solid
jazz-style swinging, but only after every other aspect of the symphony
orchestra has been exploited. If there is a theme to this piece, it is
Mulligan's style of improvisation; throughout there are references to
his favorite styles of playing, with allusive quotes to the approaches
he has taken in so many different contexts over the past forty years.
On the other hand, "The Sax Chronicles" pays tribute to his writing,
particularly the distinctive melodic lines he has devised in songwriting over these same decades. The classical compositions are a collaboration with Harry Freedman, and there's a bit of whimsy involved as
the suite is constructed according to the hypothetical proposition that
composers from Bach to Debussy might have written symphonic ma-

terial for the baritone sax had Mulligan been around to influence
them as a virtuoso performer (in the manner that many important
classical works were created with specific star soloists of the day in
mind, incorporating their own flourishes of style as part of the theme).
In this way "Sun on the Bach Stairs" uses the melody from Mulligan's
"Sun on Stairs" (*Little Big Horn*) to create a Bach-like effect, the
strings answering his bari line as did Dave Grusin's piano (itself im-
itating Chet Baker's trumpet). As befits the tonal abstractions of a
later composer's work, "Sax in Debussy's Garden" quotes no discern-
able Mulligan theme, but "Sax in Mozart Minor" finds that Gerry's
"Festive Minor" is already amazingly close to that composer's spirit.
There is even a more publicly Viennese taste to Mulligan's work, as
revealed by the interpolation of "Taurus Moon" (*Idol Gossip*) with
"Under a Star" (*Little Big Horn*) in "Sax and Der Rosenkavalier,"
showing how the two lines reflect each other and how the latter lends
itself to a grand-waltz treatment worthy of the finest Strauss melody.
Finally, "A Walk with Brahms" quotes the thematic line from *La
Menace*, Mulligan's last major composition before undertaking these
chronicles and thus tying together these two aspects of his work.

The most recent period of Gerry Mulligan's development, then,
has been as various and multifaceted as any segment in his career. In
the late 1940s he was gigging with smaller groups at the forefront of
jazz innovation at the same time he was still selling conventionally
drafted yet imaginatively original big-band arrangements to Claude
Thornhill and Elliot Lawrence. Even in the midst of his next key
development, the pianoless quartet with Chet Baker, he could organize, write for, and record a substantial number of songs with a
tentette playing a style of music vastly different from the material he
and Baker had been introducing Monday nights at the Haig. The later
1950s and the 1960s had seen more of the same behavior as Mulligan
worked with groups as large as the Concert Jazz Band and as small as
the "*Jeru*" rhythm section with his solitary horn out front. Now, in
the *Age of Steam* era, which had begun with the Beaver and Krause
rock-jazz fusion album and quickly led to his own rhythmically based
the electronically enhanced groups, he had proceeded through several albums devoted almost entirely to his fusion-based compositions
but played by an ever-changing instrumentation, ranging from quartet to fifteen-piece big band, with never the same format twice. He
could collaborate with Italian avant-gardists and write a score for a
French film yet still share a stage with Chet Baker; equally comfortable with Barry Manilow or the Houston Symphony, his playing could

span the range of American musical expression yet never lose its integral jazz character.

It is fitting, therefore, that in 1986 this broadly talented musician, whose career had spanned three distinct eras in the history of jazz—from big-band swing through bebop and its resulting forms of cool and progressive jazz to the fusion age now at hand—could record an album simply for his own enjoyment, yet an LP that would prove as rewardingly listenable as any of the newer directions he'd been exploring for the past decade and a half. Since the late 1940s his happiest and most relaxed playing had been in the company of his close friend Zoot Sims, recorded testimony to which graces their albums with Chubby Jackson (1950), the sextet (1954–1956), the Concert Jazz Band (1960), and lastly their *Something Borrowed, Something Blue* (1966) album, Mulligan's one valid project in a sad mid-decade of disappointment and awkward compromise. With Sims's death, such work was no longer possible, but in company with a new tenor sax star, Scott Hamilton, the feeling of Sims and Mulligan's playing is virtually re-created, a hint that the best of such music just might be immortal.

- **Scott Hamilton–Gerry Mulligan:** "Soft Lights and Sweet Music," "Gone," "Do You Know What I See?," "I've Just Seen Her," "Noblesse," "Ghosts," and "Port of Baltimore Blues," from *Gerry Mulligan Meets Scott Hamilton: Soft Lights and Sweet Music,* Concord Jazz CJ-300, January 1986. Scott Hamilton (tenor), Gerry Mulligan (baritone): saxophones; Mike Renzi: piano; Jay Leonhart: bass; Grady Tate: drums.

Scott Hamilton's tenor playing is similar to Zoot Sims's in its breathy lyricism, but it is also a style born out of Ben Webster and Coleman Hawkins rather than just Lester Young, though all four influences are central to the younger man's work. Yet those imitative features alone would scarcely be sufficient to create such special opportunities for collaboration with a musician of Gerry Mulligan's stature, for Mulligan had played with the originals himself. What happens on this LP is that Gerry brings along five new compositions drafted in the style of his late 1950s "meetings," numbers designed with the guest player's special strengths and stylistic hallmarks in mind; also on the docket are two standards with similar qualities. As a result, the album exudes a sense of loose swinging and easy relaxation, both in the unison themes (on which Mulligan's baritone takes on a tenor-sax coloring and Lester Young flavor) and during the solos. Most crucial, however, is the way Mulligan exploits his old practice of trading phrases, eights, fours, and twos with Sims, the only horn player with whom he played this way; each of the new album's seven cuts has Mulligan and Hamilton trading off, to the exaggerated extent that neither horn ever plays a complete segment alone, for even their individual solos are traded back and forth in several sixteen-bar portions. Such trading adds immensely to the album's relaxed feeling and encourages even more mutual enjoyment between the players.

Traces from the earlier *Gerry Mulligan Meets . . .* projects abound. "Gone" draws an easy walking line in variation from the Mulligan-Ben Webster collaboration "Go Home," while "Noblesse" is such a classic Zoot Sims-Stan Getz style of ballad that Mulligan gives its initial theme entirely to Scott Hamilton's appropriately respectful tenor. Nearly all of the pieces are reminiscent of the *Something Borrowed* LP, from the pert ditty, "Do You Know What I See?" to the Beiderbeckian feel that characterizes "Port of Baltimore Blues."

That Gerry Mulligan can write and play this way is significant when one considers the challenges that culture, history, and fate have thrown up to his continuing work. The "meetings" from which the tradition of this Scott Hamilton date developed were originally just a happy vehicle for financing a much more "serious" project, the Concert Jazz Band; yet thirty years later the CJB had been out of business for some jazz players' lifetimes, while Mulligan could still draw inspiration from this originally catch-as-catch-can format that had broadened his own playing to a range unsuspected when he'd been producing those masterpieces in miniature with Chet Baker just a few years before. The original quartet had ended in disappointment, with Mulligan jailed for narcotics and Baker taking off for immediately greener fields. But then so many of Gerry Mulligan's projects had seemed to be short-term busts: the Miles Davis *Birth of the Cool* ensemble, which couldn't get enough gigs to survive, Mulligan's writing for Stan Kenton, his romance and musical collaboration with Judy Holliday, his premature attempts at fusion with pop-rock and easy listening music in the mid-1960s. The list goes on to include successful groups aborted by his own choice, including the mid-fifties sextet that made him fear for comfortable boredom and the Concert Jazz Band's 1957 precursor, which somehow didn't sound quite right.

Yet as the 1990s dawned, almost everything with which Gerry Mulligan had been associated had turned to gold. The *Birth of the Cool* recordings had shaped an entire era in jazz, and the Concert Jazz Band's records were still considered sufficiently important to be kept in print during an era when tax laws and inventory expenses (not to mention the pressures of mass marketing) made even important jazz classics unavailable. His fusion work was deemed a success by both jazz critics and the Grammy Awards panels. Even his long-unreleased album with Judy Holliday was earning praise and meriting exceptionally wide distribution as a compact disc, a new form of technology that flattered Mulligan's purity of sound.

Like America itself, whose history as a nation can be spanned by the lifetimes of three septuagenarians and whose development can be so readily traced from specific sources, jazz provides a manageable tradition, the extent of which can be comprehended by even an un-trained listener who may, on a given night in a city such as New Orleans, hear the full extent of that tradition being played by veterans still alive and working, from a Dixieland band in Preservation Hall and a dance band playing at the Hotel Roosevelt to a combo gigging off Bourbon Street and a student-led fusion group at Tulane. Within this scope Gerry Mulligan comprises the greater part of its full range. As Dave Brubeck commented to critic Leonard Feather, when Gerry Mulligan plays, you can hear the entire history of jazz.

COMPOSING A LIFE OF MUSIC

Gerry Mulligan's first recording dates from 1945 with the Elliot Lawrence band. His forty-five years' worth of albums are a remarkable archive, even more so when measured against the entire history of recorded jazz, which dates only from the February 1917 sessions of the Original Dixieland Jazz Band for Victor, with jazz itself existing as an identifiable musical form only for a few short years before that. Of the seventy-some years in the history of jazz records, Mulligan's four-and-a-half decades are the greatest part, missing only one epochal style, Dixieland, while including the swing era, in which he debuted, and all the various developments since.

Swing, bop, progressive, cool, fusion—Mulligan not only experiences them all but contributes to them as an innovator and draws on their new styles for his own playing and writing. He is one of the few important jazz musicians who can sound utterly contemporary in 1945, 1959, 1971, and in the present, and whose work has the feel of anticipating what's to come. His vast canon of LPs serves as an archive of a major part of jazz history, providing not just enjoyable listening but a culturally illustrative soundtrack reviewing all the ground covered over the past half-century, with special attention to all the formative steps along the way.

No one would suggest that in Mulligan's dance-band writing of 1945 can be heard the excitement of V-E Day and the tremors of atomic detonation over Japan. That's something for the movies, and though even a very good one—Martin Scorsese's *New York, New*

York—dramatizes the emergence of bop out of just such excitement and moral disruption, the relation of jazz to American culture is an immensely more subtle matter. But the fact remains that Gerry Mulligan's evolving music was at the heart of changes in American jazz, changes that revolutionized the art form and brought it to its greatest period of confidence and maturity. And all this happened during the century's central decades that initiated an epoch with names of its own. Postwar, atomic, postmodern, contemporary—the specific terminology is still unsettled, but the period itself is a historically and culturally distinct one. The marvel is that in the 1990s one can look back and see so many changes within the lifetime of Americans just now in their prime. Because Gerry Mulligan's work went through the same range of development, comprising so much of the history of jazz, and yet is still with us in an eminently current way, his music makes the perfect aural backdrop to this half-century of transformation.

For example: Is there a definitive transition from swing to bop, coincidental with (if not causally related to) the general quickening of pace and tempering of mettle in the immediate postwar years? Though Mulligan's work for Elliot Lawrence shows many such facets, a good place to start is with that band's recording of the first tune Gerry ever wrote, the brisk, upbeat "Elevation." In a way that might have surprised some swing-era dancers, it starts right off with a trumpet section theme, without so much as an introductory drum beat, bass note, or piano chord. Why so? Because for this tune tempo is everything, a point the arrangement keeps clearly in view as the solidly cooking ensemble introduces each solo by taking the first four bars as a section riff, making the band and its spotlighted instruments clear partners in the service of wholehearted driving swing.

Rarely are the solos and ensemble work in big-band jazz so closely knitted together, a forecast of the harder playing that bands would be asked to do in the coming bebop era. Nicely enough, "Elevation" becomes, in 1947, the first Mulligan number to be performed by such musicians, in this case the hardcore innovators known as Red Rodney's Beboppers, consisting of Rodney on trumpet, Allen Eager on tenor sax, and Serge Chaloff on baritone, plus a rhythm section of Al Haig, Chubby Jackson, and Tiny Kahn. Here Mulligan's line, which had worked so well in propelling the Elliot Lawrence band, serves as a comparatively easier piece for the 52nd Street crowd, which uses a slightly slower tempo and a piano introduction to frame the theme as taken in unison by the three horns, where it sounds as authentically bebop as anything Charlie Parker or Dizzy Gillespie may have intro-

duced that same year (Rodney was Parker's trumpet player as the
forties ended).

There are greater parallels with the style of American life than just
tempo and severity, ones that reach into the changing natures of both
music and society. The big-band era of jazz runs from the early 1930s
to the mid-1940s, years during which the major social concerns were
the economic reformation and recovery of the Great Depression and
the fighting of World War II. Is it too obvious to point out that each,
like big-band music itself, is a collective effort both for performers
and audience? During these times group organization was the key
principle and collectively integrated response its essense of practice.
The music was written for and played by an aggregation of a dozen-
and-a-half players, all working as a team rather than as individuals. Its
audience was another collective, functioning together on the dance
floor, quite literally moving in step to the same beat. Listening involved physical participation, and that participation, because it was in
group form, demanded organization and order. Variation was expected, and even a certain amount of disruption was possible—if kept
within the larger bounds that lined up fifteen to eighteen musicians
on the bandstand and any number of couples dancing on the floor.
Similar principles structured the economic and military efforts of
these same years.

In the years immediately following 1945, the need for these principles no longer exists, and as social life changes, so does the music.
The earliest signs in the latter, while still in the big-band format, are
the expansions of limits and modifications of content that characterize
Gerry Mulligan's own writing in transition. Consider his work for
Gene Krupa in 1946 and into 1947. There's the crispness and melodic
invention of "How High the Moon," where the sections play as distinctly as a single instrument yet state thematic lines as complicated
as any of the bebop head charts—a lesson Mulligan teaches by having
Krupa's band move flawlessly into Charlie Parker's "Ornithology" for
the number's second phrase. Near the end, just before a restatement
of the standard melody takes the band out, Mulligan writes his own
variation on the theme, a bridge that has the feeling that would
characterize his solos in decades to come. Although the hit tune he
supplied turned out to be "Disc Jockey Jump," its anticipation of the
Woody Herman "Four Brothers" sound is somewhat less reflective of
his best work than the sharper attack in this older standard, the
properties of which would be helping to inspire the bebop revolution
as well.

Yet there is another dimension to Mulligan's work from his years with Elliot Lawrence and Gene Krupa, and that's his sense of structural inventiveness and oddball humor, two qualities that complement themselves in charts like "Sometimes I'm Happy" (for Krupa) and "Between the Devil and the Deep Blue Sea" (for the Lawrence orchestra). The more familiar the melody, Mulligan reasons, the more radically he can rearrange its parts, following the age's growing practice of setting aside collective integration and highlighting instead the individuality of collage, each element retaining its own identity and forming a whole more by a system of contrasts, even outrageous ones, than by smoothly coherent, virtually seamless functioning. Such works count for at least half of Mulligan's contributions to the Krupa catalog, a sign of that band's interest in music that was intellectually listenable as well as danceable.

Humor becomes, for both Mulligan and his cultural age, not just something for its own delight, such as relieving depression during the Great Depression or boosting morale in the war, but a way of drawing attention to the properties of sound. It is during this next phase that the solo voice of his surprisingly lyrical baritone sax emerges as the distinctive one—a fresh choice, given the dance-band era's spotlighting of clarinet and trumpet while the saxophone solos went to alto or tenor. It is funny to hear that big blatty bari for the first time, but Mulligan soon transforms that rude surprise into a work of beauty, taking the space opened by comedy and filling it with something else the collective nature of dance-band music had not previously emphasized: the qualities of texture and timbre that, in the decades following Duke Ellington's tonal experiments of the late 1920s, had shared an increasingly smaller part of the stage with the swinging and stomping of section work. One last tour of big-band writing becomes necessary for these parts to fall into place. The orchestra was Claude Thornhill's and the senior writer was Gil Evans, whose duty was to provide arrangements keyed on sound rather than purely melodic effects and that drew on the reshapings of musical theory being worked by bebop innovators such as Miles Davis, Charlie Parker, and Dizzy Gillespie. At the same time Miles Davis was looking in a complementary direction, seeking ways to expand his small-group ideas into a larger orchestral format. Discovering their common interest, Evans and Davis began to hang out together, talking and experimenting and gathering around them some of the sharper sidemen in Thornhill's group, chief among them Gerry Mulligan. What resulted was a powerful cross-fertilization that benefited both ensembles but even more so Mulligan personally. His "Jeru" survives as a recording for both Thornhill's big band and Davis's nine-piece group and is also recalled as the nickname the innovative trumpeter fashioned for him. Its melody is a relaxed but bop-like line, and for Thornhill Mulligan intermixes the theme with solos and in addition has the orchestra do its solo backups in full ensemble rather than by sections and play lines instead of chords, all of which contributes to an underlying sense of complexity, yet one that never disrupts the tune's smooth flow. This delicacy of balance characterizes his work for the Thornhill band and is the key element he transposes to the Miles Davis *Birth of the Cool* materials, where "Jeru" serves as the first cut on the nonet's album, the initial track recorded on its studio debut from 21 January 1949. Tempo and line survive intact, the latter's complexity actually enhanced by the smaller ensemble that allows Mulligan to stack the trumpet, alto, French horn, trombone, and tuba in a unique, airy-sounding choir. His own solo fits this breathy mood, sliding effortlessly along the chord changes in four-bar trades with the trumpet-led ensemble.

Working with Davis is characteristic of Mulligan's general move to take part in the next phase of jazz development, small combos. Between 1949 and 1951 one finds him moving among several groups of musicians and various sizes of groups, from Kai Winding's sextet and septet, through the nine-piece Miles Davis ensemble and his own tentette, to a twelve-man session with Chubby Jackson. Of the dozen cuts with Winding, the best numbers are those that point toward Mulligan's later practice, with his sextet, of orchestrating the several horns in a stacked ensemble as tight as a close-fisted piano chord, yet loose enough that one can distinguish the tonality and timbre of each separate instrument. On "Mud Bug," from the Winding group's 20 May 1949 session featuring the Lester Young style blowing of tenorist Brew Moore, Mulligan's new ensemble sound is complemented by his own emerging solo style; hearing the two reinforce each other makes one think it's already 1956.

The smooth lyricism yet subtly insistent swing of Lester Young's tenor playing works its influence on more than just Gerry's playing and writing for the Kai Winding group; it marks the difference between the intellectual complexities and sometimes precious effects of the *Birth of the Cool* recordings and the looser swing of the Winding-Brew Moore sessions that Mulligan would carry with him into the 1950s. It's the style most apparent on his 1950 work with the Chubby Jackson All-Stars, a twelve-piece group whose organization along the sectional lines of big-band convention is corrected, in a more forward-looking fashion, by the Young-like determination of its players to swing along with the solos. This session catches Mulligan looking both backward and forward, his pleasant "I May Be Wrong" (soon to be a quartet favorite) here charted in the smooth and glossy tones he made famous with Elliot Lawrence, while "So What" (another title for "Apple Core") finds the trumpets written out and nearly all of the tune given to traded fours between himself and Zoot Sims, with riffs from Kai Winding and J. J. Johnson behind their solos anticipating the sextet's style, in which no horn player would ever find himself without something to do.

Such emphasis on individuality and even spontaneity are consequences of the developing age—in these cases quite direct results of changing conditions as the economy of jazz music shifted from big bands to small groups, forcing one or two horns to do what had been handled previously by entire sections. The new responsibilities were accepted gladly, for there was now plenty of room for doing the job one's own way. In Mulligan's work with Kai Winding and in Chubby Jackson's ensemble, and most emphatically in his New York tentette recording in 1951 (where "Roundhouse" devises contrasting timbres and tonalities for melodies and bridge while his baritone sax rides the rhythm with a new sense of confidence and direction), one finds a strongly vocal presence that characterizes the material as his own. These were the same years, after all, that Jackson Pollock and others were changing the subject matter of painting from represented objects to the action of their own paint on the canvas, glorying in the great field of activity now open in the wake of confining tradition swept away by social (and not just artistic) changes. No more great armies—just small groups inspiring each other's innovations. No grand marches across enemy territory—rather a commitment to organize such tactics on intellectual terms. A cold war. Cool jazz.

In retrospect, it seems no accident that Gerry Mulligan looked West to his next stage of development, coinciding with a demographic shift away from New York City and the East Coast as the sole centers of American business, politics, and culture. In previous decades California had made its impact on the country through Hollywood, but with the 1950s it was effecting infrastructural changes in the shape of American life. Build out, not up; replace high-density concentration with openness and a minimalism that risked the charge of vacancy. Ease off, quiet down; continue looking westward, not from New York's perspective at the head of a continent (with its back to the Atlantic) but from California's situation gazing out across the Pacific, a life conducted on the beach with the ever-present reminder of such emptiness so near at hand. From the congestion of 52nd Street one moves the bandstand to the Lighthouse, Howard Rumsey's jazz club at Hermosa Beach, where the din of taxi horns is replaced by the ebbing tides and rolling surf. It seems silly to take note of, but sociologists might find meaning in Mulligan's appearances at the Haig on Wilshire Boulevard: for the first time in his life, he was working in a jazz club with a parking lot, where listeners arrived in cars rather than in cabs or on the A train. How did he get there from New York? Like Jack Kerouac's characters in *On the Road*, by car, hitching his way and getting an even closer feel for the landscape traversed.

Once there, he finds himself acting out another role, to Stan Kenton as the young "rebel without a cause" who finds himself unable to fit into the older man's confining structures. Had Mulligan clicked with Kenton, he could have followed the path of writers Bill Holman and Johnny Richards, leading straight from the last days of the swing era to the academically secure life of stage-band scoring and music education. As it happened, the older leader and the young arranger had strongly different musical visions and conflicting personalities to boot, so that only a few Mulligan charts survive within the Kenton canon. Although "Young Blood" is the famous one, the originals Mulligan would almost immediately transpose for his four-piece group are more noteworthy in terms of personal development, especially the arrangement of "Swing House," which lightens up the Kenton band considerably and creates a viable small-group feel for the five minutes of solo by six of the band's featured players.

Looking back to his last two years in New York, one sees that Mulligan had been swirling amid a wide conflux of sources, from the Thornhill band's alumni gravitating toward Miles Davis, Davis himself, and Charlie Parker to the entirely different group of players active on the Kai Winding and Chubby Jackson dates—Zoot Sims, J. J. Johnson, Al Porcino, Brew Moore, and Don Ferrara among them—who would be taking jazz in a more lyrical yet determinedly swinging direction. It is along this latter route that Mulligan proceeds yet never forgetting the idiosyncracies picked up among the more hardline hipsters of the bop revolution. That key difference may explain his own work's special angularity that one never finds in the playing of such a close associate as Zoot Sims and also anticipates his ability to play future sessions with Thelonious Monk and Charles Mingus.

In June 1952 these forces are funneled into an extremely narrow opening: the tiny stage at a Los Angeles jazz club called the Haig, where Mulligan fronts his smallest group ever: just himself and trumpeter Chet Baker, supported by the thinnest of rhythm sections, bass and drums. Dropping the piano had many consequences, but chief among them was the sense of exquisite miniaturization the Gerry Mulligan Quartet was able to achieve, both for familiar standards (where the listener's memory could fill in the obvious gaps) and the leader's new compositions, whose catchy melodies had to carry the greater burden of each number's presence. With so many cuts to choose from, especially from such a stylistically even catalog of material, it's tempting to fill an entire hour with a dozen or more of them. But since the key effect is brevity and fineness, it's best to stick with just one, "Nights at the Turntable," for here Mulligan shows how such a short number, lasting just two minutes and forty-eight seconds, could sound like a much more complex work, thanks to the constant interweavings and exchanges between Baker's horn and his own. Hardly a single four-bar stretch passes without a change of sorts, whether from unison to harmony, solo or polyphony, or one horn or the other in the lead. Nor are any distributions repeated; where the bari has the lead, next time it goes to trumpet, with the same for contrasting high and low parts in the harmony. When Mulligan organized another ten-piece group and took it to the studio in January 1953, a bridge was built between his similarly sized (but differently orchestrated and voiced) New York group of two years before and the quartet, whose personnel formed the nucleus of this new group. Here again the sheer beauty of the band's material begs for multiple cuts, but for the one most representative in Gerry's development, the choice should be "Walkin' Shoes," both for its quality of sound and for the seamless manner in which the lead is passed among solo horns and ensemble.

When Mulligan heads back East after his year in Los Angeles, it is with the typical brashness of a young man coming home from his first extended trip away. He'd experienced a new style of life and gone through several changes himself; New York could still be a base for him, but his work would be somewhat different, just as the country itself had been changed by the era's Californiazation of American life. But if Gerry Mulligan returns a new man, he at once reshapes his California style as well—for how this happens, one need listen to any of the *Paris Concert* cuts with Bob Brookmeyer, whose valve trombone not only replaces Chet Baker's trumpet but adds a new dimension to the quartet's work. Brookmeyer's instrument itself is a major contribution, able to be sharply articulate and gutty at the same time, allowing for ensemble parts the more extended bottom that escaped Mulligan when writing for his earlier groups. Plus, Bob's style has the major effect of loosening up the quartet, knocking its precious miniaturization into a raft of fragments, each one of which has its own crazy appeal. Where Chet Baker would play just a few notes, soft and pretty, Brookmeyer could gasp and wheeze all over his horn, delighting in its range with an adolescent's fondness for rude noises and surprises. This exuberance inspires a similar relaxing play in Mulligan, who now swings with the rhythm and takes special pleasure in coming down hard on a number's rocking beat. It heats up the California cool to cracking temperature, taking each aspect of the Baker-Mulligan collaboration and deconstructing it for rephrasing in the new group's style, one that both expresses the California side of Gerry Mulligan and critiques it as it happens. Throughout, these pieces from the *Paris Concert* LP and expecially "Open Country" from the Storyville album a bit later sail along with a sense of bounce the Baker combo could only program; here it comes across as thoroughly natural.

As the middle 1950s, before the economic recessions of 1957 and 1959, were years of stability and confidence, so too does Mulligan grow from the various-sized ensembles and reorchestrated quartets to a position where he finds what might seem to be the ideal jazz group. His sidemen recall the 1955–1956 sextet as Mulligan's happiest combo, and listening to "Elevation," Gerry's first composition and one already heard in versions by Elliot Lawrence and Red Rodney, shows why. The ensemble is a unique one, producing an extremely tight sound, yet one in which each instrument can be distinguished for the qualities that characterize each player's unique style. The first phrase sounds much like Lawrence's or Rodney's, a unison line from the bari and valve trombone, with Mulligan's clear tone and Brookmeyer's articulation in evidence. But then, like suddenly having a black-and-white TV switched to color, the ensemble is enriched by the addition of trumpet and tenor sax, Don Ferrara's round but soft-edged tone combining with Zoot Sims's breathy clarity to yield a full range of textures that nevertheless come together in the service of the song's snappy tempo and brisk melody. The greatest benefit is to Mulligan's own playing, for his solo rides along with its most confident feeling ever, drawing energy from the rhythm and new inspirations from the horns riffing behind him, a style of support that threatens at any moment to erupt into spontaneous polyphony, his favorite contrivance in the light-handed arrangements that characterize this group from start to finish.

Why the sextet would ever come to an end stumps some listeners, but Mulligan's disinclination to stay in any one mode too long is part of it, plus his eyes were set again on big-band writing, this time for his uniquely designed Concert Jazz Band. His journey from the sextet to the CJB, however, would have to make pauses for some interruptions, although they would be nothing like hitchhiking from New York to California over several months, then getting sidetracked into some frustrating work with Stan Kenton, getting in trouble with the law such as put an end to the quartet with Chet Baker and left a year-long gap before the appearances in Paris with Bob Brookmeyer. The 1957–1960 period finds him in a stage of development coherent and diverse all at once, meeting a broad range of famous jazz personalities for a series of one-on-one albums. Hearing one cut from each makes for quite a sampling of the age's talent, but one should keep an ear open to what Mulligan picks up from each player. With Teddy Wilson at Newport, Gerry finds that he can swing along in "Sweet Georgia Brown" with a fully unassuming sense of Benny Goodman-era liveliness, just as he can go head to head with Harry Carney and let the audience know that neither distinctive style of bari playing loses a thing in close reflection. Likewise for Paul Desmond's ethereal, brainy style of alto sax, which swings right along with Mulligan's sextet-bred looseness on "Blues Intime." Things tighten up a bit with Thelonious Monk, but hearing Gerry work his way around the odd chord changes of " 'Round Midnight" reveals that his customary angularity and wit share features with Monk's arcane style of jazz. When he switches horns with Stan Getz for "Too Close for Comfort," one hears in Mulligan's tenor work a hint of Brew Moore but even more of Lester Young, with whom Gerry will share the TV screen on CBS's "The Sound of Jazz." As with the deep bluesiness shared with Ben Webster and Jimmy Witherspoon during their own meeting, Mulligan tells his listeners something very important: that when asked to work with the historic legends of jazz, he need never play down to them. With Young and especially Billie Holiday on "Fine and Mellow," we find his brilliance in being completely himself, building one of his most characteristic solos that starts in double time, climbs up the chord structure, and finally slides around on its top.

These meetings tell us a lot about the times. Jazz itself in the late 1950s is considered stable—no one is scratching their heads over Ornette Coleman just yet. Though there are perceived stylistic differences and emphatically historical epochs to contend with, they are viewed in terms of continuity rather than disruption. Why not team Monk with Mulligan? Despite the great contrast in musical personalities, they both play within a diatonic scale and according to measurable time signatures. And why not put Lester Young and Gerry Mulligan into the same combo? Though figures of different eras, they have evolved in the same line according to the same precepts. Most of all, there is the living sense of presence. During this heydey of performance, both in public and on records, jazz can gather virtually all of its artists to interact—not just contemporary stars of vastly different styles but legends from the past who, thanks to the music's concise span of history (which in the late 1950s means reaching back just two generations), might actually play together quite integrally, as happens on the CBS show. No matter how distinct their dialects and personal idiosyncracies of usage, they all speak a common language; and so, with an agreed-upon grammar and syntax in place, an infinite amount of jazz music can be generated.

All that would change, of course, when a new generation of players brought with them an entirely new set of rules. With the 1960s, nearly everything else in society's consensus was challenged as well. For music, the common terminology would no longer be there in a decade that Lester Young and Billie Holiday, Mulligan's colleagues from "The Sound of Jazz," would not live to see. Along with so many other changes in American life during this decade, jazz takes some hard hits: its records are issued in dwindling numbers, radio play almost vanishes, club dates become fewer, and the festival scene degenerates into a malevolence of violent misbehavior climaxing with the destruction of stage set and piano following Mulligan and Dave Brubeck's aptly titled *The Last Set at Newport* in 1971, where one of Brubeck's compositions bears the sadly ironic title, "Open the Gates (Out of the Way of the People)." That Gerry Mulligan and his music would not only survive the 1960s but actually grow and develop through these years is especially significant. Like the country itself, he would gain from the new age's advances but also be sufficiently cautious to avoid being swept up in (and away by) its more frivolous aspects.

It will take a major work of vast sociological range and purpose to sort out the American 1960s and their impact on history, but for Mulligan's part it is possible to note how and why he succeeded. For such an understanding it is crucial to see the position of strength he had achieved in 1959 with perhaps his finest quartet, his great ambitions (and achievements) in 1960–1961 with the Concert Jazz Band, and the series of deep disappointments suffered in both his personal and professional life as the 1960s began (coincidentally) to heat up. That his hopes for the 1960s—the CJB—could not be sustained was not the mortal blow to development other artists might suffer. Instead, Mulligan would look to the very culture that had frustrated his plans, finding roots for a style of jazz that could be new and deeply traditional at the same time.

First for his strengths. With trumpeter Art Farmer Mulligan finds an apt partner for taking the musicianship and inspiration Gerry had marshalled through the 1950s and placing it back in the context of a trumpet-and-baritone pianoless quartet, as happens on *What Is There to Say?* (1959). The title track's delicately strong voice and the hard-hitting "Blueport" anticipate resources that the Concert Jazz Band would exploit, drawing as they do on Mulligan's vocal lyricism and newly percussive playing, both of which make the most of these songs' contrasting slow and upbeat tempos and rhythmic shifts. Art Farmer's trumpet proves a good complement, its breathiness recalling Chet Baker's style but here combined with a harder-hitting style of play that makes something like "Blueport," Farmer's own composition, possible.

Extensive and diverse, the work of Mulligan's Concert Jazz Band deserves sufficient sampling to reveal at least three of the major styles it pursued: the concerto grosso effect of framing his quartet with Bob Brookmeyer, Gerry's own solo horn persisting in its featured role throughout a number, and the band's larger ability to perform virtual orchestral suites. For the first, there's "Sweet and Slow," where the ease and quiet of the opening bass line forms the principle on which the entire subsequent tune is based. The featured horns are Mulligan's and Brookmeyer's, but not just for solos—each is introduced leading a section that allows the player's distinctive tonality and phrasing to come through. The solos themselves move back and forth among supporting lines from the sections, with the saxes surrounding a clarinet and the trombones harmonizing in the old-fashioned Duke Ellington manner. In this way the core of Mulligan's quartet works as equal partners with the band, with the result as manageable as anything Mulligan and Baker put together on the Haig's tiny stage in 1952. It's hard to believe there's a thirteen-piece band in the studio, so efficient is the use of each of its parts.

For Mulligan's featured role in the Concert Jazz Band, "Come Rain or Come Shine" is the obvious choice, partly because the way has been prepared by Zoot Sims on the tour album; here Gerry is challenged to match Zoot's lighter horn and breathier intonation but instead prevails with his most characteristic style of playing, expressed with a deeply resonant tone that makes his bari sound more vocal than ever. A quarter-century later this approach would be embraced by a larger public through his work with Barry Manilow and then with the Houston Symphony, two contexts in which a solo baritone sax lead was as surprising as hearing bari and trumpet playing without harmonic support back in the summer of 1952. Looking back through this range of performances, one realizes how much Mulligan has done to legitimize the lead voice of what before his time had often been regarded as a novelty instrument when taken out of its normal context as a sectional bottom. "Come Rain or Come Shine" is the watershed for this development.

The ten-and-a-half minutes of "All about Rosie" reveal the CJB's greatest dimensions as a vehicle for the involved yet swinging writing for which Mulligan wanted his band to be a laboratory and performance vehicle. Here the soloists hang out until the third and final movement, although individual horns play a key role in stating the themes of part one (trumpet) and two (bari). Unlike so much of conventional big-band writing, George Russell's arrangement (of his own composition) never uses the same voicing twice, re-forming the trombones at one point by including the bass clarinet in their line and pulling out a single alto sax to play a melody that might sound trite were the full section to do it. The final effect is compositional, not just in terms of the component melodies and rhythms but in how the different elements of the band are recombined with the same sense of originality.

That the Concert Jazz Band could be sustained for just three years might count in some records as a failure, but its influence becomes an enduring element in Gerry Mulligan's playing in the years afterwards. The middle 1960s were not his most innovative years by far, but the manner in which he remained productive bears special notice. Because of the greater role listening had assumed during the late fifties "meetings" and the early sixties CJB work, his session playing would now share direction with his cohorts on each date. Consider how Bob Brookmeyer's lusty, sweeping valve trombone style sets the mood for "I Believe in You," inspiring Mulligan to a more broadly rhythmic style than before; as far as tighter and possibly busier rhythmic effects, there's the shift in Gerry's playing that occurs on the *"Jeru"* album with pianist Tommy Flanagan and Alec Dorsey's congas in tandem with drummer Dave Bailey—their "Capricious" reveals a new, lighter style of baritone sax playing that Mulligan carries back to the quartet with Brookmeyer and the new style of sextet with Brookmeyer, Art Farmer, and guitarist Jim Hall, where "Morning of the Carnival" draws on these same Latin rhythms while "In the Wee Small Hours of the Morning" shows just how quiet the group can be and still make its point. That these musicians can also achieve an up-tempo hard swing becomes evident on a third cut, "Old Devil Moon," making one wish this particular combo had survived for more than an album and a half. Yet throughout the period Mulligan was reacting strongly to a diverse set of influences: few contrasts are as strong as between his equally legitimate playing with Paul Desmond on a tune from their second meeting, "The Way You Look Tonight," where their lines become so abstract as to be virtually unrecognizable, and the open-armed embrace of Roger Miller's pop melody in "King of the Road," played on the *If You Can't Beat 'Em* album with studio rocker Johnny Gray. Even Zoot Sims shows up to reimpress his own influence on his old jam-session buddy with the *Something Borrowed, Something Blue* LP, on which "Davenport Blues" stands as a creditable Beiderbeckian piece of indulgence one cannot imagine Mulligan attempting before this time. For Gerry himself, the most personal of these influential involvements had come at the very start of the sixties, while the Concert Jazz Band was in full flower: his romance and musical collaboration with Judy Holliday. Earlier work with singers Annie Ross and Jimmy Witherspoon had shown how his own strongly vocal style could stand up respectably in the company of theirs, but with Judy there appears a deeper sense of delicacy and emotion, just slightly sharpened with a barb of irony in a tune like "Blue Prelude," a fitting complement of her voice with his tone.

Cancer would take Judy Holliday out of Mulligan's life but not out of his music. The tragedy of her loss would cripple lesser spirits, but Gerry Mulligan manages to continue with his life of music—not forgetting her, but drawing on her art and the special qualities the two of them shared in work that would take him through the decade and into the more rewarding years beyond. Likewise for the Concert Jazz Band, having to fold because of the era's transformed economics, which did not count the support of a big band as a priority (or, in Mulligan's case, even a possibility). From the CJB Gerry drew a new confidence in placing his distinctively voiced horn in new contexts, which by the dawn of the 1970s would include enhanced rhythm and jazz-rock fusion effects. But even in terms of Mulligan's less brilliant activities of these confusing years, such as his popwash of Roger Miller tunes and syrupy treatments of Broadway show tunes with strings, there is a benefit to accrue: while others were turning their backs on middle-class culture, Gerry Mulligan was staying in touch with it and thereby forming a historical bridge between generations of the past raised on Rodgers and Hart, the Gershwins, and Harold Arlen and those who would appreciate Stephen Sondheim and Andrew Lloyd Webber. If nothing else, Mulligan's experience with this mini-era shows not just how a mainstream figure can survive but that absolutely everything of the old style need not be thrown out, given the chance true genius has in transforming it.

Gerry Mulligan's last encounter of the 1960s would be his most musically fruitful, a collaboration with Dave Brubeck that ran from 1968 through 1972 and produced five albums, one of which premiered the first of the baritone saxophonist's new fusion compositions. Here the transitional element is rhythm and the source is Brubeck, one of the heaviest and most percussive piano players in jazz. With Alan Dawson and Jack Six, the new quartet was even more rhythmically inclined and, combined with Dave's intellectualism, created effects more complex than Mulligan had previously worked with. Their initial LP, *Compadres*, boasts a Mexican flavor that keeps both the drummer and bassist busier than usual. Brubeck finds it all quite natural and uses the occasion to play a tune developed from his California ranching youth, "Indian Song." Its boldly percussive nature and rolling $\frac{6}{8}$ beat prohibit the use of most of Mulligan's familiar stylistic techniques; instead, he is forced to be responsive to the playing that surrounds him, a facility he'd been developing through his late fifties "meetings," the context of the Concert Jazz Band, and his various involvements throughout the sixties. The effect carries over to "Unfinished Woman," one of the numbers central to his coming *Age of Steam* fusion-based band but first publicly performed with Brubeck during their final European tour. Like "Indian Song," the melody is a simple one, with the song's complexity resulting from the rhythmic action taking place around it. With fewer chord changes, Mulligan has less excuse to meander among the melodic permutations and is encouraged to improvise with the beat instead. As a result his baritone sax playing reveals new properties, both of the instrument and his imagination; his presence on the big horn now includes that last dimension, rhythm, completing his solo voice and making it virtually self-sufficient.

This stylistic fulfillment brings Mulligan into the 1970s and 1980s, a consistently productive stretch of years in which he is almost constantly writing new material and shaping new formats for his decidedly contemporary-sounding group. Throughout the *Age of Steam*, *Walk on the Water*, and *Little Big Horn* albums one finds him expanding and contracting the size of his ensembles, from four to as many as eighteen yet always playing new compositions that exploit those particular groups' rhythmic properties. "One to Ten in Ohio," from *The Age of Steam*, is the logical successor to both Brubeck's "Indian Song" and his own "Unfinished Woman," for its almost total lack of chordal progression places the greatest emphasis possible on rhythm. For this debut of his fusion band Mulligan even gives the first solo to tenorist Tom Scott, whose funky booting serves to teach the group how a saxophone has inherently rhythmic properties. Gerry's own solo is not as rhythm-and-bluesish but still does plenty of popping back and forth from the low to high registers in the manner developed by players such as King Curtis and Junior Walker, here coupled with the more usual practice of slipping in additional notes.

There's yet another dimension to Mulligan's new style of playing, and that's his willingness to extend notes to a bar's length and, more, letting the deep, clear tone of his bari sax, so close to that of a deep male voice, resound above both the rhythm and orchestral support. With the larger resources of his *Walk on the Water* band, he's able to exploit this talent to its fullest in "Song for Strayhorn," an extremely moving piece whose melody is a sentimental tribute to Ellington's chief arranger and to his important influence on Mulligan's writing and horn work as well. Had Mulligan done this number twenty years earlier, it would have been an attractive tune; now, thanks to his deep resonance and his courage to sustain the song on this tone alone, it becomes an exceptionally emotional testament to both Strayhorn's music and Mulligan's own work within its resources. Playing both within and around the full orchestral effects, Gerry is able to make his horn sound as rich as the full choir of trumpets, another step toward the bari's independence as a feature solo voice.

Rounding out this sample from the *Age of Steam* era is the cut from *Little Big Horn* that proves Mulligan's playful wit still has room for full exercise: "Another Kind of Sunday," where his horn romps around the catchy backbeat melody played throughout by a tight studio horn section. He works on the beat, ahead of it, and behind it, listening all the time for the little nuances in phrasing that allow him to superimpose time signatures on the section's own, multiplying the dimensions of this otherwise simple tune until it is as complex yet swingingly flowing as Gerry's solo style itself. A constant in his *Age of Steam* work is to show how much can be done with so little, with the "so little" part of it keeping jazz close to its rhythmic roots.

By the late 1980s, as Mulligan begins his fifth decade as a recording jazz artist, one finds him in two unlikely places: working with pop singer Barry Manilow and with the Houston Symphony Orchestra. Yet a common element unites the two occasions: what Gerry has made of his baritone sax, which is now a strongly personal voice that on "What Am I Doin' Here" can match its sound with an exceedingly well-fashioned vocal tone yet also have the lyric strength and integrity to sustain itself as the lead element in a twelve-minute, classically conceived piece, "Entente for Baritone Sax and Orchestra." On both cuts Gerry plays almost all the time yet never dominates or seems out of place. Quite the contrary: his horn not only adds key elements to each performance but, even with Manilow, lends a sense of personality to the larger musical piece. From the start Gerry Mulligan has been idiosyncratic. As his career moves toward a full half-century in jazz, as many years as that teenaged baritone saxophonist and arranger back in 1945 could count to the turn-of-the-century pianists in New Orleans whose ragtime music bore the first anticipations of Dixieland, his work assumes the stature of true character, a hallmark that can be mistaken for none other in the now very long history of jazz.

DISCOGRAPHY

The following is a physical description of my own collection of Gerry Mulligan's commercially recorded performances and arrangements, supplemented by a survey of my materials undertaken by Gerry Mulligan and by the world's leading collector of Mulligan's music, Gordon Jack of London, England. In cases where I have not seen the item in question, Jack's descriptions are indicated. Both of us are aware of and grateful for the several partial discographies in print and include acknowledgment of these sources where we have drawn upon them:

Astrup, Arne. *Gerry Mulligan Discography*. Soeburg, Denmark: Bidstrup Discographical Publishing Company, 1989.

Jepsen, Jorgen Grunnet. *Jazz Records 1942–1965*. Holte, Denmark: Emil Knudsen, 1966.

Middleton, Tony. "Discography." In *Gerry Mulligan's Ark*, Raymond Horricks. London: Apollo Books, 1986.

Ruppli, Michel. *The Clef/Verve Labels*. Westport, Conn.: Greenwood Press, 1986.

Tercinet, Alain. "Discographie de Gerry Mulligan." *Jazz Hot* no. 335 (March 1977): 25–29; no. 336 (April 1977): 20–23.

Mulligan's film work available on record or video cassette has been compared with listings in the second edition of David Meeker's *Jazz in the Movies* (New York: DaCapo Press, 1981); readers interested in Mulligan's film scores and performances available only on film are referred to this work.

The structure of this discography is album by album (some of which comprise tracks from several decades) and is ordered in terms of Mulligan's own historical progression; for example, a 1958 recording of 1946–1947 arrangements is listed with other material from the late forties.

Although all known sources have been studied, no claim can be made for the absolute completeness of this discography. Collectors who know of additional material are urged to notify me at the Department of English, University of Northern Iowa, Cedar Falls, Iowa 50614-0502.

Tommy Tucker and his Orchestra (Circle Records CLP15); 1945.

[Not seen. Mulligan recalls "Brass Hats" as the only surviving recorded example of his earliest professional arranging.]

Elliot Lawrence and His Orchestra (Hindsight HRS-182); 1945.

[Not seen. Middleton mentions "three 1945 Gerry Mulligan scores including 'Indiana,' reported to be Mulligan's first paid arrangement."]

Elliot Lawrence and His Orchestra: "Sugar Beat" (Big Band Archives LP-1219); 1945–1954.

The Old Night Owl; Listen to Lawrence*; The Night Is Young and You're So Beautiful; March from *Carmen*; How High the Moon*; Someone to Watch over Me; Hand Me Five; If You Are But a Dream; The Song Is You*; Lawrence Leaps*; Chloe; Between the Devil and the Deep Blue Sea*

ARRANGEMENTS*: Gerry Mulligan
TRUMPETS: *Red Rodney, John Dee, Paul Cope*
TROMBONES: *Frank Rodowicz, Joe Verrechico, Herb Collins*
SAXES: *Ernie Cantonucci, Buddy Gentiles, Gerry Mulligan, Pete Sansone, Mike Donio*
FRENCH HORN: *Ernie Angelucci*
PIANO: *Elliot Lawrence*
BASS: *Andy Riccardi*
DRUMS: *Max Spector*   Recorded 1945, NYC

Box 155
TRUMPETS: *Alec Fila, John Dee, Walt Stuart*
TROMBONES: *Frank Rodowicz, Vince Forrest, Willie Dennis*
SAXES: *Ernie Cantonucci, Mike Giamo, Jerry Fields, Bruno Rondelli, Louis Giamo*
FRENCH HORN: *Tony Ryya*
OBOE: *Bert Gassman*
BASSOON: *Earl Shuster*
PIANO: *Elliot Lawrence*
BASS: *Louis Palombi*
DRUMS: *Marty Masters*
GUITAR: *Louis Melia*   Recorded 16 September 1946, NYC

Sugar Beat
TRUMPETS: *Alec Fila, John Dee, Fred Edwards*
TROMBONES: *Barney Liddell, Tony Lala, Vince Forrest*
SAXES: *Leon Cohen, Mike Giamo, Bruno Rondelli, Danny Melia, Merle Bredwell*
FRENCH HORN: *John St. Amour*
OBOE: *Harold Feldman*
PIANO: *Elliot Lawrence*
BASS: *Louis Palombi*
DRUMS: *Marty Masters*
GUITAR: *Louis Melia*   Recorded 3 February 1947, NYC

Elevation
ARRANGEMENT: Gerry Mulligan
TRUMPETS: *Joe Techner, John Dee, Jimmy Padget*
TROMBONES: *Sy Berger, Vince Forrest, Chuck Harris*
SAXES: *Joe Soldo, Phil Urso, Bruno Rondelli, Gerry Mulligan, Merle Bredwell*
FRENCH HORN: *Bill Danzien*
PIANO: *Elliot Lawrence*
BASS: *Tommy O'Neil*
DRUMS: *Howie Mann*
GUITAR: *Bob Karch*   Recorded 13 April 1949, NYC

Cool Days
TRUMPETS: *Don Leight, Bernie Glow, Stan Fishelson*
TROMBONES: *Eddie Bert, Ollie Wilson, Tyree Glenn*
SAXES: *Sam Marowitz, Hal McKusick, Al Cohn, Charlie O'Kane*
PIANO: *Elliot Lawrence*
BASS: *Russ Saunders*
DRUMS: *Don Lamond*
GUITAR: *Sam Herman*   Recorded 13 December 1954, NYC

[Mulligan believes what the album notes describe as 1947–1949 recording sessions in NYC are in fact 1946–1947 WCAU air-checks from Philadelphia, and that "Elevation" is an air-check from an engagement at Bop City in New York.]

Gene Krupa 1945–1946 (Vee Jay RJL-2641); 1945–1946.
Begin the Beguine; Birdhouse
TRUMPETS: *Red Rodney, Joe Triscari, Vince Hughes, Jimmy Millazzio*
TROMBONES: *Bob Ascher, Dick Taylor, Nick Gaglio, Tasso Harris*
SAXES: *Harry Terrill, Charlie Kennedy* (alto), *Charlie Ventura, Buddy Wise* (tenor), *Joe Koch* (bari)
PIANO: *Teddy Napoleon*

GUITAR: *Mike Triscari*
BASS: *Irv Lang*
DRUMS: *Gene Krupa, Joe Dale*

Recorded late 1945, early 1946, NYC

Margie
TRUMPETS: *Red Rodney, Joe Triscari, Ray Triscari, Tony Anelli*
TROMBONES: *Ziggy Elmer, Dick Taylor, Warren Covington, Ben Seaman*
SAXES: *Harry Terrill, Charlie Kennedy (alto), Charlie Ventura, Buddy Wise (tenor), Jack Schwartz (bari)*
PIANO: *Teddy Napoleon*
GUITAR: *Mike Triscari*
BASS: *Bob Munoz*
DRUMS: *Gene Krupa, Joe Dale*   Recorded May 1946, NYC

[Mulligan recalls these materials as air-checks from mid-1946 or later, perhaps from the 400 Club in New York.]

Elliot Lawrence and His Orchestra: "Elevation" (First Heard FH38); 1946–1947.

Elevation
TRUMPETS: *Alec Fila, John Dee, Fred Edwards*
TROMBONES: *Barney Liddell, Vince Forrest, Tony Lala*
FRENCH HORN: *John St. Armour*
REEDS: *Bud Pecha (oboe), Joe Soldo, Louis Giamo (alto), Andy Pino, Joe Dee, or Bruno Rondelli (tenor), Merle Bredwell (bari)*
PIANO: *Elliot Lawrence*
GUITAR: *Louis Melia*
BASS: *Louis Palombi*
DRUMS: *Howie Mann*   Recorded live 2–5 December 1947, Palladium Ballroom, Hollywood, California

Gerry Mulligan: The Arranger (Columbia JC-34803); 1946–1947.

How High the Moon (Gene Krupa and His Orchestra)
TRUMPETS: *Red Rodney, Joe Triscari, Ray Triscari, Tony Anelli*
TROMBONES: *Bob Ascher, Dick Taylor, Warren Covington, Ben Seaman*
SAXES: *Harry Terrill, Charlie Kennedy (alto), Charlie Ventura, Buddy Wise (tenor), Jack Schwartz (bari)*
PIANO: *Teddy Napoleon*
GUITAR: *Mike Triscari*
BASS: *Bob Munoz*
DRUMS: *Gene Krupa*   Recorded 21 May 1946, NYC

Disc Jockey Jump (Gene Krupa and His Orchestra)
TRUMPETS: *Don Fagerquist, Ray Triscari, Ed Badgley, Al Porcino*
TROMBONES: *Clay Harvey, Dick Taylor, Emil Mazanec, Jack Zimmerman*
SAXES: *Harry Terrill, Charlie Kennedy (alto), Buddy Wise, Mitch Melnick (tenor), Jack Schwartz (bari)*
PIANO: *Buddy Neal*
GUITAR: *Bob Lesher*
BASS: *Bob Strahl*
DRUMS: *Gene Krupa*   Recorded 22 January 1947, NYC

[Album also contains material from Mulligan's work with Elliot Lawrence in 1946 and 1947 and with his own big band in 1957. Descriptions follow below in detail.]

Gene Krupa Plays Gerry Mulligan Arrangements (Verve MGV-8292); 1946–1947.

Bird House; Margie; Mulligan Stew; Yardbird Suite
TRUMPETS: *Al DeRisi, Ernie Royal, Doc Severinsen, Al Stewart*
TROMBONES: *Eddie Bert, Billy Byers, Jimmy Cleveland, Kai Winding*
SAXES: *Phil Woods, Sam Marowitz (alto), Frank Socolow, Eddie Wasserman (tenor), Danny Banks (bari)*
PIANO: *Hank Jones*
GUITAR: *Barry Galbraith*
BASS: *Jimmy Gannon*
DRUMS: *Gene Krupa*   Recorded 20 October 1958, NYC

Begin the Beguine; Sugar; The Way of All Flesh; Birds of a Feather; Sometimes I'm Happy; How High the Moon; If You Were the Only Girl in the World; Disc Jockey Jump
Same personnel, except that trumpeter Markie Markowitz and uncredited tubaist are added, while trombonists Willie Dennis and Urbie Green replace Eddie Bert and Billy Byers.
Recorded 20 November 1958, NYC

Gerry Mulligan: The Arranger (Columbia JC-34803); 1946–1949.

Elevation (Elliot Lawrence and His Orchestra)
TRUMPETS: *Joe Techner, John Dee, Jimmy Padget, Bill Danzien*
TROMBONES: *Sy Berger, Vince Forrest, Chuck Harris*
SAXES: *Joe Soldo, Louis Giamo (alto), Phil Urso, Bruno Rondelli (tenor), Merle Bredwell (bari)*
PIANO: *Elliot Lawrence*
BASS: *Tommy O'Neil*
DRUMS: *Howie Mann*   Recorded 13 April 1949, NYC

Between the Devil and the Deep Blue Sea
  Same personnel as above, except Frank Hunter and Gene Hessler
  replace Vince Forrest and Chuck Harris on trombones, and Gerry
  Mulligan on bari replaces Louis Giamo on alto sax.

                                    Recorded 10 October 1949, NYC

  [This recording is identical to the cut on the Elliot Lawrence "*Sugar
  Beat*" LP described above as a 1945 session, and which Mulligan
  believes may be a 1946 air-check. Tercinet notes the 13 April 1949
  recording of "Elevation" and adds two cuts arranged by Mulligan for
  vocalists Rosalind Patton and Jack Hunter, "Gigolette" (Hunter) and
  "Ev'ry Night Is Saturday Night" (vocal group), released as Columbia
  38497 and 38522 respectively. Tercinet notes the 10 October 1949
  recording of "Between the Devil and the Deep Blue Sea" and adds
  three cuts on which Mulligan plays and may have arranged (Nelson
  Riddle is also credited as an arranger for the session) "Your Life Is My
  Life" (vocal by Danny Ricardo), "Got You Where I Want You" (vocal
  by Rosalind Patton), and "Ritual Fire Dance," released as Columbia
  36829-A, 36829-B, and 38664 (as the B side of "Between the Devil
  and the Deep Blue Sea"). Mulligan recalls not playing on the latter
  three cuts and having arranged "Got You Where I Want You" only
  after the vocal section, previous parts being Elliot Lawrence's work;
  he also disclaims arranging "Your Life Is My Life" and "Ritual Fire
  Dance."]

Elliot Lawrence Plays Gerry Mulligan Arrangements (Fantasy 3-206/OJC-
117); 1945–1951.

  Happy Hooligan; The Rocker; Elegy for Two Clarinets; The Swinging
  Door
    TRUMPETS: *Dick Sherman, Bernie Glow, Al DeRisi, Stan Fishelson*
    TROMBONES: *Eddie Bert, Ollie Wilson, Paul Seldon*
    FRENCH HORN: *Fred Schmidt*
    SAXES: *Sam Marowitz, Hal McKusick* (alto), *Al Cohn, Ed Wasser-
      man* (tenor), *Charlie O'Kane* (bari)
    PIANO: *Elliot Lawrence*
    BASS: *Russ Saunders*
    DRUMS: *Don Lamond*   Recorded 4 March 1955, NYC

  Bye Bye Blackbird, Strike Up the Band; Mullenium; But Not for Me
    TRUMPETS: *Nick Travis, Bernie Glow, Al DeRisi, Stan Fishelson*
    TROMBONES: *Eddie Bert, Ollie Wilson, Paul Seldon*
    FRENCH HORN: *Tony Miranda*
    SAXES: *Sam Marowitz, Hal McKusick* (alto), *Al Cohn, Ed Wasser-
      man* (tenor), *Charlie O'Kane* (bari)
    PIANO: *Elliot Lawrence*
    BASS: *Buddy Jones*

DRUMS: *Don Lamond*   Recorded 1 July 1955, NYC

Apple Core; Bweebida Bwobbida; My Silent Love; Mr. President
Trombonist Al Robertson replaces Paul Seldon
Recorded 5 July 1955, NYC

Mulligan Arrangements Played by Claude Thornhill and His Orchestra
(MCA 3147 [Japan]); 1947–1951.

[Not seen, listed by Middleton.]

Two Sides of Claude Thornhill (Kapp KL-1058); 1947–1951.

Jeru; Rose of the Rio Grande; Poor Little Rich Girl; Five Brothers
TRUMPETS: *Dale Pierce, Sonny Rich, Dick Sherman*
TROMBONES: *Owen Massingill, Billy Ver Planck*
FRENCH HORNS: *Al Antonucci, Sandy Siegelstein*
TUBA: *Bill Barber*
REEDS: *Ralph Aldridge (tenor, clarinet), Med Flory, Gene Quill
(alto), Dave Figg, Ray Norman (tenor), Dick Zubach (bari,
clarinet)*
PIANO: *Claude Thornhill*
GUITAR: *Barry Galbraith*
BASS: *Bob Peterson*
DRUMS: *Winston Welch*   Recorded 28–29 April 1953, NYC

Red Rodney's Be-Boppers (Keynote 670; Mercury Compact Disc 830 922-2);
1947.

Elevation
TRUMPET: *Red Rodney*
TENOR SAX: *Allen Eager*
BARITONE SAX: *Serge Chaloff*
PIANO: *Al Haig*
BASS: *Chubby Jackson*
DRUMS: *Tiny Kahn*   Recorded 29 January 1947, NYC

Dave Lambert and Buddy Stewart with the Five Bops (Sittin' in With 508;
Vogue V-2050; Mainstream M-56025); 1948.

Hot Halavah; Deedle*; In the Merry Land of Bop
TROMBONE: *Benny Green*
TENOR SAX: *Allen Eager*
BARITONE SAX AND COMPOSER*: *Gerry Mulligan*
GUITAR: *Jimmy Raney*
PIANO: *Al Haig*
BASS: *Clyde Lombardi (or Ben Russo)*

DRUMS: *Charlie Perry*
VOCALS: *Dave Lambert, Buddy Stewart, Blossom Dearie*
Recorded late 1948, NYC

[Not seen; described by Jepsen under listings for Dave Lambert and for the Five Bops.]

Claude Thornhill and His Orchestra / The Song Is You (Hep 17); 1948.

Anthropology, Baia; Arab Dance; Royal Garden Blues; Polka Dots and Moonbeams; Sometimes I'm Happy; September Song; Godchild; Robbin's Nest; The Song Is You; April in Paris; La Paloma; Loverman; Elevation

TRUMPETS: *Emil Terry, Johnny Vohs, Bob Peck*
TROMBONES: *Johnny Torrick, Allan Langstaff*
TUBA: *Bill Barber*
FRENCH HORN: *Sandy Siegelstein*
SAXES: *Danny Polo, Lee Konitz (alto), Mickey Folus, Jerry Sanfino (tenor), Gerry Mulligan (tenor and bari)*
PIANO: *Claude Thornhill*
BASS: *Russ Saunders*
DRUMS: *Billy Exner*   Recorded Spring 1948, NYC

[Not seen; described by Jack, who indicates Mulligan's bari solos on "Anthropology" and "Elevation" plus both bari and tenor sax solos on "Godchild"; Mulligan recalls not being with Thornhill at this time.]

Miles Davis Nonet: Jazz Live (Cicala BLJ-8003); 1948.

Why Do I Love You; Godchild*; S'il Vous Plait; Moon Dreams; Hallucinations (Budo)

ARRANGEMENT*: *Gerry Mulligan*
TRUMPET: *Miles Davis*
TROMBONE: *Mike Zwerin*
FRENCH HORN: *Junior Collins*
TUBA: *Bill Barber*
SAXES: *Lee Konitz (alto), Gerry Mulligan (bari)*
PIANO: *John Lewis*
BASS: *Al McKibbon*
DRUMS: *Max Roach*
VOCAL: *(on "Why Do I Love You"): Kenny Hagood*
Recorded live 4 September 1948, NYC

Move; Darn That Dream*; Moon Dreams; Hallucinations (Budo)
Same personnel as above, except Curley Russell replaces Al McKibbon on bass; Kenny Hagood sings "Darn That Dream."
Recorded live 18 September 1948, NYC

[Not seen; Jepsen describes the 4 September session as a broadcast, adding "Mood" (which Tercinet correctly identifies as "Move" but indicates was not issued on Cicala); Tercinet further identifies location as the Royal Roost club; Astrup lists "Chasin' the Bird" as an unissued cut from 18 September and describes a third session on 21 September that yielded four unissued cuts: "Half Nelson," another take of "Chasin' the Bird," "You Go to My Head," and "Broadway Theme." Jack notes that these last four numbers are performed by a sextet within the band consisting of Davis, Konitz, Mulligan, Lewis, Russell, and Roach, with Hagood as vocalist on "You Go To My Head"; Jack believes "Half Nelson" dates from 25 September. Throughout these and the other Miles Davis Nonet sessions Mulligan indicates "Budo" as his arrangement, while other sources credit John Lewis.]

Miles Davis and His Orchestra: The Complete Birth of the Cool (Capitol Jazz Classics M-11026); 1949–1950.

Jeru*; Move; Godchild*; Budo
ARRANGEMENTS*: *Gerry Mulligan*
TRUMPET: *Miles Davis*
TROMBONE: *Kai Winding*
FRENCH HORN: *Junior Collins*
TUBA: *Bill Barber*
SAXES: *Lee Konitz (alto), Gerry Mulligan (bari)*
PIANO: *Al Haig*
BASS: *Joe Shulman*
DRUMS: *Max Roach*   Recorded 21 January 1949, NYC
Venus de Milo*; Rouge; Boplicity; Israel
Trombonist J. J. Johnson replaces Kai Winding, French horn player Sandy Siegelstein replaces Junior Collins, pianist John Lewis replaces Al Haig, bassist Nelson Boyd replaces Joe Shulman, and drummer Kenny Clarke replaces Max Roach   Recorded 22 April 1949, NYC
Deception; Rocker*; Moon Dreams; Darn That Dream*
French horn player Gunther Schuller replaces Sandy Siegelstein, bassist Al McKibbon replaces Nelson Boyd, drummer Max Roach replaces Kenny Clarke, and vocalist Kenny Hagood performs on "Darn That Dream."   Recorded 9 March 1950, NYC

Georgie Auld and His Orchestra (Discovery LP-3007, Savoy MG-12089, JS LP-50001); 1949.

You've Got Me Jumpin'; Darn That Dream; Hollywood Bazaar; They Didn't Believe Me*
TRUMPET: *John Anderson*

TROMBONE: *Billy Byers*
SAXES: *John Rotella (alto), Georgie Auld (alto and tenor), Irv Roth
       (tenor), Pete Terry (bari)*
PIANO: *Jimmy Rowles*
BASS: *Joe Mondragon*
DRUMS: *Al Stoller*
BONGOS: *Karl Kiffe*
ARRANGERS: *Gerry Mulligan*, Hal Vernon*
                                    Recorded 17 January 1949, LA

Nashooma; Vox Bop; Mild and Mellow; Settin' the Pace
Same personnel as above, except Neal Hefti replaces John Anderson
on trumpet and Clint Neagley replaces John Rotella on alto sax.
                                    Recorded 21 March 1949, LA

[Not seen; described by Jepsen.]

Georgie Auld and His Orchestra (Swing House SWH-25); 1949.

So What's New; Sweet Thing; Nashooma; Lullaby in Rhythm; Blues for
Me; Mo Mo; You Got Me Jumpin'; Flying Home; So What Can Be New
Now
TRUMPET: *Neal Hefti*
TROMBONE: *Billy Byers*
SAXES: *Clint Neagley (alto), Georgie Auld, Pete Terry (tenor),
       Gerry Mulligan (bari)*
PIANO: *Jimmy Rowles*
BASS: *Joe Mondragon*
DRUMS: *Alvin Stoller*
BONGOS: *Karl Kiffe*   Recorded live in April 1949, LA

[Not seen; described as a recorded broadcast by Astrup, who also
indicates a Mulligan solo on "Blues for Me." Mulligan recalls playing
in a larger Auld orchestra but not with this smaller unit.]

The Brothers: Stan Getz and His Four Brothers (Prestige P-7022/OJC-008); 1949.

Five Brothers; Four and One Moore
TENOR SAXES: *Stan Getz, Zoot Sims, Al Cohn, Allen Eager, Brew
             Moore*
BARITONE SAX: *Stan Getz (on chorus of "Five Brothers")*
PIANO: *Walter Bishop*
BASS: *Gene Ramey*
DRUMS: *Charlie Perry*
ARRANGER: *Gerry Mulligan*   Recorded 8 April 1949, NYC

Early Modern: The Kai Winding Sextet (Jazztone J-1263); 1949.

Bop City; Sleepy Bop; Crossing the Channel; Wallington's Godchild
TROMBONE: *Kai Winding*
SAXES: *Brew Moore (tenor), Gerry Mulligan (bari)*
PIANO: *George Wallington*
BASS: *Curley Russell*
DRUMS: *Max Roach*   Recorded 10 April 1949, NYC

[Tercinet describes a 15 April 1949 broadcast from the Bop City club
of "Bop City" and "Godchild"; Jack adds that these cuts were issued
on Bomo 4953.]

George Wallington Septet (Regal 1196, Savoy XP8112, MG-12081); 1949.

Knockout; Igloo
TRUMPET: *Jerry Lloyd*
TROMBONE: *Kai Winding*
SAXES: *Brew Moore (tenor), Gerry Mulligan (bari)*
PIANO: *George Wallington*
BASS: *Curley Russell*
DRUMS: *Charlie Perry*
VOCAL (ON "KNOCKOUT"): *Buddy Stewart*
                                   Recorded 9 May 1949, NYC

Gene Roland Boppers (DeLuxe [unissued]); 1949.

Oh Them Saxes; Hold Them Trumpets; Blues in Our Times; Symphony
Sid's Symphonette
TRUMPETS: *Gene Roland (doubling on valve trombone and piano),
          Dan Blue, Dan Baxter, Jerry Lloyd, Dale Pierce*
SAXES: *Al Cohn, Stan Getz, Zoot Sims (tenor), Gerry Mulligan
       (bari)*
PIANO: *Gene DiNovi*
BASS: *Red Kelly*
DRUMS: *Tiny Kahn*   Recorded 17 May 1949, NYC

[Not seen; described by Jepsen.]

Brew Moore et al.: Brothers and Other Mothers, Vol. 2 (Savoy 2236); 1949.

Mud Bug; Gold Rush; Lestorian Mode; Kai's Kid (two cuts each)
TRUMPET: *Jerry Lloyd*
TROMBONE: *Kai Winding*
SAXES: *Brew Moore (tenor), Gerry Mulligan (bari)*
PIANO: *George Wallington*
BASS: *Curley Russell*
DRUMS: *Roy Haynes*   Recorded 20 May 1949, NYC

Kai Winding et al.: Early Bones (Prestige P-24067); 1949.

A Night on Bop Mountain; Waterworks; Broadway; Sid's Bounce
TRUMPET: *Jerry Lloyd*
TROMBONE: *Kai Winding*
SAXES: *Brew Moore (tenor), Gerry Mulligan (bari)*
PIANO: *George Wallington*
BASS: *Curley Russell*
DRUMS: *Roy Haynes*   Recorded 23 August 1949, NYC

Brew Moore: Brewer's Blew (Bomo 4953); 1949–1950.

Bop City; Godchild; Indianola; OW
TRUMPET: *Jerry Lloyd*
TROMBONE: *Kai Winding*
SAXES: *Brew Moore (tenor), Gerry Mulligan (bari)*
PIANO: *George Wallington*
BASS: *Curley Russell*
DRUMS: *Roy Haynes*   Recorded live in 1949 and 1950, NYC

[Not seen; described by Jack as a recorded broadcast from either the Royal Roost or Bop City club.]

Mary Ann McCall with Al Cohn's Band (Roost 511 and 514); 1950.

I Cried for You; The Sky Is Crying; After I Say I'm Sorry; Until the Real Thing Comes Along
TRUMPET: *Red Rodney*
TROMBONE: *Earl Swope*
SAXES: *Al Cohn (tenor), Gerry Mulligan (bari)*
PIANO: *Al Haig*
BASS: *Curley Russell*
DRUMS: *Jeff Morton*
VOCALS: *Mary Ann McCall*   Recorded 1 February 1950, NYC

[Not seen; described by Jepsen.]

Chubby Jackson: Sextet and Big Band (Prestige PR-7641); 1950.

Flying the Coop; Why Not; So What; I May Be Wrong; New York; Leavin' Town; Hot Dog; Sax Appeal
TRUMPETS: *Howard McGhee, Al Porcino, Don Ferrara (section does not play on "So What")*
TROMBONES: *J. J. Johnson, Kai Winding*
SAXES: *Charlie Kennedy (alto), Zoot Sims, Georgie Auld (tenor), Gerry Mulligan (bari)*
PIANO: *Tony Aless*
BASS: *Chubby Jackson*
DRUMS: *Don Lamond*   Recorded 15 March 1950, NYC

Gene Roland Band: The Band That Never Was (Spotlite 141).

Stardust (three takes); It's a Wonderful World (four takes); Just You Just Me

TRUMPETS: *Miles Davis, Kenny Dorham, Dizzy Gillespie, Al Porcino, Red Rodney*

TROMBONES: *Eddie Bert, Jimmy Knepper, plus four other unnamed trombonists*

SAXES: *Joe Maini, Charlie Kennedy, Charlie Parker (alto), Al Cohn, Zoot Sims, Don Lanphere, Billy Miles (tenor), Gerry Mulligan, Bob Newman (bari)*

GUITAR: *Sam Herman*

BASS: *Buddy Jones*

DRUMS: *Phil Arabia, Charlie Perry*

ARRANGER AND CONDUCTOR: *Gene Roland*

Recorded 3 April 1950, NYC

[Not seen; described by Tercinet, who adds two untitled numbers performed by Parker and rhythm; date corrected from March by Jack. Mulligan recalls being present but disclaims playing.]

Stan Getz and His Orchestra (Charlie Parker CP-503); 1950.

Four Brothers; Early Autumn; My Gentleman Friend

TRUMPETS: *Stan Fishelson, Al Porcino, Idrees Sulieman*

BASS TRUMPET: *Johnny Mandel*

SAXES: *Don Lanphere, Zoot Sims, Stan Getz (tenor), Gerry Mulligan (bari)*

PIANO: *Billy Taylor*

BASS: *Tommy Potter*

DRUMS: *Roy Haynes*

VOCAL: (on "My Gentleman Friend"): *Sarah Vaughan*

Recorded live 17 August 1950, NYC

[Not seen; described by Jack as a show recorded at the Apollo Theater.]

Charlie Parker: The Verve Years, 1950–51 (Verve VE-2-2512); 1950.

Rocker

ALTO SAX: *Charlie Parker*

OBOE: *Tommy Mace*

VIOLINS: *Sam Caplan, Ted Bloom, Stan Karpenia*

VIOLA: *Dave Uchitel*

CELLO: *Bill Bundy*

HARP: *Wallace McManus*

PIANO: *Al Haig*

BASS: *Tommy Potter*

DRUMS: *Roy Haynes*
ARRANGER: *Gerry Mulligan*

Recorded live 16 September 1950, NYC

Gerry Mulligan All Stars: Mulligan Plays Mulligan [reissued as **Historically Speaking**] (Prestige 7006 [7251]); 1951.

Funhouse; Ide's Side; Roundhouse; Kaper; Bweebida Bobbida; Mullenium; Mulligan's Too

SAXES: *Allen Eager (tenor), Max McElroy, Gerry Mulligan (bari)*
TRUMPETS: *Jerry Hurwitz [Lloyd], Nick Travis*
TROMBONE: *Ollie Wilson*
PIANO: *George Wallington*
BASS: *Phil Leshin*
DRUMS: *Walter Bolden*
MARACAS: *Gail Madden*   Recorded 27 August 1951, NYC

["Funhouse" and "Mullenium" omit trumpets and trombone; "Mulligan's Too" omits trumpets, trombone, and McElroy's bari. All discographies indicate an initial take of "Kaper" as rejected. Jepsen dates the session as 21 September 1951; Tercinet indicates 27 August 1951; both Middleton and the album's liner notes by Les Davis say 17 August, but the recently issued compact disc (Prestige OJCCD-003-2) with notes by Ira Gitler specifies 27 August and modifies the conventional shorthand of "NYC" to indicate recording in Hackensack, New Jersey. French discographers name the band Gerry Mulligan New Stars, while others say Gerry Mulligan All Stars. Mulligan recalls New York as being correct location.]

One Night Stand with Stan Kenton's Concert in Miniature No. 9 and 10 (Joyce 1087); 1952.

Limelight; I've Got You under My Skin; Young Blood

TRUMPETS: *Buddy Childers, Maynard Ferguson, Conte Candoli, Reuben McFall, Don Dennis*
TROMBONES: *Bob Burgess, Frank Rosolino, Bill Russo, Keith Moon, George Roberts (bass trombone)*
SAXES: *Dick Meldonian, Vinnie Dean (alto), Lee Elliot, Bill Holman (tenor), Bob Gioga (bari)*
PIANO: *Stan Kenton*
GUITAR: *Sal Salvador*
BASS: *Don Bagley*
DRUMS: *Stan Levey*

Recorded live 29 July 1952 at Steel Pier, Atlantic City, N.J. (first two cuts), and 5 August 1952 at Club 86, Geneva, N.Y.

[Mulligan does not recall "I've Got You under My Skin" as his arrangement.]

Stan Kenton and His Orchestra (Capitol EAP 1-383 and W 569-7); 1952.

Young Blood; Swinghouse

Same personnel as *One Night Stand* above, except that Lee Konitz and Richie Kamuca replace Dick Meldonian and Lee Elliot on alto and tenor sax respectively.

Recorded 10 and 15 September 1952, Chicago

[Not seen; described by Tercinet.]

Stan Kenton and His Orchestra: Europe—'Fifty Three (First Heard FH49); 1952.

Young Blood; Walking Shoes

TRUMPETS: *Buddy Childers, Vince Minichiello, Conte Candoli, Don Dennis, Don Smith*

TROMBONES: *Bob Burgess, Frank Rosolino, Bill Russo, Keith Moon, Bill Smiley (bass trombone)*

SAXES: *Dave Schildkraut, Lee Konitz (alto), Bill Holman, Zoot Sims (tenor), Tony Ferina (bari)*

PIANO: *Stan Kenton*

GUITAR: *Barry Galbraith*

BASS: *Don Bagley*

DRUMS: *Stan Levey*   Recorded live 16 September 1953, Munich

Stan Kenton: Contemporary Concepts (Creative World ST-1003); 1952.

Limelight

TRUMPETS: *Ed Leddy, Al Porcino, Sam Noto, Stu Williamson, Bob Clark*

TROMBONES: *Bob Fitzpatrick, Carl Fontana, Kent Larsen, Gus Chappell, Don Kelly*

SAXES: *Lennie Niehaus, Charlie Mariano (alto), Bill Perkins, Dave VanKriedt (tenor), Don Davidson (bari)*

PIANO: *Stan Kenton*

GUITAR: *Ralph Blaze*

BASS: *Max Bennett*

DRUMS: *Mel Lewis*   Recorded 20 July 1955, Chicago

Kenton '56: The Concepts Era (Artistry AR-103); 1952.

All the Things You Are; Swing House; Young Blood; Walking Shoes

TRUMPETS: *Ed Leddy, Dennis Grillo, Lee Katzman, Phil Gilbert, Billy Catalano*

TROMBONES: *Bob Fitzpatrick, Kent Larsen, Jim Amlotte, Kenny Schroyer (bass trombone)*

TUBA: *Jay McAllister*

FRENCH HORNS: *Irving Rosenthal, Erik Kessler*

SAXES: *Lennie Niehaus (alto), Bill Perkins, Richie Kamuca (tenor),*
         Pepper Adams (bari)
PIANO: *Stan Kenton*
GUITAR: *Ralph Blaze*
BASS: *Don Bagley*
DRUMS: *Mel Lewis*
               Recorded live 5 November 1956, San Francisco

[Jepsen lists a concert at Cornell University recorded on a Cornell Jazz 10-inch LP, 15 April 1953, including Mulligan's "Young Blood," "Walking Shoes," and "Bweebida Bobbida."]

Vic Lewis and His Orchestra: Mulligan's Music (Decca LF-1157, London LB-980, Mole 9); 1952.

Walkin' Shoes; Bweebida Bobbida; Limelight; Nights at the Turntable; Westwood Walk; Sextet; Bark for Barksdale; Line for Lyons
TRUMPETS: *Dave Loban, Ronnie Baker, Les Condon, Colin Wright*
TROMBONES: *Lad Busby, John Watson, Jack Botterall, Laurie*
           Franklin
SAXES: *Ronnie Chamberlain, Bernard Allen (alto), Wes Wigfield*
         (tenor), Tubby Hayes, Brian Rogerson (tenor and bari)
PIANO: *Don Riddell*
BASS: *Dave Willis*
DRUMS: *Kenny Hollick*
CONDUCTOR: *Vic Lewis*
                 Recorded 13 and 14 January 1954, London

[Not seen; described by Middleton and Tercinet and supplemented by Jack; first three cuts are Mulligan's arrangements, while the balance consists of Johnny Keating arrangements of Mulligan numbers.]

Jazz Superstars: Jam Session Record No. 102 (Jam Session JS-102); 1952.

Tiny's Blues; I Cover the Waterfront; I'm in the Mood for Love
TENOR SAXES: *Gerry Mulligan and Dave Pell*
TRUMPET: *Ted Ottison*
PIANO: *Paul Smith*
BASS: *Joe Mondragon*
DRUMS: *Bill Wilson*

Out of Nowhere; Our Delight; Lullaby of the Leaves; Blues
BARITONE SAX: *Gerry Mulligan*
PIANO: *Jimmy Rowles*
GUITAR: *Howard Roberts*
BASS: *Joe Mondragon*
DRUMS: *Tommy Rundell*   Recorded live 27 May 1952, LA

The Complete Pacific Jazz and Capitol Recordings of the Original Gerry Mulligan Quartet and Tentette with Chet Baker (Mosaic MR5-102, five LP discs); 1952–1953.

Get Happy; 'S Wonderful; Godchild
BARITONE SAX AND PIANO: *Gerry Mulligan*
BASS: *Red Mitchell*
DRUMS: *Chico Hamilton*

Haig and Haig [version based on "Dinah"]; She Didn't Say Yes, She Didn't Say No
BARITONE SAX: *Gerry Mulligan*
TRUMPET: *Chet Baker*
PIANO: *Jimmy Rowles*
BASS: *Joe Mondragon*   Recorded 9 July 1952, LA

Bernie's Tune; Lullaby of the Leaves; Utter Chaos #1
BARITONE SAX: *Gerry Mulligan*
TRUMPET: *Chet Baker*
BASS: *Bob Whitlock*
DRUMS: *Chico Hamilton*   Recorded 16 August 1952, LA

Aren't You Glad You're You; Frenesi; Nights at the Turntable; Freeway [unedited version]; Soft Shoe; Walkin' Shoes
Same personnel as above.   Recorded 15–16 October 1952, LA

A Ballad; Westwood Walk; Walkin' Shoes; Rocker
SAXES: *Bud Shank (alto), Gerry Mulligan, Don Davidson (bari)*
TRUMPETS: *Chet Baker, Pete Candoli*
VALVE TROMBONE: *Bob Enevoldsen*
FRENCH HORN: *John Graas*
TUBA: *Ray Siegel*
BASS: *Joe Mondragon*
DRUMS: *Chico Hamilton*   Recorded 29 January 1953, LA

Takin' a Chance on Love; Flash; Simbah; Ontet
Same personnel as above, except drummer Larry Bunker replaces Chico Hamilton.   Recorded 31 January 1953 LA

[The eight above cuts also exist as *Gerry Mulligan Tentette* (Capitol Jazz Classics Vol. 4, M-11029) and as part of *Gerry Mulligan Tentette and Quartet* (Quintessence Jazz Series QJ-25321).]

Makin' Whoopee; Cherry; Motel; Carson City Stage [unedited]
BARITONE SAX: *Gerry Mulligan*
TRUMPET: *Chet Baker*
BASS: *Carson Smith*
DRUMS: *Larry Bunker*   Recorded 24 February 1953, LA

Festive Minor; My Old Flame; All the Things You Are
Same personnel as above.   Recorded 27 March 1953, LA

[Jack believes first and last tracks are from December 1957.]

Love Me or Leave Me (alternate and master); Swing House; Jeru, Utter Chaos #2

Same personnel as above.   Recorded 27 April 1953, LA

Darn That Dream [unedited master and alternate]; I May Be Wrong [master and alternate]; I'm Beginning to See the Light [alternate and master]; The Nearness of You; Tea for Two

Same personnel as above.   Recorded 29–30 April 1953, LA

Five Brothers [unedited]; I Can't Get Started; Ide's Side, Haig and Haig [version based on "Funhouse"]; My Funny Valentine [unedited]

Same personnel as above.   Recorded live 20 May 1953, LA

Aren't You Glad You're You; Get Happy; Poinciana; Godchild

Same personnel as above, except drummer Chico Hamilton replaces Larry Bunker   Recorded live 20 May 1953, LA

[*Gerry Mulligan Quartet* (World Pacific PJ-1207) features twelve of the above cuts: "Frenesi," "Nights at the Turntable," "Lullaby of the Leaves," "Jeru," "Cherry," "Swinghouse," "I May Be Wrong," "Aren't You Glad You're You" (studio version), "I'm Beginning to See the Light," "The Nearness of You," "Makin' Whoopee," "Tea for Two."]

Too Marvelous for Words; Lover Man; I'll Remember April; These Foolish Things; All the Things You Are; Bernie's Tune

SAXES: *Lee Konitz (alto), Gerry Mulligan (bari)*
TRUMPET: *Chet Baker*
BASS: *Carson Smith*
DRUMS: *Larry Bunker*   Recorded live June 1953, LA

[Mosaic liner notes speculate these recordings as dating from either January or June, while Jepsen follows the original World Pacific issue by listing 25 January 1953; others suggest June and are supported by aural evidence plus the memory of producer Richard Bock, who recorded the date.]

Almost Like Being in Love; Sextet; Broadway

Same personnel as above.   Recorded June 1953, LA

[Mosaic lists January or June, but an errata sheet specifies 23 and 30 January and 1 February.]

I Can't Believe That You're in Love with Me; Lady Be Good [master and alternate]

Same personnel as above, except bassist Joe Mondragon replaces Carson Smith.   Recorded 10 June 1953, LA

[*Lee Konitz Plays with the Gerry Mulligan Quartet* (World Pacific PJM-406) includes "I Can't Believe That You're In Love With Me," "Broadway," "Almost Like Being in Love," "Sextet," "Lady Be Good," "Too Marvelous for Words," "Lover Man," "I'll Remember April," "These Foolish Things," and "All the Things You Are."]

Gerry Mulligan, Featuring Chet Baker, Chico Hamilton (Fantasy 3-220; Prestige PR-20416, less "Utter Chaos"); 1952–1953.

> Line for Lyons; Carioca; My Funny Valentine; Bark for Barksdale; Utter Chaos
>> BARITONE SAX: *Gerry Mulligan*
>> TRUMPET: *Chet Baker*
>> BASS: *Carson Smith*
>> DRUMS: *Chico Hamilton*   Recorded 2 September 1952, LA
>
> Limelight; The Lady Is a Tramp; Turnstile; Moonlight in Vermont
>> Same personnel as above.   Recorded 3 January 1953, LA

Boots Brown [pseudonym for Shorty Rogers] and His Blockbusters (Victor 20-5110; LPM-1071; Groove LG-100); 1952.

> Block Buster; Shortnin' Bread; Oh Happy Day; Dynamite
>> TRUMPET: *Shorty Rogers*
>> TROMBONE: *Milt Bernhart*
>> SAXES: *Bud Shank (alto), Jimmy Guiffre (tenor), Gerry Mulligan (bari)*
>> PIANO: *Marty Paich*
>> GUITAR: *Jimmie Wyble*
>> BASS: *Howard Rumsey*
>> DRUMS: *Roy Harte*
>> VOCAL: *Joe Joe Johnson (Shad Turner)*
>>> Recorded 19 November 1952, LA
>
> [Not seen; described by Jepsen under Boots Brown.]

Gerry Mulligan with Chet Baker (GNP Crescendo GNPS-56); 1953.

> Varsity Drag; Speak Low; Half Nelson; Lady Bird; Love Me or Leave Me; Swing House
>> BARITONE SAX: *Gerry Mulligan*
>> TRUMPET: *Chet Baker*
>> BASS: *Carson Smith*
>> DRUMS: *Larry Bunker*   Recorded 7 May 1953, LA

The Fabulous Gerry Mulligan Quartet: Paris Concert 1954 (Vogue Jazz Series K18P-6755/6, two record set); 1954.

> I May Be Wrong; Five Brothers; Gold Rush; Lullaby of the Leaves; Makin' Whoopee; Laura; Motel [mistakenly listed as "Soft Shoe"]; The Nearness of You; Limelight; Come Out Wherever You Are; Love Me or Leave Me; Bernie's Tune; Walkin' Shoes; Moonlight in Vermont; The Lady Is a Tramp; Bark for Barksdale
>> BARITONE SAX: *Gerry Mulligan*

VALVE TROMBONE: *Bob Brookmeyer*
BASS: *Red Mitchell*
DRUMS: *Frank Isola*   Recorded live 1–7 June 1954, Paris

[*Gerry Mulligan Quartet: Paris Concert* (Pacific Jazz PJ-1210) includes "Come Out Wherever You Are," "Five Brothers," "Laura," "Love Me or Leave Me," "Utter Chaos" (not included on the Vogue issue), "Bernie's Tune," "Walkin' Shoes," "Moonlight in Vermont," "The Lady Is a Tramp," and a second version of "Utter Chaos"; *Gerry Mulligan: Paris Concert* (Pacific Jazz PJ-10102) adds to this selection "Soft Shoe" (not included on the Vogue issue) and "Motel" (which the Vogue issue lists as "Soft Shoe").]

Gerry Mulligan and His Quartet, Featuring Guests Zoot Sims and Bob Brookmeyer: California Concerts (World Pacific PJ-1201); 1954.

Blues Going Up; Little Girl Blue; Piano Blues; Yardbird Suite; Utter Chaos
BARITONE SAX AND PIANO: *Gerry Mulligan*
TRUMPET: *Jon Eardley*
BASS: *Red Mitchell*
DRUMS: *Chico Hamilton*
            Recorded live 3 December 1954, Stockton, California

[Liner notes misdate this concert as 12 November. *Jazz West Coast* World Pacific K18P-9258 adds "Soft Shoe."]

Western Reunion; I Know, Don't Know How; The Red Door
SAXES: *Zoot Sims (tenor), Gerry Mulligan (bari)*
VALVE TROMBONE AND PIANO: *Bob Brookmeyer*
TRUMPET: *Jon Eardley*
BASS: *Red Mitchell*
DRUMS: *Larry Bunker*
            Recorded live 14 December 1954, San Diego, California

Gerry Mulligan: California Concerts Volume 1 (Pacific Jazz/Capitol compact disc CDP-7-46860-2); 1954.

Blues Going Up; Little Girl Blue; Piano Blues; Yardbird Suite; Blues for Tiny; Soft Shoe; Makin' Whoopee; Darn That Dream; Ontet; A Bark for Barksdale
Same personnel, date, and location as 3 December 1954 above.

Gerry Mulligan: California Concerts Volume 2 (Pacific Jazz/Capitol compact disc CDP-7-46864-2); 1954.

Makin' Whoopee; Nights at the Turntable; Blues for Tiny; Frenesi; Limelight

Same personnel, date, and location as 3 December 1954 above.

People Will Say We're in Love; Western Reunion; I Know, Don't Know How; The Red Door; Polka Dots and Moonbeams; I'll Remember April; There Will Never Be Another You; It Don't Mean A Thing (If It Ain't Got That Swing); In a Sentimental Mood/Flamingo/Moon Mist

Same personnel, date, and location as 14 December 1954 above.

John Graas: Jazz Studio 3 (Decca ED-2190 and 2192; MCA Coral 6.22070); 1954.

Mulliganesque; $\frac{6}{4}$ and Even; My Buddy

TRUMPET: *Don Fagerquist*
FRENCH HORN, ARRANGER, AND CONDUCTOR: *John Graas*
BARITONE SAX: *Gerry Mulligan*
PIANO: *Marty Paich*
GUITAR: *Howard Roberts*
BASS: *Red Mitchell*
DRUMS: *Larry Bunker*   Recorded 16 December 1954, LA

[Not seen; described by Jepsen and Tercinet, with trumpet and piano sitting out on "My Buddy."]

Gerry Mulligan: New York December 1960 (Musidisc Europe Jazz Anthology JA-5236); 1955.

Everything Happens to Me

BARITONE SAX: *Gerry Mulligan (accompanied by a large unidentified orchestra)*

Bernie's Tune

BARITONE SAX: *Gerry Mulligan with his sextet, personnel not identified*   Recorded live 3 March 1955, NYC

[Tercinet identifies the occasion as a broadcast of the Steve Allen television show and speculates that the trumpet player on "Bernie's Tune" is Jon Eardley; he lists Alto 717 as the original recording issued; other instruments identifiable on "Bernie's Tune," in addition to Mulligan's baritone sax and Eardley's trumpet, are piano, guitar, bass, and drums.]

Presenting the Gerry Mulligan Sextet (EmArcy MG-36056); 1955.

Mud Bug; Sweet and Lovely; Apple Core; Bernie's Tune

SAXES: *Zoot Sims (tenor), Gerry Mulligan (bari)*
VALVE TROMBONE: *Bob Brookmeyer*
TRUMPET: *Jon Eardley*
BASS: *Peck Morrison*
DRUMS: *Dave Bailey*   Recorded 21 September 1955, NYC

Nights at the Turntable; Broadway; Everything Happens to Me; The
Lady Is a Tramp
    Same personnel as above.   Recorded 31 October 1955, NYC

Gerry Mulligan Sextet: The Vibes Are On (Chazzer 2005); 1955.
    The Red Door; Soft Shoe; Makin' Whoopee; Bernie's Tune
    Same personnel as *Presenting* above.
                Recorded live 12 December 1955, NYC

[Not seen; Jack describes the session as recorded at the Basin Street
East club in NYC, as does Astrup, who notes unissued takes of
"Theme" (most likely "Utter Chaos") and "I Don't Know Why" (most
likely "I Know, Don't Know How") and describes an unissued October 1955 broadcast from the same location with the same personnel, playing "Theme," "Apple Core," "Moonlight in Vermont," and a
fadeout of "Broadway."]

Mainstream: Gerry Mulligan and His Sextet (EmArcy MG-36101); 1955–
1956.
    Blue at the Roots
    Same personnel as above, except Mulligan plays piano instead.
                Recorded 22 September 1955, NYC
    Mainstream; Ain't It the Truth
    Same personnel as above, except Mulligan is back on baritone sax and
    bassist Bill Crow replaces Peck Morrison.
                Recorded 25 January 1956, NYC
    Elevation; Igloo; Lollypop
    Same personnel as above, except trumpeter Don Ferrara replaces
    Jon Eardley.   Recorded 26 September 1956, NYC

A Profile of Gerry Mulligan (Mercury MG-20453); 1955–1956.
    Duke Ellington Medley (Moon Mist; In a Sentimental Mood)
    Same personnel, date, and location as 21 September 1955 above.
    Westwood Walk; Blues (described by Jepsen as an alternate take of
    "Blue at the Roots")
    Same personnel, date, and location as 22 September 1955 above.
    Demanton
    Same personnel, date, and location as 31 October 1955 above.
    La Plus Que Lente; Makin' Whoopee
    Same personnel, date, and location as 26 September 1956 above.

    [A three-volume Japanese reissue titled *Mainstream* (EmArcy 195J-
34, 35, 36) includes all material from the above three sextet albums

plus adds alternate takes of "Blues," "Everything Happens to Me," "The Lady Is a Tramp," and "Broadway." *Mainstream* (EmArcy compact disc 826 933-2) adds alternate takes of "Westwood Walk and "La Plus Que Lente" to a selection of sextet recordings.]

Gerry Mulligan Quartet: Recorded Live in Boston at Storyville (Pacific Jazz PJ-1228); 1956.

Bweebida Bwobbida; Birth of the Blues; Baubles, Bangles, and Beads; Rustic Hop; Utter Chaos; Open Country; Storyville Story; That Old Feeling; Bike Up the Strand; Utter Chaos (second version)

BARITONE SAX AND PIANO: *Gerry Mulligan*

VALVE TROMBONE: *Bob Brookmeyer*

BASS: *Bill Crow*

DRUMS: *Dave Bailey*   Recorded live 1–6 December 1956, Boston

[*The Genius of Gerry Mulligan* (Pacific Jazz PJ-8) includes "Blue at the Roots," another take from the Storyville sessions with Mulligan on piano; the Japanese Pacific Jazz version of Storyville (CP32-5358) includes this and the other cuts plus "Ide's Side," "I Can't Get Started" (Gerry on piano), "Frenesi," "Flash" (Gerry on piano), "Honeysuckle Rose" (Bob on piano), and "Limelight/Utter Chaos."]

Billy Taylor with the Quincy Jones Orchestra / My Fair Lady (ABC Paramount ABC-177); 1957.

Show Me; The Rain in Spain; I Could Have Danced All Night; Get Me to the Church on Time [plus five other tracks without Mulligan]

TRUMPETS: *Ernie Royal, Don Elliott*

TROMBONE: *Jimmy Cleveland*

FRENCH HORN: *Jim Buffington*

TUBA: *Jay McAllister*

SAXES: *Tony Ortega (alto and tenor), Gerry Mulligan (bari)*

PIANO: *Billy Taylor*

GUITAR: *Al Cassamenti*

BASS: *Earl May*

DRUMS: *Ed Thigpen*   Recorded 5 February 1957, NYC

[Not seen; described by Jepsen under Billy Taylor.]

Manny Albam and the Jazz Greats of Our Time, Volume One (Coral CRL-57173); 1957.

My Sweetie Went Away; See Here Miss Bromley; Poor Dr. Millmoss; All Too Soon; Minor Matters; Latined Fractured; Blues from Neither Coast

TRUMPETS: *Nick Travis, Art Farmer*

VALVE TROMBONE: *Bob Brookmeyer*
SAXES: *Phil Woods (alto), Zoot Sims (tenor), Gerry Mulligan (bari),*
     Al Cohn (ténor and bari)
PIANO: *Hank Jones*
BASS: *Milt Hinton*
DRUMS: *Osie Johnson*   Recorded 2–4 April 1957, NYC
Am I Blue?
Same personnel as above.   Recorded 2 April 1957, NYC.

[Released as part of *Leonard Feather Presents: An Encyclopedia of Jazz on Records, Vol. 5* (MCA2-4063, two-record set).]

Gerry Mulligan: The Arranger (Columbia JC-34803); 1957.
Thruway; All the Things You Are; Mullenium; Motel
TRUMPETS: *Don Ferrara, Don Joseph, Jerry Lloyd, Phil Sunkel*
TROMBONES: *Bob Brookmeyer (valve), Jim Dahl, Frank Rehak*
SAXES: *Lee Konitz, Hal McKusick (alto), Charlie Rouse, Zoot Sims*
     (tenor), Gene Allen, Gerry Mulligan (bari)
PIANO: *Gerry Mulligan*
BASS: *Joe Benjamin*
DRUMS: *Dave Bailey*   Recorded 19–20 April 1957, NYC

[Jack notes an alternate take of "Thruway" on Columbia CL-1765, *Who's Who in the Swinging Sixties*; Gus Johnson replaces Dave Bailey on "Mullenium."]

Gerry Mulligan in Sweden (Jazz Information CAH-4003/4, two-record set); 1957.
Birth of the Blues; Open Country; I Can't Get Started; Interview: Gerry Mulligan-Olle Helander; Frenesi; Baubles, Bangles, and Beads; Yardbird Suite; Walkin' Shoes; My Funny Valentine; Blue at the Roots; Come Out Wherever You Are; Moonlight in Vermont; Lullaby of the Leaves; Bernie's Tune
BARITONE SAX AND PIANO: *Gerry Mulligan*
VALVE TROMBONE: *Bob Brookmeyer*
BASS: *Joe Benjamin*
DRUMS: *Dave Bailey*   Recorded live 17 May 1957, Stockholm

[Astrup notes unissued takes of "As Catch Can," "Just in Time," "What Is There to Say," and "Utter Chaos," although these titles imply the subsequent quartet with Art Farmer.]

The Teddy Wilson Trio and Gerry Mulligan Quartet with Bob Brookmeyer at Newport (Verve MGV-8235); 1957.
Sweet Georgia Brown
BARITONE SAX: *Gerry Mulligan*

PIANO: *Teddy Wilson*
BASS: *Milt Hinton*
DRUMS: *Specs Powell*

My Funny Valentine; Utter Chaos
BARITONE SAX: *Gerry Mulligan*
VALVE TROMBONE: *Bob Brookmeyer*
BASS: *Joe Benjamin*
DRUMS: *Dave Bailey*

Recorded live 6 July 1957, Newport, Rhode Island

[Astrup notes an unissued take of "Motel."]

Jazz Giants '58 (Verve MGV-8248); 1957.

Chocolate Sundae; When Your Lover Has Gone; Candy; Ballade (medley of Lush Life; Lullaby of the Leaves; Makin' Whoopee; It Never Entered My Mind); Woodyn' You
SAXES: *Stan Getz (tenor), Gerry Mulligan (bari)*
TRUMPET: *Harry Edison*
PIANO: *Oscar Peterson*
GUITAR: *Herb Ellis*
BASS: *Ray Brown*
DRUMS: *Louis Bellson*

Recorded 31 July 1957, NYC

The Gerry Mulligan-Paul Desmond Quartet (Verve MGV-8246); 1957.

Blues Intime; Body and Soul; Wintersong
SAXES: *Paul Desmond (alto), Gerry Mulligan (bari)*
BASS: *Joe Benjamin*
DRUMS: *Dave Bailey*

Recorded 1 August 1957, NYC

Standstill; Line for Lyons; Battle Hymn of the Republican; Fall Out
Same personnel as above.

Recorded 27 August 1957, NYC

[Ruppli indicates unissued tracks of "Now Here" and "These Foolish Things" from the 1 August session.]

Mulligan Meets Monk (Riverside RLP-1106); 1957.

Rhythm-a-ning; Straight, No Chaser; I Mean You
BARITONE SAX: *Gerry Mulligan*
PIANO: *Thelonious Monk*
BASS: *Wilbur Ware*
DRUMS: *Shadow Wilson*

Recorded 12 August 1957, NYC

'Round Midnight; Sweet and Lovely; Decidedly
Same personnel as above.

Recorded 13 August 1957, NYC

[*Thelonious Monk/Gerry Mulligan* (Milestone M-47067) adds alternate takes of "Straight, No Chaser," "Decidedly," and "I Mean You."]

Gerry Mulligan and Bob Brookmeyer Play Phil Sunkel's Jazz Concerto Grosso (ABC Paramount ABC-225); 1957.

Jazz Concerto Grosso
>   TRUMPETS: *Nick Travis, Al Stewart, Don Stratton, John Wilson*
>   TROMBONES: *Bob Brookmeyer (valve), Frank Rehak, Eddie Bert*
>   *(bass)*
>   TUBA: *Don Butterfield*
>   SAXES: *Dick Meldonian (alto), Cliff Hoff, Bill Slapin (tenor), Gene*
>   *Allen, Gerry Mulligan (bari)*
>   CORNET: *Phil Sunkel*
>   BASS: *Milt Hinton*
>   DRUMS: *Osie Johnson*   Recorded 14 October 1957, NYC

Something for the Ladies; Song for Cornet
>   CORNET: *Phil Sunkel*
>   FLUEGELHORN: *John Wilson*
>   VALVE TROMBONE: *Bob Brookmeyer*
>   SAXES: *Jim Reider (tenor), Gerry Mulligan (bari)*
>   BASS: *Wendell Marshall*
>   DRUMS: *Harold Granowsky*   Recorded 15 October 1957, NYC

Getz Meets Mulligan in Hi-Fi (Verve MGV-8249); 1957.

>   Let's Fall in Love; Anything Goes; Too Close for Comfort; That Old
>   Feeling; This Can't Be Love; Ballad
>   SAXES: *Stan Getz (tenor), Gerry Mulligan (bari) [the two switch*
>   *horns for the first three cuts]*
>   PIANO: *Lou Levy*
>   BASS: *Ray Brown*
>   DRUMS: *Stan Levey*   Recorded 22 October 1957, LA

Stan Getz and Gerry Mulligan / Stan Getz and the Oscar Peterson Trio (Verve MGV-8348); 1957.

>   Scrapple from the Apple; I Didn't Know What Time It Was
>   Same personnel, date, and location as above.

>   [Jepsen describes these cuts but states incorrectly that they were not
>   issued; Verve MGV-8349 includes liner notes stating that this album,
>   numbered in fact just before it, is shortly forthcoming; as such, it
>   includes the Getz-Mulligan cuts on side A, while side B consists of
>   four numbers by Stan Getz with the Oscar Peterson Trio. All eight
>   Getz-Mulligan tracks are collected on the two-record set, *Gerry Mul-
>   ligan: Mulligan and Getz and Desmond* (Verve VE-2-2537), which
>   also includes the material with Paul Desmond from Verve MGV-8246
>   described above.]

The Gerry Mulligan Songbook, Vol. 1 (World Pacific PJ-1237); 1957.

Four and One Moore; Crazy Day; Turnstile; Sextet; Disc Jockey Jump; Venus de Milo; Revelation

SAXES: *Lee Konitz (alto), Zoot Sims, Allen Eager (alto and tenor), Al Cohn (tenor and bari), Gerry Mulligan (bari)*
GUITAR: *Freddie Green*
BASS: *Henry Grimes*
DRUMS: *Dave Bailey*   Recorded 4–5 December 1957, NYC

Gerry Mulligan with Vinnie Burke's String Jazz Quartet (Pacific Jazz DJ-2); 1957.

The Preacher
BARITONE SAX: *Gerry Mulligan*
VIOLIN: *Dick Wetmore*
CELLO: *Calo Scott*
GUITAR: *Paul Palmieri*
BASS: *Vinnie Burke*
DRUMS: *Dave Bailey*   Recorded 5 December 1957, NYC

[Not seen; listed by Jepsen as a promotional release for disc jockeys and recorded in August 1958; Michael Cuscuna supplies the correct recording date and adds the titles of as yet unreleased material: "Out of Nowhere," "Mayreh," "I'll Remember April," "Bags' Groove," "Lullaby of Rhythm," "I Can't Get Started," "Body and Soul," and "Good Bait."]

Gerry Mulligan Quartet: Reunion with Chet Baker (World Pacific PJ-1241); 1957.

Reunion; My Heart Belongs to Daddy; When Your Lover Has Gone; Stardust; Jersey Bounce; Surrey with the Fringe on Top; Travelin' Light; Ornithology

BARITONE SAX: *Gerry Mulligan*
TRUMPET: *Chet Baker*
BASS: *Henry Grimes*
DRUMS: *Dave Bailey*   Recorded 3 and 11 December 1957, NYC

[The Pacific Jazz/EMI Manhattan compact disc reissue (CDP 7-46857-2) adds an alternate take of "Travelin' Light," the previously unreleased numbers "The Song Is You," "I Got Rhythm," and "All the Things You Are," and two cuts previously released only on Playboy records, "People Will Say We're in Love" (PB-1958) and "Gee Baby, Ain't I Good to You" (PB-1959), plus an alternate take of "Gee Baby, Ain't I Good to You." Jack indicates that "All the Things You Are" is an unedited version of the same number listed in the Mosaic collection as a 27 March 1953 session in LA and cites aural evidence for the true date being 1957, as here.]

The Real Sound of Jazz (Pumpkin 116); 1957.
Fast and Happy Blues; Dickie's Dream
TRUMPETS: *Roy Eldridge, Joe Newman, Joe Wilder, Doc Cheatham, Emmett Berry*
TROMBONES: *Vic Dickenson, Dickie Wells, Benny Morton*
SAXES: *Earle Warren* (alto), *Ben Webster, Coleman Hawkins* (tenor), *Gerry Mulligan* (bari)
PIANO: *Count Basie*
GUITAR: *Freddie Green*
BASS: *Eddie Jones*
DRUMS: *Jo Jones*
Fine and Mellow
VOCALIST: *Billie Holiday*
TRUMPETS: *Roy Eldridge, Doc Cheatham*
TROMBONE: *Vic Dickenson*
SAXES: *Coleman Hawkins, Ben Webster, Lester Young* (tenor), *Gerry Mulligan* (bari)
PIANO: *Mal Waldron*
GUITAR: *Danny Barker*
BASS: *Milt Hinton*
DRUMS: *Osie Johnson*   Televised 8 December 1957, NYC

[Astrup notes "My Man" and "Blues Medley" as unreleased. Similar material by partly different personnel, dating from this show's rehearsal session, has been released under similar titles by other labels.]

Annie Ross Sings a Song With Mulligan! (World Pacific WP-1253); 1957–1958.
How About You; This Time the Dream's On Me; Let There Be Love; Between the Devil and the Deep Blue Sea; It Don't Mean a Thing
BARITONE SAX: *Gerry Mulligan*
TRUMPET: *Chet Baker*
BASS: *Henry Grimes*
DRUMS: *Dave Bailey*
VOCAL: *Annie Ross*   Recorded 11 and 17 December 1957, NYC

[Dates are from Michael Cuscuna, working from the labels on studio tapes and correcting Jepsen and Middleton.]
I Feel Pretty; I've Grown Accustomed to Your Face; All of You; Give Me the Simple Life; This Is Always

Same personnel as above, except Art Farmer replaces Chet Baker on trumpet and Bill Crow replaces Henry Grimes on bass.

Recorded December 1957, NYC

[*The Genius of Gerry Mulligan* (Pacific Jazz PJ-8) adds "The Lady's in Love With You" with Ross, Mulligan, Grimes, and Bailey, recorded 17 December 1957, NYC, according to producer Richard Bock's 1960 liner notes. The compact disc of *Annie Ross Sings a Song with Mulligan!* (Pacific Jazz / EMI Manhattan CDP 7 46852 2) adds previously unreleased tracks of "I Guess I'll Have to Change My Plans," "You Turned the Tables on Me" (with Grimes but no trumpet), and an alternate version of "I've Grown Accustomed to Your Face" (with Grimes but no trumpet), plus a previously unreleased "My Old Flame" (with Farmer and Crow), an alternate version of "This Is Always" (with Baker and Grimes), and an unedited version of "It Don't Mean a Thing." The CD notes are by Michael Cuscuna, circa 1988.]

Timex Jazz Show (Kings of Jazz KLJ-20031); 1958.

St. Louis Blues
TRUMPET AND LEADER: *Louis Armstrong*
TROMBONE: *Jack Teagarden*
CLARINET: *Edmond Hall*
PIANO: *George Shearing*
VIBES: *Lionel Hampton*
BASS: *Mort Herbert*
DRUMS: *Danny Barcelona*
VOCAL: *Jaye P. Morgan*

Night Watch [incorrectly titled "Night Walk"]
BARITONE SAX: *Gerry Mulligan*
TRUMPET: *Art Farmer*
BASS: *Henry Grimes*
DRUMS: *Dave Bailey*   Recorded live 30 April 1958, NYC

[Not seen; described by Tercinet as a recording of the Timex Jazz Show on CBS Television.]

Gerry Mulligan: The Jazz Combo from "I Want to Live!" (United Artists UAL-4006); 1958.

Black Nightgown; Theme from *I Want to Live!*; Night Watch; Frisco Club; Barbara's Theme; Life's a Funny Thing
TRUMPET: *Art Farmer*
TROMBONE: *Frank Rosolino*
SAXES: *Bud Shank (alto and flute), Gerry Mulligan (bari)*

PIANO: *Pete Jolly*
BASS: *Red Mitchell*
DRUMS: *Shelly Manne*
ARRANGER: *Johnny Mandel*   Recorded 24 May 1958, LA

Duke Ellington and His Orchestra: Newport 1958 (Columbia CL 1245); 1958.

Prima Bara Dubla
TRUMPETS: *Cat Anderson, Harold Baker, Clark Terry, Ray Nance*
TROMBONES: *Quentin Jackson, John Sanders, Britt Woodman*
REEDS: *Jimmy Hamilton (clarinet), Johnny Hodges, Russell Procope (alto sax), Paul Gonsalves (tenor sax), Harry Carney, Gerry Mulligan (bari sax)*
PIANO: *Duke Ellington*
BASS: *Jimmy Woode*
DRUMS: *Sam Woodyard*
                Recorded live 3 July 1958, Newport, Rhode Island

Pete Johnson and the Newport Blues Band (Jackson 1206); 1958.

Pete's Boogie Woogie; Feelin' Happy; Corinne Corinna
PIANO AND VOCAL: *Pete Johnson*
TRUMPETS: *Buck Clayton, Lonnie Johnson*
TROMBONE: *Jack Teagarden*
CLARINET: *Tony Scott or Rudy Powell*
SAXES: *Earle Warren (alto), Georgie Auld, Buddy Tate (tenor), Gerry Mulligan (bari)*
BASS: *Tom Bryant*
GUITAR: *Kenny Burrell*
DRUMS: *Jo Jones*
VOCAL: *Joe Turner*
                Recorded live 5 July 1958, Newport, Rhode Island

[Not seen; described by Tercinet.]

Newport Jazz Festival (CBS 88605); 1958.

As Catch Can; Bernie's Tune; Baubles, Bangles, and Beads; Line for Lyons
BARITONE SAX: *Gerry Mulligan*
TRUMPET: *Art Farmer*
BASS: *Bill Crow*
DRUMS: *Dave Bailey*
                Recorded live 6 July 1958, Newport, Rhode Island

[Not seen; described by Middleton; also noted by Tercinet as a broadcast, dropping "As Catch Can" and adding "Blueport"; Astrup notes

"Blueport," "Moonlight in Vermont," and repeats of "Bernie's Tune" and "Baubles, Bangles, and Beads" as unissued.]

Billie Holiday at Monterey, 1958 (Black-Hawk BHK-50701); 1958.

I Only Have Eyes for You; Good Morning Heartache; Them There Eyes; Billie's Blues; Oh What a Little Moonlight Can Do; Lady Be Good; Trav'lin' Light; Lover Come Back to Me

VOCALS [ON ALL BUT "LADY BE GOOD," WHICH IS A BRIEF INSTRU-MENTAL THEME]: *Billie Holiday*
CLARINET: *Buddy DeFranco*
SAXES: *Benny Carter (alto), Gerry Mulligan (bari)*
PIANO: *Mal Waldron*
BASS: *Eddie Kahn*
DRUMS: *Dick Berk*

Recorded live 5 October 1958, Monterey, California

[A brief instrumental introduction and four other numbers by Holiday precede these selections; Mulligan joins her and the rhythm section for "I Only Have Eyes for You" and "Good Morning Heartache"; this group is then joined by DeFranco and Carter for the balance of the program.]

The Gerry Mulligan Quartet: What Is There to Say? (Columbia CL-1307); 1958–1959.

Blueport
BARITONE SAX: *Gerry Mulligan*
TRUMPET: *Art Farmer*
BASS: *Bill Crow*
DRUMS: *Dave Bailey*   Recorded 17 December 1958, NYC

My Funny Valentine
Same personnel as above.   Recorded 18 December 1958, NYC

Utter Chaos; As Catch Can
Same personnel as above.   Recorded 23 December 1958, NYC

Just in Time; What Is There to Say?; Festive Minor; News from Blueport
Same personnel as above.   Recorded 15 January 1959, NYC

Gerry Mulligan Meets Ben Webster (Verve MGV-8343); 1959.

Chelsea Bridge; Who's Got Rhythm; Go Home
SAXES: *Ben Webster (tenor), Gerry Mulligan (bari)*
PIANO: *Jimmy Rowles*
BASS: *Leroy Vinnegar*
DRUMS: *Mel Lewis*   Recorded 3 November 1959, LA

[Ruppli notes "In a Mellotone," "What Is This Thing Called Love," and "For Bessie" as unreleased takes.]

The Cat Walk; Sunday; Tell Me When
Same personnel as above.   Recorded 2 December 1959, LA

Gerry Mulligan Meets Johnny Hodges (Verve MGV-8367); 1959.

Bunny; What's the Rush; Back Beat; What's It All About; Eighteen Carrots for Rabbit; Shady Side
SAXES: *Johnny Hodges (alto), Gerry Mulligan (bari)*
PIANO: *Claude Williamson*
BASS: *Buddy Clark*
DRUMS: *Mel Lewis*   Recorded 17 November 1959, LA

[Ruppli notes "TWA" and an untitled number as unreleased takes; Mulligan does not play on "What's the Rush."]

Witherspoon, Mulligan, Webster: At the Renaissance (HiFi Jazz J-426); 1959.

Time's Gettin' Tougher Than Tough; How Long; Corina-Corina; C. C. Rider; Roll 'Em Pete; Every Day; Outskirts of Town; Goin' to Kansas City; Trouble in Mind; St. Louis Blues
VOCALIST: *Jimmy Witherspoon*
SAXES: *Ben Webster (tenor), Gerry Mulligan (bari)*
PIANO: *Jimmy Rowles*
BASS: *Leroy Vinnegar*
DRUMS: *Mel Lewis*   Recorded live 2 December 1959, LA

[Jepsen dates this session as either 2 or 9 December 1959; Astrup prefers 2 December; Tercinet chooses 9 December.]

The Subterraneans: Original Sound Track (MGM Records E-3812ST); 1959.

Why Are We Afraid; A Rose and the End; Analyst; Two by Two
PERSONNEL: *orchestra conducted by André Previn, with parts by Gerry Mulligan (bari), Art Pepper (alto), Jack Sheldon (trumpet), Bob Enevoldsen (valve trombone), André Previn (piano), Red Mitchell (bass), and Shelly Manne (drums)*

Bread and Wine; Things Are Looking Down
SAXES: *Art Pepper (alto), Bill Perkins (tenor), Gerry Mulligan (bari)*
TRUMPET: *Art Farmer*
VALVE TROMBONE: *Bob Enevoldsen*
PIANO: *Russ Freeman*

BASS: *Buddy Clark*

DRUMS: *Dave Bailey*   Recorded late 1959, LA

[Astrup dates these sessions as July 1959; others say end of year.]

Mulligan: Gerry Mulligan (Nippon Columbia Compact Disc 33C38-7682); 1960.

Festive Minor

BARITONE SAX: *Art Farmer*

BASS: *Bill Crow*

DRUMS: *Dave Bailey*

Recorded live May or June 1960, Stockholm

[Liner notes by Yuzo Fujimoto do not specify date or place, but Tercinet describes this number and personnel as part of a broadcast.]

Jeru

BARITONE SAX: *Gerry Mulligan*

PIANO: *Claude Williamson*

BASS: *Buddy Clark*

DRUMS: *Mel Lewis*   Recorded live July 1960, LA

[This cut also appears on *Europa Jazz: Dizzy Gillespie, Gerry Mulligan* listed with 1966 material below; the disc also includes "Rose Room" from 1966, described below; Jack advises that "Jeru" is in fact "Round House/Out of Nowhere"; Fujimoto's liner notes guess at the date, claiming that other material by this same personnel exists from July 1960; Astrup says July 1960 and locates the session in Los Angeles.]

Gerry Mulligan: The Concert Jazz Band (Verve MGV-8388); 1960.

I'm Gonna Go Fishin'

TRUMPETS: *Danny Stiles, Don Ferrara, Phil Sunkel*

TROMBONES: *Bob Brookmeyer (valve), Wayne Andre (slide) Alan Raph (bass)*

REEDS: *Gene Quill (alto and clarinet), Dick Meldonian (alto), Jim Reider (tenor), Gene Allen, Gerry Mulligan (bari)*

BASS: *Bill Takas*

DRUMS: *Dave Bailey*   Recorded 28–29 May 1960, NYC

Sweet and Slow; Bweebida Bobbida; Manoir des mes Rêves (D'Jango's Castle); You Took Advantage of Me; Out of This World; My Funny Valentine; Broadway

TRUMPETS: *Nick Travis, Don Ferrara, Conte Candoli*

TROMBONES: *Bob Brookmeyer (valve) Wayne Andre (slide) Alan Raph (bass)*

REEDS: *Gene Quill (alto and clarinet,) Dick Meldonian (alto), Zoot*
        Sims (tenor), Gene Allen, Gerry Mulligan (bari)
BASS: **Buddy Clark**
DRUMS: *Mel Lewis*   Recorded 25–27 July 1960, LA

[Ruppli notes "Barbara's Theme," "Walkin' Shoes," "I Know, Don't
Know How," "Utter Chaos," "Young Blood," and "Black Nightgown"
as unreleased takes.]

**Gerry Mulligan and the Concert Jazz Band on Tour: Guest Soloist, Zoot
Sims** (Verve V/V6-8438); 1960.

    Go Home; Barbara's Theme; Apple Core
    Same personnel as 25–27 July 1960 above, except trombonist Willie
    Dennis replaces Wayne Andre, alto saxophonist Bob Donovan re-
    places Dick Meldonian, tenor saxophonist Jim Reider is added to take
    Zoot Sims's section parts, baritone saxophonist Gene Allen doubles
    on bass clarinet, and Gerry Mulligan doubles on piano.
                      Recorded live November 1960, Milan
    Theme from *I Want to Live!*
    Same personnel as above.   Recorded live November 1960, Berlin
    The Red Door; Come Rain or Come Shine; Go Home (second version)
    Same personnel as above.
            Recorded live late 1960, Santa Monica, California

Gerry Mulligan and the Concert Jazz Band: Live at the Village Vanguard
(Verve V-8396); 1960.

    Blueport; Body and Soul; Black Nightgown; Come Rain or Come Shine;
    Lady Chatterly's Mother; Let My People Be
    Same personnel as above, except trumpeter Clark Terry replaces
    Conte Candoli, bassist Bill Crow replaces Buddy Clark, and Zoot
    Sims is omitted.   Recorded live 10 December 1960, NYC

    [Ruppli notes "Mother's Day," "Eighteen Carrots for Rabbit," "Body
    and Soul," "Come Rain or Come Shine," "Piano Blues," "Utter
    Chaos," "Barbara's Theme," "Black Nightgown," and "Walkin'
    Shoes" as unreleased takes or unissued alternates; Tercinet notes
    "Utter Chaos" as released on Verve MGV-8567.]

**André Previn and the MGM Studio Orchestra: Music from "The Four Horse-
men of the Apocalypse"** (catalog unspecified, but possibly Columbia CL-
1782/8583); 1961.

    Main Title; Love Theme; The Four Horsemen
    PERSONNEL: *Gerry Mulligan (baritone sax), Art Farmer (trumpet),*
    and André Previn (piano) with a large unidentified orchestra.
                   Recorded circa 1960–1961, LA

[Not seen; described by Astrup incompletely. The soundtrack album, MGM 3993, is conducted by Previn but does not include Mulligan or Farmer. Mulligan disclaims all involvement with this film.]

Holliday with Mulligan (DRG Records SL-5191); 1961.

What's the Rush; Loving You; Lazy; It Must Be Christmas; The Party's Over; It's Bad for Me; Supper Time; Pass That Peace Pipe; I've Got a Right to Sing the Blues; Summer's Over; Blue Prelude

VOCALS: *Judy Holliday*

TRUMPETS: *Nick Travis, Don Ferrara, Al DeRisi*

TROMBONES: *Bob Brookmeyer (valve), Alan Raph (bass)*

FRENCH HORNS: *Gunther Schuller, Earl Chapin, Fred Klein*

REEDS: *Walter Levinsky (clarinet and alto sax), Al Klink (flute and tenor sax), Don Asworth (oboe and tenor sax), Gene Allen (bass clarinet and baritone sax), Gerry Mulligan (baritone sax)*

PIANO: *Bernie Leighton*

BASS: *Bill Crow*

DRUMS: *Dave Bailey*   Recorded 10–17 April 1961, NYC

[Ruppli notes "Hong Kong Blues" as an unissued take from 11 April and "While We're Young" as an unissued take from 12 April.]

Gerry Mulligan: New York December 1960 (Musidisc Europe Jazz Anthology JA-5236); 1961–1962.

Bweebida Bobbida [as "Wee Bit of Bopita"]; My Funny Valentine; Out of This World; Lady Chatterly's Mother [as "Lady Chatterly's Sister"]

TRUMPETS: *Don Ferrara, Conte Candoli, Nick Travis*

TROMBONES: *Bob Brookmeyer (valve), Willie Dennis (slide), Alan Raph (bass)*

SAXES: *Gene Quill, Bob Donovan (alto), Jimmy Reider (tenor), Gene Allen (bari and bass clarinet), Gerry Mulligan (bari)*

BASS: *Bill Crow*

DRUMS: *Mel Lewis*   Recorded live 13 May 1961, NYC

Barbara's Theme [as "Blue Theme"]; Chuggin'

Personnel probably same as above.

Recorded live 28 April 1962, NYC

[Record title's dates are incorrect; Tercinet describes these cuts (and their mistitlings) as broadcasts from Birdland and as first issued on Alto 717 and King of Jazz KJ-20021, with "Theme From *I Want to Live!*" substituted for "Barbara's Theme." Astrup notes these unissued takes: "Castle of My Dreams," "I'm Gonna Go Fishin'," "Summer's Over," and "You Took Advantage of Me." Personnel for both

dates cannot be confirmed, though both Astrup and Jack believe Al
Cohn takes a tenor sax solo on "Bweebida Bobbida."]

Gerry Mulligan Presents a Concert in Jazz: The Concert Jazz Band (Verve
V-8415); 1961.

All about Rosie; Weep; I Know, Don't Know How; Chuggin'; Summer's
Over; Israel

Same personnel as for 10 December 1960, except trumpeter Doc
Severinsen replaces Clark Terry and saxophonist Bob Donovan doubles on flute.   Recorded 10–11 July 1961, NYC

Carol Sloane (Columbia CL 1766); 1961.

Prelude to a Kiss; Aren't You Glad You're You; Little Girl Blue; Who
Cares; My Ship; Will You Still Be Mine; The More I See You; Deep
Purple; Life Is Just a Bowl of Cherries; My Silent Love; Night and Day

VOCALS: *Carol Sloane*
TRUMPET: *Nick Travis*
FLUEGELHORN: *Clark Terry*
VALVE TROMBONE: *Bob Brookmeyer*
SAXES: *Al Klink (tenor), Gerry Mulligan (bari)*
PIANO: *Bernie Leighton*
GUITAR: *Barry Galbraith, Jim Hall*
BASS: *Art Davis, George Duvivier*
DRUMS: *Walter Perkins*
ARRANGERS: *Bob Brookmeyer, Bill Finegan, and unnamed others*
                                           Recorded December 1961, NYC

[Not seen; described by Jack.]

The Gerry Mulligan Quartet (Verve V/V6-8466); 1962.

I Know, Don't Know How

BARITONE SAX: *Gerry Mulligan*
VALVE TROMBONE: *Bob Brookmeyer*
BASS: *Bill Crow*
DRUMS: *Gus Johnson*   Recorded live 25 February 1962, NYC

[Ruppli notes that in a NYC session on the day preceding this the
same group recorded the following unissued takes: "Baubles, Bangles, and Beads," "I Believe in You," "My Funny Valentine," "Spring
Is Sprung," and "When Your Lover Has Gone"; from the Village
Vanguard session on 25 February Ruppli notes these takes as unissued: "My Heart Belongs to Daddy," "Strike Up the Band." Mulligan
does not recall session being live, despite aural evidence, nor does he
recall Ruppli material.]

I'm Getting Sentimental over You; Piano Train; Lost in the Stars; I Believe in You; Love in New Orleans
> Same personnel as above, plus Brookmeyer doubles on piano.
>> Recorded 14–15 May 1962, NYC

> [Ruppli notes the following unissued takes: "Five Brothers," "Come Out Wherever You Are," "Straight, No Chaser," "Subterranean Blues," "Waltz," "I'll Never Forget What's His Name," "Bye Bernie," "Limelight."]

"Jeru": Gerry Mulligan (Columbia CL-1932/CS-8732); 1962.

> Capricious; Here I'll Stay; Inside Impromptu; You've Come Home; Get Out of Town; Blue Boy; Lonely Town
> BARITONE SAX: *Gerry Mulligan*
> PIANO: *Tommy Flanagan*
> BASS: *Ben Tucker*
> CONGAS: *Alec Dorsey*
> DRUMS: *Dave Bailey*   Recorded 30 June 1962, NYC

Paul Desmond and Gerry Mulligan: Two of a Mind (RCA Victor LPM/LSP-2624); 1962.

> The Way You Look Tonight; Blight of the Fumble Bee
> SAXES: *Paul Desmond (alto), Gerry Mulligan (bari)*
> BASS: *John Beal*
> DRUMS: *Connie Kay*   Recorded 26 June 1962, NYC

> [Tercinet includes "Easy Living" as an issued cut on this recording, but Astrup identifies it correctly as an unissued take; Astrup also describes the following unused material from an 8 June 1962 session in NYC (confirmed by Tercinet) adding guitarist Jim Hall and replacing drummer Connie Kay with Ed Shaughnessy: "All the Things You Are," "Untitled Blues."]

> All the Things You Are; Stardust
> Same personnel as 26 June 1962 above, except bassist Wendell Marshall replaces John Beal.   Recorded 3 July 1962, NYC

> Two of a Mind; Out of Nowhere
> Same personnel, except bassist Joe Benjamin replaces Wendell Marshall and drummer Mel Lewis replaces Connie Kay.
>> Recorded 13 August 1962, NYC

Gerry Mulligan Quartet: Spring Is Sprung (Phillips PHM 200-077); 1962.

> Jive at Five; Four for Three; Seventeen-Mile Drive; Subterranean Blues; Spring Is Sprung; Open Country

BARITONE SAX AND PIANO: *Gerry Mulligan*
VALVE TROMBONE AND PIANO: *Bob Brookmeyer*

[Bassist and drummer are not indicated, but Tercinet identifies them as Bill Crow and Gus Johnson, as confirmed by Mulligan.]

Recorded 11–12 December 1962, NYC

Gerry Mulligan '63: The Concert Jazz Band (Verve V/V6-8515); 1962.
Little Rock Getaway; Ballad; Big City Life; Big City Blues; My Kind of Love; Pretty Little Gypsy; Bridgehampton South; Bridgehampton Strut
TRUMPETS: *Clark Terry (doubling on fluegelhorn), Nick Travis, Don Ferrara, Doc Severinsen*
TROMBONES: *Bob Brookmeyer (valve), Willie Dennis (slide), Tony Studd (bass)*
REEDS: *Gene Quill (clarinet and alto), Eddie Caine (flute and alto), Jim Reider (tenor), Gene Allen (bass clarinet and bari), Gerry Mulligan (clarinet and bari)*
PIANO: *Gerry Mulligan, Bob Brookmeyer*
GUITAR: *Jim Hall*
BASS: *Bill Crow*
DRUMS: *Gus Johnson*   Recorded 18–21 December 1962, NYC

Gerry Mulligan Sextet (Musica Jazz FD4-1025); 1963.
Beaver
BARITONE SAX: *Gerry Mulligan*
TRUMPET: *Art Farmer*
VALVE TROMBONE: *Bob Brookmeyer*
GUITAR: *Jim Hall*
BASS: *Bill Crow*
DRUMS: *Dave Bailey*
Recorded live 5 July 1963, Newport, Rhode Island

[Not seen; described by Jack.]

Gerry Mulligan: Night Lights (Phillips PHM 200-108); 1963.
Night Lights; Wee Small Hours; Festive Minor
BARITONE SAX AND PIANO: *Gerry Mulligan*
TRUMPET AND FLUEGELHORN: *Art Farmer*
VALVE TROMBONE: *Bob Brookmeyer*
GUITAR: *Jim Hall*
BASS: *Bill Crow*
DRUMS: *Dave Bailey*   Recorded July or September 1963, NYC
Morning of the Carnival from *Black Orpheus*; Prelude in E Minor; Tell Me When
Same personnel as above.   Recorded 3 October 1963, NYC

Gerry Mulligan: Butterfly with Hiccups (Limelight LM-82004); 1963–1964.
The Ant Hill; Crazy Day
> Same personnel, date, and location as July or September 1963 session above.

Old Devil Moon
> Same personnel, date, and location as 3 October 1963 session above.

Butterfly with Hiccups
> Same personnel as above.   Recorded 11 October 1963, NYC

You'd Be So Nice to Come Home To; Theme for Jobim; Blues for Lynda; Line for Lyons
> Same personnel as above, omitting Farmer and Hall.
>   Recorded 25 June 1964, NYC

Gerry Mulligan, Pee Wee Russell (I.A.J.R.C. 28); 1964.
Blues
> CLARINET: *Pee Wee Russell*
> TENOR AND BARITONE SAX: *Gerry Mulligan*
> BASS: *Jimmy Bond*
> DRUMS: *Nick Nerow*
>   Recorded live September 1964, Monterey, California

[Not seen; described as a recording from the Monterey Jazz Festival by Jack. Mulligan does not recall performing on tenor sax.]

Gerry Mulligan: If You Can't Beat 'Em, Join 'Em (Limelight LM-82021); 1965.
> King of the Road; Engine Engine No. 9; Hush Hush Sweet Charlotte; I Know a Place; Can't Buy Me Love; A Hard Day's Night; If I Fell; Downtown; Mr. Tambourine Man; If You Can't Beat 'Em Join 'Em
> BARITONE SAX: *Gerry Mulligan*
> PIANO: *Pete Jolly*
> GUITAR: *Johnny Gray*
> BASS: *Jimmy Bond*
> DRUMS: *Hal Blaine*
>   Recorded 22 and 26–28 July 1965, Hollywood

Gerry Mulligan: Feelin' Good (Limelight LM-82030); 1965.
> The Lonely Night (Night Lights); Please Don't Talk about Me When I'm Gone; The Second Time Around; Not Mine; P. S. I Love You; The Song Is Ended (But the Melody Lingers On); Love Walked In; Feeling Good from *The Roar of the Greasepaint, the Smell of the Crowd*; Love Is the Sweetest Thing; I'll Walk Alone; The Shadow of Your Smile
> Same personnel as above, except that Gerry Mulligan doubles on clarinet, is accompanied by a ten-piece string section conducted by

Harry Bluestone, and guitarist Jimmy Helms substitutes on some cuts for Johnny Gray.   Recorded 20–22 October 1965, Hollywood

Mulligan: Gerry Mulligan (Nippon Columbia Compact Disc 33C38-7682); 1966.

Rose Room
TRUMPET: *Ruby Braff*
SAXES: *Bud Freeman (tenor), Gerry Mulligan (bari)*
PIANO: *Billy Taylor*
BASS: *Benny Moten*
DRUMS: *Osie Johnson*
Recorded live 1 July 1966, Newport, Rhode Island

[Liner notes by Yuzo Fujimoto do not speculate on date, but Jack identifies the cut as issued earlier (with date and place) on I Giganti del Jazz 42.]

Europa Jazz: Dizzy Gillespie, Gerry Mulligan (Europa Jazz EJ-1024); 1960.

I Never Knew
TRUMPET: *Ruby Braff*
SAXES: *Bud Freeman (tenor), Gerry Mulligan (bari)*
PIANO: *George Wein*
BASS: *Jack Lesberg*
DRUMS: *Buddy Rich*
Recorded live 1 July 1966, Newport, Rhode Island

[Album's liner notes date this session incorrectly as 1961; Jack identifies the cut as issued earlier (with date and place) on I Giganti del Jazz 30.]

Four Brothers
TRUMPETS: *Bill Byrne, Marvin Stamm, Bill Chase, Lyn Biviano, Dave Gale*
TROMBONES: *Jerry Collins, Henry Southall, Carl Fontana*
CLARINET, ALTO SAX, AND LEADER: *Woody Herman*
SAXES: *Bob Pierson, Frank Vicari, Sal Nistico (tenor), Tom Anastas (bari)*
PIANO: *Nat Pierce*
BASS: *Mike Moore*
DRUMS: *Ronnie Zito*
GUEST SAXOPHONISTS: *Al Cohn, Zoot Sims, Stan Getz (tenor), Gerry Mulligan (bari)*
Recorded live 3 July 1966, Newport, Rhode Island

[Album's liner notes date this session incorrectly as 1961 and lists incorrect personnel for Woody Herman's orchestra; Jack identifies the cut as issued earlier (with correct date, place, and personnel) on

I Giganti del Jazz 30; album's title reflects two cuts by Dizzy Gillespie on the B side.]

Gerry Mulligan: Something Borrowed, Something Blue (Limelight LS-86040/LM-82040); 1966.

Davenport Blues; Sometime Ago; Take Tea and See; Spring Is Sprung; New Orleans; Decidedly

SAXES: *Zoot Sims (tenor), Gerry Mulligan (alto and bari)*
PIANO: *Warren Bernhardt*
BASS: *Eddie Gomez*
DRUMS: *Dave Bailey*   Recorded 19 July 1966, NYC

[Tercinet notes "Lillibut" (Astrup: "Lili Beth") as an unissued take.]

Gerry Mulligan Quintet in Stockholm (Ingo Six); 1966

Lullaby of the Leaves; Body and Soul; All the Things You Are
BARITONE SAX: *Gerry Mulligan*
PIANO: *Burt Adams*
GUITAR: *Dean Wright*
BASS: *Eddie Gomez*
DRUMS: *Dave Bailey*   Recorded live 1966, Stockholm

[Not seen; described by Middleton; Jack advises a NYC location, as does Astrup, who dates it as a summer 1955 session.]

The Fortune Cookie (United Artists UAL-4145); 1966.

The Bad Guys; One Million Dollars; The Detectives (plus eight other tracks without Mulligan)
BARITONE SAX: *Gerry Mulligan (with unidentified musicians conducted by André Previn)*
                    Recorded 1966, Hollywood

[Mulligan disclaims involvement with this film.]

Luv (RCA/Columbia Pictures Home Video); 1967.

[Mulligan plays his own original score with a big band; orchestrations are by Bill Holman.]

Gerry Mulligan with the Dave Brubeck Quartet (Oxford OX-3024); 1968.

Out of the Way; These Foolish Things; Jumpin' Bean; St. Louis Blues
BARITONE SAX: *Gerry Mulligan*
PIANO: *Dave Brubeck*
BASS: *Jack Six*
DRUMS: *Alan Dawson*   Recorded live 17 May 1968, New Orleans

[Not seen; described by Jack, who corrects the liner notes' mistaken personnel and identifies a further cut, "Get Out of Town," as coming from Mulligan's set with Hampton Hawes in 1971.]

Compadres: The Dave Brubeck Trio Featuring Gerry Mulligan (Columbia CS-9704); 1968.
>Jumping Bean; Adios, Mariquita Linda; Indian Song; Tender Woman; Amapola; Lullaby de Mexico; Sapito; Recuerdo
>Same personnel as above.
>>Recorded live later May 1968, Mexico City

[Jack notes "Theme for Jobim" issued on the Brubeck compilation, CBS 564377.]

Blues Roots: The Dave Brubeck Trio Featuring Gerry Mulligan (Columbia CS-9749); 1969.
>Limehouse Blues; Journey; Cross Ties; Broke Blues; Things Ain't What They Used to Be; Movin' Out; Blues Roots
>Same personnel as above.   Recorded 1969, NYC

Dave Brubeck Trio with Gerry Mulligan and the Cincinnati Symphony Orchestra (MCA Records MACS-4954); 1970.
>Happy Anniversary; The Duke; Blessed Are the Poor; Forty Days; Elementals
>Same personnel as above with the Cincinnati Symphony Orchestra conducted by Erich Kunzel.
>>Recorded live 26 May 1970, Cincinnati

[Not seen; described by Tercinet.]

Dave Brubeck–Gerry Mulligan Quartet (Muza SXL-0696); 1970.
>Jumpin' Bean; St. Louis Blues
>Same personnel as Brubeck-Mulligan quartet sessions above.

[Not seen; described by Tercinet.]

Dave Brubeck Trio and Gerry Mulligan: Live at the Berlin Philharmonic (Columbia KC-32143); 1970.
>Things Ain't What They Used to Be; The Sermon on the Mount; Indian Song; Limehouse Blues; Lullaby de Mexico
>Same personnel as above.
>>Recorded live 7 November 1970, Berlin

[Tercinet adds the following numbers on a CBS European release: "The Duke," "New Orleans," "St. Louis Blues," "Out of the Way of the People," "Basin Street Blues," "Take Five."]

Beaver and Krause: *Gandharva* (Warner Brothers WS-1909); 1971.

Gandharva; By Your Grace; Good Places; Short Film for David; Bright Shadows

SAXES: *Gerry Mulligan (bari), Bud Shank (alto and flute)*
HARP: *Gail Laughton*
GUITAR: *Howard Roberts*
PIPE ORGAN: *Paul Beaver*
MOOG SYNTHESIZER: *Bernard L. Krause*

Recorded 10–11 February 1971, San Francisco

Gerry Mulligan: *The Age of Steam* (A & M Records SP-3036); 1971.

One to Ten in Ohio; K-4 Pacific; Grand Tour; Over the Hill and Out of the Woods; Country Beaver; A Weed Grows in Disneyland; Golden Notebooks; Maytag

SAXES: *Bud Shank (alto and flute), Tom Scott (tenor and soprano), Gerry Mulligan (bari and soprano)*
VALVE TROMBONE: *Bob Brookmeyer*
TRUMPET: *Harry Edison*
PIANO: *Gerry Mulligan, Roger Kellaway*
GUITAR: *Howard Roberts*
BASS: *Chuck Domanico*
DRUMS: *John Guerin, Joe Porcaro*
ADDITIONAL PERCUSSION: *Joe Porcaro, Emil Richards*
ADDITIONAL HORNS: *Ernie Watts, Kenny Schroyer, Jimmy Cleveland, Roger Bobo*

Recorded between February and July 1971, Hollywood

The Dave Brubeck Quartet Featuring Gerry Mulligan: *The Last Set at Newport* (Atlantic SD-1607); 1971.

Blues for Newport; Take Five; Open the Gates (Out of the Way of the People)

Same personnel as earlier Brubeck-Mulligan quartet sessions.

Recorded live 3 July 1971, Newport, Rhode Island

Gerry Mulligan Quartet: *"The Shadow of Your Smile"* (Moon Records MLP-003-1); 1971.

Get Out of Town; It's Sandy at the Beach; The Shadow of Your Smile; Blues in B ♭; Bright Boy Blues (I Got Rhythm)

BARITONE SAX: *Gerry Mulligan*
PIANO: *Hampton Hawes*
BASS: *Henry Franklin*
DRUMS: *Michael Garvin*   Recorded 17 July 1971, Pescara, Italy

[Not seen; described by Jack, who corrects several errors among album's list of numbers.]

The Hot Rock (soundtrack): Quincy Jones (Prophesy SD-6055); 1972.
Main Title Track; Seldom Seen Sam; Parole Party; Miasmo; Sahara Stone; Slam City; Listen to the Melody/Dixie Tag; End Title (plus four other tracks without Mulligan)
TRUMPET: *Clark Terry*
SAXES: *Jerome Richardson (soprano, tenor, and clarinet), Gerry*
           Mulligan (bari)
TROMBONE: *Frank Rosolino*
PIANO: *Clare Fisher*
VIBES: *Victor Feldman, Emil Richards (also percussion)*
GUITAR: *Dennis Budimir*
BASS: *Ray Brown, Chuck Rainey, Carol Kaye*
DRUMS: *Grady Tate*
SYNTHESIZER: *Mike Melvoin*
PERCUSSION: *Tommy Tedesco, Bobbi Porter, Milt Holland*
LEADER AND COMPOSER: *Quincy Jones*   Recorded 1972, LA

[Astrup says December 1972, which is unlikely, as both film and soundtrack recording were 1972 releases.]

Charles Mingus: Mingus and Friends in Concert (Columbia KG-31614, two record set); 1972.
Honeysuckle Rose; Jump Monk; E. S. P.; Ecclusiastics; Eclipse; Us Is Two; Mingus Blues; Little Royal Suite; E's Flat Ah's Flat Too; Ool-ya-koo
TRUMPETS: *Lonnie Hillyer, Eddie Preston, Jon Faddis, Lloyd*
           Michaels
BASS TROMBONE: *Eddie Bert*
FRENCH HORNS: *Sharon Moe, Richard Berg*
TUBA: *Robert Stewart*
FLUTE: *James Moody*
SAXES: *Charles McPherson, Lee Konitz, Richie Perri (alto), George*
           Dorsey, Gene Ammons (tenor), Bobby Jones (tenor and clar-
           inet), Gerry Mulligan (baritone sax), Howard Johnson (bar-
           itone sax and tuba)
PIANO: *John Foster, Randy Weston*
BASS: *Charles Mingus, Milt Hinton*
DRUMS: *Joe Chambers*
VOCALS: *Honey Gordon, Dizzy Gillespie, Bill Cosby*
CONDUCTOR: *Teo Macero*
           Recorded live in Town Hall, 4 February 1972, NYC

Newport in New York '72: Volume 3 (Cobblestone CST 9026-2); 1972.

Perdido; Misty; Now's the Time; Roll 'em Pete

TRUMPETS: *Joe Newman, Nat Adderley*
TROMBONE: *Tyree Glenn*
SAXES: *Illinois Jacquet, Buddy Johnson (tenor), Gerry Mulligan (bari)*
PIANO: *Jaki Byard*
BASS: *Chubby Jackson (on first two numbers), Al McKibbon (on last)*
DRUMS: *Elvin Jones*
VOCAL: *Jon Hendricks (on "Roll 'em Pete")*

Recorded live 6 July 1972, NYC

[Hendricks and "Roll 'em Pete" are described by Tercinet but not included on the American issue of this album.]

Illinois Jacquet: Birthday Party (JRC 11434); 1972.

On the Beach; Birthday Party Blues; Robbin's Nest; Blues for Louisiana; The Shadow of Your Smile

TRUMPETS: *Joe Newman, Art Farmer (sit out on last number)*
SAXES: *Illinois Jacquet, James Moody (tenor and flute), Gerry Mulligan (bari)*
PIANO AND ORGAN: *Jimmy Smith*
GUITAR: *Kenny Burrell*
BASS: *Jack Six*
DRUMS: *Roy Haynes*   Recorded live 6 October 1972, Tokyo

[Not seen; described by Tercinet. Recalled by Mulligan as a studio session.]

Gerry Mulligan Quintet: Newport Jazz Festival in Japan (Elec JRC-11436); 1972.

Mulligan Stew

BARITONE SAX: *Gerry Mulligan*
PIANO: *Jimmy Smith*
GUITAR: *Kenny Burrell*
BASS: *Jack Six*
DRUMS: *Roy Haynes*   Recorded live October 1972, Tokyo

[Not seen; described by Jack.]

Dave Brubeck, Gerry Mulligan, Paul Desmond: We're All Together Again for the First Time (Atlantic SD-1641); 1972.

Truth; Unfinished Woman; Take Five

Same personnel as Brubeck-Mulligan quartet albums above, with the addition of alto saxophonist Paul Desmond.

Recorded live 4 November 1972, Berlin

Rotterdam Blues

Same personnel as above.

Recorded live 28 October 1972, Rotterdam

[Album includes two numbers on which Gerry Mulligan does not play: "Koto Song" and "Sweet Georgia Brown."]

T-Bone Walker: Very Rare (Reprise 2 XS 6483); 1972.

Just a Little Bit

TRUMPETS: *Marvin Stamm, Danny Styles*

SAXES: *Joe Farrell, Frank Vicari (tenor and flute), Seldon Powell (tenor, bari, flute), Gerry Mulligan (bari)*

PIANO: *James Booker*

CLAVINET: *Warren Bernhardt*

GUITAR: *David T. Walker*

ELECTRIC SITAR: *John Tropes*

BASS: *Wilton Felder*

DRUMS: *Paul Humphrey*

CONGAS: *King Errison*

VOCAL: *T-Bone Walker, The Sweet Inspirations*

Stormy Monday

Same personnel minus Bernhardt, Errison, D. T. Walker, and the Sweet Inspirations, plus Charles Brown on Fender Rhodes piano and T-Bone Walker on guitar.   Recorded 1972, Hollywood and NYC

[Not seen: described by Tercinet, who explains the dual recording site as Mulligan having dubbed his part across the country in NYC.]

The Last Days of Man on Earth (Embassy Home Video VHS-4033) 1973.

[Mulligan plays baritone sax on one number and during the final credits in a score by Paul Beaver and Bernard L. Krause.]

Recorded 1973

Gerry Mulligan, Astor Piazzolla: Summit (Tango Nuevo) (Atlantic ATL-50168); 1974.

Twenty Years Ago; Close Your Eyes and Listen; Years of Solitude; Deus Xango; Twenty Years After; Aire de Buenos Aires [composed by Mulligan]; Reminiscence; Summit

BARITONE SAX: *Gerry Mulligan*

BANDONEON: *Astor Piazzolla*

PIANO, ELECTRIC PIANO, ORGAN: *Angel "Pocho" Gatti*

GUITARS: *Fillipo Dacco, Bruno de Filippi*
BASS: *Giuseppe Prestipino*
DRUMS AND PERCUSSION: *Tulio de Piscopo*
MARIMBAS: *Alberto Baldan, Gianni Zilioli*
FIRST VIOLIN: *Umberto Benedetti Michelangeli*
FIRST VIOLA: *Renato Riccio*
FIRST CELLO: *Ennio Miori*
Recorded 24–26 September and 1–4 October 1974, Milan

Gerry Mulligan, Chet Baker: Carnegie Hall Concert, Volumes 1 and 2 (CTI Records CTI-6054 and 6055-S1); 1974.

Line for Lyons; Song for an Unfinished Woman; My Funny Valentine; Song for Strayhorn
BARITONE SAX: *Gerry Mulligan*
TRUMPET: *Chet Baker*
PIANO: *Bob James*
BASS: *Ron Carter*
GUITAR: *John Scofield*
VIBES AND PERCUSSION: *Dave Samuels*
DRUMS: *Harvey Mason*

It's Sandy at the Beach; Bernie's Tune; K-4 Pacific; There Will Never Be Another You
Same personnel as above, except Gerry Mulligan is replaced by trombonist Ed Byrne for Chet Baker's vocal on "There Will Never Be Another You." Recorded live 24 November 1974, NYC

Gerry Mulligan Meets Enrico Intra (Pausa PR-7010); 1975.

Nuova Civilta; Fertile Land; Rio One [Mulligan's composition]; Champoluc
BARITONE AND SOPRANO SAXES: *Gerry Mulligan*
SOPRANO SAX AND FLUTE: *Giancarlo Barigozzi*
PIANO: *Enrico Intra*
GUITAR: *Sergio Farina*
BASSOON: *Pino Prestipino*
PERCUSSION: *Tulio de Piscopo*
Recorded 16–17 October 1975, Milan

Jazz Gala Concert (Atlantic SD-1693); 1976.

Song for Strayhorn; Festive Minor
FEATURED BARITONE SAX: *Gerry Mulligan*
FEATURED TRUMPET: *Art Farmer*
TRUMPETS: *Rick Kiefer, Ron Simmonds, Derek Watkins, Ack Van Rooyen*

TROMBONES: *Jiggs Whigham, Otto Bredl, Slide Hampton, Albert Mangelsdorff, Peter Herbolzheimer*
SAXES: *Herb Geller, Ferdinand Povel, Johnny Griffin, Wilton Gaynair, James Towsey*
CLAVIERS: *Wolfgang Dauner*
GUITAR: *Volker Kriegel*
BASS: *Niels-Henning Ørstedt Pedersen*
DRUMS: *Grady Tate*
PERCUSSION: *Nippy Noya, Alex Riel*
 Recorded live 18 January, Hanover, and 23 January, Wiesbaden

[Tercinet notes an unissued take of "Maytag."]

Gerry Mulligan's New Sextet: Idol Gossip (Chiaroscuro CR-155); 1976.
 Idol Gossip; Strayhorn Two; Walk on the Water; Waltzing Mathilda; Out Back of the Barn; North Atlantic Run; Taurus Moon
 BARITONE AND SOPRANO SAXES: *Gerry Mulligan*
 VIBES: *Dave Samuels*
 GUITAR: *Mike Santiago*
 PIANO: *Tom Fay*
 BASS: *George Duvivier*
 DRUMS: *Bob Rosengarden* Recorded 27 November 1976, NYC

Pelé (Atlantic SD-18231); 1977.
 Meu Mundo é Uma Bola (My Life Is a Ball); Voltando a Baurú (Back to Baurú); A Tristeza do Adeus (The Sadness of Goodbye) [two versions]; Amor e Agressão (Love and Aggression); Meu Mundo é Uma Bola (My Life Is a Ball) [second version]
 LEADER AND COMPOSER: *Sergio Mendes*
 BARITONE AND SOPRANO SAXES: *Gerry Mulligan*
 GUITAR: *Pelé, Oscar Castro Neves*
 KEYBOARDS: *Chico Spider*
 DRUMS: *Jimmy Keltner*
 PERCUSSION: *Steve Forman, Laudir de Oliveira, Chacal*
 BASS: *Bill Dickinson*
 VOCALS: *Pelé, Gracinha Leporace, Carol Rogers*
                Recorded 1977

[Astrup locates session in Hollywood, but film was Mexican.]

Lionel Hampton Presents: Gerry Mulligan (Who's Who in Jazz WWLP-21007); 1977.
 Apple Core; Song for Johnny Hodges; Blight of the Fumble Bee; Gerry Meets Hamp; Blues for Gerry; Line for Lyons
 BARITONE AND SOPRANO SAXES: *Gerry Mulligan*

VIBES: *Lionel Hampton*
GUITAR: *Bucky Pizzarelli*
PIANO: *Hank Jones*
BASS: *George Duvivier*
CONGAS: *Candido Camero*
DRUMS: *Grady Tate*   Recorded 29 October 1977, NYC

[The Who's Who compact disc WWCO 21007 adds "Walking Shoes" and "Limelight"; Jack notes that Kingdom Gate 7015 adds these cuts plus "Ain't Misbehavin.'"]

Lionel Hampton Presents: The Music of Charles Mingus (Who's Who in Jazz WWLP-21005); 1977.

Just for Laughs (part 1); Peggy's Blue Skylight; Caroline Keikki Mingus; Slop; Just for Laughs (Part 2); Fables of Faubus; Duke Ellington's The Sound of Light; Farewell, Farewell
TRUMPETS: *Jack Walrath; Woody Shaw*
FRENCH HORN: *Peter Matt*
SAXES: *Ricky Ford, Paul Jeffrey (tenor), Gerry Mulligan (soprano and bari)*
VIBES: *Lionel Hampton*
PIANO: *Bob Neloms*
BASS: *Charles Mingus*
DRUMS: *Dannie Richmond*   Recorded 6 November 1977, NYC

[Jack notes that Gateway GSLP 7026, *The Music of Charlie Mingus: His Final Work*, adds "So Long Eric" and that Gateway GSLP-10113 adds "It Might as Well Be Spring."]

Michel Legrand & Co.: Le Jazz Grand (Gryphon G-786-0798); 1978.

Basquette; Southern Routes: North, West, East, South (Suite)
TRUMPETS: *Jon Faddis, Joe Shepley, Burt Collins, John Gatchell*
TROMBONES: *John Clark, Albert Richmond, Brooks Tillotson*
HARP: *Gloria Agostini*
TUBA: *Tony Price*
SAXES: *Phil Woods (alto), Gerry Mulligan (bari)*
KEYBOARDS: *Bernie Leighton, Tom Pierson*
GUITAR: *Harry Leahey*
BASS: *Ron Carter*
DRUMS: *Grady Tate*
PERCUSSION: *"Crusher" Bennett, Portinho*
VIBES: *Don Elliott*
ARRANGER AND CONDUCTOR: *Michel Legrand*

La Pasionaria [featuring Phil Woods]; Malagan Stew [featuring Gerry Mulligan]; Iberia Nova [featuring Jon Faddis]

TRUMPET: *Jon Faddis*
SAXES: *Phil Woods (alto), Gerry Mulligan (bari)*
PIANO: *Michel Legrand*
BASS: *Ron Carter*
DRUMS: *Jimmy Madison*
PERCUSSION: *Portinho*   Recorded March 1978, NYC

Jay McShann Septet: The Big Apple Bash (Atlantic SD-8804); 1978.

   Crazy Legs and Friday Strut; Georgia on My Mind
   PIANO (AND VOCAL ON "GEORGIA ON MY MIND"): *Jay McShann*
   SOPRANO AND BARITONE SAXES: *Gerry Mulligan*
   TENOR SAX AND FLUTE: *Herbie Mann*
   GUITAR: *John Scofield*
   BASS: *Jack Six*
   DRUMS: *Joe Morello*
   PERCUSSION: *Sammy Figueroa*   Recorded August 1978, NYC

Gerry Mulligan and His Orchestra: Walk on the Water (DRG Records SL-5194); 1980.

   For an Unfinished Woman; Song for Strayhorn; 42nd & Broadway; Angelica; Walk on the Water; Across the Track Blues; I'm Getting Sentimental over You
   TRUMPETS: *Laurie Frink, Barry Ries, Tom Harrell, Mike Davis, Danny Hayes*
   TROMBONES: *Keith O'Quinn, Dave Glenn, Alan Raph (bass)*
   SAXES: *Gerry Niewood (alto), Ken Hitchcock (alto, tenor), Gary Keller (tenor), Ralph Olson, Seth Broedy, Eric Turkel (soprano), Gerry Mulligan (bari and soprano), Joe Temperly (bari)*
   PIANO: *Mitchel Forman*
   BASS: *Jay Leonhart, Mike Bocchicchio*
   DRUMS: *Richie DeRosa*   Recorded September 1980, NYC

Mel Tormé and Friends Recorded at Marty's in New York City (Finesse W2X-37484, two record set); 1981.

   Real Thing; Medley ("Line for Lyons," "Venus de Milo," "Walking Shoes") [eighteen other tracks omit Mulligan]
   BARITONE SAX: *Gerry Mulligan*
   PIANO: *Mike Renzi*
   BASS: *Jay Leonhart*
   DRUMS: *Donny Osborn*
   VOCAL: *Mel Tormé*   Recorded live May 1981, NYC

Aurex Jazz Festival (Aurex EWJ-80208); 1981.

Bag's Groove

SAXES: *Stan Getz (tenor), Gerry Mulligan (bari)*
TRUMPET: *Freddie Hubbard*
VALVE TROMBONE: *Bob Brookmeyer*
PIANO: *Roland Hanna*
VIBES: *Milt Jackson*
BASS: *Ray Brown*
DRUMS: *Art Blakey*   Recorded live 3 September 1981, Tokyo

[Not seen; described by Jack, who notes "Woody 'n You" as an unissued cut from the previous day in Osaka and again from the Tokyo concert.]

Bernie's Tune

BARITONE SAX: *Gerry Mulligan*
VALVE TROMBONE: *Bob Brookmeyer*
BASS: *Ray Brown*
DRUMS: *Art Blakey*   Recorded live 3 September 1981, Tokyo

Song for Strayhorn

Same personnel as above, except Hanna substitutes on piano for Brookmeyer on valve trombone.

Recorded live 6 September 1981, Yokohama

[Jack notes "Walkin' " as unissued from this session.]

Aurex Jazz Festival (Aurex EWJ-80254); 1981.

Woody 'n You

Same personnel as above.

Recorded live 6 September 1981, Yokohama

Gerry Mulligan: "La Menace" Original Motion Picture Soundtrack (DRG Records MRS-506); 1982.

Dance of the Truck; Introspect; Watching and Waiting; Trucking Again; New Wine; The Trap; Theme from *La Menace*; Vines of Bordeaux; The House They'll Never Live In; Watching and Waiting (reprise); The Pantomimist; Introspect (reprise); Vines of Bordeaux (reprise)

BARITONE AND SOPRANO SAXES, CLARINET, KEYBOARDS: *Gerry Mulligan*
KEYBOARDS: *Dave Grusin, Derek Smith, Tom Fay*
DRUMS: *Bob Rosengarden, Michael Di Pasqua*
BASS: *Jack Six, Jay Leonhart*
MOOG SYNTHESIZER: *Peter Levin*
OBERHEIM SYNTHESIZER: *Edward Walsh*

Recorded 1982, Weston, Connecticut

Ornella Vanoni: Uomini (C. G. D. 20376); 1983.

Uomini; Io Capito Che Ti Amo
BARITONE SAX: *Gerry Mulligan*
KEYBOARD: *Fio Zanotti*
GUITARS: *Paolo Gianolio, Moreno Ferrara*
BASS: *Davide Romani*
DRUMS: *Mauro Gherardi*
VOCAL: *Ornella Vanoni* Recorded 26 March 1983, Milan

Gerry Mulligan: Little Big Horn (GRP Records GRP-A-1003); 1983.

Little Big Horn; Another Kind of Sunday
BARITONE SAX: *Gerry Mulligan*
KEYBOARDS: *Dave Grusin*
BASS: *Anthony Jackson*
DRUMS: *Buddy Williams*
HORN SECTION: *Marvin Stamm, Alan Rubin (trumpets), Keith O'Quinn (trombone), Lou Marini (alto sax), Michael Brecker (tenor sax), Gerry Mulligan (bari sax)*

Under a Star
BARITONE SAX: *Gerry Mulligan*
PIANO AND OBX SYNTHESIZER: *Dave Grusin*
BASS: *Jay Leonhart*
DRUMS: *Buddy Williams*

Bright Angel Falls
Same personnel as above, except bassist Anthony Jackson replaces Jay Leonhart, Dave Grusin plays just electric piano and not synthesizer, and acoustical pianist Richard Tee is added.

Sun on Stairs
BARITONE SAX: *Gerry Mulligan*
PIANO: *Dave Grusin*
BASS: *Jay Leonhart*
DRUMS: *Butch Miles*

I Never Was a Young Man
Same personnel as above, except Gerry Mulligan sings as well, and drummer Butch Miles is replaced by Buddy Williams.

Recorded 1983, NYC

Barry Manilow: 2:00 AM, Paradise Café (Arista AL8-8254); 1984.

Paradise Café; Where Have You Gone; Say No More; Blue; When October Goes; What Am I Doin' Here; Good-bye My Love; Big City Blues; When Love Is Gone; I've Never Been So Low on Love; Night Song

VOCALS AND PIANO: *Barry Manilow*
BARITONE SAX: *Gerry Mulligan*
GUITAR: *Mundell Lowe*
PIANO: *Bill Mays*
BASS: *George Duvivier*
DRUMS: *Shelly Manne*   Recorded 20–21 April 1984, LA

[Mel Tormé sings with Barry Manilow on "Big City Blues"; Gerry Mulligan does not play on the duet with Sarah Vaughan, "Blue"; Jack notes a videotape of the rehearsal, The Video Collection VC 4008 PAL.]

Gerry Mulligan Meets Scott Hamilton: Soft Lights and Sweet Music (Concord Jazz CJ-300); 1986.

Soft Lights and Sweet Music; Gone; Do You Know What I See?; I've Just Seen Her; Noblesse; Ghosts; Port of Baltimore Blues
SAXES: *Scott Hamilton (tenor), Gerry Mulligan (bari)*
PIANO: *Mike Renzi*
BASS: *Jay Leonhart*
DRUMS: *Grady Tate*   Recorded January 1986, NYC

Barry Manilow: Swing Street (Arista AL-8527); 1987.

One More Time

[Gerry Mulligan's baritone sax track, recorded in NYC in 1987, is added to the LA track recorded by Barry Manilow and an accompanying orchestra; Mulligan does not play on the album's other cuts.]

Symphonic Dreams: Gerry Mulligan and His Quartet/Houston Symphony Orchestra, Erich Kunzel, Conductor (Pro Acoustic Digital Recordings PAD-703); 1987.

Entente for Baritone Sax and Orchestra; The Sax Chronicles ("Sun on the Bach Stairs," "Sax in Debussy's Garden," "Sax in Mozart Minor," "Sax and der Rosenkavalier," "A Walk with Brahms")
BARITONE SAX: *Gerry Mulligan, accompanied by the Houston Symphony Orchestra*

Song for Strayhorn; K-4 Pacific
BARITONE SAX: *Gerry Mulligan*
PIANO: *Bill Mays*
BASS: *Dean Johnson*
DRUMS: *Rich DeRosa*

Recorded live 6–7 February 1987, Houston

[The Houston Symphony Orchestra accompanies the quartet.]

Cincinnati Pops Big Band Orchestra: Big Band Hit Parade (Telarc compact disc CD-80177); 1988.

In the Mood; Take the "A" Train; Begin the Beguine; Sentimental Journey; One O'Clock Jump; Caravan; Let's Dance; You Made Me Love You; Woodchopper's Ball; Sing Sing Sing; I'm Getting Sentimental over You; Well Git It!; Artistry in Rhythm; Moonlight Serenade; St. James Infirmary; When the Saints Go Marchin' In

TRUMPET: *Doc Severinsen*
TROMBONE: *Buddy Morrow*
REEDS: *Eddie Daniels (clarinet and tenor), Gerry Mulligan (bari)*
PIANO: *Dave Brubeck*
BASS: *Ray Brown*
DRUMS: *Ed Shaughnessy*
VOCAL: *Cab Calloway*   Recorded 3 August 1988, Cincinnati

Happy Anniversary, Charlie Brown (GRP Records compact disc GRD-9596); 1989.

Rain, Rain, Go Away
BARITONE SAX: *Gerry Mulligan*
PIANO: *Bill Charlap*
BASS: *Dean Johnson*
DRUMS: *Rich DeRosa*   Recorded in 1989, NYC

BIBLIOGRAPHY

Bourne, Michael. "Gerry Mulligan: Singing a Song of Mulligan." *Down Beat* 56, (January 1989): 23–25.

Carey, Gary. *Judy Holliday: An Intimate Life Story.* New York: Seaview Books, 1982.

Charters, Samuel B., and Leonard Kunstadt. *Jazz: A History of the New York Scene.* New York: Doubleday, 1962.

Coryell, Julie, and Laura Friedman. *Jazz-Rock Fusion.* New York: Delacorte Press, 1978.

Easton, Carol. *Straight Ahead: The Story of Stan Kenton.* New York: William Morrow, 1973.

Feather, Leonard. *The New Edition of the Encyclopedia of Jazz.* New York: Horizon Press, 1960.

———. *The Encyclopedia of Jazz in the Sixties.* New York: Horizon Press, 1966.

———, and Ira Gitler. *The Encyclopedia of Jazz in the Seventies.* New York: Horizon Press, 1976.

Gitler, Ira. *Jazz Masters of the Forties.* New York: Macmillan, 1966.

———. *Swing to Bop.* New York: Oxford University Press, 1985.

Gordon, Robert. *Jazz West Coast.* London: Quartet Books, 1986.

Harrison, Max. "Gerry Mulligan: An Ensemble Style for White Jazz." In *These Jazzmen of Our Times*, edited by Raymond Horricks, 58–79. London: Victor Gollancz, 1959.

———, Alun Morgan, Ronald Atkins, Michael James, and Jack Cooke. *Modern Jazz.* London: Aquarius Books, 1975.

Hentoff, Nat. "In the Mainstream: A Profile of Gerry Mulligan," *The New Yorker* 35 (21 March 1959); *The New Yorker* 35 (28 March 1959).

Hodeir, Andre. *Jazz: Its Evolution and Essence.* New York: Grove Press, 1956.

Holtzman, Will. *Judy Holliday: A Biography.* New York: Putnam's, 1982.

Horricks, Raymond. *Gerry Mulligan's Ark.* London: Apollo Books, 1986.

————. *Profiles in Jazz from Sidney Bechet to John Coltrane.* New Brunswick, New Jersey: Rutgers University Press; Transaction Publishers, 1990.

Lee, William F. *Stan Kenton: Artistry in Rhythm.* Los Angeles: Creative Press, 1980.

McCarthy, Albert, et al. *Jazz on Record.* New York: Oak Publications, 1968.

Simon, George T. *The Big Bands.* New York: Macmillan, 1971.

INDEX

C